Strategies for Managing Computer Software Upgrades

Neal G. Shaw
University of Texas-Arlington, USA

IDEA GROUP PUBLISHING
Hershey • London • Melbourne • Singapore

Acquisition Editor: Mehdi Khosrowpour
Managing Editor: Jan Travers
Development Editor: Michele Rossi
Copy Editor: Maria Boyer
Typesetter: Tamara Gillis
Cover Design: Deb Andree
Printed at: Sheridan Books

Published in the United States of America by
Idea Group Publishing
1331 E. Chocolate Avenue
Hershey PA 17033-1117
Tel: 717-533-8845
Fax: 717-533-8661
E-mail:cust@idea-group.com
Web site: http://www.idea-group.com

and in the United Kingdom by
Idea Group Publishing
3 Henrietta Street
Covent Garden
London WC2E 8LU
Tel: 44 20 7240 0856
Fax: 44 20 7379 3313
Web site: http://www.eurospan.co.uk

Library of Congress Cataloging-in-Publication Data

Shaw, Neal G., 1975-
Strategies for managing computer software upgrades / Neal G. Shaw.
p. cm.
Includes bibliographical references and index.
ISBN 1-930708-04-1
1. Software maintenance--Management. I. Title.

QA76.76.S64 S613 2001
005.1'6--dc21 00-054136

British Cataloguing in Publication Data
A Cataloguing in Publication record for this book is available from the British Library.

Strategies for Managing Computer Software Upgrades

Table of Contents

Preface

On the surface, this is a book about software upgrades; however, at its core, this is a book about organizations and the people, processes, and technology that compose them. Thus, this is a book about information systems (IS) and the management of information technology (IT). I began my career in information technology by working at an IT help desk. Eventually, I moved into software development and then into consulting. Now, I have moved into academia to pursue research interests, specifically research in software upgrades. In each position that I have held, and in each company for which I have performed consulting work, I have seen the impact of changing technology, and I am certain that all readers have seen its impact as well. Unfortunately, even though changes in technology are a given in today's society, there is a lack of mainstream knowledge about how to manage effectively the organizational changes associated with changes in technology.

Upgrading software is only one type of technological change, but it is certainly one of the most prevalent in modern organizations, given the rapid pace with which software vendors release new versions. Every single IT manager with whom I have discussed software upgrades points to the need for successful management of end users, management support, proper training, and other organizational issues as critical success factors in the management of software upgrades. This is consistent with findings by IS researchers who have identified these factors and others as key factors in the success of any IS implementation. Although there are many technical issues that must be resolved as well, including deployment options and accompanying hardware/software changes, this book focuses primarily on the presentation of tips, techniques, and strategies to help IS managers deal with the user and organizational problems that are often associated with software upgrades.

Why focus on primarily non-technical aspects of upgrades? Quite simply, this book was written at the request of practicing IT managers. There are many, many books that deal with the technical aspects of upgrading specific packages. For example, all the technical aspects of upgrading from one version of Microsoft Windows, to another can be found in books from Microsoft Corporation as well as numerous third parties. On the other hand, there are few, if any, books to help an IT manager deal with the organizational issues associated with the transition. There is a great deal of research to help the practicing manager, but to find it, one has to consult numerous periodicals and books to synthesize and interpret the relevant information.

This book has two major features: (1) a discussion and analysis of the most current techniques for managing software upgrades based upon recent field research, (2) an in-depth treatment of critical topics through carefully selected research papers. Through these two vehicles, my goal is for the reader to take from this book an enhanced understanding of the state-of-the-art in knowledge about managing the user and organizational aspects of software upgrades. In the interest of readability, I have purposely omitted the details of the statistical procedures used to analyze the data collected in the survey; however, I will be more than happy to share this information with any reader who is interested. The same holds true for details of the theoretical development of the model in the book along with a comprehensive literature review. Please feel free to contact me if you are interested in the details of the data analysis or literature review (or anything else), and I sincerely hope that you find this book both thought-provoking and useful.

Chapter 1

Introduction

Neal G. Shaw
University of Texas, Arlington, USA

> *[Howard Selland, President of Aeroquip Corp.] issues a blistering attack on the reliability and hidden costs of today's software. He recently calculated the full cost of upgrading his company's 50-person research lab in Ann Arbor, Mich., to Microsoft Corp.'s Windows 95 from Windows 3.1. The bill was $20,000 a person, or a total of $1 million. Such is the seductive pull of technology, however, that Aeroquip just kept rolling out the new [technology] (Wysocki, 1998).*

Windows 3.1. Windows 3.11. Windows 95. Windows 98. Windows 2000. Will it ever end? Should it ever end? The "it," of course, is the seemingly endless chain of software versions released by virtually every company in the software industry. New versions of existing software provide updates, corrections, and enhancements that are designed to significantly increase the productivity of individual users, which should in turn lead to increased productivity at the organizational level. In recent years, however, the software industry has faced growing resistance to the rapid release of software versions due to high implementation and conversion costs (Wysocki, 1998). Unfortunately, many organizations are forced to upgrade to current versions in order to maintain compatibility and interoperability among not only internal systems but also links to external suppliers, customers, etc., in an effort to maintain consistent and functional levels of information technology (IT) infrastructure development.

Until recently, the problems and challenges associated with the rapid changes in IT have not been studied in great detail (Benamati, Lederer, & Singh, 1997); however, recent studies have shown that the speed with which companies are introducing new IT products is having a substantial impact on the management of the IT function in organizations

(Lederer & Benamati, 1998). The recognition of the problems associated with new IT is consistent with the problematic nature of IT infrastructure development which is often cited as one of the major problems of IS management in organizations (Brancheau, Janz, & Wetherbe, 1996). With increasing demands on infrastructure components such as hardware and software, there does not seem to be a simple way of maintaining a responsive IT infrastructure because endless upgrades to meet the demands not only incur significant monetary costs, but also they are practically impossible to support with staff and expert knowledge. Thus, in general, infrastructure problems represent one of the largest domains of open problems in the IS field (Zmud, 1997).

The problem of maintaining a responsive IT infrastructure is often attacked with numerous hardware and software upgrades to meet increasing demands on the IS staff and the information system (IS) in general; however, there has been relatively little research in industry or academia to evaluate the efficiency and effectiveness of such a solution. Thus, it seems reasonable to question the logic behind the endless hardware and software upgrades to which many organizations are resigned. Accordingly, in order to help practicing IT managers better understand the individual and organizational impacts of software upgrades, this book presents a view of the state-of-the-art in knowledge of the organizational management of software upgrades, including the results of a study that surveys a large number of organizational software users. Specifically, the book seeks to address the following major questions:

- Do software upgrades enhance the productivity of employees and an organization as a whole?
- What problems typically arise during the implementation of software upgrades?
- What steps can an organization take to minimize productivity losses during software upgrades?

The investigation of these questions is important to a wide variety of people and organizations, specifically (1) end-users seeking to become more productive from software upgrades, (2) managers deciding whether or not to purchase a software upgrade for an organization, (3) software vendors wishing to understand customer perceptions of upgrades, (4) information systems professionals needing to determine an optimal strategy for upgrading software, and (5) researchers studying phenomena associated with implementation of technology in organizations.

The book is organized into three major parts. Part I provides an introduction to the most current organizational research on software upgrades along with a set of factors that, based upon current knowledge, should be good predictors of successes/failures associated with software upgrades. Part II presents some basic research findings about users and their experiences with upgrades, and Part III provides a more in-depth look at some research results along with a discussion of upgrade strategies that can be deduced from the findings. In addition, Part III discusses some future trends and possible new technologies that could change the nature of software upgrades.

PART I: THE SOFTWARE UPGRADE PHENOMENON

When considering changes in software, one notion that might come to mind is the concept of evolution as proposed by biologist Charles Darwin. He postulated that animal species undergo gradual changes to evolve into more advanced forms. His theories have been used to explain the tendency of mankind to improve and advance the current state of societies and technology. In the specific case of information systems, one can easily argue that the same phenomenon takes place. In fact, changes in computer technology are becoming more and more rapid over time (Benamati et al., 1997). Using such reasoning in IS gives rise to many different questions. For example, one might wonder why such changes occur. Similarly, questions about the nature of the changes themselves seem relevant. This book is concerned about the degree to which such changes occur. That is, given that such changes occur, what makes one particular change more dramatic than others?

If we consider again the evolution of species as studied by Darwin, one of the most fundamental components that shapes the evolution of a species is the environment in which that species develops. The environment has a significant impact on the outcome of the change in species. In computing, one would expect the same result. That is, it seems natural that the environment, and more specifically the organization, will impact computing changes in the same manner proposed by Darwin. Additionally, the characteristics of the particular species in question will no doubt have an impact on the changes and outcome of the evolution of the species. Again, in computing, one would certainly expect that the characteristics of the software in question will have an impact on the changes caused by evolution. Finally, Darwin's theory also suggests that the process of evolution that the species undergoes will have an impact on the transformation. Similarly, in IS, the evolution process and its effect on users should certainly be expected to impact the changes in the overall organization caused by a software upgrade.

Factors Expected to Impact Software Upgrades

Although Darwin's theories seem particularly relevant, there is very little prior work in information systems on computing evolution. Thus, given the lack of previous IS research in the area of software upgrades, there is no major model, theory, or framework to serve as a foundation for a model to help IT managers identify the factors that must be controlled in a successful software upgrade. Consequently, the approach to the analysis of upgrades taken by this book is based on concepts and ideas proposed in other areas of information systems research. As discussed previously, the goal of this book is to expose practicing managers to IS research that will help to ease the process of transitioning from one software package to another, and a large body of work in IS research has focused on the implementation of information systems. For example, Kwon and Zmud (1987) propose three major types of research in information systems: factors research, process research, and political (environmental) research. The factor approach to research in IS implementation is further developed by Cooper and Zmud (1990) as user factors, technical factors, organizational factors, etc. This approach coincides with one of the most prominent IS research frameworks (Ives, Hamilton, & Davis, 1980) that proposes three major categories of information systems components for study. The three categories are as follows.

1. *Process Variables*—Process variables refer to the interaction between the information system and its environment. For example, users interact with the system when they use it to obtain information. Characteristics of such an interaction are classified as process variables.
2. *Environmental Variables*—Environmental variables refer to the characteristics that define the resources and constraints under which the information subsystem must function.
3. *Information System Subsystem (ISS) Variables*—ISS variables refer to application and information subsystem characteristics such as content, form, and time. In general, this category can be described as representing the information system itself.

These categories, because they apply to all information systems (Ives et al., 1980) and because they have been shown to affect the implementation process (Kwon & Zmud, 1987), seem to be a logical starting point for groupings of factors that affect software upgrades, given the lack of prior work in the area. This book defines three categories of factors that affect software upgrades. IT factors, environmental factors, and user factors represent a level of abstraction to separate the critical factors into logical groupings. In addition, several key factors within each category have been identified as the most important factors affecting software upgrades. These individual factors are derived from previous work in other areas of information systems research, where possible; however, there are without question some factors which are unique to the study of software upgrades and are developed here for the first time. Figure 1 shows a conceptual model of the factors that affect software upgrades, and further explanations of the categories, the factors, and the relationships are given in the following paragraphs.

Transparency of Software Upgrades

The dependent variable in this is the transparency of software upgrades. An IT manager would likely be concerned with any change in productivity as a result of an upgrade, and to establish practical relationships, the model assumes that a high degree of change would result in an initial loss of productivity. This line of reasoning comes from the Shannon-Weaver entropy model developed as part of the early work on information theory (Shannon & Weaver, 1963). The idea is straightforward: a loss of information causes disruption, or a higher level of entropy, which in turn causes chaos, or in this case a lack of productivity. So, if an organization's information infrastructure is disrupted, the amount of information in the system falls, and the entropy of the system increases. Information theory has been used previously in a similar manner to evaluate the effectiveness of adoption and diffusion approaches (Richards, 1995), so a precedent exists for claims such as those that are made in this research. In general, an organization should attempt to maximize the transparency of upgrades to keep productivity as close to pre-upgrade levels as possible.

IT Factors

The first category of factors focuses on the characteristics of the particular software package that is undergoing change. This category has strong foundations in the IS literature, including a direct link to the Ives, Hamilton, and Davis research framework discussed previously. The information subsystem variables from their research framework lend support to the necessity of having a general category of factors related to the information technology itself (Ives et al., 1980). In addition, literature on the adoption and diffusion of innovations in organizations has shown that the characteristics of a particular innovation are one of the largest determinants of the manner and speed with which the innovation is introduced into the organization (Chau & Tam, 1997; Fichman, 1992; Fichman & Kemerer, 1997; Grover & Goslar, 1993; Grover, Goslar, & Segars, 1995; Leonard-Barton, 1988). Indeed there is sufficient agreement that the particular characteristics of an innovation must be key considerations in any study of adoption and diffusion of innovations.

Logically, the influence of IT factors on the degree of change in an organization is easily observed by using simple examples from typical organizational upgrade problems. For example, suppose an organization decides to upgrade its word processing platform to a new version of its existing word processing software. If the organization wants to know what will happen to the overall infrastructure as a result of the new software, it is clear that the specifications of the new software must be considered. If the new software has a substantially different interface than the old software, then the degree of overall change will be higher than if the interfaces were relatively the same. Similarly, if the file format of the new software is not compatible with the file format of the old software, conversion problems will certainly have to be overcome. Also, additional features of the new software might require learning and training time as well as time for the user to become reasonably comfortable with the new software.

Clearly, for both practical and theoretical reasons, the characteristics of the specific IT software must be considered. The following paragraphs describe the particular issues that must be considered when evaluating the transparency of an upgrade relative to the characteristics of the software.

A change in functionality from one software package to the next refers to additional features, sophistication, and options that were not available in the original package. Functionality is defined here to mean tasks that can be performed with the software. In more simplistic terms, this factor refers to anything that the new software can do that the first software could not do. For example, when Microsoft released the 1997 edition of its popular Microsoft Office software suite, a significant amount of additional functionality was added with the integration of World Wide Web (WWW) functionality into the product. Users familiar with Office '95 were forced to accept the WWW additions in the new software. A

Figure 1: A Conceptual Model of Factors Affecting Software Upgrades

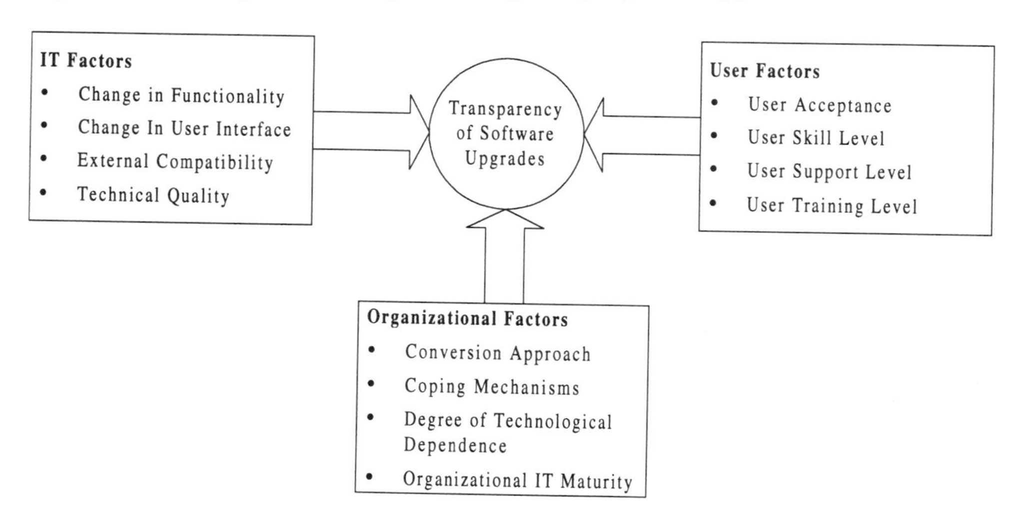

user unfamiliar with the WWW might well have been dismayed by the additional functionality and complexity of the new software.

Also, one must consider any loss in functionality. That is, there is a real possibility that the new software might have removed some functionality available in the old software. As an example, consider the release of Netscape Navigator 4.0. Immediately upon its release, many companies migrated immediately to the new version of the software from an existing version, such as Navigator 2.0 or 3.0. One of the undocumented idiosyncrasies of such an upgrade, however, was the omission of certain user functions by Netscape. The new version changed the functionality of many existing command buttons and eliminated many keyboard shortcuts because they were needed to implement more sophisticated functionality in other parts of the software.

There are few arguments against the claim that new software adds significant functionality. In today's marketplace, this is an absolute necessity in order for companies to remain competitive (Porter, 1980). What must be shown, however, is that such changes in functionality affect the degree of organizational change caused by an upgrade. There is little theoretical work on which to base such a claim because of the lack of prior research in this area. Still, one can argue that the relationship is strong enough that a logical argument is sufficient to justify the inclusion of this factor in the conceptual model that will be empirically validated at a later stage of the research.

The second IT factor included in the conceptual model is the degree of change in the user interface from the old software to the new software. Obviously, some types of software will have little or no change in user interface; however, in general, this factor will likely have a substantial impact upon the overall degree of change involved in an upgrade. For example, consider again the scenario of upgrading operating system software from Microsoft Windows 3.1 to Microsoft Windows '95. There is a major change in the user interface when changing versions of this software, and this presents problems for users as they make the transition to the new software. Keyboard shortcuts and mouse clicks to which users are accustomed no longer function as they once did. The user is forced to undergo a learning process to determine how to complete tasks which were routine before the upgrade.

The third factor that can be classified as an inherent characteristic of the new software is the degree of external compatibility. External compatibility refers to the potential for incompatibility in interfaces for the new software. For example, the file format for the new software may be different than the file format of the old software. An external incompatibility is created because file conversion problems might occur, and potentially the organization might not be able to share data as easily if some users still use the old format.

The final IT factor, technical quality, is a construct that captures the correctness of the construction of a software package. For example, software with high technical quality would have high performance (good use of memory, etc.), few bugs (technical glitches), and few systems crashes, among other characteristics. Conversely, low quality software would exhibit poor performance, bugs, and/or many system crashes. Although there are few empirical studies to show the relationship of technical quality to constructs such as user transparency (Chen et al., 1996), one can easily see the relationship. The level of technical quality can certainly be expected to have an impact on the transparency of software upgrades, since users will see problems occurring with low quality software. Thus, a change to low quality software would be expected to have a low degree of transparency.

Organizational Factors

The second category of factors, organizational factors, refers to the intraorganizational environmental components of the information system as defined by the Ives, Hamilton, and Davis framework (Ives et al., 1980). There are two fundamental types of environmental factors (Ives et al., 1980; Lederer & Mendelow, 1990): intraorganizational environment factors and interorganizational environment factors.

1. *Intraorganizational*—Intraorganizational environment factors refer to those resources and constraints dictated by the environment within the organization. Examples of intraorganizational environment factors include users (Benamati et al., 1997; Ives et al., 1980; Lederer & Mendelow, 1990) as well as organizational structural configuration, and organizational maturity levels (Gibson & Nolan, 1974; Herbsleb, Zubrow, Goldenson, Hayes, & Paulk, 1997).
2. *Interorganizational*—Interorganizational factors refer to environmental factors that are between organizations or are external to the organization. Typical interorganizational environmental factors include political forces and legal issues. Although it is likely that interorganizational environmental factors such as market factors will affect software upgrades, they are not of interest in this study. As noted earlier, this study does not focus on the environmental factor grouping proposed by Cooper and Zmud (1990). It assumes that external environmental factors are negligible, if they exist. Future empirical research will be necessary to examine the validity of this assumption.

The influence of the intraorganizational environment on the management of information systems has been demonstrated both theoretically and empirically in previous IS research, and thus, it is clear that the environment has an impact on the management of IS in virtually all cases. Moreover, it has recently been shown that the environment plays an even more critical role in the management of emerging technologies in information systems (Benamati et al., 1997; Lederer & Benamati, 1998). Thus for this research, the environment seems to be an especially important issue to consider. Four particular components of the intraorganizational environment have been shown to have an impact on the development and use of software, and the following subsections discuss these particular issues in detail.

The first organizational factor refers to the conversion approach chosen by the organization for the new software package. Organizations have a number of options in converting to a new information system, including phased conversion approaches, big bang approaches, etc. The manner in which the conversion takes place has been shown to impact the outcome of the overall implementation. Thus, the conversion approach will likely have a significant impact on the degree of change caused by a change in software.

The second organizational factor is again a newly defined factor which has not been studied in detail in the information systems literature. The degree of dependence, first defined as part of a telecommunications research initiative (Shaw & Yadav, 1998), refers to the degree to which the organization is dependent upon the software being replaced. Some software packages have a low degree of dependence because they are not critical to the organization. For example, very little organizational disruption is likely to take place if an upgrade is made to a seldom used software package on one user's workstation. On the other hand, an upgrade of an enterprise resource planning (ERP) system will undoubtedly have a profound effect on the organization because the organization's core operations can be affected.

The third organizational factor is a measure of how well the organization copes with the problems caused by the other environmental factors. As discussed previously, IS researchers have shown that the major method for handling environmental issues used by IT managers is to use some form of coping mechanism (Benamati et al., 1997; Lederer & Mendelow, 1990). The reason for introducing this factor into the conceptual model is that it is imperative to be able to capture any processes or procedures that the organization has put in place to reduce the effect of environmental problems. In this manner, the potentially damaging effect of technical failures or lack of user skill can potentially be overcome with coping mechanisms.

The fourth organizational factor that is likely to have a major impact on software upgrades, organizational IT maturity, is a measure of the IT capabilities of the organization itself. Logically, an organization that is mature in the area of information technology will almost certainly show a more effective transition process between software packages than organizations that are less mature. For example, suppose someone is comparing two organizations to determine which one will have more success in upgrading software. If one organization has reached a mature stage of IT development and has an established and tested IT development and diffusion process, that organization would likely produce a more effective upgrade than an organization with immature IT processes. Nolan's stage of growth model (e.g., Gibson and Nolan, 1974) and the Capability Maturity Model (Herbsleb et al., 1997) are two sample reference models that can be used to gauge the level of organizational IT maturity.

User Factors

The third category, user factors, refers to a category of factors that can be found at the intersection of information technology and its intraorganizational environment. For example, users have been previously identified as part of the intraorganizational environment. Also, characteristics of software have been identified as part of the IT factors. Then, in this research, to be consistent with Cooper and Zmud's (1990) categories, a user factor refers to a concept such as the manner in which the user uses the software.

One major difference between the user factors and the other categories of factors is the ability of a firm to control some of the user factors within the organization such as user training level and user support level. The other classes of factors, organizational factors and IT factors, are largely beyond the control of the individual firm. Many of the IT factors are mandated by the marketplace and the vendors that produce software. The organizational factors are largely predetermined characteristics of the organization. Obviously the firm has a certain level of control over intraorganizational factors such as coping mechanisms; however, the level of success of these options may not be known beforehand. With user support and user training, in general, the organization will have direct control over the levels of these factors. In other words, if a specified degree of change is required, the organization might be able to manipulate the user factors such as support level and training level to achieve a desired level of evolution and productivity. There are four major user factors that have been identified, and the details of each factor are given in the following paragraphs.

The first user factor, user acceptance, refers to the usage of an information system by the intended users. The Technology Acceptance Model (TAM) shows that perceived usefulness and perceived ease of use of a new technology from the user perspective can predict the usage of a system by the end users (Davis, 1989). In software implementation studies, such constructs have not been applied to study the degree of overall change; however, if the level of system usage changes due to the introduction of a new technology, then the degree of overall change will necessarily be affected as well. This argument also can be easily understood from the perspective of user resistance to change. If a user resists the change to the new technology, i.e., refuses to accept the new technology, then there will undoubtedly be problems caused by the introduction of this technology.

The second critical user factor, user skill level, can be traced to the work of Ives et al. (1980) and Lederer and Mendelow (1990). The user skill level is defined as the degree of information technology skill possessed by the user of the new software. While user skill and performance have been studied in some areas of IS research (Dillon & Morris, 1996; Goodhue & Thompson, 1995), user skill has not been specifically studied in the context of a software upgrade. Based on a logical argument, however, it seems reasonable to expect that user skill level will have a major impact on the degree of change effected by the change in a software package. For example, consider again the word processor upgrade scenario referenced several times previously. A skilled user is likely to need less time to adapt to the new word processor than an unskilled user because the skilled user is likely already familiar with the fundamental terminology, concepts, etc., needed to use the word processor. The new system will take time to learn, obviously, but it seems apparent that the unskilled user, who has little prior knowledge in the problem domain, will take longer to learn the nuances of the new software than the skilled user.

The third user factor refers to the level of support provided by the information systems function as the organization goes through the upgrade process. Prior research in the diffusion of innovations in information systems has shown that the level of support can have a significant impact on the implementation process (Benamati et al., 1997; Dillon & Morris, 1996; Grover & Goslar, 1993; Lederer & Mendelow, 1990). The importance of information systems support is logically significant as well. An organization with many support resources devoted to the implementation of a software upgrade should be able to lessen the severity of any negative impact on the organization. This factor can be manipulated by the organization to moderate the effect of other factors.

The fourth and final user factor, user training level, is very similar to the user support level described previously. Emerging technology research has shown that user training (or lack thereof) is a significant determinant in the perceived problems associated with a technological innovation (Benamati, 1997; Benamati et al., 1997). In addition, since this factor can be manipulated by the organization, i.e., by giving users more training, the transparency of an upgrade seems particularly susceptible to the user training level given previously shown relationships among user training and IS implementation (Cooper & Zmud, 1990; Lee, Kim, & Lee, 1995; Nelson & Cheney, 1987).

SUMMARY

In summary, we now have a proposed conceptual model of software upgrades by identifying 12 factors, grouped into three categories, that affect the transparency of upgrades and consequently affect organizational productivity. The model has both theoretical and practical foundations, as it was designed to be primarily an aid to IT managers in the evaluation of software upgrade scenarios but also a theoretical foundation for researchers investigating further software upgrade issues. The primary limitation of the model is that it has not been constructed to be a dynamic model to incorporate structural changes over time. That is, the long-term effects of software upgrades might not be accurately captured by the model.

Detailed Research

The following set of articles provides a more in-depth introduction to the software upgrade phenomenon through the presentation of related research findings. The first article, by Lederer and Benamati, argues for the importance of treating new and emerging technologies as special entities, which implies a need for IT managers to focus specifically on changes in hardware and software such as upgrades. Then, Coe presents five secrets to information systems success, and Doudikis reinforces the same principles as he discusses IT trends in small businesses. LeBlanc provides an example of the selection process for making a change in microcomputer software, and Lane, Palko, and Cronan do an excellent job of summarizing recent research in IS implementation. All of these chapters are presented here because they succinctly represent a large part of the most commonly accepted principles of information systems, information systems implementation, and software upgrades.

Chapter 2

What's New? The Challenges of Emerging Information Technologies

Albert L. Lederer
University of Kentucky, USA

John Benamati
Miami University (Ohio), USA

Fifty years have passed since the introduction of the digital computer. During that time, information technology has evolved beyond belief. Continued evolution seems highly likely. New information technologies—new hardware, software, and data management tools—have offered and will continue to offer great opportunities to organizations that choose to implement them. In fact, the failure to implement them will likely create disadvantages for other organizations.

However, along with the opportunities of new information technologies come the challenges. These challenges are many and diverse. Perhaps, IT professionals have not done a very good job of managing these challenges. In fact, until recently IT researchers have not recognized them.

What are these challenges of emerging information technologies? That is, what makes applying and managing them arduous and problematic when they are initially introduced? Here are some examples of these challenges.

First and foremost, IT specialists—database administrators, tech support specialists, systems analysts, programmers, and project managers—simply are not familiar with them. This is because the technologies are new and unused, and thus, the technical experts have yet to learn to use them well. Moreover, they have not seen the flaws in the technologies. They do not know the little quirks and necessary tricks that are not well documented, but are still absolutely essential to making them perform correctly.

Often, in their early releases, new information technologies do not perform as expected. They may abort unexpectedly. They may run too slowly. Some may even produce

This chapter previously appeared in the Journal of Database Management, vol. 9, No. 1. Copyright © 1998, Idea Group Publishing.

incorrect results.

Perhaps their failure to meet expectations is a result of the competition among vendors to deliver new information technology quickly. However in their rush, the vendors do so prematurely. Perhaps vendors market new information technology before debugging thoroughly. Perhaps they rely too heavily on their initial users to find the errors and performance problems. Finding these problems will enable the vendors to develop the stable versions that ultimately become popular, but discovering them will be problematic for the users who do so.

On the other hand, maybe the failure of new information technologies to perform as expected results from the exaggerated promises of their vendors. Competitive forces may drive vendors to make claims that cannot always be met.

Moreover, when the new information technology does not perform as expected, large numbers of customers may be affected. These customers may seek help almost simultaneously, but the vendors may not able to support them all. Thus vendor neglect can be one of the challenges of emerging information technology.

Even when developing new applications with sufficient vendor support, an organization may face its own support shortage. It needs more hours from IT professionals. It may also need more of these professionals, and it likely needs them with the skills in the new information technology. That means either the education of current IT professionals or the hiring of new ones. Of course, the skills may not exist yet because the information technologies are so new.

In addition to the need to spend more hours or employ more IT professionals with new skills, the acquisition of one information technology may produce the unexpected need to acquire another one. For example, perhaps a new program runs with the prescribed main memory requirement but does so slowly; more memory is really needed. Perhaps a database management system requires more storage space than was expected. Such cascading needs can be unanticipated and costly.

In addition to needing more IT professionals to manage new information technologies and to apply the technologies to develop new applications, the organization may also need them to integrate the new information technologies with existing ones. This integration process—with any number of possible existing information technologies—can be a challenge all its own.

Many IT professionals might find the use of the new information technologies attractive. They might see it as providing them opportunities for advancement or mobility. However, other IT professionals might resent the new information technologies. They may prefer not to be forced to learn them, but instead to continue using whatever has worked well in the past for them.

Even in organizations where all IT professionals accept emerging information technology, the decision to acquire a new product and the choice of the particular product may be difficult. An organization may be torn between buying too early (and risking the problems of an unstable product) and waiting until the product is stable (and risking that competitors will gain an edge by acquiring it).

Finally, as organizations acquire more and more new information technologies, they create a labyrinth of what will become old information technologies to support. Will they have the necessary skills in the future to maintain this variety of new products?

Thus, it is evident that the challenges of implementing new information technologies are great. The failure to meet the challenges is eventually played out in three ways. First, projects cost more than their budgets. Second, they are completed after their target dates. Third, their quality is not as high as had they understood the new information technologies and managed their implementation smoothly.

In fact, it may be that IT managers and other professionals plunge into the acquisition process with less consideration about these problems than they should have. Their enthusiasm for new information technology might blind them to the challenges. Perhaps like the vendors who are under pressure to sell new information technologies, these managers and other professionals face pressure to provide new information technologies.

Despite these challenges, little academic research has been done on this subject. Earlier this year however, Benamati, Lederer, and Singh's "Changing Information Technology and Information Technology Management" in *Information and Management* (volume 31, 1997, pp. 275-288) considered the challenges. Benamati's doctoral dissertation ("Managing Information Technology in a Changing Information Technology Environment," unpublished doctoral dissertation, University of Kentucky, 1997) also makes an initial effort to understand the challenges and to identify the coping mechanisms that IT managers might use to deal with them.

More research is clearly needed in this area to help IT managers deal with change. Research might make a serious contribution to the management of IT in the organizations that face the challenges of emerging IT.

Chapter 3

Five Small Secrets to Systems Success

Larry R. Coe
University of Illinois, USA

A pervasive theme today regarding the performance of new systems is "many systems are technical successes, but organizational failures." Systems that are well designed often fail to meet user expectations at implementation. This chapter details and analyzes the implementation of a major operations support system at a large U.S. firm that fits this theme. Measurements (of success) from a quasi-experiment are used to accurately measure user performance and user expectations pre- and post-system implementation. These measurements offer solid proof that the system achieved key user defined objectives. ... And yet, the system is widely viewed as a failure. This chapter highlights the "organizational chaos" that "technically successful" systems often cause in user organizations when the Systems Delivery process (how systems are delivered to users) is ineffectual. In effect, systems are dropped off at the users' doorsteps. A prescriptive model using five key guidelines is proposed for effective management of the Systems Delivery process. These five relatively small secrets can save corporations millions in investment dollars, reduce negative impacts to customer service, and enhance employee morale and systems acceptance.

CALL CENTERS UNITED (CCU) INTRODUCTION

During the early 1980s, five mid-size call center companies combined to form a large call center conglomerate called CCU (Call Centers United). The combined company served more than 10 million customers and employed over 60,000 employees. With the formation of CCU, the company found itself with a hodgepodge of systems—various mainframe vendors, five different system architectures, multiple telecommunications software products, 37 different types of workstations, 600 million lines of application code to maintain, and escalating systems costs. Service Representatives were required to understand and use 250,000 service order codes in order to respond to customer requests for products and services.

This chapter originally appeared in the Information Resources Management Journal, vol. 9, no. 4.

COMMON SYSTEMS STRATEGY

In 1985, a key corporate strategy was initiated to combine all of CCU's systems into a "common" CCU approach. One of the most challenging "commonization" efforts was converting the massive billing and ordering systems from the five original companies to one common system. After eight years of requirements gathering and validation, joint application development sessions with user groups, system design, coding and testing, and pre-installation testing—the deployment of a common Billing and Ordering System (BOS) began in 1993 in a phased company by company approach.

Before merging, each company used a distinct billing and ordering system to process customer bill inquiries and orders. From 1993 to November 1995, CCU implemented BOS to replace all of these systems.

The expected benefits of BOS were many. CCU combined its ordering and billing systems staffs, reduced system maintenance costs, and allowed new services to be provided faster throughout the five company area. System changes now required modifications to one system instead of five or ten. The consolidation of systems and staffs was certainly significant to the Systems department. However, to the Sales and Services organizations within CCU (the user departments), the critical measure of success for BOS was a reduction in the average call handling time required to satisfy customer phone inquiries and orders.

CCU receives 45 million service calls a year. Before BOS, the average time to handle a call was 7.3 minutes. To handle these calls CCU employed a work force of 5,000 Service Representatives (Service Reps). BOS enhancements to the bill inquiry and service order processes would allow Service Reps to handle customer calls more quickly, which would lead to a reduction in the number of Service Reps. Anticipated savings due to average call handling time was actualized in early 1995, as the Service Rep work force was reduced to take maximum advantage of expected time savings from BOS.

Unfortunately, average call handling time did not decrease with the implementation of BOS, but increased. Despite tremendous investment in human and financial resources and eight years of development and planning, the implementation of BOS was a very painful experience for CCU. Contrary to plan, average call handling time increased as Service Reps struggled to use/learn the new system. As call lengths increased, hold time for customers waiting to talk to a Service Rep grew proportionately. The system was deemed defective, poorly designed and difficult to use. The company president, referring to BOS, concluded "our systems have failed us."

WHAT HAPPENED? Why did average call handling time increase instead of decrease? Why did the consolidation of ten disparate systems into one common system degrade CCU's service instead of improve it? Was the system defective? Was BOS poorly designed? Why did users have such a difficult time using the system? With eight years of planning, why did the system fail to meet expectations/user measurements of success?

BOS IMPACT ON CUSTOMER SERVICE

The implementation of BOS caused CCU's Service Reps and customers great pain. Service Reps had a very difficult time learning the system. They complained *bitterly* about the complexity and difficulty of using the system. BOS seemed plagued with defects. The following complaints about BOS were collected via a survey of Service Reps at one of CCU's offices one week after converting over to BOS:

- Just want to cry, very confused and frustrated
- Fix problem on SUM1 screen; installation charges incorrect

- More SMEs in office to assist us post-training
- Managers should understand the system to assist us
- More clarity about the differences between SAV and STR orders
- More on how to find the waivers screen
- Change the PF12 key so I don't lose my work
- Get rid of the BOS User Guide—it is useless!
- Non-translatables are a nightmare!
- Phone numbers come up too late
- When you get out of sequence, you are lost
- Eliminate multiple log-ons to so many systems
- Tell us how terrible training is going to be upfront
- Need more help taking calls the first day out of training
- It's a challenge to move back and forth between systems
- S/R key and F/B keys are not consistent between systems—causes confusion
- There is no way to know if we made service order errors
- The screen flow is so very different from prior system
- Adjustments are impossible to do
- Can't sleep at night worrying about BOS and my orders and my adherence; afraid I might lose my job
- Computing rates in the middle of a contact is difficult
- Hate working between systems
- Too many screens to remove service
- Closed after every call to get help

Service Reps throughout CCU strongly disliked the new system. External customers also complained. After waiting a half hour on hold and then having to talk to a Service Rep who was unfamiliar with the system, was intolerable. Customer complaints flooded into the company. Newspapers published articles detailing the company's service and system problems. One company oversight commission fined CCU $10,000/day for failing to meet negotiated service levels. The implementation of BOS was a huge problem for CCU.

Why did BOS fail to meet user expectations? Why do systems in general fail to meet user expectations?

WHY SYSTEMS FAIL

A significant amount of research has been conducted on why systems fail or succeed. A wide range of theories have been proposed. In these studies, a key ingredient for successful systems is the relationship/involvement of the user groups and system designers in the system development process. While early theorists (Churchman and Schainblatt, 1967) proposed that successful systems could be developed with neither designer nor user understanding each other, later literature (Bean and Radnor, 1979) recommended the use of functional intermediaries between designers and users to ensure successful systems. Another group of researchers hypothesized that top management support or user attitudes towards a new system were the key factors in determining systems success: Lucas (1975), Neal and Radnor (1973), Ives and Olson (1984).

Strong user involvement is the preeminent approach used today in the majority of systems development projects. User involvement was a major focus of the BOS project, including extensive user requirements documentation and numerous joint application development sessions. Research supporting this approach includes Baronis and Louis (1988), Tait and Vessey (1988), Robey and Zeller (1978), and Ginzburg (1981). However, the influence of user involvement on system success is not very well identified. For example, Lucas (1993) concludes that "the notion of user involvement is intuitively appealing, however there is little evidence on how it affects implementation success." The plethora of theories on how to successfully design and develop systems is confusing, conflicts with other studies, and often lacks supportive empirical evidence.

DETERMINING MEASURES OF SUCCESS

HOW DO WE DETERMINE SYSTEMS SUCCESS? What measurements determine if a system has succeeded or failed? Four generally accepted measurements for assessing system success are:

- Use of system measured by intended or actual use of system
- Favorable attitudes toward system on part of users
- Degree to which system accomplishes its original objective
- Payoff to the organization

All measures do not apply to all systems. It is important to consider the type of system, key system applications, and whether system usage is mandatory or voluntary when establishing measures of success. Important system distinctions include:

- System type: transaction oriented system, information providing system, or decision support type system?
  –Transaction processing systems: Transaction-oriented systems used to perform and process key organizational functions such as service orders, bill handling, payroll applications.
  —Information providing systems: electronic mail systems, bulletin boards, and Lotus Notes® type applications.
  —Decision support systems: Modeling applications like investment analysis programs, and executive information systems.
- The system is primarily centralized or decentralized?
  Centralized systems: Actual information processing is done at a central location and is generally mainframe based.
  Decentralized systems: Actual information processing is done locally often using mid to small sized computers.
- System usage is mandatory or voluntary?
  —Voluntary usage: System is not required for user to accomplish his or her job.
  —Mandatory usage: System is required for user to perform job.

System distinctions are critical in determining measures of success for a system. Most research today concentrates on decentralized type systems where usage is primarily voluntary; thus, the key measure of system success is employee usage. A usage measurement is, however, irrelevant to the success of mandatory usage, mainframe-based (centralized) systems like BOS.

How can we determine if BOS was successful or not? What are appropriate measurements of success for BOS? Reviewing the initial Service Rep complaints and the very negative impacts on CCU's customers, BOS initially looks to be a disaster. However, this data is cursory, and a more in-depth and longer term review of actual Service Rep performance data reveals a very different assessment of BOS.

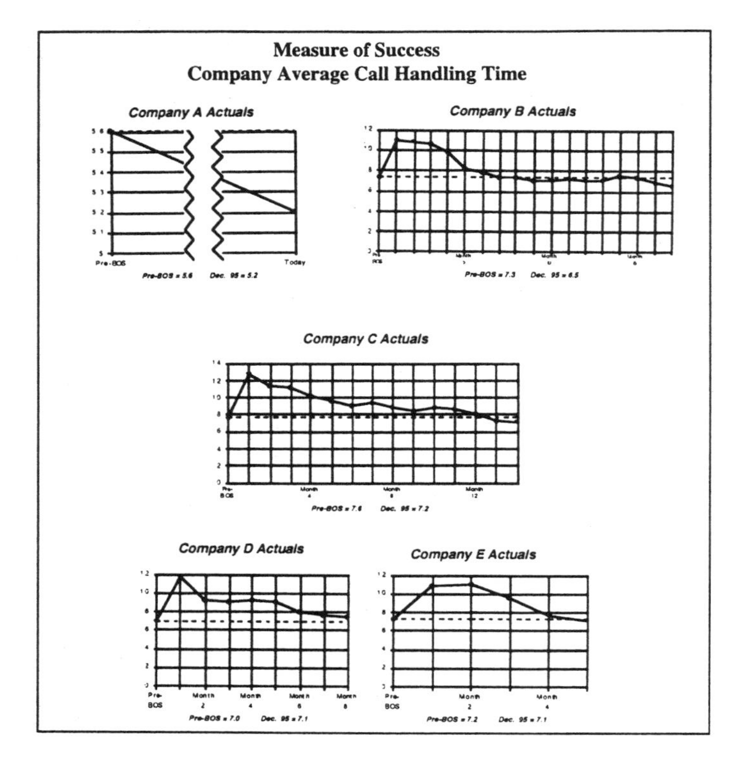

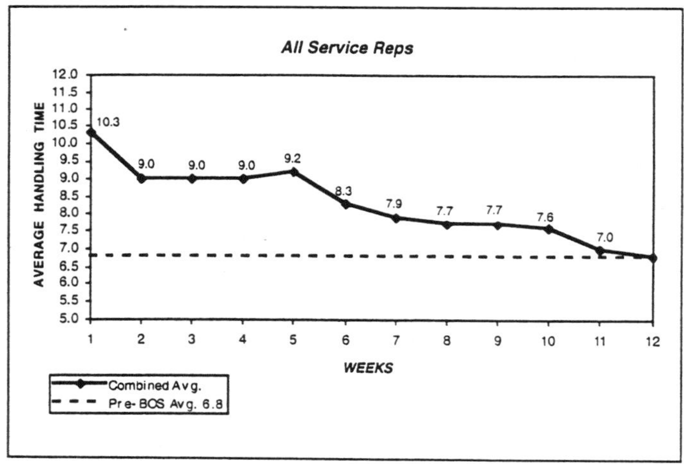

MEASURE OF SUCCESS: COMPANY LEVEL AVERAGE CALL HANDLING TIME

The charts above document the monthly impacts of BOS on average call handling time as the system was phased into each company. The pre-BOS number is the benchmark for average call handling performance over the 12-month period prior to BOS.

The key measure of success for BOS from the user organization perspective was a reduction in average handling time. With the exception of Company D, every state's average handling time has been reduced. Company D is very close to reaching a reduced average call handling time.

Initial system implementation caused average call handling times to escalate dramatically from pre-BOS levels. After five to eight months of learning the system, average handling time dropped below pre-BOS performance levels in each company. Combining current call handling in all five companies, BOS is saving CCU approximately 30 seconds per call and continues to slowly trend downward. A reduction of 30 seconds per call times 45 million calls per year is quite significant (equates to salary savings of 18¢ on each call x 45,000,000 calls/year = $8.1 million/year). This is a significant measure of success. Of course the question arises whether these improvements should have been immediate or at least earlier than five to eight months. The answer to this question is the key finding of this research effort and is addressed in the section "Effective Systems Delivery."

MEASURE OF SUCCESS: SERVICE REP AVERAGE CALL HANDLING TIME

In an effort to gain a more in-depth understanding of the effects of BOS on individual Service Rep performance, a quasi-experimental study was conducted on the performance of 36 Service Reps during the BOS conversion. Average call handling measurements for the group and each individual Service Rep were documented one month prior to implementing the new system and for 12 weeks after BOS was implemented. Average handling time performance levels and the effects of BOS implementation are graphed below.

The average handling time measurements of all service reps indicate a marked increase in average handling time per call with the introduction of BOS and a steadily declining learning curve towards decreased average handling time over the 12-week period since BOS implementation. This learning curve effect closely mirrors the state measurements as well. At Week 12 (the time of this report), the group average of 6.8 minutes equaled the pre-BOS average of 6.8 with further declines likely as additional weeks progress from the time of this report. These results correlate with our findings that BOS, given three to four months, will reduce average call handling time per Service Rep. The learning curve for each state was lengthened because the conversion of two to four million accounts and training of 5,000 Service Reps was phased in week by week.

NOTES ON QUASI-EXPERIMENTAL RESEARCH DESIGN

Service Rep selection for this experiment was not totally random. Thirty-six Service Reps were selected from one office based on their normal training rotation schedules. These schedules may be somewhat biased by seniority. A comparison of the pre-BOS average handling time for the combined 36 Service Reps of 6.8 minutes compares very generally to the total office Service Rep pool (130 Service Reps) average of 6.6 minutes.

The collection of data for this experiment began on August 1 for all Service Reps involved in the experiment. Average call length measurements are tracked daily for each Service Rep as a normal part of the job. Obtaining and recording this data was totally unobtrusive to the Service Rep performance. Call lengths are tracked electronically by computer switches as calls come in and exit from a Service Rep's console board. Supervisors heavily monitor extended calls or absences from the console. The measurement equipment and process has been in place for more than 20 years and is quite reliable. This equipment is monitored and serviced for peak performance as a normal part of the call center's operations and was not changed during any part of this study. Performance data from these switches is replicable as history files are maintained in the switch databases and reports continue to be printed weekly. Call types to our service centers are always random as customers feel a need to call for service.

Assignment of call types to Service Reps is done by the switches in a round robin mode of next available. Total calls (observations) measured before the experiment for three weeks exceeded 26,000. Total calls for the ten weeks measured after the introduction of BOS was 61,000.

By measuring the Service Rep's performance very closely to the point of implementing the system, the experimenter made concerted efforts to control for changes in employee attitudes, job stresses, seasonality, Service Rep work hour shifts over time, problems on the job, at home, happiness levels, etc. The assumption being that whatever factors were influencing the Service Rep one month and up to the change variable would continue to influence the Service Rep 10 to 12 weeks after the experiment. Thus, Service Rep performance changes would more likely be caused by the experimental variable (BOS) than fluctuations in these extraneous external variables. One Service Rep retired and two others transferred to different departments in the company. Data for these three Service Reps were removed from both the pre-BOS and post-BOS measurements to ensure consistency. The original experimental group size was 39. Thus the same specific persons are involved throughout the experiment, minimizing selection as a source of main effect.

MEASURE OF SUCCESS: USER ATTITUDE

These observations were further confirmed by the following interview results conducted with 29 of the 36 remaining Service Reps in our group study 10 weeks after converting to BOS:

(1) Honestly, after having worked with the new system for two months now, if it were your choice, which system would you choose? (Prefer BOS or prior system):
Prefer BOS = 20
Prefer prior system = 9

(2) Briefly, can you tell me why you chose ______?

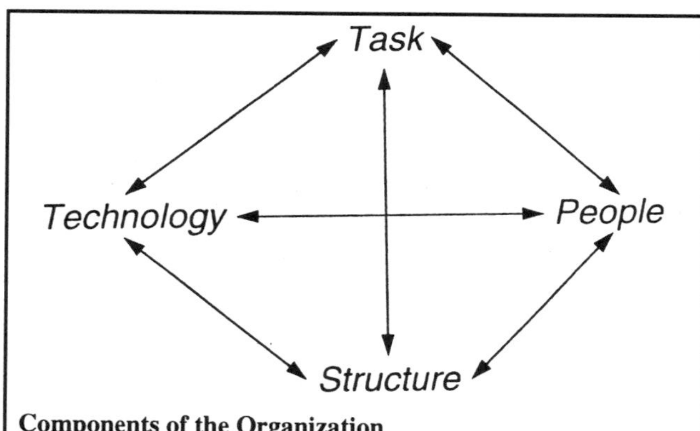

Components of the Organization
- Task, Technology, People and Structure are interrelated and mutually adjusting
- Technology changes Ooften cause other components to adjust and dampen impact of innovation

Source: Peter Keen, Sloan School of Management, MIT, "IS and Organizational Change," January 1981

The Leavitt Diamond Model

Prefer BOS because: BOS is faster, easier, not as much work as prior system, screens flow easier, all information is there to serve customer.

Prefer prior system because: Orders (what Service Reps are paid on) were easier to do in prior system and you can't track orders well in BOS.

(3) Note: To change the subject, the next question was: How long have you been using computers, any kind of computer?

(4) Which system do you feel, from your experience, allows you to better serve customers?
BOS is better to serve customers: = 21
Prior system is better to serve customers: = 7
Systems about the same: = 1

(5) Briefly, why is ______ better for serving customers?
Question 4 answers mirrored Question 2 on both systems.

These responses and results were very surprising. The complaints noted earlier in this chapter were actually made by the same Service Reps surveyed above. After working with BOS for 2.5 months, the majority of Service Reps found BOS to be (of all things) easier to use, simpler, and better designed to serve customers. This is a significant turnaround in user satisfaction with the system. Given no major changes or fixes to the system during this interim period - this data lends significant credence to the hypotheses that the average handling time increase was not due to poor design, system defects, or any major system inadequacy.

NOTES ON INTERVIEW RESEARCH

The interviewer (the author) explained at the beginning of each interview who he was, why the interview was being conducted and the overall purpose of the study. Responses to interview questions were recorded on the spot and immediately for accuracy. In an attempt to provide the interviewee with a sense of confidentiality, a tally sheet was visibly used to record many responses. No names were recorded and comments were collected in a tally sheet format as well, making it difficult to attribute ownership to a specific person. This data was recorded in full view of the interviewee.

MEASURES OF SUCCESS VS. USER EXPECTATIONS

It was not how BOS was designed, developed or its technical problems that led to CCU's widespread service problems, but rather it was the methods used to deploy the system into user organizations. The observations above point to a flawed systems implementation process.

The data illustrate that average call handling time decreased in each of the original companies. The survey results demonstrate that employee dissatisfaction with BOS has dramatically shifted to satisfaction with the system after a learning curve effect. Based on these two critical measurements of success and given time for the learning curve effect, BOS should now be regarded as a success by users. This is not the case.

How do we explain this disparity between successful results and user expectations/dissatisfaction with the system? The answer to this problem lies in the methodology used to implement systems. This answer also explains why many systems are technical successes and organizational failures.

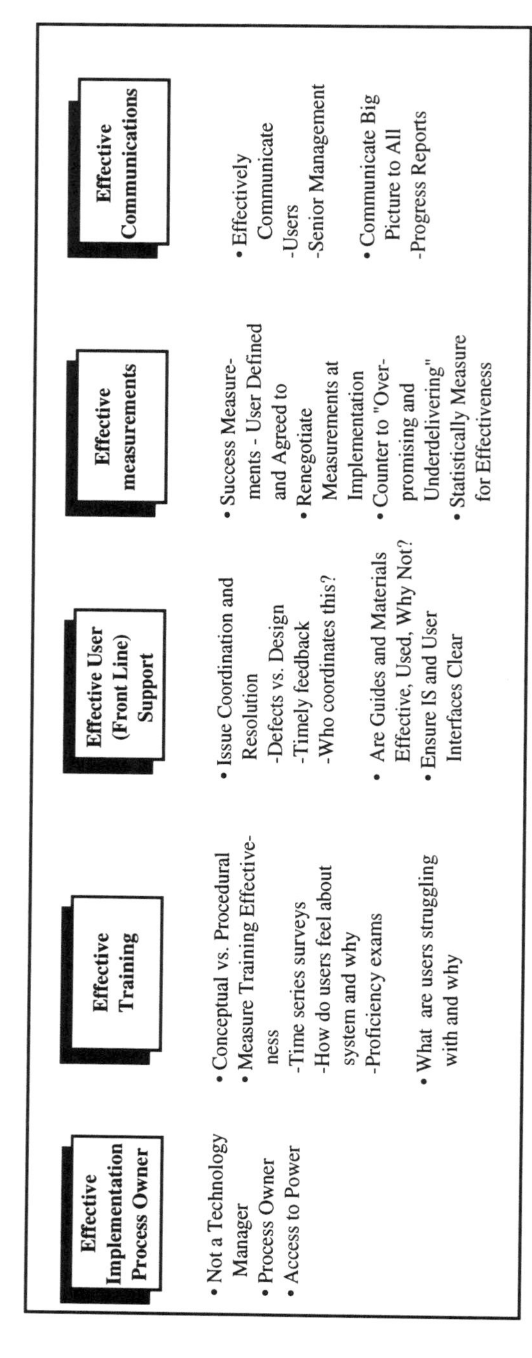

Effective Systems Delivery

SILOISM

The traditional methodology of developing and implementing systems in an assembly line process is depicted.

Each phase represents a silo of activity with unique personnel and unique functional inputs and outputs. Outputs from one phase such as user requirements are gathered and documented by business analysts. These documents are then handed over to designers as input to the next phase: Design. Designers use the requirements to create data models and entity programs that are, in turn, handed to programmers for coding and testing. A major problem with the silo approach of systems development is the discontinuance of user involvement throughout the project. The timeframe to develop and deliver large systems often exceeds one to two years. Many changes in company personnel, in company processes, and in system requirements are likely to have evolved by the time the system is ready for implementation. Requirements gathered in earlier phases are likely to be outdated, inadequate, and possibly non-applicable. A silo approach exacerbates the already difficult problem of trying to keep up with ever-evolving system requirements.

Prior to the 1980s, users were primarily involved in the requirements phase of the development process. Their next experience with the process was during implementation. This approach to systems development was found to be flawed and radically changed in the 1980s. Most projects today use Joint Application Development (JAD) which stresses user involvement in the requirements, design, and code and testing phases. Programmers today often sit with users to gain a better understanding of the functions they are coding into a new system. This joint IS and user involvement has led to systems which at implementation *technically* meet user requirements. Unfortunately, this successful teaming of IS and users in the front end of the systems development process ends at the implementation phase. Once the systems are successfully coded and tested, they are handed over to users for implementation in their organizations. This approach of dropping systems off at the users' doorsteps is a primary cause of many system failures at implementation.

IMPLEMENTATION IS A PROCESS CHANGE, NOT A SYSTEM CHANGE

It is important to recognize that technically beautiful systems are not the reason companies invest millions in systems development projects. Systems are essential components of key corporate processes that enable the successful delivery of company services and products. The implementation of new technology into an organization causes change in that organization. The Leavitt Diamond Model illustrates the important interrelationship of components in an organization and how the components often shift to dampen the effects of the introduction of changes, including technology enhancements.

PRESCRIPTIVE MODEL FOR EFFECTIVE SYSTEMS DELIVERY

Companies underestimate and often fail to plan for the changes that accompany the implementation of a new system. The complexity of systems implementation, organizational shifts and overall process changes are difficult challenges for most companies to manage. An effective systems delivery model must address all the components of a process to ensure successful goal attainment. The following model is prescriptive for managing process change. The model contains a comprehensive set of guidelines for successfully managing the complex and shifting issues of systems implementation, organizational shifts, and process change.

Implementation Process Manager

Given the best systems design and/or designers, it is highly unlikely that the process being mechanized will be perfectly captured by the new system. Organization and responsibility shifts, changes in tasks, and most importantly, user reactions and resistance must be managed effectively. A key proposal of this chapter is the establishment of an Implementation Process Owner to manage process changes and adjustments.

An Implementation Process Owner is critical to effectively delivering systems to the user organization. The Implementation Process Owner owns, directs, and adjusts the process to correspond to shifting organizational changes. The Implementation Process Owner must be skilled in both technology and organization dynamics and have access to power. He or she must be able to resolve issues that overlap organization boundaries such as those that occur between IS and the user organization during systems implementation and process change.

Valuable resources and energies are wasted as employee groups debate responsibilities, system deliverables, measurements, and timeframes. During the implementation of BOS at CCU, service center managers (users) and IS systems managers argued ad nauseam over system "glitches." On a daily basis, the users argued the system was not working as it should. IS argued and produced documentation detailing that so-called "defects" were never included in the systems design. At CCU, the debate on "issues vs. defects" consumed an extensive and expensive number of employee hours. An effective process for resolving these debates did not materialize.

The Implementation Process Owner must be accountable for and resolve issues that span organizational boundaries. These issues generally cannot be solved at lower and middle-level management. The Implementation Process Owner must quickly take ownership of such issues, come to a resolution, and effectively communicate and implement the decision. This ownership and resolution of complex issues avoids hours of wasted time in bickering, frustrated employees, and non-productive corporate resources.

Effective Training

Effective training is a bottom-line financial issue. Companies can either take the time and expenses to adequately train employees up front, or allow employees to learn the new processes on the job— negatively impacting customer service, and increasing employee dissatisfaction with the system and company. CCU cut plans to train its employees from ten days to six. Employees felt training was rushed and inadequate. Employee morale and customer service dropped. At best, it took them 12 weeks to learn the system. Many offices instituted paid Saturday training to review lessons covered in the original six-day BOS training. Other offices simply set aside days to retrain BOS material.

Ensuring that users are effectively trained is critical to effective systems delivery. Inadequate or improper training is a key reason users reject and resist the implementation of new systems. Although there is no panacea for correct training, as different people learn best by various instructional means, a number of effective training techniques can be employed to ensure training effectiveness. Formal training is preferred to self-taught. Users allowed to train themselves often form mental models of how the system works based on incomplete, oversimple and "superstitious" experiences with the system. Hands-on training is clearly more effective than straight lecture-based instruction. Many companies continue to err by using procedural training, which explains exactly how a user is to use the system based on required functions. A better approach is conceptual model training in which users are presented with overviews of how the system is organized and how the system works. A road map of the system is presented in addition to basic procedural commands. With a conceptual knowledge of the system, the user is able to perform more complex tasks in which all the steps needed to perform a task have not been spelled out. This empowers users to solve problems on their own and dramatically improves user proficiency and satisfaction with the system.

Measuring training effectiveness ensures that the training program is accomplishing key objectives. Effective tools for measuring user knowledge of the system are time series surveys and proficiency exams. Use surveys at various intervals to ask users how they feel about the training, the system, and why. Very valuable concerns and problems with the system are likely to surface. Training and support can be adjusted accordingly before users are serving customers. Proficiency exams can identify areas users are struggling with and identify additional training/coaching that is required. Effective training provides a significant return on investment when implementing new processes.

Effective User (Front Line) Support

Service Reps at CCU felt very frustrated as they identified problems with using the system, but often responses back were very slow or their issues went unaddressed. Non-resolution of these problems precipitated subtle, but stifling organizational finger pointing. Users blamed IS for creating systems that were too complex and not user friendly, while IS suggested the user groups lacked the ability to use the valuable new technologies at their fingertips. Instead of cooperation and teamwork, user attitudes degenerated to nonproductive finger pointing and process effectiveness degraded. The Implementation Process Owner must ensure that support and problem resolution procedures are effective.

Mechanization in and of itself does not constitute effectiveness. The mechanization of functions, and methods and procedures does not guarantee an improved process. Front-line user support during implementation and ongoing is very important to systems success. Are user guides and materials effective? Can users understand them? More importantly, do users use them? Why or why not? A fast, new on-line handbook that replaced numerous cruddy old service order manuals was not used at CCU because Service Reps couldn't find the information they were looking up. The same products and services had different names in each of the five companies. The combined Index and Handbook had standardized to one name per service/order. After valiant efforts to guess at the names for many products, Service Reps often reverted to keeping hand notes or hunted furiously in old closets for those cruddy old manuals.

Manuals, guides, and methods and procedures (M&P), whether mechanized or not, must be monitored and measured for effectiveness. Survey front-line users to ascertain if they use these materials. Why or why not? If not, fix. These are key resources intended to help users more effectively use the system and serve customers. Who updates these materials? How do changes and adjustments to the process get reflected in these materials?

Ensure that on-site support is adequate. Clearly identify the key IS organization interfaces and user organization interfaces. Establish and clearly communicate procedures for front-line questions and issues to be handled. Clearly establish the chain of command for problem resolution. Establish, track, and reward timeliness measurements for response back to and resolution of front-line employee issues with the system and process.

Effective Measurements

An important goal in establishing measurements of success is that they're established for the most part by the user organization, and not the systems organization. Successful BOS system integration and staff consolidations were insufficient and inadequate in making BOS a success at CCU.

The primary measures of success from the user organization's perspective was reducing average contact handling time and not negatively impacting customer service. Although these were the expectations the system was judged by, these measures of success were neither well communicated nor documented. Many systems development projects like BOS often exceed one to two years. User needs, requirements, and expectations are very likely to have changed or shifted from the time the system requirements and business goals were gathered. The implementation Process Owner must reevaluate and probably renegotiate measures of success at systems implementation. Key performance indicators must be established and agreed to by key company stakeholders and users. A plan using statistical methods to measure performance (to avoid chasing outliers) must be implemented. Ensuring that these objectives are realistic and achievable, the Process Owner must effectively communicate these to everyone.

Effective Communications

Effective communications is the silver bullet to allay system expectations of "overpromising and underdelivering." What are the measurements of success for the system? When will they be realized? All these questions can easily be answered and effectively communicated by the Implementation Process Owner. As shifts in measurements occur (user changes), these changes must be documented and communicated in a timely manner to all. System and implementation process objectives and timelines must be communicated to both users and key stakeholders. It is not enough and probably unwise to assume that senior managers are ensuring that lower level mangers and users are in the information loop. A very wise technique is to visit and sit with users of the system periodically and ask how things are going. Adjust the communication process and flow accordingly.

CONCLUSION

The Five Small Secrets identified above are offered as a prescriptive model for successfully implementing centralized, transaction-oriented, mandatory usage type systems like BOS. The need for such a model has been exacerbated by today's business climate of downsized organizations. Many companies gamble that they can fix the problems of systems implementation post facto. This is a huge mistake. The implementation of a new system is a Moment of Truth for the long-term success of most system projects. Users forced to suffer through system implementations when they are poorly trained, inadequately supported, not sure of system measurements and objectives, are likely to subvert the system's efforts for years to come. The effort to reclaim their faith is probably best invested in the next system.

The cost to implement a Process Owner, effective training, effective communications, effective user support and effective measurements is small. The return on this small investment is huge. Implementing the Five Small Secrets to systems success can save corporations millions in investment dollars, reduce negative impacts to customer service, and enhance employee morale and systems acceptance.

REFERENCES

Adams, Dennis, Nelson, R. Ryan and Todd, Peter (1992). "Perceived Usefulness, Ease of Use and Usage of Information Technology: A Replication." *MIS Quarterly,* 16(2), 227-248.

Ahituv, N. (1980). "A Systematic Approach Towards Assessing the Value of an Information System." *MIS Quarterly*, 4(4), 61-75.

Baronas, A. M., & Louis, R. (1988). "How User Involvement Leads to Systems Acceptance." *MIS Quarterly,* 12(1), 111-123.

Bean, A. S., & Radnor, M. (1979). "The Role of Intermediaries in the Implementation of Management Science." *TIMS Studies in the Management Sciences,* 13, 121-37.

Bardach, E. (1977). *The Implementation Game: What Happens After a Bill Becomes a Law.*" MIT Press, Cambridge, Mass.

Burkhardt, M. E. and Brass, D. J. (1990). "Changing Patterns or Patterns of Change: The Effects of a Change in Technology on Social Network Structure and Power." *Administrative Science Quarterly,* 35, 104-127.

Churchman, C. W., & Schainblatt, A. H. (1967). "On Mutual Understanding." *Management Science,* 12(2), B40-42.

Davis, Fred D. (1989). "Perceived Usefulness, Perceived Ease of Use and User Acceptance of Information Technology." *MIS Quarterly*, 13(3), 319-339.

Delone, W. H. (1988). "Determinants of Success for Computer Usage in Small Business."*MIS Quarterly,* 12(1), 51-61.

Dunn, C. S. (1983). "The Influence of Instructional Methods on Concept Learning." *Science Education,* 67(5), 647-656.

Gattiker, U. E. and Paulson, D. (1987). "The Quest For Effective Teaching Methods: Achieving Computer Literacy for End Users." *INFOR,* 24(3), 256-272.

Ginzberg, M. J. (1981). "Early Diagnosis of MIS Implementation Failure: Promising Results and Unanswered Questions." *Management Science*, 27(4), 459-478.

Gist, M. E., Schwoerer, C. E. and Rosen, B. (1989). "Effects of Alternative Training Methods on Self-Efficacy and Performance in Computer Software Training." *Journal of Applied Psychology*, 74, 884-891.

Ives, B., & Olson, M. (1984). "User Involvement and MIS Success: A Review of Research." *Management Science,* 30(5), 586-603.

Jones, L. H. and Kydd, C. T. (1988). "An Information Processing Framework for Understanding Success and Failure of MIS Development Methodologies." *Information and Management*, 15(5), 263-271.

Latham, G. P. and Saari, L. M. (1979). "Application of Social Learning Theory to Training Supervisors Through Behavioral Modeling." *Journal of Applied Psychology*, 64(3), 239-246.

Lucas, Jr., H. C. (1993). *Information Systems Implementation.* New Jersey: Ablex Publishing Corporation.

Lucas, Jr., H. C. (1975). *Why Information Systems Fail.* New York: Columbia University Press.

Mayer, R. E. (1981). "The Psychology of How Novices Learn Computer Programming." *Computing Surveys*, 13(1), 121-141.

Neal, R. D., & Radnor, M. (1973). "The Relation Between Formal Procedures for Pursuing OR/MS Activities and OR/MS Group Success." *Operations Research*, 21(2), 451-74.

Nelson, R. R., and Cheney, P. H. (1987). "Training End Users: An Exploratory Study." *MIS Quarterly,* 11(4), 547-559.

Pettigrew, A. M. (1972). "Implementation Control as a Power Resource." *Sociology*, 6(2), 187-204.

Rivard, S. and Huff, S. L. (1988). "Factors of Success for End User Computing." *Communications of the ACM*, 31(5), 552-561.

Robey, D. and Taggert, W. (1981). "Measuring Managers Minds: The Assessment of Style in Human Information Processing." *Academy of Management Review,* 6(3), 375-384.

Robey, D., & Zeller, R. (1978). "Factors Affecting the Success and Failure of an Information System for Product Quality." *Interfaces,* 8(2), 70-75.

Sein, M. K. and Bostrom, R. P. (1989). "Individual Differences and Conceptual Models in Training Novice Users." *Human Computer Interaction,* 4, 197-229.

Tait, P., & Vessey, I. (1988). "The Effect of User Involvement on Systems Success: A Contingency Approach." *MIS Quarterly,* 12(1), 91-108.

Wexley, K. N. (1984). "Personnel Training." *Annual Review of Psychology*, 35, 519-551.

Chapter 4

Trends in Information Technology in Small Businesses

Georgios I. Doukidis
Athens University of Economics and Business, Greece

Steve Smithson
London School of Economics, UK

Takis Lybereas
Warwick Business School, UK

It is widely recognized that IT has made considerable inroads into large organizations, such that the majority now rely on IT for their day-to-day operations. The position regarding small businesses is less clear as they face somewhat different opportunities and constraints. In particular, the approach to the introduction of IT into small firms in less developed national IT environments has received little attention in the literature. This chapter reports on the results of a survey of the approaches adopted by small firms in Greece. The findings are analyzed in terms of previous experience with computers, factors influencing the decision to adopt IT, advice received, staff involvement in IS development, training, and problems encountered and the solutions adopted. The results are compared with a study performed five years earlier in order to identify recent trends.

During the last 20 years, there has been considerable growth in the number and prosperity of small businesses (SBs) throughout Western economies, including Europe (Sengenberger, Loveman and Piore, 1991). This has been noticeable regardless of the political complexion of the national government. This growth, which is in line with the teachings of management theorists such as Drucker (1989) and Porter (1990), has been seen in both the manufacturing and services sectors. Across Europe, SBs are employing an increasing proportion of the total working population and are becoming increasingly identified with new products and new production processes, thus contributing to exports,

This chapter originally appeared in the Journal of End User Computing, vol. 6, no. 4.

national wealth and competitiveness. Many governments (at national, state and local levels) have recognized the benefits of SB growth and have attempted to provide a relevant support infrastructure in terms of local enterprise agencies or small business development centers (Gibb and Manu, 1990). SBs comprise the vast majority of businesses throughout Europe (taking the widest definition of a business, including all the self-employed), counting for more than 90 percent of businesses in the UK, Italy, Germany, Belgium, Holland and Greece.

Information technology (IT), ranging from mainframe-based transaction processing systems to office information systems based on local area networks, and ranging from computer-integrated manufacturing to communications-based applications such as videoconferencing and electronic mail, has made considerable inroads into large organizations. The majority of such organizations now rely on IT for their day-to-day operations. This diffusion of technology has been credited with significant cost reductions, gains in productivity and organizational effectiveness plus, in some cases, a definite competitive advantage (Earl, 1989). While considerable successes have been achieved, there have also been a number of technical and commercial disasters. Angell and Smithson (1991) argue that IT needs to be viewed in terms of both opportunities and risks, where the risks may outweigh the promised opportunities.

There is no reason to believe that these issues apply any less to small enterprises than to the largest multinational. Meyer and Boone (1987) outline numerous cases where small companies have benefited through the use of external databases, office automation applications (e.g., spreadsheets), and project management software. The general trend away from costly mainframe computing, based on in-house programs, towards cheaper user-friendly microcomputers, with standard software packages, means that sophisticated tools are becoming increasingly available to SBs, without the need for advanced programming skills.

However, it is less clear to what extent these advantages are realized in practice by firms in less developed national IT environments such as Greece, or how such firms approach IT in order to reap the rewards. In this chapter, we report on a survey started in the summer of 1989 that collected information on the introduction and use of microcomputers in Greek SBs. We concentrated on microcomputers since this is the technology that dominates this sector. We wished to 'paint a picture' of the situation confronting SBs, including their previous experience with computers, the factors that influenced their decision to adopt IT, the type of advice they received, the amount of staff involvement in IS development, and the type of problems they frequently encountered.

In order to identify recent trends, the results are compared with an earlier study which surveyed SBs in Greece, Denmark and Ireland in 1984 (CEC 1985). This latter study examined the approaches taken to the adoption of IT by 50 companies in each country.

Although our study uses different firms, we carefully selected the firms and designed the interview questionnaire in such a way as to render the studies as comparable as possible.

INFORMATION TECHNOLOGY AND SMALL BUSINESSES

Concerning the use of IT, Heikkila, Saarinen and Saaksjarvi (1991) propose three major differences between SBs and large organizations:

- SBs tend to use computers more as tools and less as a communications medium;
- the few stakeholders involved in SBs mean that there are likely to be fewer problems in terms of organizational politics;

• SBs have many fewer resources available to implement IT solutions.

While it is hard to dispute the lack of resources, the other points are less clearcut. Firstly, the treatment of computers as tools may only be a temporary phase as networks promise considerable gains for SBs in terms of collaboration with other firms. Lacking their own resources but with normally a plentiful supply of entrepreneurialism, SBs rely more on short-term subcontracting and other temporary arrangements to satisfy the needs of their customers. Secondly, SBs are not totally free of organizational conflict and family politics can be just as bitter as the politics found in bureaucracies.

Wroe (1987) argues that small firms possess certain potential advantages in making use of the technology, since they are able to complete the transition process much faster and they possess greater flexibility to undertake any reorganization required to realize the full benefits of the technology (Poutsma and Walravens, 1989). Furthermore, the flexibility of new technologies facilitates small batch, tailored or niche-focused production, the preserve of the small firm. It has been argued (Dwyer, 1990; Clark, 1987) that IT promises considerable gains for SBs, allowing them to increase their market scope and secure their position within the industry through improved communication with both large firms and other small firms. Through accurate and systematic record-keeping, IT can help SBs in areas of traditional concern: the collection of outstanding payments, stock control, increased sales, and improved after-sales service. Although Lincoln and Warberg (1987) found that, in practice, SBs failed to utilize the marketing data that they possessed, Poutsma and Walravens (1989) argue that IT can help an SB to develop its markets, increase turnover, raise profitability, and still remain a small firm able to realize the benefits of that smallness in service and flexibility.

These views are further supported by Cornford and Whitley (1991) who identify the following benefits IT offers to SBs:

- improved productivity and performance within the enterprise;
- greater internal control of operations;
- the possibility of new ways of managing activities;
- improved management perception and penetration of business environments;
- the possibility of new organizational forms (e.g., networked organizations);
- the delivery of a valued and high quality package of product and service;
- the extension of available markets;
- the redefinition of existing businesses or the spawning of whole new businesses.

On the other hand, SBs have particular problems in adopting and using IT. Typically they do not have the appropriate skills available in-house and thus have to train existing staff or purchase those skills in the marketplace. IT is usually associated with a systematic approach to management and decision-making, and its introduction requires careful planning, whereas much SB management practice is based on short-term, informal, ad hoc lines (Hill et al., 1984). Although the technology is much cheaper than before, it still represents a considerable investment for SBs, which traditionally lack such funds. The introduction of IT, which may lead to dramatic changes in the business's fundamental activities, requires an awareness and basic knowledge within the management function, but many owners of SBs appear to be too busy 'surviving' to invest time in such projects. Therefore, there is a significant risk that such efforts to introduce IT will be unsuccessful and the cost of such a failure may be fatal for the small firm lacking adequate financial and productive cushioning (Scholhammer and Kuriloff, 1979). Thus, it is hardly surprising that until recently many SBs have avoided such risks by ignoring IT.

SURVEY METHODOLOGY

Our criteria for selecting companies to include in the study were as follows:

- they should employ less than 100 staff;
- they should have used microcomputers for between six months and five years;
- they should make up a sample that was comparable with the earlier study in terms of industrial sectors (i.e. manufacturing, services, retail and distribution).

On this basis, 50 companies were selected from membership lists of chambers of commerce, from which we excluded wholly owned subsidiaries of large companies and publicly owned companies. Based on the economic statistics available at the time, this sample was fairly representative of Greek SBs as a whole. Like the majority of companies and computer systems in Greece, most of the respondents were located in the greater Athens area (Attiki). As can be seen from the profile (Table 1), the companies comprised a wide range of SBs in terms of industrial sector, size, age of the company, and length of microcomputer experience. These statistics are comparable to those of the earlier study; for example, for the latter study, the distribution of cases across sectors was: retail and distribution (42 percent), services (36 percent) and manufacturing (22 percent); while the number of employees was: below 20 (54 percent), 21-40 (10 percent), 41-60 (24 percent), and 61-100 (12 percent).

The survey was conducted through semi-structured interviews based on a questionnaire similar to the one used by the earlier study. The questionnaire was a balance between 'open' and 'closed' questions and was divided into the following main areas: previous experience with IT, factors influencing the decision to adopt IT, advice obtained, staff

Table 1: Profile of Companies Surveyed (n=50)

Sector	%	No. of employees	%	Years of trading	%	Years using microcomputers	%
Retail &		Below 20	38	1 - 10	26	Below 1	22
distribution	40	21 - 40	14	11 - 20	34	1 - 2	32
Services	32	41 - 60	28	21 - 50	26	2 - 3	26
Manufacturing	28	61 - 100	20	over 50	14	3 - 4	14
						4 - 5	6

Table 2: Profile of Respondents (n=50)

Title	%
Owner	38
General Manager	26
Manager	16
Accountant	12
Other	8

involvement, training issues, and problems encountered in implementation and their solutions. We chose to use interviews to allow the respondents to provide a contextual interpretation of the issues raised. The questionnaire was tested through pilot interviews. The interviewees were generally managers responsible for the introduction and/or operation of the microcomputers; their organizational positions are shown in Table 2. The title 'general manager' includes managing directors and chief executives. In SBs, owners and general managers are often the same person; in this case, the respondent was referred to as the owner. In this table, 'manager' denotes someone responsible for a single department, although for the remainder of this chapter, the term will be used as a synonym for 'respondent', reflecting the general level of the respondents.

Each interview was quite detailed, lasting from one to three hours. In many cases, other company staff were invited to contribute regarding specific details. The questionnaire was used to structure the discussion and, where necessary, follow-up telephone calls were used to clarify any outstanding or ambiguous issues.

The results were analyzed in terms of simple frequency distributions and compared with the findings of the earlier study. The results are interpreted in light of the qualitative comments of the respondents themselves.

PREVIOUS EXPERIENCE WITH COMPUTERS

There had been a considerable increase in respondents' and companies' previous experience of computers since the earlier (1984) study (Table 3). In 1989, more than three-quarters (76 percent) of the companies had had some experience, compared to the 1984 situation, when only one-fifth had any previous experience. Personal experience had similarly grown considerably, with the majority of respondents (56 percent) claiming substantial or extensive experience, as opposed to the position in 1984 when the majority had had no experience at all with computers.

Personal experience had usually been obtained at a university, through a training course, or through the use of computer bureau services. Almost half of the companies had used, or were still using, a computer bureau service, in comparison with 10 percent in the earlier survey. University courses are likely to continue to play an important role but, in many cases, personal experience had been gained in positions previously held in other companies. The influence of the younger generation was important; we encountered cases where a manager or key employee had been encouraged to work with IT by their children's familiarity with microcomputers (through school studies or hobbies). Even computer games seemed to have facilitated this familiarization. Stair, Crittenden and Crittenden (1989) found that the majority of U.S. owners/managers of small businesses surveyed had no formal IT education or training. From our interviews, it was apparent that this considerable increase in previous experience (both company and personal) had changed people's expectations of IT and consequently their approach to its introduction, as will be discussed below.

This increased experience would seem intuitively to indicate a greater likelihood of successful systems development although the literature is somewhat ambivalent concerning the various aspects of this factor. On the basis of their survey in Finland, Heikkila, Saarinen and Saaksjarvi (1991) found that there was little substitute for experience; prior experience with computers meant that users were more likely to evaluate the packages in advance (perhaps by consulting existing users), more likely to obtain the benefits of integration, by applying the software over a number of linked applications, and were less dependent upon vendors' training facilities. They found that problems were most likely when inexperienced users failed to give sufficient consideration to the acquisition and requirements specification phases.

However, other writers argue that, taken by itself, the length of time an organization has used IT has either no effect on success (DeLone, 1988; Montazemi, 1988) or a slightly negative effect (Raymond, 1985). They argue that expertise and skills are more important than the passage of time. For example, Raymond (1985) found that satisfaction increased when organizations developed and operated more applications in-house. Lees (1987) claims that successful IS development in SBs is related to the employment of technical experts (either internal staff or outside consultants) who have a good knowledge of systems analysis, design and implementation, backed up by extensive vendor support. Montazemi (1988) found that satisfaction increased when end users were computer literate, while DeLone (1988) argued that it was the expertise and knowledge of the chief executive that was important. DeLone also advocated increased attention to the coordination of planning and control over computers, a skill that is often lacking in SBs (Stair, Crittenden and Crittenden, 1989).

FACTORS INFLUENCING THE DECISION TO ADOPT IT

The increased number of factors prompting the initial decision to acquire a microcomputer (Table 4) may demonstrate the increased experience of SBs with IT. Respondents expected IT to provide information on actual production costs, and details of sales and customers. In most cases, they expected IT to provide this essential management information not only faster and when needed, but also in various formats, depending on the manager's decision-making preferences. Similarly, Farhoomand and Heryeyk (1985) found that 'information overload' was a key incentive to computerize. The increasing realization of IT's value as a productivity tool can be seen in our correspondents' increased emphasis on 'time saving and coping with workload'. This reflects two inherent problems of SBs: lack of in-house expertise for specific tasks and a continuous fight for survival in a competitive world. This can also be seen in the demands for improved stock control procedures and greater accuracy.

Improved accounting procedures were mentioned less often, reflecting a realization that computers are much more than glorified adding machines. While accounting applications are still often among the first to be implemented, the benefits of other applications are becoming increasingly well known. The shift in expectations from staff reductions to other cost reductions also reflects the growing experience and maturity regarding IT.

A majority (54 percent) of the companies reported no reservations at all about the introduction of computers (Table 5), reflecting increased awareness and perceived improvements in the technology. Despite a general increase in experience, more than 20 percent of

Table 3: Previous Experience with Computers (n = 50)

Level	Company		Personal	
	1984 %	1989 %	1984 %	1989 %
Extensive/substantial	6	34	8	56
Moderate	6	24	12	18
Little	8	18	26	12
None	80	24	54	14

respondents still felt that a lack of computer experience remained a constraint. However, there was less concern with the problem of software and hardware selection, mostly as a result of improved access to information through consultancy, magazines, and exhibitions. However, this was less true in the case of smaller companies who typically cannot afford the services of an IT consultant and must rely on the personal efforts of the owner/manager. This is an extra burden on the owner/manager who is usually a 'jack of all trades' with very little time to explore the relatively new world of IT. Nevertheless, Heikkila, Saarinen and Saaksjarvi (1991) argue that software selection is still a key decision. They found that success was more likely when users evaluated software packages in advance to ensure that the package matched the information requirements and met the criteria of usability and adaptability.

'Potential implementation problems' refers to fears about the changeover period, mostly due to perceived shortcomings in the existing (manual) system. The relatively unstructured way in which most SBs are managed (Yap 1989) can make such implementation a considerable problem. Worries over the cost of IT are not surprising given the very limited

Table 4: Factors Influencing the Initial Decision to Computerize (n=50)

Factors	**1984 %**	**1989%**
Improved processing & availability of information	40	50
Time savings and coping with workload	18	42
Improved stock control procedures	24	24
Greater accuracy	12	22
Improved accounting procedures	40	18
Cost reduction	0	16
Staff reduction	12	6
Total	**146**	**178**

Table 5: Major Reservations (n=50)

Reservations	**1984%**	**1989%**
None	40	54
Lack of computer experience	24	22
Software and hardware selection	36	20
Potential implementation problems	8	16
Cost	-	8
Adequate service	14	6
Other	8	20

investment funds typically available to SBs. This may also be a reflection of past experiences, especially if past projects have exceeded their budgets. Another important fear (included in the 'other' category) was the anticipated resistance to change primarily from older staff who may be reluctant to learn new working practices. Our findings are mostly in line with those of other researchers. For example, apart from aspects of cost and lack of expertise, Gable and Raman (1992) also noted a belief among some CEOs of small businesses that IT was unnecessary for them, based on a misunderstanding of the benefits and a reluctance to pay for consultancy and software. In addition, Baker (1987) found that small businesses were constrained by a feeling that technology was changing too fast, by a lack of knowledge about the technology, a lack of confidence in the claims of the vendors, and a mistrust of future vendor support.

One way of reducing such uncertainty is to carry out a formal feasibility study. The present study found that the proportion of companies that performed a feasibility study, prior to the purchase and introduction of their first microcomputer, increased from 40 percent to 60 percent. In light of the risks involved, it could be argued that such a proportion is still inadequate, but it does indicate that Greek SBs are taking a more systematic and professional attitude towards such important decisions. Only 30 percent of the respondents used outside consultants, which is partly due to a traditional reluctance of Greek managers (from both large and small companies) to pay for external services and a lack of appropriate consultants. Very few of the smaller SBs performed a feasibility study, due partly to the costs of hiring a specialist but, perhaps more importantly, many of these managers did not understand the concept of a feasibility study. They preferred to base their decision on an informal exchange of ideas with other managers and whatever information they could discover through personal 'research' into the IT market.

Although it was difficult to give a precise number of man-days spent in reaching the decision to purchase IT, only 16 percent spent less than a week, 26 percent spent two to three weeks, and 36 percent spent over three weeks (20 percent of respondents were unable to answer as they did not keep such records). By SB standards, this activity consumes a considerable amount of effort, especially on the part of the owner/manager, reflecting the problems IT poses for SBs.

Table 6: Type of Advice Sought (n=50)

Type of advice	**1984%**	**1989%**
Type of computer	86	52
Type of software	72	50
Staff training	44	44
Staffing the project	18	20
Company/job reorganization	2	18
Decide on the need	8	14
Other	0	20

ADVICE RECEIVED

SBs still actively sought advice on the selection of hardware and software (Table 6), although to a much lesser extent than before. The reduction doubtless again reflects the increased experience and greater availability of information. It is encouraging to see an increasing demand for advice on non-technological aspects, such as the potential company/ job reorganization that may arise with the introduction of new technology. There seemed to be a growing realization that IT can have a considerable impact on all aspects of the working and social environment, including the non-automated and informal components (Liebenau and Backhouse, 1990). These results suggest that many SB managers are beginning to take the introduction of IT seriously.

There was still a high demand for advice about training and other staffing issues, as staff and skill availability can constrain SBs in their attempts to change the way they work. In most cases, the manager has little time to develop yet another skill and it may not be possible to free key employees from their current jobs without risking interruptions in the operation of the business. Advice on training mainly concerned 'what' training should be given and 'by whom'. The importance of training can be illustrated, for example, when a new word-processor is introduced. If the secretaries are insufficiently trained, they may feel a lack confidence which may result in such a loss of job satisfaction that they resign, throwing the central administration of the business into chaos. 'Deciding on the need' for IT applied particularly to those SBs where quality of customer service was highly valued and loss of personal service was a major concern.

The high percentage of 'other' advice covers two very recent trends. The first concerns the growth in IT other than computers, including telephones, fax machines, photocopiers, typewriters and calculators, in addition to data communications networks and production technology. The second concerns advice that does not involve the use of IT; for example, the redesign of paper forms or changes in the structure or operating procedures may significantly improve the operation of a company's manual systems. This suggests that business analysis and management consultancy skills are equally (if not more) important than programming and 'hands-on' computer skills.

An SB typically cannot afford to hire an independent IT expert/consultant, leaving the responsibility for the analysis and design of information systems with the owner or senior

Table 7: Obtaining Advice from External Organizations (n=50)

Source of Advice	1984%	1989%
Software houses	20	50
Hardware suppliers	84	44
Outside consultants	18	28
Neighboring companies	36	16
Training companies	0	6
Support organizations	0	6
Other	22	12

Table 8: Number of Staff Involved in the Project Phases (n=50)

Staff involved	Decision		Selection		Implementation	
	1984	1989	1984	1989	1984	1989
Manager/owner	54	33	47	25	31	16
Accountant	7	12	8	13	20	10
Other	24	8	14	10	34	26
Total	85	53	69	48	85	52

manager. Understanding the problems involved in these tasks and finding appropriate solutions represents a considerable responsibility. Many SBs rely on their IT suppliers (Table 7), believing that they possessed the necessary expertise. This belief can often be misplaced as suppliers frequently lack the independence and the understanding of the user's business that are crucial to successful analysis and design.

As shown in Table 7, software houses, which grew quickly in Greece during the second half of the 1980s, replaced hardware suppliers as the main external source of advice. The use of outside consultants has increased but remains relatively low.

Frankenhuis (1977) found that organizations did not only hire consultants because of a lack of expertise, but they also valued an independent view and may well be looking for staff savings. While many consultants are both knowledgable and reputable, SBs are concerned not only about the cost and competence of consultants, but also the dangers of becoming dependent upon them. Furthermore, for many owner/managers of SBs, calling in a consultant is perceived as an admission of personal failure and lack of competence. Similarly, Gable (1991) found that clients were typically worried about consultants' lack of commitment and experience, their unsystematic approach and their inadequate appraisal of suppliers. He warns of the misconceived views clients had of the role of consultants including the belief that the client merely had either to provide information or terms of reference to the consultant for a solution to appear miraculously. This extreme reliance on consultants is bound to lead to failure (see also Lees and Lees 1987). Raymond (1985) also notes that consultants are not always the answer.

The increasing availability of professional advice seemed to have led to a decline in the popularity of the more informal advice from neighbouring companies. The limited role of training companies and support organizations (such as chambers of commerce, professional associations and public bodies) in providing a significant level of real assistance should be noted. The latter agencies do offer limited IT advisory services, although many SBs appeared to be unaware of the existence of such services. Elsewhere such schemes seem to be more successful; Gable and Raman (1992) discuss the success of a Singapore government scheme to support the introduction of IT into SBs.

In general, fewer companies were satisfied with the advice provided, with the proportion satisfied falling from 72 percent to 53 percent. This may be because increased experience has led to higher expectations. The reason most often mentioned for dissatisfaction was 'misunderstanding of real needs' and 'incompetence of suppliers'. In one case, this resulted in an unacceptable delay costing the user company several million drachmas. It was only due to the owner/manager's convictions regarding the benefits of IT, together with the effective organizational structure of the company, that the IT plan survived. However, there appeared to be a relatively high rate of satisfaction with external consultants and software houses when the SB was relatively experienced. In these cases, the user was able to formulate questions better, as well as gain greater insight from the advice received.

STAFF INVOLVEMENT IN IS DEVELOPMENT

In addition to the external advisors, the 50 respondents were asked how many user staff (including managers and owners) were involved in the three main phases of the project (Table 8): decision, selection and implementation. As can be seen, fewer SB staff were involved in each phase compared to the 1984 study. This was partly because of the increasing use of external professionals.

The decision phase includes identifying possible areas for improvement, assessing the potential for using microcomputers in the company, and evaluating associated costs/benefits and acceptability to staff. Managers/owners continued to dominate this stage but there were an increasing number of accountants involved. Many applications are in the accounting area and accountants are becoming increasingly expert in the use of IT. Compared to the earlier study, fewer other employees were involved in this stage because of the increased use of external advisors, an increased awareness of IT's importance and the increased knowledge of managers. Of the staff involved in this stage, 58 percent possessed some background knowledge, in comparison with 15 percent in 1984.

The selection phase includes tasks such as satisfying company requirements, reviewing products/suppliers in the marketplace, and negotiating the final contract. This is a time-consuming process and hence the reduction in managerial involvement is understandable. Accountants still played an important role, linked to their expertise in contracts and contract terms. Although fewer staff in total were involved in this phase (compared to 1984), there was an increase in the proportion with background knowledge/training (from 15 percent to 55 percent).

The implementation phase encompasses all activities required after the basic software has been installed. Typically, it includes the setup and conversion of files, testing and verification of new systems, changes to clerical procedures, and staff training. In general, there was less involvement by top management except where the owner had been heavily involved from the beginning. However, managers from one-third of the companies still managed to devote part of their scarce time to these activities. In some cases, this resulted in a delay in the completion of the project because the owner/manager 'could not find the time to supervise it.'

Senior managers/owners play a uniquely important part in the running of the smaller business, and their personal influence has a much wider impact than their counterparts in large firms. In the absence of other managers or armies of administrators, the chief executive of an SB may well be the main information user and decision maker, and he/she needs to be directly involved in any computerization. DeLone (1988) found that the key factor for the successful introduction of IT was the chief executive's familiarity and involvement with IT, and thus the reduction in involvement by our respondents may give rise for concern. DeLone argues that there is no substitute for the executive's knowledge of the business and their understanding of where IT will achieve the greatest benefit. This is because care has to be taken to ensure that the model built into the IS is a sound reflection of the owner/manager's

Table 9: Major Problems Encountered (n=50)

Problem	1984 %	1989%
Insufficient training	14	28
Power failures	8	22
Supplier incompetence	34	20
Staff	8	16
Software	2	8
Hardware	12	2
Other	22	4

'real world'. In Borovits and Neumann's (1988) case study, they attribute the success to the commitment of top management, high levels of user involvement (especially at the design stage), an evolutionary approach to development, and a concern with managing the change to avoid employee resistance.

Gable (1991) found that where consultants were employed by small firms, the involvement of managers from the firms was the key to successful projects. In his study, the hours of client involvement ranged from 35 to 300 hours. He argues that SB owners should accept the responsibility for directing projects rather than relying excessively on the consultants. Montazemi (1988) found that user involvement was likely to improve the prospects of developing a successful system in an SB, although DeLone (1988) concluded that success was not related to high levels of employee acceptance.

On the other hand, managers of SBs must be careful to avoid investing too much of their time in setting-up complex systems that may only produce a marginal benefit. Such a trade-off can only be managed sensibly where owner/managers have a high level of awareness and confidence in the technology. Martin (1989) identified five markedly different involvement patterns among top managers of small firms. Involvement increases from complete noninvolvement (Level 1), through goal-setting (Level 2), close involvement in implementation (Level 3), and direct involvement in development—e.g. programming - (Level 4), up to the top level of routine 'hands-on' interaction with the technology. We found examples of all levels of involvement, but the majority of our managers (about 60 percent) belonged to Level 2 where they were involved only in a managerial capacity, identifying goals and setting targets.

PROBLEMS ENCOUNTERED AND SOLUTIONS

Training is now recognized as the major problem (Table 9), with that provided by suppliers perceived as inadequate. This was followed by electrical power failures, which was rather surprising as it is a problem more often associated with less developed countries. Many companies had installed special devices to allow systems to continue working for long enough to save the necessary data.

Supplier incompetence, which was perceived as a lesser problem than in 1984, included the inability to determine the necessary machine capacity and their inability to understand the user's procedures. Staff problems related to perceived job threats due to a lack of confidence in the new technology. Software problems included programming errors, complex programs that were difficult to use, and poor documentation. Many of these problems resulted from the inability of the developer to comprehend the problem in hand or their lack of understanding of the user's business. Many SBs believed that, since their procedures and goals differ from other (especially larger) businesses, an understanding of both SBs and the industry sector is imperative. This seems to be increasingly recognized by the software houses, a number of which have set up special departments for specific sectors. There was a significant reduction in hardware and other problems.

It should be noted that many of the companies which had the most difficulties with these problems had not performed any form of feasibility study and had not sought any external advice. Some had no software support or hardware maintenance contracts, which worsened the impact of the problems. It seems essential for Greek SBs to understand the need for support in this area. Without sufficient expertise within the firm, the in-house policy followed by many SBs resulted in bigger problems.

When asked about ways in which these problems could have been avoided, the most popular suggestions included: improved staff training, a more detailed feasibility study, a more careful choice of suppliers, and the clarification of suppliers' responsibilities. The fact that very few mentioned 'seeking independent advice' serves to underline the deeply ingrained 'in-house' attitude of many Greek SBs and the lack of appropriate consultants and related advice-giving organizations. Heikkila, Saarinen and Saaksjarvi (1991) also mentioned the problems of inadequate training and support from suppliers, but remarked that a need for extensive training may be indicative of a fundamentally poor package. DeLone (1988) found that success was not related to the amount of employee training, nor to the level of external support provided. Nazem (1990) found that most U.S. small business users were fairly satisfied with packaged software in spite of the inadequate support and training provided.

CONCLUSION

It is widely believed that SBs are crucial to any nation's economic health because of their importance for innovation and job creation. However, it is also recognized that SBs face particular problems in realizing the opportunities offered by the use of information technology. This study has highlighted the trends within Greece, which is assumed to be typical of other small European countries (Cornford and Whitley, 1991; Heikkila, Saarinen and Saaksjarvi, 1991). Nevertheless, many of the issues raised are likely to be common to SBs internationally although particular national cultures may have strong mediating effects. However, such cultural factors are likely to manifest themselves in complex, subtle and unexpected ways and should be the subject of further research.

Our survey showed a number of changes since the earlier study in 1984. In general, there was an increased experience and awareness of IT among SBs. This increased maturity was visible both in a greater general level of confidence as well as an awareness of the nontechnical problems associated with IT. This suggests that many owner/managers have passed the stage of fascination/terror with the technology and are now actively implementing useful systems. There was an increased use of feasibility studies and external consultants, although the public support organizations seemed to have had little impact. Software houses have become very important to the SB sector, in terms of providing advice and training as well as the software itself. As expected, the attitude of the managers of SBs was somewhat different from that of large organizations. Doukidis, Smithson and Naoum (1992) show that the main preoccupation of IS managers from larger organizations in Greece surrounds issues of strategic management rather than technology management.

It is evident from this study that non-IT specialists (the owner/managers and accountants) dominate the first two stages of IT projects in SBs, that is decision and selection. Their position is difficult as they have to take potentially far-reaching decisions on the basis of limited expertise and little assistance. The results reported here have formed an input to a project (Doukidis and Karakoulas, 1994; Whitley, Poulymenakou and Cornford, 1992) to develop knowledge-based tools to assist managers of SBs to understand IT planning and the formulation of their IT needs with regard to their own business priorities.

By carrying out this research, it became clear that SBs generally have little regard for IT planning. The results reported here have formed an input to another project (Doukidis, Mylonopoulos, and Lybereas, 1993) which investigates IT planning in small and medium-sized enterprises which have distinctive entrepreneurial organizational cultures. We believe that the traditional 'stage' models (e.g., Nolan, 1979) of IT diffusion based on large bureaucratic organizations do not match the experiences of small businesses. Thus, we would argue that new frameworks need to be developed to guide the planning and implementation of IT in SBs.

A major problem with many respondents is dissatisfaction with the training provided by vendors. Similarly, there was a decline in the proportion of respondents satisfied with the advice obtained. In addition, difficulties with electrical power failures and relationships with suppliers give cause for concern. Compared to the earlier study, the smaller proportion of owner/managers involved in the introduction of IT gives rise to some concern where this reflects a lack of interest. We believe that these issues are worrying, even though, firstly, the divergence between the surveys could be explained by the fact that the underlying survey samples are not identical and, secondly, optimists could shrug off the results on the grounds that the sample size is too small to provide conclusive evidence. We believe that the risks and opportunities regarding the introduction of IT into SBs are too important to ignore and the current situation can be summarized as one full of potential but requiring further professional support.

Note: An earlier version of this chapter was presented at the Thirteenth International Conference on Information Systems (ICIS 1992) in Dallas, Texas, in December 1992.

REFERENCES

Angell, I.O., and Smithson, S. (1991). *Information Systems Management: Opportunities and Risks*. Basingstoke, UK: Macmillan.

Baker, W.H.(1987). Status of information management in small business. *Journal of Systems Management*, 38(4), 10-15.

Borovits, I., and Neumann, S. (1988). "Airline management information system at Arkia Israeli Airlines". *MIS Quarterly*,12(1), 127-137.

CEC (1985). *Microcomputers in the Administration and Management Processes in Smaller Business*. Luxembourg: Office for Official Publication of the European Communities. CB-44-85-800-EN-C.

Clark, A. (1987). *Small Business Computer Systems*. London: Hodder and Stoughton.

Cornford, A., and Whitley, E. (1991). *A Review of IT Strategies within the UK SME Sector*. Internal research paper for the ESPRIT project smEsprit (No. 5639). London: The London School of Economics.

Delone, W.H. (1988). "Determinants of success for computer usage in small business." *MIS*

Quarterly, 12(1), 151-61.
Doukidis, G.I., Smithson, S. and Naoum, G.(1992). "Information system management in Greece: Issues and perceptions." *Journal of Strategic Information Systems*, 1(2), 63-75.
Doukidis, G.I., and Karakoulas, G. (1994). "Feasibility study and impact assessment for a knowledge-based information technology planning system." *Knowledge-Based Systems*, 7(1), 27-36.
Doukidis, G.I., Mylonopoulos, N., and Lybereas, P. (1993). "Information systems planning within medium environments: A critique of IS growth models." Paper presented at IFORS XIII Conference, Lisbon, Portugal, July.
Drucker, P.F.(1989). *New Realities*. New York: Heinemann.
Dwyer, E. (1990). *The Personal Computer in the Small Business: Efficient Office Practice*. Oxford: NCC Blackwell.
Earl, M. (1989). *Management Strategies for Information Technology*. New York: Prentice Hall.
Farhoomand, F., and Heryeyk, G.P.(1985). "The feasibility of computers in the small business environment." *American Journal of Small Business*, 9(4), 15-22.
Frankenhuis, J.P.(1977). "How to get a good consultant." *Harvard Business Review*, Vol.55, Nov-Dec, 133-139.
Gable, G.G.(1991). "Consultant engagement for computer systems selection: A pro-active client role in small businesses." *Information and Management*, Vol. 20, 83-93.
Gable, G.G., and Raman, K.S.(1992). "Government initiatives for IT adoption in small businesses." *International Information Systems*, 1(1), 68-93.
Gibb, A.A., and Manu, G.(1990). "Design of extension and support services for small scale enterprise development." *International Small Business Journal*,8(3), 10-27.
Heikkila, J.; Saarinen, T.; and Saaksjarvi, M.(1991). "Success of software packages in small business: an exploratory study." *European Journal of Information Systems*, 1(3), 159-169.
Hill, S., Blyton, P.,Patrick, C. and Peregrine, J.(1984). *Decision-Making in the South Wales Engineering Industry: A Survey*. Cardiff: UWIST Discussion Papers in Business and Economics, UWIST.
Lees, J.D.(1987). "Successful development of small business information systems." *Journal of Systems Management*, September, 32-39.
Lees, J.D., and Lees, A.D. (1987). "Realities of small business information system implementation." *Journal of Systems Management*, January, 6-13.
Liebenau, J., and Backhouse, J.(1990). *Understanding Information: An Introduction*. Basingstoke, UK: Macmillan.
Lincoln, D.J., and Warberg, W.B.(1987). "The role of microcomputers in small business marketing." *Journal of Small Business Management*, 25(2), 8-17.
Martin, C.J.(1989). "Information Management in the smaller business: The role of the top manager." *International Journal of Information Management*, Vol.9, 187-197.
Meyer, N.D., and Boone M.E.(1987). *The Information Edge*. New York: McGraw Hill.
Montazemi, A.R.(1988). "Factors affecting information satisfaction in the context of the small business environment." *MIS Quarterly*, 12(2), 239-256.
Nazem, S.M.(1990). "Sources of software and levels of satisfaction for small business computer applications." *Information and Management*, 19(2), 95-100.
Nolan, R.L.(1979). "Managing the crises in data processing." *Harvard Business Review*, 57(2), 115-126.
Porter, M.E.(1990). "The competitive advantage of nations." *Harvard Business Review*,

March/April, 73-93.

Poutsma, E., and Walravens, A (eds.) (1985). *Technology and Small Enterprises: Technology Autonomy and Industrial Organization*. Delft, Holland: Delft University Press, 1989.

Raymond, L. "Organizational characteristics and MIS success in context of small business." *MIS Quarterly*, 9(1), 37-52.

Scholhammer, H., and Kuriloff (1979). A.H. *Entrepreneurship and Small Business Management*. New York: Wiley.

Sengenberger, V.; Loveman, G.W.; and Piore, M.J.(1991). *The Re-emergence of Small Enterprises: Industrial Restructuring in Industrialized Countries*. Geneva, Switzerland: International Institute for Labour Studies.

Stair, R.M.; Crittenden, W.F.; and Crittenden, V.L.(1989). "The use, operation and control of the small business computer." *Information and Management*, Vol.16, 125-130.

Whitley, E.A.; Poulymenakou, A.; and Cornford, A.(1992). "The Spring model for knowledge based systems analysis: A case study involving small and medium-sized enterprises." *Data Base*, 23(2), 1-5.

Wroe, B.(1987). *Successful Computing in a Small Business*. Manchester: NCC Publications.

Yap, C.S.(1989). "Computerisation problems facing small and medium enterprises: The experience of Singapore." *Proceedings of the Twentieth Annual Meeting of the Midwest Decision Sciences Institute*, Miami University, Ohio, April 19-21, 128-134.

Chapter 5

Armadillo Power & Light: A Software Evaluation and Selection Case Study

Louis A. LeBlanc
University of Arkansas at Little Rock, USA

Armadillo Power & Light Company (AP&L), headquartered in Hondo (TX), provides electric service to the lower half of the Lone Star State. AP&L is a wholly owned subsidiary of Texas Power Corporation, an electric utility holding company.

The General Accounting (GA) Department of AP&L is primarily responsible for closing the company books on a monthly basis. After the books are closed, GA is responsible for providing senior management with data relating to key operating results. This data includes a comparative income statement, analysis of rate of return on common equity, analysis of operating revenues and megawatt hours (MWH) sales (as shown in Figure 1), analysis of sources and disposition of energy, and analysis of operation and maintenance expenses by function.

Some of this data is used by senior management in their quarterly meetings with the Board of Directors. Senior management officials also use this data in presentations to banks when obtaining short-term financing. Since the professional construction and presentation of this data is of utmost importance, it is to the advantage of the GA staff to have this data neatly prepared with tabular and graphical analyses.

GA currently uses the Lotus Corporation's Symphony 2.2 software package with Allways, a graphics add-in for the Lotus spreadsheet. This

Figure 1: Armadillo Power and Light Analysis of Operating Revenues and Megawatt Hours (MWH) Sales —September 30, 1992

	Revenues	MWH
Residential	$53,690	579
Commercial	30,967	409
Industrial	32,313	505
Government& Municipal	1,850	25
Sales for Resale	37,261	1,516
Other Electric Sales	1,768	
Total Electric Revenues	*$157,849*	*3,305*

This chapter previously appeared in the Journal of End UserComputing, vol. 7, no. 2.

combination has proven to be a very capable as well as flexible program that combines five functions in one package. These capabilities are: 1) word processing—a tool for writing letters, reports, memorandums and other business correspondence; 2) spreadsheet—a tool that performs the numeric and financial analyses needed for planning and decision making; 3) graphics—a tool that converts numeric data into graphs and charts for analyzing financial data; 4) database management—a tool for storing, organizing, and managing information electronically; and, 5) telecommunications— the ability to exchange information with other computers.

GA at AP&L is equipped with the following hardware:

1) Six IBM Personal System/2 computers, Model 70/386, with Disk Operating Systems (DOS) Version 5.0;
2) Each computer has a VGA monitor and mouse;
3) A Hewlett Packard 7550a graphics monitor;
4) A Hewlett Packard LaserJet Series II;
5) A Hewlett Packard Laser Jet III,
6) An IBM Proprinter II XL; and,
7) An IBM Quietwriter printer.

Recent technological improvements in software, combined with the need for data to be professionally arranged and presented, has shifted the company's standard toward software compatible with Microsoft Windows, a graphical user interface. GA has decided to initiate a software evaluation and selection project for a spreadsheet package with advanced graphics, worksheet publishing, and Windows compatibility, since it current software package (Symphony) does not have these features.

INITIAL SCREENING CRITERIA

Senior management uses the data provided by GA in presentation to both the Board of Directors and banking officials. Therefore, it is in the best interest of AP&L to provide all technical and financial data in a most attractive and comprehensible manner.

The currently used spreadsheet package does not have the extensive worksheet publishing and graphics capabilities that senior management requires to prepare easy-to-read and attractive visuals. However, advanced spreadsheet packages are now available with worksheet publishing features which allow information to be summarized into concise tables with borders using high resolution fonts. These tables are much easier to read and interpret than just multiple rows and columns of numbers. A variety of graphs are available in the advanced packages ranging from simple line graphs, pie charts, bar and column graphs to scattergrams.

Spreadsheet software compatible with Windows may also be used to enhance document preparation. These features allow the display of multiple worksheets in windows that can be sized, moved, zoomed, and stacked. GA is extremely interested in this area, as management feels that windowing features are the wave of the future in advanced spreadsheet software.

There are several such spreadsheet packages on the market today. GA believes that it is time to initiate a software evaluation and selection project to find a spreadsheet package that will meet the current and future needs of the department. Although AP&L has its own Information Systems (IS) department that could design custom software, GA users are willing to accept the standardized functions and procedures associated with these spreadsheet packages. They want to take advantage of the decreased implementation time, decreased costs, and the potential for vendor maintenance services associated with packaged software.

A project team of three members was formed. The members represent different areas of the AP&L organization. One of the members is from GA as a representative of the direct users of the package. A second member, from financial management, will provide feedback on the usefulness and appeal of the final products generated for use in management presentations. The third member, representing the IS department of AP&L, serves as the expert in software/hardware features and functions.

The stages involved in application software evaluation include screening of potential packages, evaluation of the best available software, and the confirmation of the final selection. The project team's responsibilities in the screening stage are threefold. They will first verify that packaged spreadsheet software can be used. Next, they will identify the packages available on the market. Finally, they will attempt to narrow the field of choices to the best two or three packages that should be seriously considered and evaluated in detail.

The initial screening matches the unique requirements of GA with unique capabilities of available software packages. Criteria must be established to pare an initial long list of software packages to a more manageable short list for ease of comparison. The various criteria can be classified into four categories: 1) technical; 2) functional; 3) documentation and training; and, 4) vendor-related information. Each of these categories are described in the following paragraphs.

Technical Requirements

The software selected must be compatible with the current hardware in GA. The spreadsheet package must be able to run on an IBM Personal System/2, Model 70/386 with a hard disk drive and operated by DOS version 5.0. It must also support Hewlett Packard Laser Jet printers and plotters, in addition to the IBM Proprinter II XL and Quietwriter printer.

It is management's decision not to change any of the hardware at this time because the department expects to switch to a local area network (LAN) system in the future. Therefore, the spreadsheet software chosen should have a LAN version (or will have in the near future). The software should also have strong windowing capabilities (i.e., operate under Microsoft's Windows 3.1 graphical user interface) to facilitate the advanced functional requirements.

Functional Requirements

The spreadsheet package selected must have strong worksheet publishing capabilities and extensive graphing functions. Worksheet publishing capabilities allow the creation of enhanced worksheets by varying fonts, styles, shading, boxes, etc.

Since the current spreadsheet package is Symphony, the new software must be able to import existing Symphony files. The selected package should have consolidation and linking capabilities. Linking is the ability to link cells in different spreadsheet files so that when a change is made on one worksheet, the same change is made in all supporting worksheets. This eliminates the need to consolidate spreadsheets manually. This capability allows smaller worksheets or modules, thereby freeing primary memory which would be otherwise consumed by a very large worksheet.

Documentation and Training

It is important that good documentation and training be available so that GA will not lose productive time while switching to the new spreadsheet software. Therefore, training should be available to assist the users in quick implementation of this package.

Vendor Information

The reputation of the software vendor should be considered along with their stability. The length of time that the company has been in business, its financial position, and the reputation of its product are appropriate indicators in this area.

A most important step in the software evaluation is the initial screening process. This screening step significantly reduces the amount of time spent in the evaluation process as it focuses attention on the top two or three packages to be considered in detail. This eliminates the confusion that may develop when many alternatives are considered.

Figure 2 lists the nine screening criteria and whether or not each package provides each criteria. Figure 3 summarizes why each package was eliminated.

SHORT LIST EVALUATION

Now that the list of potential spreadsheet packages has been narrowed to two or three finalists, an extensive evaluation should be performed. The initial screening process determines whether or not critical features were present. Additional criteria must be added to each of the four categories to provide a detailed comparison of the finalists. In this detailed

Figure 2: Initial Screening Criteria Grid

Technical	**Package A**	**Package B**	**Package C**	**Package X**
IBM Compatible/DOS 5.0	X	X	X	X
Future Networking Capacity	X	X	X	X
Windows Compatibility	—	X	X	X
Functional				
Graphics	X	X	X	X
Symphony Import/Export	—	—	X	X
Linking Capability	X	—	X	X
Worksheet Publishing	X	X	—	X
Documentation & Training				
Training	X	X	X	X
Vendor				
Reputation/Stability	X	X	X	X

Note: This grid would have as many columns as there are potential spreadsheet packages. For a package to be selected for the short list (i.e., retained as a finalist), that software must include each criteria as illustrated by "Package X." Failure to offer any screening criteria will eliminate a package.

(X) Indicates that criteria is present in package.
(—) Indicates that criteria is not present in package.

Figure 3: Initial Screening—Elimination Summary

Software Package	Elimination Category	Reason for Elimination
Package A	#1	No Windows Compatibility
Package B	#2	No Symphony Import/Export
Package C	#3	No Worksheet Publishing
Package X		Remains on Short List

Note: Elimination Categories are: 1) Technical Requirements; 2) Functional Requirements; 3) Documentation and Training; and 4) Vendor Information.

Figure 4a: Weight System for Evaluation Criteria

3 = Essential
2 = Important
1 = Optional

evaluation, each of the criteria are weighted in terms of importance to GA. The weights range from three (3) to one (1), where 3 represents an essential feature, two (2) identifies an important features, and 1 indicates an optional feature (see Figure 4a).

A rating scale ranging from five (5) to zero (0) can be used to demonstrate how the remaining spreadsheet packages compare to one another (see Figure 4b). A 5 represents an excellent score on a particular criteria and 0 indicates the criteria is not present in a software package. Total points possible are calculated by multiplying the assigned weight for each criteria by its respective maximum rating. (Note that weights are fixed for each criteria across all the packages on the short list. Rating scores on each criteria will usually vary across the packages.)

Technical Requirements

The technical requirements are now expanded to include mouse capabilities, support of VGA monitors, support of Hewlett Packard Laserjet printers and plotters, and the amount of memory used by the program (see Figure 5). The memory criteria is a low priority feature and is assigned a weight of one. The other stated criteria are important to GA and are assigned a weight of 2. The initial technical requirements identified during the screening process are also included in the detailed evaluation process. Each is considered an essential criteria and given a weight of 3. These technical requirements provide a detailed format to evaluate how well the packages match with the current system capability as well as complexity.

Functional Requirements

The functional requirements are also expanded so as to precisely determine the quantitative and qualitative attributes of each software package. Most of the detailed functional requirements fall into the following six classes.

User Interface. Functional requirements begin with the user interface (see Figure 5). The functionality of menus indicates whether the packages have Lotus style, first letter sensitive, pull-down, and/or custom menu options.

The workspace provided by the respective spreadsheets addresses their abilities to provide multiple open files, pages per worksheet, columns and rows per page, and column

Figure 4b: Rating System for Evaluation Criteria

5 = Excellent
4 = Very Good
3 = Good
2 = Fair
0 = Not Available

widths. This is considered an essential requirement. The ability to hide rows, columns and cells is classified as an important item. The automatic backup is a nice, but optional item.

Functions and Operations. Three criteria are listed under functions and operations. They include the breadth and depth of functions, recalculation strength, and advanced functions. These criteria are rated as essential, important, and optional, respectively. The recalculation strength represents a variety of features such as automatic/manual ability, background, intelligent, natural, row-wise, column-wise, and iterative recalculation abilities. Advanced functions are defined as matrix manipulation, regression analysis, what-if tables, and linear/non-linear optimization.

Linking Capabilities. In the area of linking capabilities, updating of links is considered an essential function. Saving groups of worksheets is important, and backsolving will be optional.

Database Features. Database features are not a high priority. The ability to sort and search are important while communication with external databases is optional.

Graphics. The ability to annotate with text on a wide variety of graphs is an essential functional requirement in the graphics area. The graph types include bar, line, pie, hi-lo/open-close, and scattergrams. Some spreadsheet packages even allow for the customization of graphs with free-hand drawing and clip art imports.

Worksheet Publishing. Three of the worksheet publishing features are weighted as essential: 1) WYSIWYG preview; 2) boxes and shading; and 3) multiple fonts. Landscape printing is an important consideration.

Other Functional Requirements. The ability to import/export Symphony files is an essential feature, in addition to macro programming features. Both processing speed and auditing features are important items to be considered. The various criteria, their weights and respective rating scores are listed in Figure 5.

Documentation and Training

The documentation and training criteria assess the ease of learning and using the package (see Figure 5). Training is considered to be an essential criterion. It is also essential that a clear, concise, easy-to-understand user's manual be available along with other printed support materials. Important features include on-line help and tutorials.

Vendor Information

The reputation and stability of the vendor are of primary importance in this category (see Figure 5). Since AP&L has its own IS department, the service support is important, but not essential. Price is not a determining factor at this stage of the evaluation. AP&L wants to find the best available package and will use price as a determining factor at the end of the evaluation process, if necessary.

FINAL SELECTION

The selection of the spreadsheet package that best fits GA's needs can be determined through examination of an evaluation matrix. A design for a final selection matrix is contained in Figure 5.

In order to be considered a viable choice, the spreadsheet packages must meet a minimum "hurdle" rate of 80 percent of the total possible points. Any package that fails to meet the "hurdle" rate would be eliminated from the final selection process (see Figure 6).

If there is no "clear cut" winner based on total points, the next step that can be employed to identify the best package is cost per performance point. This approach calculates the value (i.e., cost) of each performance point. In order to obtain the value of each package, a ratio of the package cost to the number of performance points is calculated. The spreadsheet package that provides the least cost per performance point would be considered the best buy or choice (see Figure 6).

If none of the finalist packages meet the criteria established by GA, and assuming that a custom-built spreadsheet is not considered an alternative, other packages may have to be sought. One approach would be to relax one or more of the initial screening criteria. This would allow additional packages to pass the initial screening phase. Another alternative is for AP&L to custom design and construct their own spreadsheet package, if they are willing to proceed in this way if no acceptable off-the-shelf spreadsheets can be identified.

CONFIRMATION

The selection process eliminates a large number of potential spreadsheet packages. First, the packages have to meet the specified initial screening criteria. The two or three packages that successfully pass this screening are then subject to a very detailed inspection and evaluation. One package remains as the best spreadsheet software.

Before making a purchase, it is necessary to confirm this choice as the best available spreadsheet. GA will work with the IS group at AP&L in obtaining a demonstration diskette from a local computer store. IS plans to conduct two training sessions for GA. The training sessions are designed to accomplish the following: 1) hands-on training on how to use the selected spreadsheet; 2) how to import Symphony spreadsheets into the "new" software; and, 3) the advantages and disadvantages of the "new" spreadsheet compared to Symphony. Note the "before" and" after" graphs found in Figures 7a and 7b and Figures 8a and 8b, which show the difference between the two packages. After completing the training sessions, GA will know if the "new" spreadsheet is the best spreadsheet for their departmental users.

GA contacted the Property Accounting (PA) Department at AP&L about the latter's experience with the possible "new" spreadsheet. PA reported that their experience has been very favorable. GA then sought the advice of the IS group. IS had evaluated the spreadsheets under consideration by GA for other departments at AP&L. After satisfactorily completing the training sessions and obtaining votes of confidence from PA and IS, GA decided to confirm their selection and make the purchase.

Figure 5: Scoring Matrix

	Weight	Ratings Package X	Package Y
Technical Requirements			
IBM Compatible/DOS 5.0	3	5	5
Future Networking Capacity	3	5	5
Windowing Features	3	5	4
Mouse Support	2	5	5
Supports VGA Color Monitor	2	4	5
Supports HP Laser Printers	2	5	5
Memory Usage	1	5	3
Documentation and Training			
Training	3	5	5
Manuals/Printed Support	3	5	5
On-Line Help	2	5	5
Tutorials	2	5	5
Vendor Information			
Reputation/Stability	3	5	5
Service Support	2	5	4
User Interface			
Functionality of Menus	3	5	5
Workspace Provided	3	5	4
Hidden Rows/Columns/Cells	2	5	4
Automatic Backup	1	5	0
Functions & Operations			
Breadth/Depth of Functions	3	5	3
Recalculation Strength	2	5	5
Advanced Functions	1	4	5
Linking Capability			
Update Links	3	5	4
Saves Groups of Worksheets	2	5	5
Backsolving	1	4	5
Database Features			
Search Features	2	5	5
Sort Features	2	4	4
Extraction/External DBs	1	4	3
Graphics			
Graph Types	3	4	5
Annotates Texts	3	5	5
Customizes Graphs	1	0	5
Worksheet Publishing			
WYSIWYG Preview	3	5	5
Boxes and Shading	3	5	5
Multiple Fonts	3	5	5
Landscape Printing	2	5	5
Import/Export Symphony Files	3	4	5
Macro Programming Features	3	5	4
Processing Speed	2	4	5
Auditing Features	2	5	4

Figure 6: Evaluation Results

	Points Possible	Package X	Package Y
Technical Requirements	80	78	75
Functional Requirements	270	252	242
Documentation & Training	50	50	50
Vendor Information	25	25	23
Total Points	425	405	390
Percent	100 %	95 %	92 %
Price		$495.00	$495.00
Price/Point		$ 1.22	$ 1.27

Figure 7a: Armadillo Power & Light Analysis of Operating Revenues—September 30, 1992

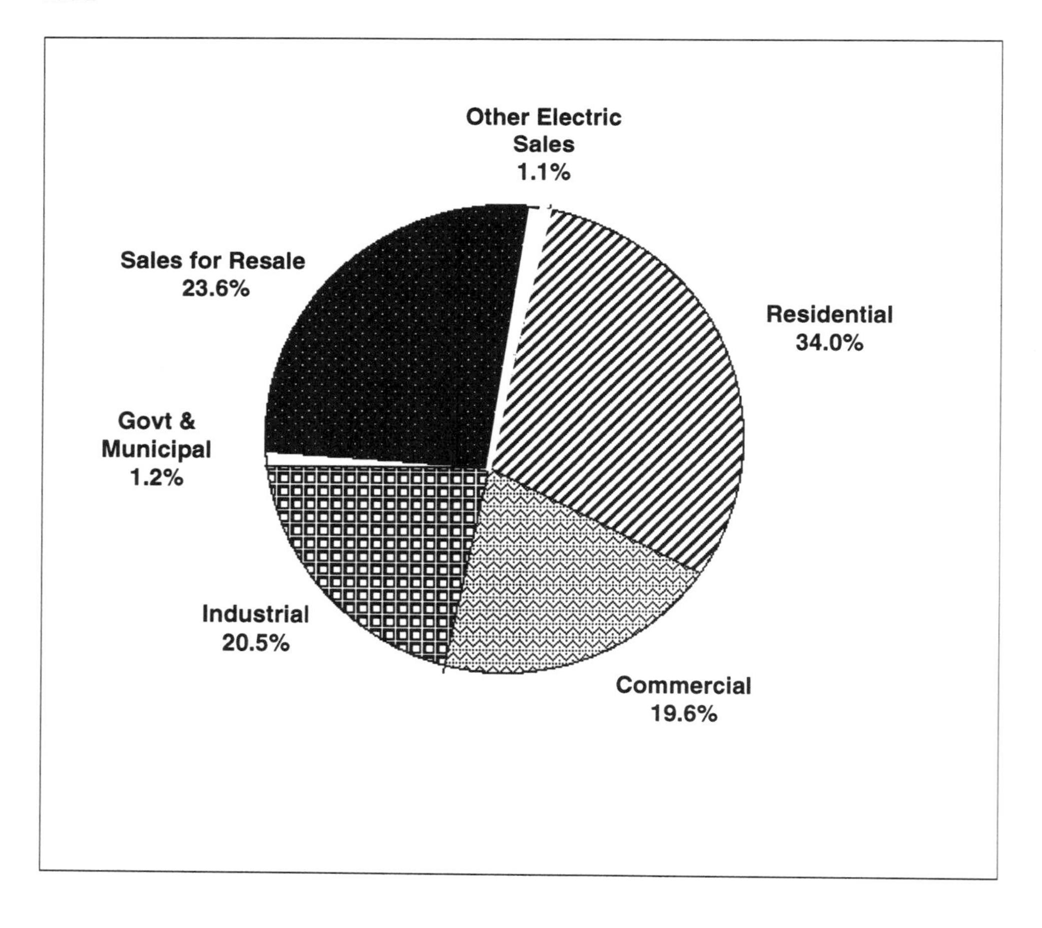

Figure 7b: Armadillo Power & Light Analysis of Operating Revenues— September 30, 1992

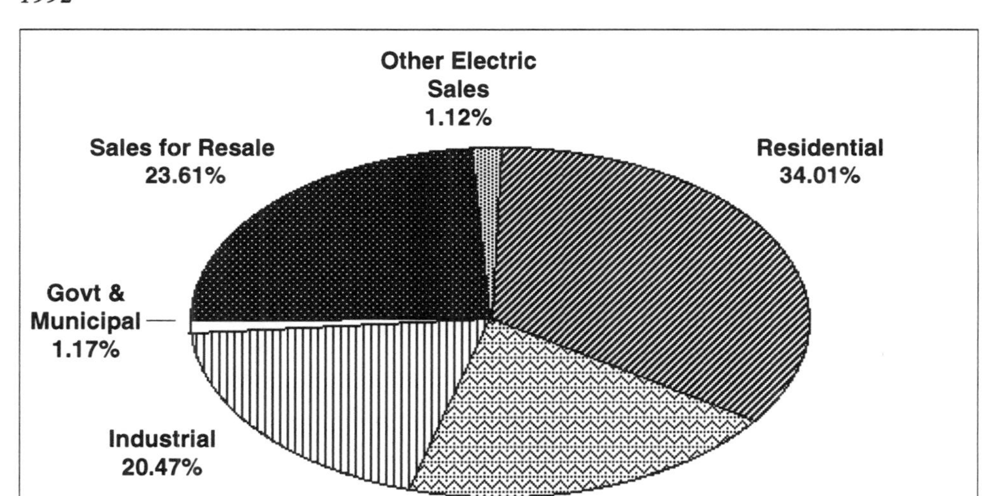

Figure 8a: Armadillo Power & Light Analysis of Megawatt Hours (MWH) Sales— September 30, 1992

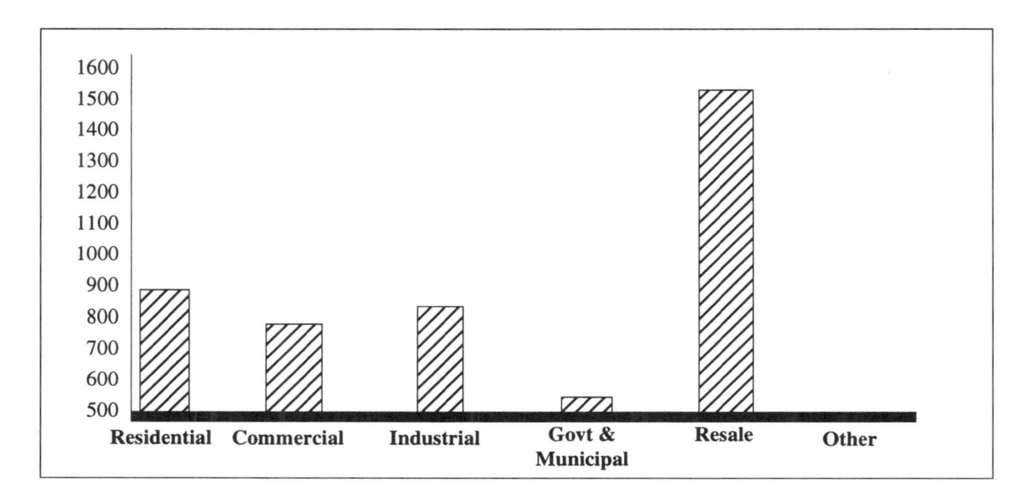

Figure 8b: Armadillo Power & Light Analysis of Megawatt Hours (MWH) Sales—September 30, 1992

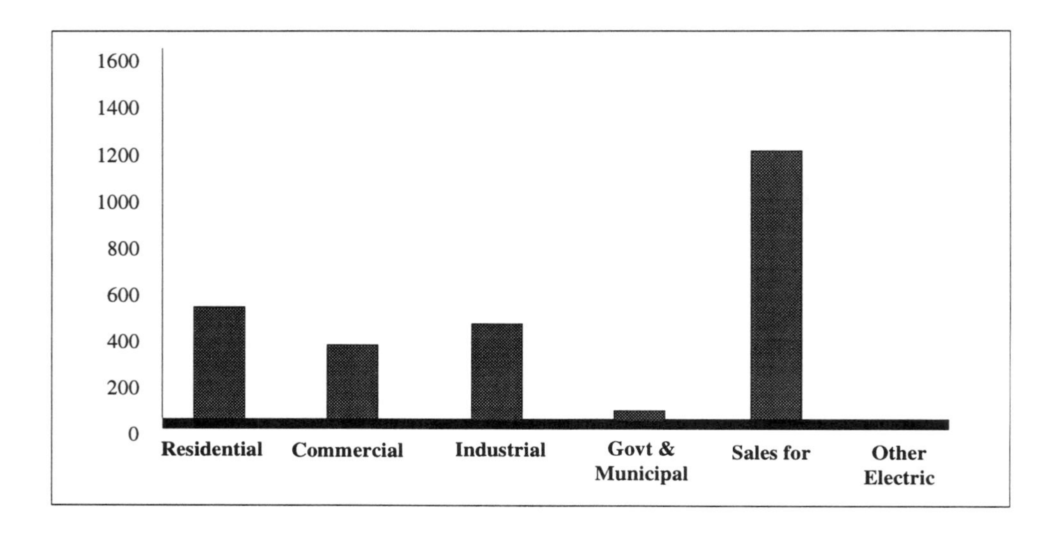

Chapter 6

Key Issues in the MIS Implementation Process: An Update Using End User Computing Satisfaction

Peggy L. Lane
Indiana University/Purdue University at Fort Wayne, USA

Jeffrey Palko
Northwestern State University of Louisiana , USA

Timothy P. Cronan
University of Arkansas, USA

Many issues that have the potential to affect the success of an information system development project have been discussed in the literature. Three issues which appeared to discriminate between successful and unsuccessful projects were identified in a 1981 study by Ginzberg. The present study enhances and expands his analysis to evaluate the stability of these issues. The purpose of this updated study is to identify which issues are associated with system development success as measured by computing satisfaction. The results indicate that although some of the issues identified by Ginzberg continue to be relevant to implementation success, their character has changed somewhat. Based on the responses from six companies, end-user computing satisfaction can be explained by the extent of project definition and planning, organizational commitment, breadth of analysis, user responsibility, and commitment to change. User ownership of the system was not considered a issue in the implementation process.

"Implementation of a computer-based information system is an on-going process which includes the entire development of the system through the feasibility study, systems analysis and design, programming, training, conversion, and installation of the system." (Lucas,

This chapter originally appeared in the Journal of End User Computing , vol. 6, no. 4.

1981). A more restricted viewpoint is offered by Swanson (1988): "Implementation is a decision-making activity that converts a design concept into an operating reality so as to provide value to the client." Implementation is a process of organizational change and refers to the ongoing process of preparing the organization for the new system and introducing this new system in such a way as to assure its successful use (Davis and Olson, 1985).

Ginzberg (1981) published an exploratory study of the issues that lead to the successful implementation of information systems. Since that time, others have addressed the problem from a variety of viewpoints (Lucas, 1981; Swanson, 1988; Markus, 1983; Tait and Vessey, 1988 and others). Their objective has been to identify variables that can affect the process of designing, developing, and installing information systems with the intent of providing designers and managers with the knowledge they need to successfully institute the organizational change inherent in bringing a system, new or modified, into production.

The purpose of this study is to provide additional insights into systems implementation success and the issues that affect it. This chapter extends and updates the study performed by Ginzberg (1981). Successful implementation issues are identified using a sample of six large companies. A method similar to Ginzberg's is used to allow comparisons. Ginzberg's issues are regressed as independent variables in a model with end user computing satisfaction as the dependent variable. Questions concerning the stability of the issues over time can be addressed. Clearly, the organizational environment for systems implementation has changed during this time which could affect the relative importance of the different issues. This study adds to the understanding of issues that affect development success. To determine which issues are associated with successful development, the following research hypothesis is tested:

H_0: There is no relationship between system development issues and system success as measured by end user computing satisfaction.

Figure 1: System Development Issues that May Affect Implementation Success

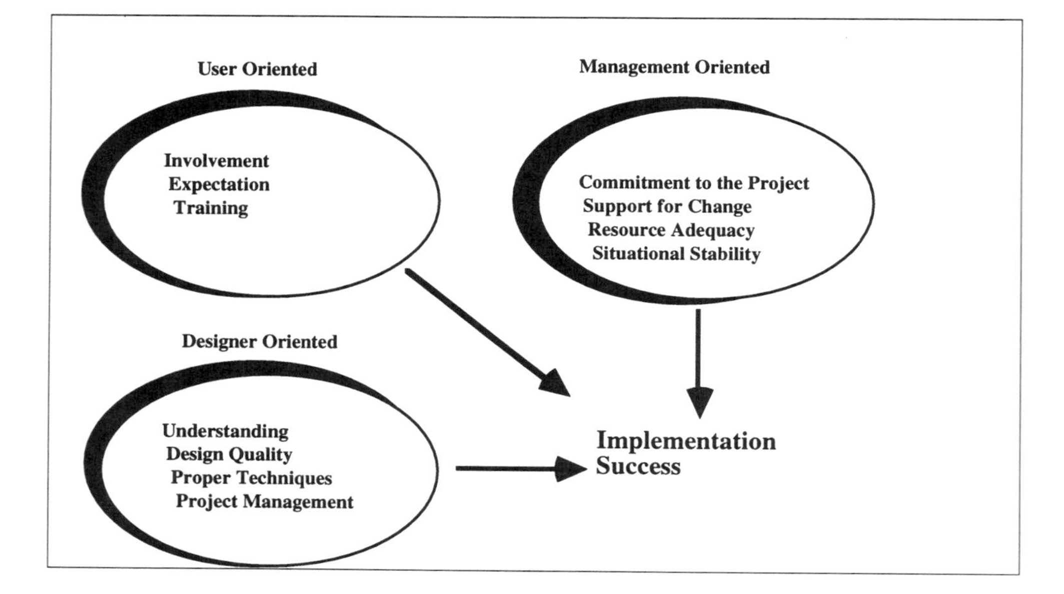

ISSUES THAT AFFECT IMPLEMENTATION

Many other issues that may affect implementation success have been identified in the information systems literature since Ginzberg's study was published. Some have been empirically verified while others remain prescriptive. This body of knowledge is a result of many years of study and represents a more thorough understanding of the systems development and implementation process. However, these findings are not always consistent with Ginzberg's results. Figure 1 presents a summary of the issues identified by Ginzberg and others. These issues can be grouped according to who controls them or is most affected by them—user-oriented, designer-oriented, and management-oriented.

User-oriented issues include user involvement, expectation, and training. Various studies have shown that user involvement is very helpful in complex projects and is effective because it restores or enhances the users' perceived control over their work (Alter, 1978; DeBrabander and Thiers, 1987; DeSanctis and Courtney, 1983; Swanson, 1988; Tait and Vessey, 1988; Zmud and Cox, 1979). User understanding of what the system is going to do is discussed by Swanson (1988), Lucas (1978), Cerveny and Sander (1986), and Ginzberg (1981). User training can help the user understand why the MIS is being introduced and how the project will affect them during and after implementation. This knowledge may make users more willing and able to contribute to an implementation effort according to Zmud and Cox (1979) and Stanford (1984).

While directly affecting users, training can also be considered a designer-oriented issue. Training is often provided to the users by the designer and should include a users' manual as well as formal training (Gunawardane, 1985; Stanford, 1984; Zmud and Cox, 1979). Other designer-oriented issues include understanding of design quality, proper techniques (e.g., use of implementor), and project management. Designers must have an understanding of users and their information needs (Cherveny and Sander, 1987; Swanson, 1988). The quality of the information system design is the responsibility of the system developers and it should affect implementation success (Gunawardane, 1985; Lees and Lees, 1987; Swanson, 1988). The impact of proper design and organizational change techniques are issues discussed by DeSanctis and Courtney (1983), DeBrabander and Thiers (1984), and Ginzberg (1981). Project management, which includes techniques for time and budget planning, was found to be one of three issues that differentiate between successful and unsuccessful MIS implementations by Ginzberg (1981). Since Ginzberg's study, Lucas (1981) and Swanson (1988) have also stressed the importance of effective project management.

Management-oriented issues include commitment to the project, support for change, resource adequacy, and situational stability. Ginzberg (1978, 1981) stressed the managers' commitment to the project. He suggests that if a manager is not willing to make a commitment to the project, it should be dropped. In his 1981 study, Ginzberg (1981) found three issues that differentiate between successful and unsuccessful MIS implementations, two of which concern management commitment—commitment to the project and commitment to change. Lucas (1978) suggests that management support should be encouraged and solicited, and top management involvement is stated as an important issue in determining the success of MIS projects by DeSanctis and Courtney (1983).

Regarding resource adequacy, Swanson (1988) states that in terms of personnel, equipment, and data, adequate resources are clearly for implementation success. The quality of the resources, not merely their quantity, is an important element of this adequacy. Situational stability represents the sensitivity of the implementation effort to situational changes that may occur (Swanson, 1988). Lucas (1978) states that personal and situational issues are likely related to success.

These newly identified issues may be the result of the many changes in information systems implementation or a more thorough investigation of the field. In either case, the question of whether the issues identified by Ginzberg are still valid should be addressed.

RESEARCH DESIGN

Sample

Seven companies were contacted to participate in the study. Four of the companies are in the oil industry, two are information service companies, and one is a major retail merchandise company. The survey instrument included general questions about the system evaluated, an end-user computing satisfaction instrument (Doll and Torkzadeh, 1988), and a series of statements about implementation issues of a system. Respondents were also asked to classify the system they were evaluating as a new system application or a maintained system. A maintained system was defined as an old system that had been redesigned and reprogrammed.

Implementation Success

In Ginzberg's study, successful and unsuccessful implementation was measured by a single question. Similar to his study, a single question regarding user feelings measured the success of the system implementation. In addition, a measure of computing satisfaction was used to determine the success of the system implementation. The measure of end-user computing satisfaction (EUCS) with an information system has recently become an important criteria for determining the success of an information system. Ives, Olson, and Baroudi (1983) presented an excellent review of the literature and proposed a short-form measure of user satisfaction. Studies that have focused on information satisfaction as a measure of success include Bailey and Pearson (1983), Baroudi, Olson, and Ives (1986), and Doll and Torkzadeh (1988). The measure of EUCS developed by Doll and Torkzadeh (1988) was used in this study to determine the success of information system development. This measure was selected because of its wide use and its focus on satisfaction with the information product by the user of the specific systems. Also, Doll and Torkzadeh (1988) suggest its use in studying relationships between EUCS and independent variables such as implementation factors. The EUCS instrument consists of a 12-item questionnaire (using a five-point scale) that measures five components of EUCS—content, accuracy, format, ease of use, and timeliness.

Specification of Issues

The design of the survey instrument is driven by the need to establish measures of the issues and then relate them to development success. These issues consist of a variety of components which may apply in a particular system project. Information from the respondents is used to establish the relative importance of the components as they relate to the specific issues. Thus, the variety of potential interpretations of a general term such as "user involvement" or "management support" does not affect the analysis. Respondents were asked to rate statements about different aspects of a specific development project with which they were recently involved. The five-point scale ranged from "very characteristic"

Table 1: Satisfaction Summary Statistics

Item	Mean	Standard Deviation
Single Item Measure	1.30	.822
End-User Computing Satisfaction		
Content	16.38	3.117
C1	4.10	.9116
C2	4.13	.9110
C3	4.05	.8149
C4	4.10	.8414
Accuracy	8.10	2.0729
A1	4.08	.9970
A2	4.03	.5060
Format	8.37	1.7928
F1	4.20	.8826
F2	4.18	.9844
Ease of Use	7.90	2.5399
E1	3.95	1.2798
E2	3.95	1.300
Timeliness	8.41	1.8169
T1	4.20	.9391
T2	4.21	1.0402
Composite	48.84	10.0160

to "very uncharacteristic." Ratings are factor analyzed to determine the issue components, and produce notated factor scores that are then regressed against the implementation success measures.

Method

In his 1981 article, Ginzberg used factor analysis with Spearman's Rho as the measure of association to identify six factors that could differentiate successfully implemented projects from those that met with failure. These six factors are: 1) extent of project definition and planning, 2) organizational commitment to the project, 3) breadth of analysis, 4) user responsibility for system, 5) commitment to change, and 6) user ownership of system. Next, he performed linear discriminant analysis to determine which factors would best predict successful and unsuccessful implementations. The six factors were the independent variables, while one overall satisfaction statement from the questionnaire was used as the dependent variable. From this analysis, three factors were found to be important for differentiating between successful and unsuccessful implementations. These three factors were commitment to the project, commitment to change, and the extent of project definition and planning (Ginzberg, 1981).

The present study compares the results of the current study with those of Ginzberg's (1981). In the present study, factor analysis identified factor loadings for the components identified in Ginzberg's analysis. His 38 statements were rated by users according to how well that statement described their specific project. Since interval scaling could not be assumed, Spearman's Rho measures were used in the analysis. These components were forced into six factors. The weighted factor scores were then used in regression analysis to determine which factors (issues) influence successful and unsuccessful implementation.

Factor scores based on results of the factor analysis were used as independent variables to determine which of the factors affected implementation success. The model is presented in equation (1).

$$IMPL = \beta_0 + \beta_1 \text{Factor1} + \beta_2 \text{Factor2} + \beta_3 \text{Factor3} + ... + \beta_N \text{Factor6} \quad (1)$$

where:

IMPL —successful and unsuccessful implementation as measured by: a single question and an end-user computing satisfaction measure (Doll and Torkzadeh, 1988).

Factor1- Factor6 - implementation factors based on the factor analysis.
β_0 - β_N- regression coefficients of the N Factors.

Multiple regression analysis was used to develop the linear implementation model described in (1) and select those factors scores which significantly explain implementation (single question and EUCS). The models used the single question and the composite score of EUCS as measures of success. Since interval scaling could not be assumed for the implementation factors and the success measures, a rank transformation[1] is appropriate. This is especially the case if the Spearman's Rho measure is determined to be appropriate for specifying the implementation factor scores.

In addition, the results of the factor analysis of the present study for Ginzberg's 38 identified components are presented. Regression analysis results for the single question and EUCS measures of success are presented and compared to Ginzberg's factors that differentiate between successful and unsuccessful implementation.

RESULTS

Sample

Six different companies with a total of 70 people were identified as potential units of a convenience sample[2]. Forty users from the companies responded to the questionnaire concerning a specific system in which the user was involved in the development process. This yielded a response rate of 56 percent. Of the 40 respondents, 85 percent were either non-programming end-users or command level end-users. Fifty-five percent of those completing the questionnaire were involved in the project from the beginning. According to the respondents, most systems are used daily or even more frequently with terminal sessions averaging over one hour each day. Fifty-five percent of the systems involved were new systems.

Implementation Success

As in Ginzberg's study, a single-item question, regarding how users feel about the system, was used to measure successful and unsuccessful implementation. Table 1 presents the mean and standard deviation for the single item measure of satisfaction which ranges from -2 (not dissatisfied) to 2 (satisfied). The mean satisfaction score was 1.30 indicating general satisfaction with the implementation process.

The EUCS (Doll and Torkzadeh, 1988) measure of success was also used to measure the success of implementation. Table 1 also presents the means and standard deviations of the composite measure of EUCS and its components. The composite score can range from 12 to 60, while all the components, except content, can range from 2 to 10. The content component can range from 4 to 20. For all measures, larger numbers indicate increased satisfaction. Based on the results, users were generally satisfied with the systems they evaluated. To determine the validity of the EUCS measure, the scores were factor analyzed and correlated with each other. Table 2 presents the factor scores for each of the components, while Table 3 presents correlation coefficients for the component questions. Based on the results, the EUCS measure appears to be a valid indicator of satisfaction. The EUCS composite score and the single item score were subsequently used as the dependent variables (IMPL) in the model.

Development Factors

Factor analysis with a varimax rotation was used to compare the results of this study with Ginzberg's. The 38 components that comprise Ginzberg's six factors were included. The results are shown in Table 4. Of the 38 components, 18 loaded in a pattern consistent with Ginzberg's findings. Factor1 (extent of project definition and planning) and Factor2 (organizational commitment to the project) are consistent with Ginsberg's Factor1 and Factor2. While most of the components loaded into factors (above the .5 cutoff used by Ginzberg), they tended to group into factors different from Ginzberg's. Although the components defined by the statements used in the 1981 study still appear to be relevant, the overall factors may not be stable over time.

System Development Model

For comparison purposes, factor scores from Ginzberg's derived factors were used in the regression analysis. As in his study, six factors were used to explain a single item question concerning the success of the system development process. A single item measure of how users feel about the system was used. Using the weighted factor scores (obtained from the factor analysis) as independent variables, regression results indicated that these factors explained 42% of the variation in success as measured by the single question (Table 5). Based on the regression analysis, the extent of project definition and planning, organizational commitment to the project, and user responsibility factors significantly explained implementation, as measured by how the users felt about the system. The first two factors are consistent with Ginzberg's results regarding MIS implementation. These results indicate that the development issues and components could have changed.

Next, regression analysis was performed with the EUCS measure of success as the dependent variable and the six weighted factor scores as the independent variables. The results of the regression analysis with all factors in the model are shown in Table 6. Based on the regression results, 63% of the variability of EUCS is explained by the implementation issues. The extent of project definition and planning, organizational commitment to the project, breadth of analysis, user responsibility, and commitment to change factors significantly explained implementation success, as measured by end-user computing satisfaction. Only Factor6, user ownership of the system, was not significant at the = .05 level. Compared to Ginzberg's results, two additional factors are important in explaining successful and unsuccessful implementation—breadth of analysis and user responsibility. This is expected since recently much emphasis has been placed in user involvement and comprehensive analysis of systems. Management commitment continues to be very important to successful implementation. If management is not willing to make a commitment, the project should be dropped. Management support and user responsibility should be encouraged.

*Table 2: Factor Loadings of EUCs Measure**

Scale	Components				
	Content	Accuracy	Format	Ease of Use	Timeliness
Content					
C1	.8015	.	.	.	.
C2	.5543	.	.	.	.
C3	.7499	.	.	.	.
C4	.	.5716	.5578	.	.
Accuracy					
A1	.	.7990	.	.	.
A2	.	.7162	.	.	.
Format					
F1	.	.	.7939	.	.
F2	.	.	.6625	.	.
Ease of Use					
E1	.	.	.	.8957	.
E2	.	.	.	.8824	.
Timeliness					
T1	.	.	.6625	.	.5111
T2	.	.	.	.	.8692

**A period (.) indicates a factor loading of .50 or less.*

Table 3: Correlation Matrix of EUCs Measure

	C1	C2	C3	C4	A1	A2	F1	F2	E1	E2	T1
C2	.797										
C3	.692	.682									
C4	.663	.853	.590								
A1	.745	.723	.468	.693							
A2	.693	.700	.363	.677	.916						
F1	.563	.733	.520	.731	.623	.616					
F2	.741	.775	.660	.721	.639	.600	.843				
E1	.613	.577	.469	.481	.665	.644	.485	.597			
E2	.625	.568	.438	.520	.715	.687	.478	.568	.938		
T1	.621	.659	.522	.655	.558	.506	.723	.737	.456	.512	
T2	.780	.746	.454	.664	.742	.772	.737	.757	.548	.540	.681

Table 4: Factor Analysis of Ginzberg's 38 Items

	Factor					
	1	**2**	**3**	**4**	**5**	**6**
Factor 1: Extent of project definition and planning						
1. In retrospect, we should have better defined what we wanted before selecting a consultant.	**.61**	-	-	-	-	-
2. It's hard to say why we chose the consultant we did for this project.	**.64**	-	-	-	-	-
3. The consultant's commitment to seeing this project through was never in doubt.	-	-	-	-	-	-
4. Leadership on this project was comfortably shared and was never a hassle.	**-.44**	-	-	.41	-	-
5. The consultant never really found out much about our business.	**.69**	-	-	-	-	-
6. Predicting the way the system would fit into our work procedures was too complex to assess in advance of implementation.	**.58**	.-	-	-	-	-
7. We didn't fully understand the system until it was up and running.	**.75**	-	-	-	-	-
8. I never was convinced that we had the best solution to our problem.	**.81**	-	-	-	-	-
9. With more effort the system could have met our original expectations.	**.41**	-	-.53	-	-	-
10. I was never sure of exactly what data we needed to evaluate this project.	**.52**	.53	-	-	-	-
11. When we started on implementing the system, we had a clear cut plan	-	-	-.53	-	-	-
12. Formal training in the use of the new system was very limited.	-	-	.60	-	-	-
13. I know this project met its goals, but we haven't collected any data to prove it.	.64	-	-	-	-	-
Factor 2: Organizational commitment to the project						
1. Changes in work routines and procedures were an important consideration in assessing the proposed system.	-	**.41**	-.51	-	-	.40
2. Our people were just too busy to participate much in problem diagnosis.	.79	-	-	-	-	-
3. There was no need to define detailed objectives for this project.	.61	-	-	-	-	-
4. When special skills were required to aid in developing the system, we tried hard to find the right people in our organization.	-	**-.52**	-	-	.51	-
5. Though many problem areas were diagnosed, we were able to work first on those that were most critical.	-	**-.47**	-	-	.46	-
6. We haven't yet done a serious evaluation of this project.	-	**.71**	-	-	-	-
7. Though we collected some data for project evaluation, we haven't done anything with it.	-	**.66**	-	-	-	-
8. I haven't yet learned to deal with the changes caused by the system in who is important around here.	-	**.69**	-	-	-	-
Factor 3: Breadth of analysis						
1. Understanding the problem required our considering a large part of the organization beyond the immediate user group.	-	-.	.76	-	-	-

Table 4 (Continued): Factor Analysis of Ginzberg's 38 Items

	Factor					
	1	2	3	4	5	6
2. We didn't realize how much effort it would take to implement this system.	.52	-	-	**.52**	-	-
3. If I were doing this project over, I would be more careful in planning how to evaluate the implemented system.	.52	-	-	-	-	-
Factor 4: User responsibility for system						
1. During implementation we felt that the consultant had the	-	-	.73	-	-	-
2. The consultant did the lion's share of the data gathering needed to pin down the requirements for this project.	-	-	-	-	-.51	
3. After the system had been turned over to us, we found there were loose ends we couldn't handle.	.48	-	-	-	.43	-
4. It was easy for us to take over responsibility for the system once it was implemented.	-	-	-	**.58**	-	-
Factor 5: Commitment to change						
1. If I had realized at the beginning the amount of resources (e.g., people, time, money) required, the project might not have been started.	.70	-	-	-	-	-
2. Right from the start, changing our working procedures was something we really didn't want to do.	.52	-	-	-	**-.53**	
3. In evaluating the system, management was interested in different measures from the ones we (the users) thought were important.	.41	-	-	-	-	-
4. As we implemented the system, we knew that some users were, unhappy but we felt the best time to deal with that was after the completed system was available.	-	-	-	-	-	-.
5. We would really find it hard to go back to our old way of doing things.	-	-.57	-	-	-	-
6. The system still doesn't fit well with our organization's way of doing things.	.64	-	-	-	-	-
Factor 6: User ownership of system						
1. I think the consultant really tried to see things my way.	-.44	-	-	.50	-	-
2. Rather than worrying about setting priorities, we dealt with each problem as it came up.	.57	-	-	-	-	-
3. It isn't clear who should be responsible for changes and additions to the system.	.55-	-	-	-	-	-
4. We feel confident in our ability to manage and use the system.	-.46	-.53	-	-	-	-

CONCLUSIONS

This study was accomplished to empirically investigate issues that might be related to the successful implementation of information systems. The intent was to provide additional insights into systems implementation success. The purpose was to expand and extend Ginzberg's study reported in 1981. This approach allowed reassessment of the issues he identified. In this study, a more comprehensive measure of success was used—the Doll and Torkzadeh end-user computing satisfaction measure which was unavailable when Ginzberg performed his study. In general, some of the same issues were found to be relevant, though changed. Other issues identified since Ginzberg's study appear to surface based on these results.

With respect to the stability of the issues identified by Ginzberg, some have changed while others remain almost the same. Issues associated with clearly defined project plans and definition and organizational commitment were again identified by this analysis. However, with respect to user understanding and involvement in this project, it seems that the involvement should span the entire project development process. Ginzberg's components of this issue tended to focus on activities at the beginning of the development process. These results included components identified with all of the development phases. This may reflect the users' improved understanding of information systems technology and the recognition that user input is essential throughout the development process.

The analysis using the factor scores for the issues identified in this study indicated only one of Ginzberg's issues that does not affect implementation success—user ownership. This issue was associated with an awareness of post implementation requirements and may reflect a relationship between the need to follow through on a project and successful implementa-

Table 5: Regression Analysis—Single-Item Question

Source	DF	Sum of Squares	Mean Square	F Value	P Value	R^2
Model	6	10.73	1.78	3.68	.0071	.416
Error	31	15.08	0.49			
Corrected Total	37	25.82				

Source	DF	Squares	F Value	P Value
Extent of Project Definition and Planning	1	3.17	6.53	.0157
Organizational Commitment to the Project	1	3.78	7.78	.0090
Breadth of Analysis	1	0.65	1.33	.2568
User Responsibility	1	2.43	5.00	.0327
Commitment to Change	1	0.69	1.42	.2429
User Ownership of System	1	0.01	0.00	.9570

Table 6: Regression Analysis—EUCs Measure

Source	DF	Squares	Mean Square	F Value	P Value	R^2
Model	6	1616.88	296.48	8.31	0.0001	.632
Error	29	940.09	32.42			
Corrected Total	35	2556.97				

Source	DF	Sum of Square	F Value	P Value
Extent of Project Definition and Planning	1	655.15	21.21	.0001
Organizational Commitment to the Project	1	216.25	6.67	.0151
Breadth of Analysis	1	279.66	8.63	.0064
User Responsibility	1	191.06	5.89	.0216
Commitment to Change	1	270.18	8.33	.0073
User Ownership of System	1	4.57	0.14	.7101

tion. Additional research is needed to refine an understanding of the issues identified here and in other studies so that managers, developers, and users can be fully informed about the process of developing and implementing information systems. More research is also needed regarding the stability of the issues themselves (factors). Based on this sample, the composition of the issues has changed. Given a more comprehensive analysis to update the issue components, implementation issues may be changing.

ENDNOTES

1 Let X_{ij} be the jth observation vector from a population i,j = 1, 2, ..., n and i = 1, 2, ..., k. The components of Xij are denoted X_{ijm}, m = 1, 2, ..., p. The rank transformation method involves ranking the mth component of all observations X_{ij} from the smallest (rank 1) to the largest (rank $N - n_1 + n_2 = ... = n_k$). Each component m = 1 to m = p is ranked separately. Stated simply, the value of a variable in a sample is replaced by rank 1 to n for all observations. Conventional regression analysis is then performed on the ranks.

2 Initially, seven companies were identified. One company declined to participate after receiving an example of the questionnaire. Since specific employees had been identified as participants, this firm was not included in the calculation of the response rate.

REFERENCES

Alter, S. (1978). Development patterns for decision support systems, *MIS Quarterly, 2(3)*, 33-42.

Bailey, J.E. & Pearson, S. (1983). Development of a tool for measuring and analyzing user satisfaction, *Management Science, 24(5)*, 530-545.

Baroudi, J.J., Olson, M.H., & Ives, B. (1986). An empirical study of the impact of user involvement on system usage and information satisfaction, *Communications of the ACM, 29(3)*, 232-238.

Baroudi, J.J., & Orlikowski, W.J. (1988). A short form measure of user information satisfaction: A psychometric evaluation and notes on use, *Journal of Management Information Systems, 4(4)*, 45-59.

Cerveny, R.P. & Sander, G.L. (1986). Implementation and structural variables, *Information and Management, 11(4)*, 191-198.

Davis, G.B. & Olson M.H. (1985). *Management Information Systems Conceptual Foundations, Structure, and Development*, Second Edition, McGraw-Hill Book Company: New York, NY.

De Brabander, B. & Thiers, G. (1984). Successful information system development in relation to situational factors which affect effective communication between MIS-users and EDP-specialists, *Management Science, 30(2)*, 137-155.

DeSanctis, G. & Courtney, J.F. (1983). Toward friendly user MIS implementation, *Communications of the ACM, 26(10)*, 732-738.

Doll, W.J. & Torkzadeh, G. (1988). The measurement of end-user computing satisfaction, *MIS Quarterly*, 12(2), 259-274.

Ginzberg, M.J. (1978). Steps towards more effective implementation of MS and MIS, *INTERFACES, 8(3)*, 57-63.

Ginzberg, M.J. (1981). Key recurrent issues in the MIS implementation process, *MIS Quarterly, 5(2)*, 47-59.

Gunawardane, G. (1985). Implementing a management information system in an extremely dynamic (and somewhat hostile) environment— a case study, *INTERFACES, 15(6)*, 93-99.

Ives, B., Olson, M.H., & Baroudi, J.J. (1983). The measurement of user information satisfaction, *Communications of the ACM, 26(10)*, 785-793.

Lees, J.D., & Lees, D.L. (1987). Realities of small business information system implementation, *Journal of Systems Management, 38(1)*, 6-13.

Lucas, H.C., Jr. (1978) Empirical evidence for a descriptive model of implementation, *MIS Quarterly, 2(2)*, 27-42.

Lucas, H.C., Jr. (1981). *Implementation: The Key to Successful Information Systems*, Columbia University Press, New York, NY.

Markus, M.L. (1983). Power, politics, and MIS implementation, *Communications of the ACM, 26(6)*, 430-444.

Rockart, J.F. & Flannery, L.S. (1983). The management of end user computing, *Communications of the ACM, 26(10)*, 776-784.

Stanford, K. Train. (1984). Document before celebrating, *Computerworld, 18(39)*, 69, 83.

Swanson, E.B. (1988). *Information System Implementation*, Irwin, Homewood, Illinois.

Tait, P. & Vessey, I. (1988) The effect of user involvement on system success: A contingency approach, *MIS Quarterly, 12(1)*, 91-108.

Zmud, R.W. & Cox, J.F. (1979). The implementation process: A change approach, *MIS Quarterly, 3(2)*, 35-43.

PART II: CURRENT TRENDS IN SOFTWARE UPGRADES

To begin investigations into the software upgrade issues described in previous chapters, a survey instrument was designed to solicit user perceptions of various aspects of the software upgrade process. First, respondents were given a brief definition of software upgrades and were asked to identify, if possible, an upgrade that had taken place within the previous 12 months at the respondent's place of employment. Then, the respondent was asked to identify both the old software package and the new software package for which the questionnaire was completed. Finally, a series of questions based upon previous IS implementation, adoption, and diffusion studies (e.g., Benamati et al., 1997; Cooper & Zmud, 1990; Davis, 1989; Fichman, 1992) were presented to the respondent. After the results of a pilot study were used to refine the instrument, a total of 62 questions remained, and the final instrument is provided in the Appendix of this book.

To solicit potential respondents, the researchers identified a list of over 660,000 registered computer software users. This particular list was chosen because of the wide variety of users and organizations represented and because of the large pool of potential respondents. Three independent, random samples were taken from the list to aid in the generalizability and replicability of the study. One of the samples was used to validate the questionnaire, leaving two samples remaining for analysis. There were no significant differences in the results between the two samples used for analysis, so the results have been combined for this book to avoid repetition. For the two analysis samples, 1,470 surveys were successfully mailed with 280 usable responses received, for a response rate of 19%. Although this response rate is less than ideal, the additional benefits gained by randomly selecting respondents were judged by the researchers to be an acceptable tradeoff. In addition, non-response bias was estimated by comparing early responders to late responders, and no significant differences were found. This, combined with the extra generalizability gained by comparing the independent samples, suggests that the study results are both generalizable and replicable.

RESPONDENT DEMOGRAPHICS

Of the users who responded, 81.1% (227) indicated that their organization had undergone some type of software upgrade within the previous 12 months, and as Figure 1 shows, the majority of upgrades involved products produced by Microsoft Corporation. An interesting point to note here is that approximately 40% of the randomly selected individuals in the study have been involved in an upgrade of Microsoft software within the last 12 months. In addition, a number of the respondents reported simultaneous transitions to new versions of more than one software package that sometimes involved Microsoft software.

To elicit further details about the population under study, respondents were asked to report the number of years that they have used computers and their individual job function within the organization. The respondents are generally quite experienced in computer use with a median of 15 years of experience using computers. Figure 2, a histogram of the self-reported computer experience of the respondents, shows that a large majority of the respondents have been using computers for five years or more. Figure 3, a breakdown of respondents by job classification, illustrates the four major job functions of the survey respondents. Somewhat surprisingly, the results cited in the book did not vary according to the respondents' computer experience or job classification. In other words, the general perceptions of upgrades reported in the book are consistent across varying levels of computer experience and job positions. This finding is noteworthy because in previous studies of packaged software implementation, similar factors have been shown to play a role in overall respondent satisfaction (Lucas, Walton, & Ginzberg, 1988).

Figure 1: Respondent Software Upgrades

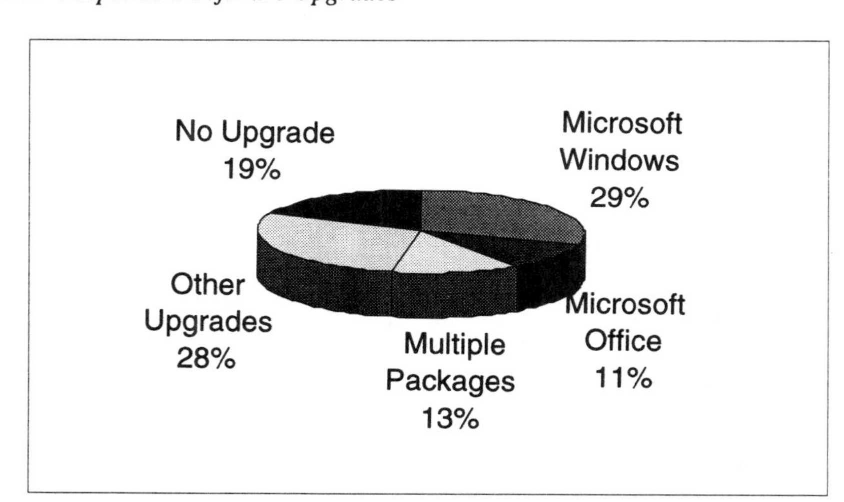

Figure 2: Respondent Computer Experience

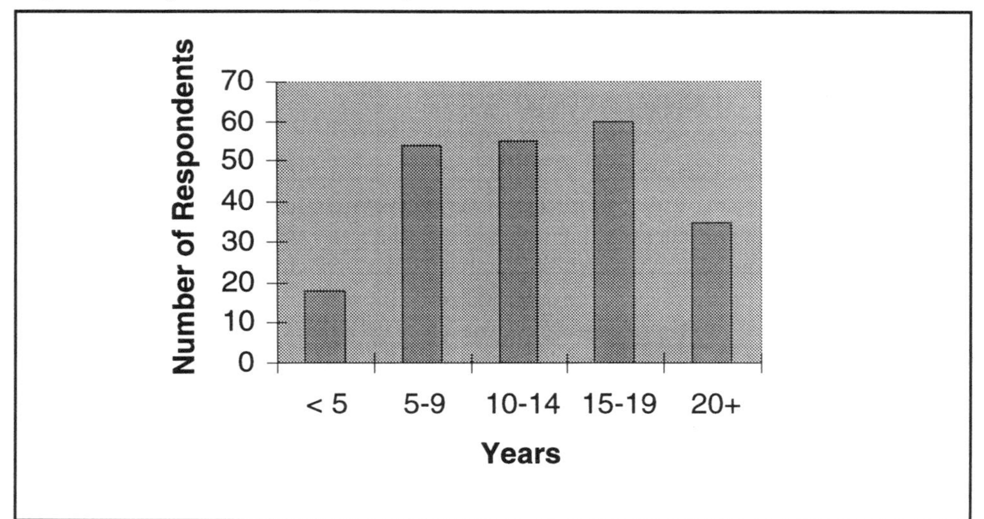

Figure 3: Respondent Job Classification

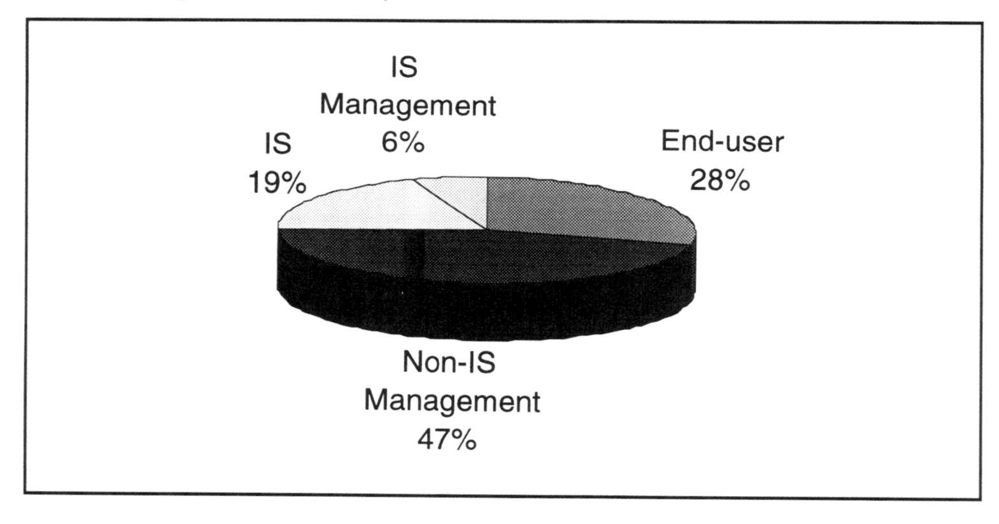

GENERAL PERCEPTIONS

Are software upgrades beneficial? Can organizations and individuals become more productive as the result of a software upgrade? To definitively answer such questions requires objective mechanisms to evaluate the benefits of an upgrade as well as any productivity changes caused by the upgrade; however, since many software benefits are intangible, and since the impacts of IS on productivity are notoriously difficult to measure (Brynjolfsson & Hitt, 1998), the survey used in this study adopted subjective measures to investigate the effectiveness of an upgrade. Respondents were asked to evaluate the upgrade to determine to what extent, if any, the upgrade was disruptive to the individual and to the organization. Similar questions were asked about the benefits and productivity changes associated with the upgrade. Finally, respondents were asked about the future impact of the upgrade. As Table 1 indicates, the respondents appeared generally to have positive perceptions of the impact of the upgrade both on their personal work and on the organization, since for each statement, a significant percentage of respondents indicated that the upgrade was not only not disruptive, but also that it increased productivity and would provide benefits now and in the future. In addition, it is worth noting that supportive sentiments were shown for individual as well as organizational impacts of the upgrade.

To further investigate the overall satisfaction with the upgrades, respondents were asked whether they wished to have the opportunity to continue using the old software package in lieu of using the new software package. Only 11.9% (27) of the respondents indicated a desire to revert to the software package that was in use prior to the upgrade. Thus, it appears that many of the respondents who did not feel that the upgrade added to benefits or productivity were still inclined to keep the new software. It is possible that these individuals might actually prefer the old software but wish to avoid the switching costs associated with another transition. Still, given the preferences shown in Table 1 and the overwhelming desire of respondents to retain the new software, there seems to be an overall trend toward acceptance of software upgrades.

Table 1: Perceptions of Software Upgrades

Statement	**Strongly Disagree**	**Disagree**	**Neutral**	**Agree**	**Strongly Agree**
The software upgrade was disruptive to my organization.	56 (25.1%)	52 (23.3%)	41 (18.4%)	51 (22.9%)	23 (10.3%)
The software upgrade was disruptive to my personal work.	63 (28.1%)	40 (17.9%)	40 (17.9%)	45 (20.1%)	36 (16.1%)
The upgrade was beneficial to my organization.	19 (8.5%)	17 (7.6%)	46 (20.5%)	68 (30.4%)	74 (33.0%)
The upgrade was beneficial to my personal work.	24 (10.7%)	27 (12.1%)	41 (18.3%)	64 (28.6%)	68 (30.4%)
My organization is more productive since the upgrade.	13 (5.8%)	34 (15.2%)	75 (33.6%)	59 (26.5%)	42 (18.8%)
I am personally more productive since the upgrade.	22 (9.8%)	39 (17.4%)	63 (28.1%)	54 (24.1%)	46 (20.5%)
I think the upgrade will be beneficial to my organization in the future.	20 (9.0%)	8 (3.6%)	45 (20.2%)	73 (32.7%)	77 (34.5%)
I think the upgrade will be beneficial to my personal work in the future.	22 (9.8%)	13 (5.8%)	46 (20.5%)	78 (34.8%)	65 (29.0%)

TYPICAL PROBLEMS

Although respondents reported a great deal of satisfaction with upgrades, there were also a number of problems reported. Respondents were asked to identify which problems, if any, occurred during the software implementation for which the survey was completed. An initial list was provided based upon a set of typical problems faced by organizations introducing new technologies (Benamati et al., 1997). Subjects were allowed to select all problems that were applicable, and they also were provided with an open-ended question to enable them to report problems other than the ones on the survey. On average, 3.6 problems were reported per respondent.

Table 2 details the problems reported by first showing the complete list of potential upgrade problems presented to respondents. The second column of the table shows the actual number of problems reported. The third column represents the percentage of all problems falling into each group, so, for example, inadequate software training accounts for 13.9% (114 / 818) of all upgrade problems reported in the study. Similarly, the final column in Table 2 shows the percentage of respondents whose upgrade involved a particular problem. Thus, inadequate software training was reported in 50.2% (114/227) of all upgrades in the study.

Furthermore, respondents were asked to estimate the nature of the majority of problems that their organization encountered, and Figure 4 shows that respondents overwhelmingly reported the majority of problems to be of a technical nature. Curiously, this subjective assessment by the respondents conflicts with the actual problems reported in Table 2.

The most common problems reported in Table 2 are inadequate software training (50.2% of upgrades), unexplained failures (46.7% of upgrades), and integration (45.4% of upgrades); however, Table 3 shows that these problems are not necessarily the ones that have the most significant impacts on the respondents' perception of the upgrades. The correlation analysis[1] suggests that vendor and support problems tend to be more closely associated with changes in upgrade perceptions than the most commonly reported problems. Similarly, although Figure 4 shows that technical problems are perceived to be widespread, the correlation analysis suggests that the effect of technical problems on upgrade perceptions does not seem to be as significant as other types of problems.

Figure 4: Perceived Nature of Upgrade Problems

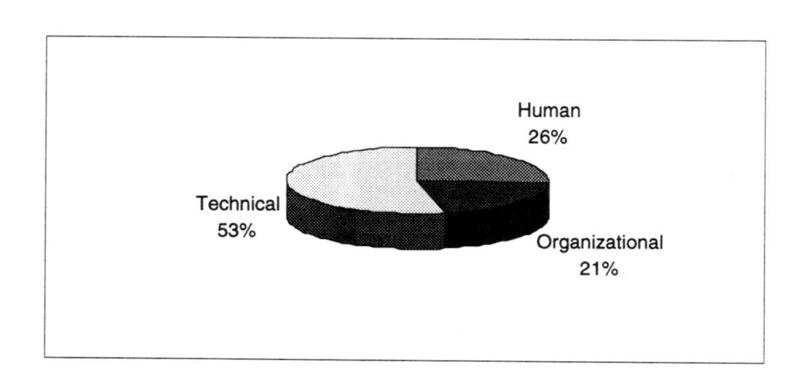

Table 2: Problems Reported

Problem	Frequency	Percentage of All Problems	Percentage of Upgrades
Inadequate software training (lack of proper training for employees)	114	13.9%	50.2%
Vendor oversell (false claims made by the software manufacturers and vendors)	49	6.0%	21.6%
Integration (making the new software work with other software on your computer)	103	12.6%	45.4%
Resistance (users who did not want to upgrade)	90	11.0%	39.6%
Purchasing problems (problems obtaining the software)	16	2.0%	7.0%
Vendor neglect (lack of support from the vendor after the sale)	35	4.3%	15.4%
Support burden (information technology staff overburdened with queries from users)	71	8.7%	31.3%
Cascading needs (purchase of new software forced purchase of other software or hardware)	79	9.7%	34.8%
Unexplained failures (software or hardware crashes with no known explanation)	106	13.0%	46.7%
Errors (known problems with the software, e.g. bugs)	86	10.5%	37.9%
Poor performance (inefficient use of memory, processor, etc.)	43	5.3%	18.9%
Other	26	3.2%	11.5%
Total	818	100.0%	—

ORGANIZATIONAL COPING MECHANISMS

Given the extensive number of problems described by the survey respondents, one might expect a proportionally negative perception of upgrades. Surprisingly, however, the overall respondent perception of upgrades remained generally positive. One possible explanation for the discrepancy is the presence of coping mechanisms, a set of reactionary measures taken by organizations in response to changes in the organizational environment (Lederer & Mendelow, 1990). It has been shown that organizations use coping mechanisms to mediate the effect of new technologies introduced into an organization (Benamati et al., 1997). In the case of software upgrades, the presence of coping mechanisms is consistent with suggestions that the major costs associated with upgrades usually do not include the actual purchase price of the software. Instead, the bulk of the costs are associated with user training, lost productivity, associated hardware upgrades, and other indirect costs (Wysocki,

Table 3: Correlation Analysis of Problems and Upgrade Perceptions

Perception	Inadequate Training	Vendor Oversell	Integration	Resistance	Purchasing Problems	Vendor Neglect
Disruptive to organization	+**		+**			
Disruptive to personal work			+*			
Beneficial to organization		-*				
Beneficial to personal work	-*	-**		-*		-*
Organization more productive						
Personally more productive						
Future benefits to organization		-**				
Future benefits to personal work		-*				

*Significant at $p < .05$ **Significant at $p < .01$

Perception	Support Burden	Cascading Needs	Unexplained Failures	Errors	Poor Performance	Other
Disruptive to organization	+**		+*		+*	
Disruptive to personal work	+*					
Beneficial to organization	-**					
Beneficial to personal work	-*					
Organization more productive	-**					
Personally more productive	-*					
Future benefits to organization	-*					
Future benefits to personal work	-**					

*Significant at $p < .05$ **Significant at $p < .01$

1998).

To investigate the effects of coping mechanisms in software upgrades, respondents were asked to identify all of the coping mechanisms used by their organization in the process of upgrading the given software package. An initial list of eleven coping mechanisms was provided based upon prior research (Benamati et al., 1997), and respondents were also encouraged to list other mechanisms via an open-ended question on the survey. An average of 2.7 coping mechanisms per upgrade were reported, and the details of these coping mechanisms are given in Table 4. The columns of Table 4 present the coping mechanism used, the number of times the mechanism was reported in total, the percentage of all coping mechanisms represented by a particular mechanism, and the percentage of all upgrades that used a given coping mechanism. The calculations for the columns in Table 4 are similar to the calculations used in Table 2 for the problems identified by the respondents.

The most commonly reported coping mechanisms were internal support (48.9% of upgrades), other users (42.7% of upgrades), and education/training (39.2% of upgrades). In contrast with the upgrade problems and perceptions reported in Table 3, however, the most popular coping mechanisms seemed to have a substantial impact on the overall perception of upgrades within the organization. Table 5 shows the correlations[2] among user perceptions and the reported coping mechanisms, and it appears that the coping mechanisms that are most closely associated with upgrade perceptions are "inaction" and "endurance," each of which signifies organizational inability to cope with the problems caused by an upgrade. Thus, although there is a lack of overwhelming evidence to support the use of any specific coping mechanism, the data suggest that perceptions of an upgrade will be substantially lowered if an organization is perceived as unwilling or unable to react to problems encountered during a software upgrade.

Table 4: Coping Mechanisms Reported

Coping Mechanism	Frequency	Percentage of All Coping Mechanisms	Percentage of Upgrades
Education and training (formal and informal training, both on-site and off-site)	89	14.3%	39.2%
Inaction (nothing was done to handle the problems)	24	3.9%	10.6%
Internal support (information technology staff provided users with support)	111	17.8%	48.9%
Vendor support (the vendor of the product was asked for help)	63	10.1%	27.8%
New procedures (new policies and/or procedures were created)	48	7.7%	21.1%
Persuasion (managers tried to persuade users and IT staff to accept the new technology)	37	5.9%	16.3%
Endurance (users wanted external support, but resources for support were unavailable)	36	5.8%	15.9%
Additional technology (additional software and/ or hardware was purchased to support the upgrade)	64	10.3%	28.2%
Consultants (external consultants were hired)	30	4.8%	13.2%
Other users (users repeatedly asked other users for help with the new software)	97	15.6%	42.7%
Staffing (additional staff were added to help with the problems)	14	2.2%	6.2%
Other	10	1.6%	4.4%
Total	623	100.0%	—

Table 5: Correlation Analysis of Coping Mechanisms and Upgrade Perceptions

Perception	Education/ Training	Inaction	Internal Support	Vendor Support	New Procedures	Persuasion
Disruptive to organization		+**				
Disruptive to personal work		+*				
Beneficial to organization		-**				
Beneficial to personal work		-**				
Organization more productive	+*	-**				
Personally more productive		-**				
Future benefits to organization		-**	+*			
Future benefits to personal work		-*				

*Significant at p < .05 **Significant at p < .01

Perception	Endurance	Additional Technology	Consultants	Other Users	Staffing	Other
Disruptive to organization	+*		+*	+**		
Disruptive to personal work	+**			+*		
Beneficial to organization	-**			-**		
Beneficial to personal work	-**					
Organization more productive						
Personally more productive						
Future benefits to organization	-**					
Future benefits to personal work	-*					

*Significant at p < .05 **Significant at p < .01

SUMMARY

In summary, the results here provide a number of useful insights into the perceptions of software upgrades in organizations. End users, managers, IS professionals, and software vendors can use the results to gain an enhanced understanding of the software upgrade phenomenon. In addition, the suggestion of previously unidentified relationships in IS implementation serve as a starting point for future research. One significant implication both for practice and for research is the indication that a staggering 81% of the organizations represented in the survey respondents had participated in some type of software upgrade within the 12 months prior to the survey. If software upgrades are as common as this result indicates, then they should likely be included as part of short-term and long-term planning and development in organizations. Many organizations include software maintenance as part of IS development budgets, and arguments have been made for the inclusion of software evolution in organizational plans (Ramamoorthy, Prakash, Tsai, & Usuda, 1988). The high percentage of upgrades reported in this study supports the idea of incorporating software upgrades as a component of IS budgets and planning.

Another interesting finding is the generally positive perception of software upgrades shown by the survey respondents. As shown in Table 1, the majority of respondents indicated that they perceived the upgrade to have a positive effect on themselves and the organization. This held true even though a large number of problems were reported throughout the upgrade process. In addition, only a handful of respondents wished to have an opportunity to revert to the old software package. There are a number of possible reasons for the respondents' perceptions. The addition of useful functionality and/or an improved user interface in the new software are two factors that could have contributed to the positive feedback received in the survey responses; however, further research is needed to make definitive claims in this area. Analysis of Table 3 and Table 5 reveals some of the ways in which upgrade perceptions can be affected by various implementation problems along with various mechanisms for coping with those problems. In general, it appears that the upgrade will be better received within an organization if the individuals within the organization feel that some actions are being taken to address the problems associated with the upgrade.

Although the findings presented here are quite informative, they should be interpreted with some caution simply due to the survey method of data collection. While the survey method increases generalizability and replicability, there is a limitation on the depth and richness of data that can be captured. Consequently, the results only describe and report user perceptions of software upgrades, and it is possible that other data-collection procedures such as case studies or field studies could show that user perceptions do not accurately capture the actual characteristics of the upgrade. Still, the findings present a useful first step in assessing the extent to which software upgrades impact organizations.

DETAILED RESEARCH

The second set of in-depth research articles focuses on a breakdown of possible explanations for the perceptions reported by the respondents in the survey above. The first chapter investigates the expectations associated with information systems and attempts to determine the reasons that users do not perceive that their needs are satisfied, even though IS staff feel that the system works fine. Similarly, the next two chapters focus on other possible reasons that users reject information technology, including personal, social, situational, and other factors. Finally, Ditsa provides some suggestions for managing user expectation by using total quality management (TQM).

ENDNOTES

1 Since the correlated data are represented by categorical variables, the Pearson Chi-square statistic was used. Thus, Table 3 presents the direction of the relationships and the statistical significance based upon the Pearson Chi-square statistic. For simplicity, only significant correlations are reported.

2 As in Table 3, the Pearson Chi-square statistic is used, and only significant correlations are reported.

Chapter 7

Our Mousetrap's Fine: So Why Aren't People Beating A Path To Our Door?

George E.M. Ditsa
University of Wollongong, Australia

R.C. MacGregor
University of Wollongong, Australia

Over the last decade, researchers of user satisfaction have continued to examine the elusive failure of information systems (IS) amidst advances in computer technology. This chapter suggests that despite the very important findings in the area of user satisfaction, very little is finding its way to the day-to-day practices. The chapter continues to suggest that even more alarming is the notion that most users expect that systems will be difficult to use and there is little demand by them for the inclusion of psychological or organisational aspects to be included in information systems. This is supported by results of a pilot study examining criteria used for repurchase of computing technology. Finally, the chapter briefly examines the organisational culture which appears to prevent users demanding more attention to user satisfaction criteria and proposes some necessary inclusions for an infrastructure; users will begin to expect and demand the inclusion of psychological and organisational aspects in the development and implementation of information systems.

Today, organisational behaviour constitutes a major challenge to information systems (Lucas, 1975; Turner, 1982; Markus, 1984; Williams, 1991). Among organisational behaviour issues, user satisfaction is considered a crucial factor affecting IS effectiveness and success (Powers and Dickson, 1973; Ives and Olson, 1984; Raymond, 1987; Abdul-Gader, 1996). However, despite the large amount of research surrounding the area of user satisfaction, studies (Franklin et al., 1992; Hornby et al., 1992; Hovmark and Norel, 1993; Williams, 1994; Markus and Keil, 1994) suggest that most systems fail to meet the objectives and aspirations held for them, not because they are not technically sound, but because psychological and organisational issues were not well addressed during the development, implementation and use of the systems.

Perhaps even more alarming is the notion put forward by Clegg (1993) who claims that most users of information systems actually expect not to find organisational or psychological factors built into the systems with which they are presented. So, despite the many important studies which have attempted to model the nature of user satisfaction, and the substantial findings which have grown out of such research, there is little demand by users for these findings to be incorporated into information systems.

This chapter will consider the results of a pilot study carried out on small to medium enterprises. The study supports the notion that organisational and psychological factors are not considered important by such organisations when the acquisition of computer technology is being carried out. The chapter begins by first looking at some of the psychological and organisational issues lacking in IS. The chapter continues by examining the nature of user satisfaction models. The chapter then discusses the use of these models in IS development, backed up by a pilot study we carried out on small to medium-size enterprises. The chapter will then briefly examine the organisational culture which maintains this lack of demand for organisational and psychological parameters by users of information systems. Finally, a set of necessary inclusions for organisational structure will be suggested. While these inclusions are far from complete, it is suggested that they form a basis such that users begin to expect the inclusion of organisational and psychological parameters in newly developed information systems.

Organisational And Psychological Factors Lacking In Information Systems Development, Implementation And Use

A number of organisational and psychological factors have been identified in the literature as lacking in IS development, implementation and use. These include lack of:

• ***Establishment of Career/Future Opportunities Associated with IS and Job Stress Reduction***. Today's high global unemployment rate has made employees concerned about the introduction of new technologies in the workplace, and the impacts that these technologies may have on their job performance and job security. A number of research studies have identified how office automation may bring about adverse working conditions, i.e., job design, which in turn could affect job stress. Sainfort (1990) in a study concludes that career/future concerns most contribute to job stress in computers users. A study by Ray et al. (1994) also reveals that both business owners and employees believe computer technology creates job stress and contributes to discomfort for users.

- ***Processes Associated with The IS: Job Design, Job Range and Job Depth Which Guarantee Autonomy, Job Satisfaction, Job Performance, Rewards and Benefits for Users.***

A number of studies (e.g., Eason, 1988; Clegg et al., 1989; Franklin et al., 1992; Markus and Keil, 1994; Williams, 1994) conclude how job design, job range and job depth (which guarantee job autonomy and job stress reduction), job satisfaction, and job performance are of much concern to computer systems users. Indeed, Hovmark and Norell (1993) point out how computer systems used for much of the working day can be expected to influence the

Figure 1: A Framework of User Satisfaction

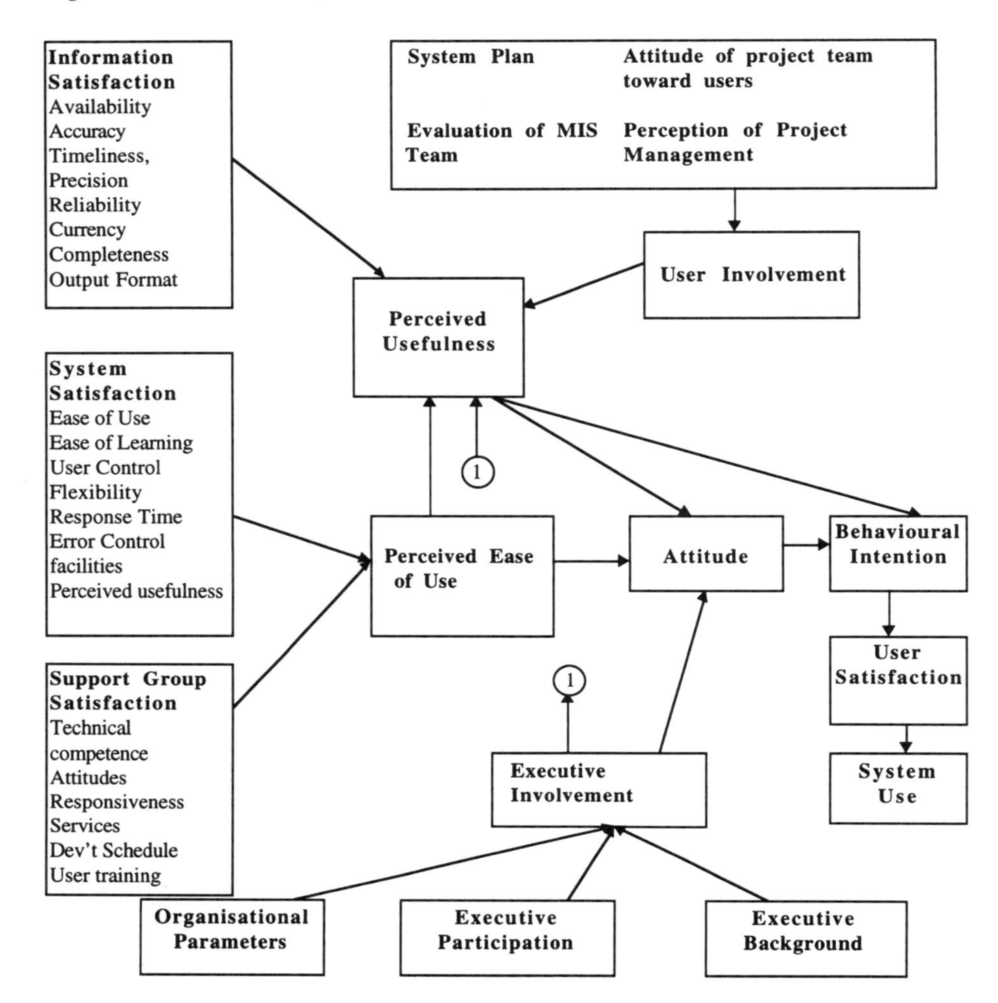

work tasks, work content, and the social and psychological work environment of system users.

Earlier survey and case study evidence (e.g., Eason, 1988; Clegg et al., 1989) also identifies lack of attention to psychological issues such as the design of jobs and the allocation of systems tasks as contributing to the problem of systems underperformance. This evidence is supported by Hornby et al. (1992) in a separate study.

- ***Addressing Causes of Individual, Group and Organisational Effectiveness and Attention to Gender-Related Issues.***

Sainfort (1990) and Williams (1994) stress the need for addressing the effectiveness of individuals and groups toward the overall effectiveness of the organisation in the design, implementation and use of IS. Williams' study reveals how different IS implementation can affect job satisfaction, job performance, as well as limiting the scope of self-managing work groups. Franklin et al. (1992) draw the attention to gender-related issues in systems development and implementation.

The organisational behaviour literature also suggests that the success or failure of any organisation should be analysed at three distinct levels of behaviour —individual, group and organisation (Etzioni, 1971; Campbell, 1979; Lewin and Minton, 1986; Cameron, 1978, 1986; Koppes et al., 1991; Ivancevich and Matteson, 1993). Behaviour is viewed as operating at individual, group and organisational levels. This approach suggests that when studying organisational behaviour, one should identify clearly the level being analysed—individual, group or organisation (see Figure 2.1). The effectiveness of the individual contributes to the effectiveness of the group, and the effectiveness of the group contributes to that of the organisation. The causes of effectiveness to these three distinct levels of an organisation are shown in Figure 2.2. It is, therefore, appropriate to view the benefits accruing from the use of IS in an organisation from these three distinct levels as shown in Figure 3. The development of management and administrative infrastructure (Figure 3) should therefore be seen as addressing the benefits that should be accruing at these three distinct levels.

- ***Socio-Technical and More Human-Centred Approaches (Instead of Technology-driven Approach) and Effective Two-Way Communication Systems Among Management, Developers and Users***

Based on Eason (1988) and Clegg's (1989) study, Hornby's et al. (1992) study reaffirms that the adoption of a technology-led approach means that human and organisational issues are unlikely to be specifically or adequately addressed as part of the systems development process. They opine that lack of attention to organisational and human issues is the major contributory factor in the underperformance of IT systems. Hornby et al. (1992) conclude that coverage of human and organisational issues is patchy in the main-stream technical methods, and methods explicitly covering the human and organisational issues are very much in the minority usage. They further conclude that analysts do not use methods according to the idealised descriptions contained in their manuals, suggesting the need to know more about how skilled analysts actually operate in practice.

Recently, technology driven systems still came under attack (Lehman, 1996; Treitler, 1996). Treitler (1996) points out that technical design of IS tends to drive the information structure and content of systems and is not driven by the social and cultural needs of end users. Treitler further emphasises a two-way communications among management, developers and users. Currie (1996) points out the need for an organisational structure to support the activities of IT.

Table 1 : Perspectives Taken by Models of User Satisfaction

Perspective	Major Emphasis	Researchers
Quality of Information in an Information System	Availability of information Accuracy of information Timeliness of information Precision of information Reliability of information Currency of information Completeness of information Output format of information	Swanson (1974) Cyert & March (1965) Bailey & Pearson (1983)
User Interface Features	Ease of Use Ease of Learning User Control Flexibility Response Time Error Control Perceived Usefulness	Goodwin (1987) Shneidermann (1987, 1992) Sless (1989) Carroll (1991) Green (1991) Carr (1992) MacGregor (1992)
Support of the User	Technical Competence Attitudes Responsiveness Service Development Schedule User Training	Green (1991) MacGregor (1992)
Effectiveness of information systems in the organisation	Availability of information Accuracy of information Timeliness of information Precision of information Reliability of information Currency of information Completeness of information Output format of information Response Time Error Control	Swanson (1974) Cyert & March (1965) Bailey & Pearson (1983)
User involvement	System planning Evaluation of the MIS team Attitude of the MIS team Project Management Communication Management of Interaction process	Avison & Fitzgerald (1990) Eliason (1990) Wysocki & Young (1990) Robey & Farrow (1982) Ives & Olson (1984) Tait & Vessey (1988) Amoako-Gyampah & White (1993)
Management Involvement	Advantages of information in organisations Recruitment of specialists Informed Management Development of centralised strategies Personal IT management Development of executive background	McFarlan et al (1983) Rockart & Flannery (1983) Doll (1985) Jarvenpaa & Ives (1991) Barki & Hartwick (1989)
Attitudes towards Information	Behavioural intentions Beliefs of Users Attitudes of users	Davis et al (1989) Netemeyer & Bearden (1992) Bagozzi et al (1992) Nataraajan (1993) Kelloway & Barling (1993) Mykytyn & Harrison (1993) Wishnick & Wishnick (1993) Saga & Zmud (1994)

Table 2: Use of Criteria In The Selection of Computer-Based Systems

Criterion	%
Performance	26.2%
Cost	20.1%
Benefits	27.9%
Ease of Use	13.9%
Future Enhancement	11.9%

Table 3: Criteria Which Would Be Adopted If Future Computer-Based Systems Are To Be Acquired

Criterion	%
Performance	25.6%
Cost	21.7%
Benefits	23.2%
Ease of Use	16.9%
Future Enhancement	12.6%

- **Formulation of Policies or Formal Rules Associated With Development, Implementation and Use of IS**

Eason (1988) and Clegg et al. (1989) identify: lack of guiding organisational and business strategies (as opposed to technical strategies); lack of end-user participation and end-user "ownership" of systems; lack of attention to education, training and awareness; and lack of organisational resources and support, concerning the "soft" infrastructures; lack of attention to organisational issues such as organisation design, organisational culture, and

Figure 2.1 Three Perspectives on Effectiveness

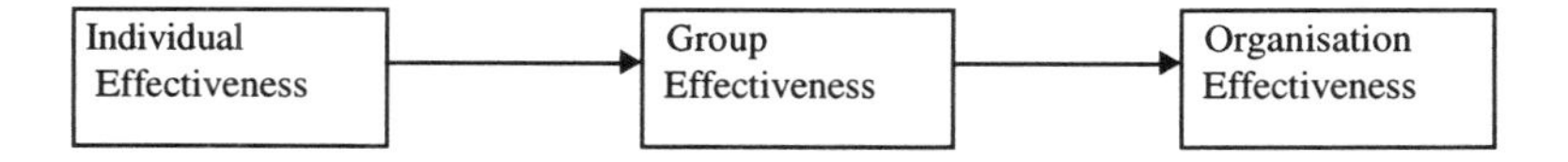

Figure 2.2: Causes of Effectiveness

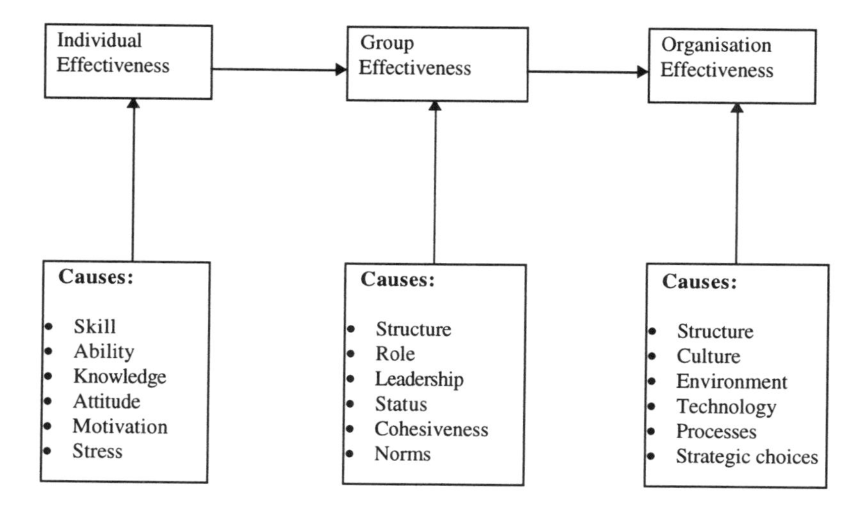

management style as contributing to the problem of systems underperformance. This is supported in a study by Hornby et al. (1992), who also conclude that analysts are constrained by many organisational factors and do not generally consider human issues to be their responsibility and, even when they do, they tend to rate them fairly low on their list of priorities. They expect users to take the lead in this area but have ambivalent feelings about the users' capacity to do so.

For IS development, implementation and use to be acceptable to users, these psychological and organisational factors above need to be adequately addressed. A management and administrative infrastructure needs to be maintained at the top level, as shown in Figure 3, to address these issues.

The Nature Of User Satisfaction Models

An examination of most models would suggest that despite their inclusion of factors such as user and management involvement, for the most part, they are technology led (Sprung, 1990; Clegg, 1993). Indeed, in a provocative summary, MacGregor (1992) likens them as:

> "...being similar to driving a multimillion dollar car, screaming 'Faster! Faster!,' while your eyes are firmly fixed on the dashboard. There is little sense of where you are or where you are going and a very good chance of doing considerable damage to the vehicle" (MacGregor, 1992, p. 276).

While perhaps overstated, an examination of most models shows that they tend to be drawn from one or more of the following perspectives:

- the quality of the information from the IS;
- the user interface features of the IS;
- the support provided by data processing staff, vendors or manuals;
- the effectiveness of the IS in the organisation;
- the involvement of the user in the planning, development and implementation of the IS;
- the involvement of management in the planning, development and implementation of the IS; and
- the user attitudes towards the IS.

For the sake of convenience, these seven perspectives have been condensed into tabular form (see Table 1). If each of the perspectives is viewed singly, it can be seen that with the exception of *User attitudes towards IS*, each relies heavily upon the technology and its uses within the organisation. While each has provided valuable data, Ditsa and MacGregor (1995) suggest that it is only when each of the perspectives are combined (see Figure 1) that a truer picture of user satisfaction can be established.

The Use Of Models In The Development Of Information Systems

Despite the development of user satisfaction models and the subsequent findings utilising such models, Underwood (1992) suggests that there is still a considerable gap between the theoretical findings and the use of them in the day-to-day information systems practice. He suggests that:

> "While the introduction of a new information system is known to have social implications for the end user, the owners of the system, and to some extent the end users, usually see the system in a technical light— a major hardware purchase, a software development project, faster processors etc. This perception is not discouraged by the major players in the information industry who make their living selling hardware and software" (Underwood, 1992, p. 268).

There are a variety of reasons given in the literature for the gap between the theoretical model and its implementation in practice. Gilb (1988) suggests that despite the attempt by designers to incorporate organisational and psychological parameters, these are consistently maintained at a broad level while technical aspects are narrowed and detailed. The result is that the organisational and psychological factors become fuzzy and are ultimately given a *back seat* or discarded entirely. Green (1991) suggests that many of the organisational and psychological factors are approached at a *veneer level* while technical aspects are examined more deeply. Underwood (1992) takes this view a stage further and suggests that organisational and psychological parameters are considered systemically (wholly), while technical factors are considered systematically (broken down and solved in parts). While conceding these views, Clegg (1993) suggests that many of the psychological and organisational aspects are pushed onto users rather than being demanded by them. Indeed, he states:

> "Looking on ourselves as suppliers of psychological and organisational expertise ...our expertise tends to be supply-pushed into the market, for example by researchers and consultants working hard at getting these ideas accepted. Such a perspective reveals a fundamental problem for professionals working in the field. My own experience is that many of us (self included) who preach the virtues of user-centred design for computing based systems, fail to practice this when working with our own users (be they managers, systems developers, end-users or whoever). We give them what we think they need because they themselves don't know" (Clegg, 1993, p. 264).

As already suggested, most user satisfaction perspectives tend to be based upon technology and its use within the organisation, rather than an attempt by designers to include psychological and organisational parameters. Based on the views of Clegg (1993) that most users do not expect psychological and organisational parameters to be included within systems, a pilot study was set up to examine the criteria considered by users as most important when systems were being acquired.

Instrument Used in the Study

Based on the views of Clegg (1993) and the early work carried out by MacGregor and Cocks (1994), a questionnaire was developed which asked respondents which two of the following:

- Performance
- Cost
- Benefits
- Ease of Use
- Future Enhancement

Figure 3: Demarginalization of Social, Psychological and Organizational Aspects of IS

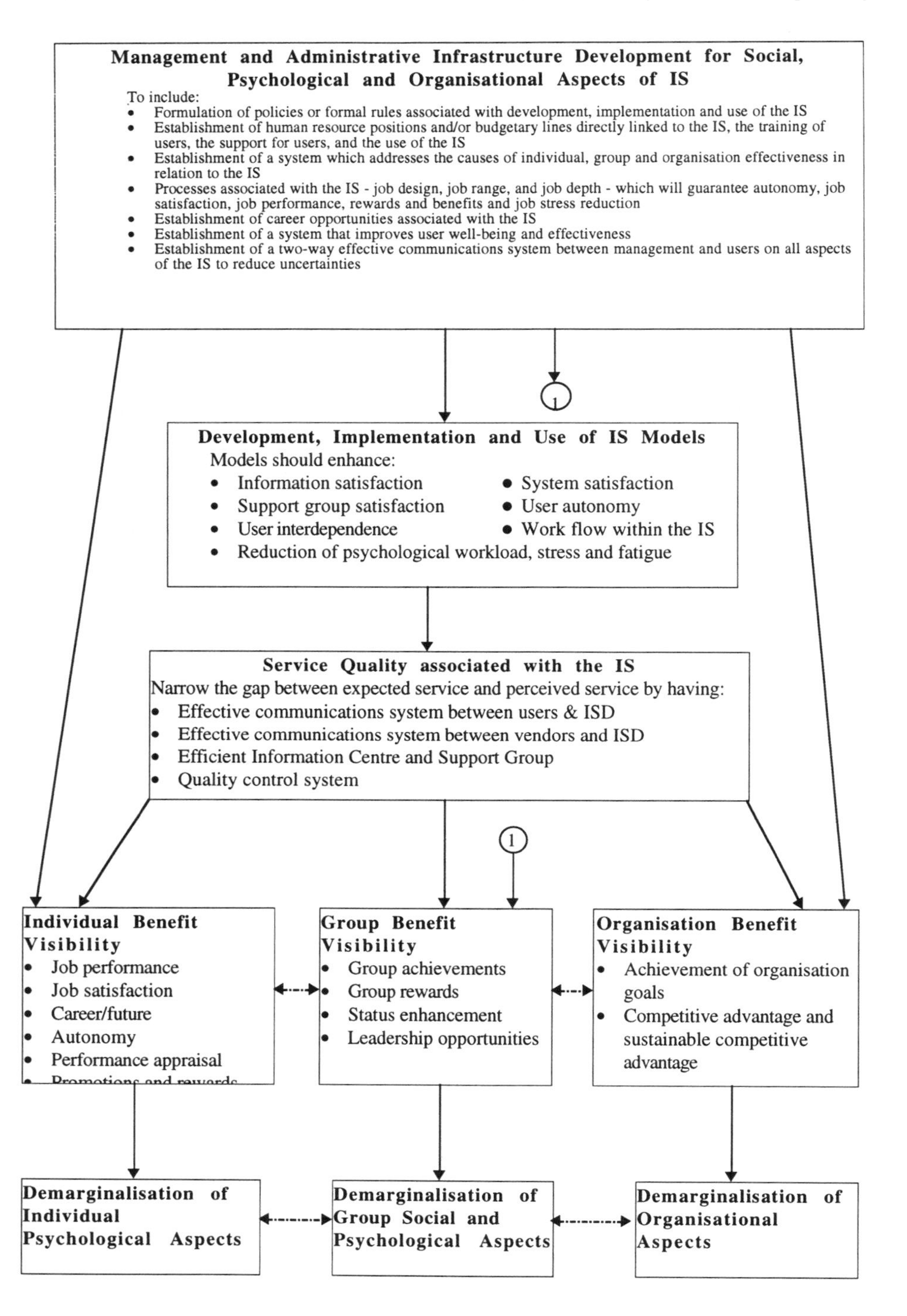

Table 4: Factors Which Should Be Introduced such that Organisational and Psychological Factors Are Removed, or at Least Marginalised in an Information System

End User Factors

- Users should be copers, even with poorly designed systems.
- The cost of poor systems should be borne by the user.
- Users should be encouraged that any adverse experience they have with the system will be repaired in the next version.
- Users should not be empowered to change practice.
- Users should not own the system.
- Users should not ever be organised and they, themselves, should be marginalised as much as possible.
- Few resources should be devoted to the bringing together of users and developers.
- Users should be perceived as sources of errors and unpredictability—All systems failures should be titled Operator Error.
- Users should be seen as problems, irrational, recalcitrant, resistant and constraints to the progress of the system.

Factors Associated with Developers/Suppliers/Experts

- The supply of technology should be new-product or functionality led, rather than performance and end-user driven.
- There should be a lot of marketing hype.
- Engineers and new technologists should be encouraged to appropriate new technology.
- Technological innovation and invention should be highly valued.
- Software industries should be encouraged to seek the brightest new brains and only these should be seen to have an exciting career path in front of them.
- The major analysis and design methods should focus on the technical to the exclusion of the organisational and psychological.
- All effort in analysis and design should be towards making the process more effective, not the final product more effective.
- The criteria for good design should be purely technical. The development process should involve multiple conflicting goals of which all psychological and organisational issues should be subservient.
- The development process should be characterised by its emergent properties, by the involvement of different people over an extended time, and by the lack of integration.
- There should be no rewards for those designers who consider the psychological or organisational components of design.

Factors Associated with Management

- Most senior managers should not understand IT nor what it can do for the business.
- Senior managers, along with accountants, should demand rapid payback on investments, these should be particularly manifested by the reduction of staff and skill levels.
- Rigorous studies of the impact of IT should be actively discouraged.
- IT should never be considered in terms of the promised performance.
- New technology should always be under funded in terms of time, money, expertise and management commitment, especially in the human aspects.
- The organisational context associated with the introduction of computer technology should be a highly political one.

(from Clegg 1993, pp 262)

they used as the primary criteria for computer purchase. The survey also asked if future systems were to be acquired, which of the criteria would be most important in the decision making process.

Method

Questionnaires were distributed to small and medium businesses in the Southern Sydney area as well as the cities of Wollongong and Nowra (population approximately. 500,000). The names and addresses were gathered from the *Illawara Business Directory* (1993), produced by the Illawara Chamber of Commerce and Industry.

Analysis of Results

A total of 600 questionnaires were distributed. Responses were obtained from 131 giving a response rate of 21.8%. All respondents indicated that they had at least 12 months experience with the use of IT in their organisations, with 87% indicating greater than two years experience.

The data was examined to determine which two criteria were used most in the selection of computer-based information systems for the organisations. Table 2 indicates the findings.

Table 3 indicates the criteria which would be used if new computer based systems were to be acquired.

The data from Tables 2 and 3 would tend to suggest the views of Clegg (1993) that, performance and financial factors tend to supersede the organisational or psychological factors when computer-based technology is being considered.

ORGANISATIONAL CULTURE WHICH SUPPORTS THE LACK OF DEMAND BY USERS

Markus and Keil (1994) lament that, though systems failures due to technical reasons (e.g., American Airlines and the Confirm Travel Reservation System) are regrettable, much more disturbing are failures that occur when people do not use systems that are technically sound. According to Markus and Keil, unused systems are generally attributed to one of two factors: software usability and implementation (the effort of line managers to ensure that the system is used). Markus and Keil, however, suggest a third major and preventable factor—bad business system design. They alluded to the fact in a case study that users (sales representatives) did not use a technically sound system because, first, they were not motivated to do what the system enabled them to do and, second, using the system made it harder for them to do what they were motivated to do. This, Markus and Keil conclude, is due to the fact that the system was wrongly placed in the organisation and the users have little or no power to demand the necessary factors that will enable them to use the system, but to completely ignore or underutilise the system.

A recent survey of 221 financial and IS executives conducted by Deloitte and Touche (Greenberg, 1995) also shows 85% recently implemented new systems with the applications falling short of user expectations, but the users did not make their demands heard. Indeed, Armstrong (1994) reaffirms that there is a basic gap between user expectations and the real-world database as experienced at the workstations. The indications are that databases are labelled in a way that users have little room in demanding psychological and organisational factors. A study by Nord and Nord (1994) also reveals that a significant percentage of end users are less pleased with the support provided by the information centre. Suh et al. (1994)

further indicate that people are actually setting up models to compensate user expectations instead of adequately addressing the issues. Oz (1994) also points out how the 3.3 million Star*Doc failed because both users and management were marginalised during the system's development. Oz referred to Lyytinen and Hirschheim's (1989) claims of how users' expectations are vaguely expressed, and are never rationalised or verbalised as real concerns because of: the great number of users; users' inability to voice their expectations because of organisational barriers; dominating ideology; lack of time or interest; or simply the unclear content of the expectations.

Blenker and Potiggia (1991) also suggest that the influence of a single organisation upon technological development is at best minimal. Thus, most organisations tend to adapt to technology and their day-to-day processes determined almost entirely by the technology employed. This view is supported by Winner (1986) and Scarberough and Corbett (1992). Hamerri (1994) suggests that one of the outcomes of this situation is that technological innovation very often stems from a narrow set of individual needs and experience. While the attempt to develop a system which includes organisational and psychological components is stated by the innovator, the result is very often a system where both of these have been developed from a narrow band of knowledge and experience. The implications on users, according to Campbell (1996), is a decrease in expectation as to the cause of use and usefulness of computer technology.

The results of our survey support most of the above studies, pointing to the fact that marginalisation of organisational and psychological factors in the development process and use of IS which contributes to systems failures still go unnoticed or are pushed to the "back seat" if noticed at all.

Given, then, that in most cases users tend not to demand the organisational or psychological components of information systems, one needs to question, "What social issues are at work?" Clegg (1993) in a polemic paper attempted to design a social system whereby users' demands were minimised and organisational and psychological factors were marginalised in the production of an information system. The resulting social system included factors associated with the user, designers and the organisation (see Table 4). While Clegg agrees that not all factors would be present in all organisations, he suggests that many of them are quite common in organisations confronted with the implementation of information technology.

A number of authors have attempted to explain why many of these factors still tend to be present. Hill (1991) suggests that introduction of technology is considered from a systems perspective. A new technology implies a new system and culture, if considered at all, is dealt with at a later date. Pacanowsky and O'Connell-Trujillo (1983) consider the management of new technology is based on the need to control, where organisation culture becomes a single variable to be manipulated along with goals, accountability, etc. Hampson (1991) suggests that while a choice is supposedly given with the introduction of a new information system, the choice possibilities are ultimately whittled down to one, based on rationality. Argyris (1980), in a similar vein, suggests that while rules are initially developed by consensus, these are ultimately bent and tightened to suit the technology which has been introduced.

THE DEVELOPMENT OF AN ALTERNATIVE

If we accept that despite the existence of models which examine user satisfaction, most users tend not to demand their use, nor the parameters that they address, then we must examine ways through which the user begins to expect the incorporation of organisational and psychological issues into information systems. A number of methods have been suggested in the literature.

Udo and Guimaraes (1994) suggest a socio-technical approach in the absorption of emerging technologies, particularly new IT, whereas Williams (1991) suggests that prior to the development of an information system, there needs to be an examination of the choices involved in the work organisation. Pliskin and Romm (1992) take this a step further by suggesting that any evaluation of the organisation must examine user beliefs and values concerning:

- innovation
- risk taking
- interdependency
- management orientation
- performance expectation
- rewards
- the level of autonomy in decision making.

To these factors Clegg adds the need for the development of policies which are concerned with information system's development and implementation, together with budgetary considerations for training and support.

It would seem, then, that in order to fully utilise the findings developed from user satisfaction models, it is important that an infrastructure be put in place which caters to the social, psychological and organisational aspects of an information system, as shown in Figure 3. As can also be seen in Figure 3, this infrastructure must contain at a minimum: policies and rules which oversee the development, implementation and use of information systems (these must be developed from social, psychological and organisational needs); establishment of human resource positions and finance for the training and support of users, using the information systems; a continuing process of examining the needs of the individual, the work group and the organisation; processes associated with the IS which examine job design, job range and job depth—which will guarantee autonomy, job satisfaction, job performance, rewards and benefits and reduction in job stress; establishment of career opportunities associated with information technology; and establishment of two-way effective communications among management, developers and users on all aspects of information technology use.

Having this infrastructure in place, the development, implementation and use of IS models should, as shown in Figure 3, enhance:

- information satisfaction
- system satisfaction
- user autonomy
- support group satisfaction
- work flow within the IS
- user interdependence
- reduction of psychological workload, stress and fatigue

In addition, as shown in Figure 3, service quality associated with the IS should narrow the gap between expected service and perceived service by having:

- effective communications system between users and the information systems department (ISD);
- effective communications system between vendors and ISD;
- efficient Information Centre and Support Group; and
- quality control system (see Pitt et al., 1995; Parasuraman et al., 1985, 1988, 1991; Zeithaml et al., 1990, 1993).

It is only when such a management and administrative infrastructure framework is developed, that the use of models and the subsequent service quality more readily benefits the individual, the work group and the entire organisation.

CONCLUSION

With the ever widening use of computer technology in organisations, user satisfaction has become an important and ongoing area of research. The literature surrounding the area of user satisfaction has given rise to a variety of models. While many of these models have begun to provide very necessary data concerning the nature of user satisfaction and we can say with some confidence "Our mousetrap's fine, thank you", it is only when an infrastructure is introduced which supports the use of these models in the day-to-day development, that users begin to expect and demand the inclusion of organisational and psychological parameters into information systems. Indeed, until the user, be they individual, group or organisation, begins to expect and demand the use of user satisfaction models and the data which has flowed from them, these models will remain marginal, at best pushed onto the user, and at worst completely ignored.

REFERENCES

Abdul-Gader, A. (1996). The Impact of User Satisfaction on Computer-Mediated Communication Acceptance: A Casual Path Model. *Information Resources Management Journal,* 9(1), 17-26.

Armstrong, C. (1994). What You See Is What You Get. *Information World Review,* (97), 29.

Argyris, C. (1980). Some Inner Contradictions in Management Information Systems in Lucas H.C. (ed) *The Information Systems Environment,* North Holland, Amsterdam.

Avison, D. & Fitzgerald, G. (1990). *Information Systems Development.* Blackwell Scientific Publications.

Amoako-Gyampah, K. & White, K.B. (July 1993). User involvement and user satisfaction. *Information & Management,* 25, 1-10.

Bagozzi, R.P., Baumgartner, H. & Yi, Y. (1992). State Versus Action Orientation and the Theory of Reasoned Action: An Application to Coupon Usage. *Journal of Consumer Research,* 18(4), 505-518.

Bailey, J.E. & Pearson, S.W. (1983). Development of a Tool for Measuring and Analyzing Computer User Satisfaction. *Management Science,* 29(5), 530-545.

Barki, H. and Hartwick, J. (1989). Rethinking the Concept of User Involvement. *MIS Quarterly* 13(1), 53-64.

Blenker, P. and Potiggia, A. (1991). Information Technology - Constructional or Strategic Resource? in Sutherland E. and Moneux Y. *Business Strategy and Information Technology,* New York: Rutledge.

Campbell, H. (1996). A Social Interactionist Perspective on Computer Implementation. *Journal of The American Planning Association,* 62(1), 99-107.

Carr, H.H. (1992). Factors that affect user-friendliness in interactive computer program. *Information & Management,* 22(3), 137-149.

Carroll, J.M. (1991) History and Hysteresis in Theories and Frameworks for HCI in Diaper D. and Hammond N. (eds) *People and Computer VI CHIí91 Proceedings,* Edinburgh, 47-56.

Clegg, C.W. (1993). Social Systems that Marginalize the Psychological and Organizational Aspects of Information Technology. *Behaviour and Information Technology*, 12(5), 261-266.

Clegg, C.W., Warr, P.B., Green, T.R.G., Monk, A., Kemp, N.J., Allison, G. and Lansdale, M. (1989). *People and Computers, How to Evaluate Your Company's New Technology*, Ellis Horwood, Chichester.

Currie, W.L. (1996). Organizational Structure and the Use of Information Technology: Preliminary Findings of a Survey in the Private and Public Sector. *International Journal of Information Management*, 16(1) 51-64.

Cyert, R.M. & March, J.G. (1965). *A Behavioral Theory of the Firm,* Englewood Cliffs, NJ: Prentice-Hall.

Davis, F.D., Bagozzi, R.P., & Warshaw, P.R. (Aug 1989). User acceptance of Computer Technology: A Comparison of two theoretical models. *Management Science,* 35(8), 982-1003.

Ditsa, G.E.M. and MacGregor, R.C. (1995). Models of User Perceptions, Expectations and Acceptance of Information Systems. *IRMA International Conference Proceedings: Managing Information and Communications in a Global Environment* (1995), Atlanta, 196-204.

Doll, W.J (March 1985). Avenues for Top Management Involvement in Successful MIS Development. *MIS Quarterly* 17-35.

Eason, K.D. (1988). *Information Technology and Organisational Change*, Taylor & Francis, London.

Eliason, A.L. (1990). *Systems Development: Analysis, Design and Implementation,* 2nd edn., Glenview, Illinois: Scott, Foresman/Little, Brown.

Franklin, I., Pain, D., Green, E., and Owen, J. (1992). Job Design Within a Human Centred (system) Design Framework. *Behaviour and Information Technology,* 1992, 11(3), 141-150.

Gilb T. (1988). *Principles of Software Information Management,* Addison Wesley, Wokingham.

Goodwin, N.C. (1987). Functionality and Usability. *Communications of the ACM*, 30, 229-333.

Green T.R.G. (1991) Describing Information Artifacts with Cognitive Dimensions and Structure Maps in Diaper D & Hammond N. (eds) *People and Computer VI CHI 91 Proceedings,* Edinburgh, 297 - 316.

Greenberg, I. (1995). Users' Bottom Line: Accounting Packages Don't Rate. *Infoworld,* 17(7), 27.

Hamerri, A.P. (1994). Using Technical Norms in Explaining Technological Action. *Technovation*, 14(8), 505-514.

Hampson I. (1991) Information Technology at Work: Industrial Democracy and Technological Determinism in Aungles S. (ed) *Information Technology in Australia*, 63 - 91.

Hill S. (1991) Technological Change and the Systematisation of Organisational Culture in Aungles S. (ed) *Information Technology in Australia,* 92 - 113.

Hornby, P., Clegg, C.W., Robson, J.I., MacLaren, C.R.R., Richardson, S.C.S. and O'Brien P. (1992). Human and Organizational Issues in Information Systems Development. *Behaviour and Information Technology*, 11(3), 160-174.

Hovmark, S. and Norell, M. (1993). Social and Psychological Aspects of Computer-aided Design Systems. *Behaviour and Information Technology,* 12(5), 267-275.

Ivancevich J. and Matteson M., (1993) *Organisational Behaviour and Management.*, Boston: Irwin.

Ives, B. & Olson, M. (May 1984). User Involvement and MIS Success: A Review of Research. *Management Science*, 30(5), 586-603.

Jarvenpaa, S. & Ives, B. (1991). Executive Involvement and Participation in the Management of Information Technology. *MIS Quarterly,* September.

Kelloway, E.K., & Barling, J. (1993). Members' participation in local union activities: Measurement, prediction, and replication. *Journal of Applied Psychology*, 78(2), 262-279.

Koppes, L.L., Trahan, W.A., Hartman, E.A., Perlman, B., and Nealon, D.J. (1991 Researching the Impact of Computer Technology in the Workplace: A Psychological Perspective in Szewczak E., Snodgrass C. & Khosrowpour M. *Management Impacts of Information Technology: Perspectives on Organizational Change and Growth,* Idea Group Publishing, Harrisburg Pennsylvania, 135-164.

Lehman, M.M. (1996). Feedback In The Software Evolution Process. *Information and Software*

Technology, 38(11) 681-686.
Lucas, H.C. (1975). *Why Information Systems Fail*, New York: Columbia University Press.
MacGregor R.C. (1992) HCI: An Overview in MacGregor R.C., Clarke R.J., Little S.E., Gould E.L. & Ang A.Y. (eds) *ISOP 92 Proceedings Third Australian Conference on Information Systems, Wollongong*, 275 - 282.
Markus, M.L. (1984). *Systems in Organizations: Bugs & Features,* Boston: Pitman Publishing.
Markus, M.L. and Keil, M. (1994). If We Built It, They Will Come: Designing Information Systems That People Want to Use. *Sloan Management Review,* 35(4) 11-25.
McFarlan, W., McKinney, J.L. & Pyburn, P. (Jan-Feb 1983). The Information Archipelago - Plotting a Course. *Harvard Business Review,* 61(1), 145-156.
MacGregor R.C. and Cocks R.S. (1994). Computer Usage and Satisfaction in the Australian Veterinary Industry. *Australian Veterinary Practitioner,* 25(1), 43-48.
Mykytyn, P.P. Jr. & Harrison, D.A. (1993). The application of the Theory of Reasoned Action to senior management and strategic information systems. *Project Management Journal,* 6(2), 15-26.
Nataraajan, R. (1993). Prediction of choice in a technically complex, essentially intangible, highly experiential, and rapidly evolving customer product. *Psychology & Marketing,* 10(5), 367-379.
Netemeyer, R.G. & Bearden, W.O. (1992). A Comparative Analysis of Two Models of Behavioral Intention. *Journal of the Academy of Marketing Science,* 20(1), 49-59.
Nord, G.D. and Nord, J.H. (1994). Perceptions and Attitudes of End-users on Technology Issues. *Journal of Systems Management,* 45(11), 12-15.
Oz, E. (1994). Information Systems Mis-Development: The Case of Star*Doc. *Journal of Systems Management,* 45(9), 30-34.
Pacanowsky M.E. & OfConnell-Trujillo N. (1983). *Organisation Communication as Cultural Performance Communications Monographs,* June, 50.
Parasuraman, A., Zeithaml, V.A., and Berry, L.L. (Fall 1985). A Conceptual Model of Service Quality and Its Implications for Future Research. *Journal of Marketing,* 41-50.
Parasuraman, A., Zeithaml, V.A., and Berry, L.L. (Spring 1988). SERVQUAL: A Multiple-item Scale for Measuring Consumer Perceptions of Service Quality. *Journal of Retailing,* 12-40.
Parasuraman, A., Berry, L.L., and Zeithaml, V.A. (1993). More on Improving the Measurement of Service Quality. *Journal of Retailing,* Spring, 140-147.
Pitt, L.F., Watson, R.T. and Kavan, C.B. (June 1995). Service Quality: A Measure of Information Systems Effectiveness. *MIS Quarterly,* 173-185.
Pliskin N. and Romm T. (1992). Organisational Culture Considerations in the Implementation of Human Resource Management Systems in MacGregor R.C., Clarke R.J., Little S.E., Gould E.L. & Ang A.Y. (eds) *ISOP 92 Proceedings Third Australian Conference on Information System,* Wollongong, 531 - 544.
Rockart, J.F. & Flannery, L.S. (Oct 1983). The Management of End-User Computing. *Communications of the ACM* 26(10), 785-793.
Powers, R.F. & Dickson, G.W. (1973). MIS Project Management: Myths, Opinions and Reality. *California Management Review,* 15(3), 147-156.
Ray, C.M., Harris, T.M. and Dye, J.L. (1994). Small Business Attitudes Toward Computers. *Journal of End User Computing,* 6(1), 16-25.
Raymond, L. (1987). Validating and Applying User Satisfaction as a Measure of MIS Success in Small Organisations. *Information and Management,* (The Netherlands), 12, 173-179.
Robey, D. & Farrow, D.L. (1982). User Involvement in Information System Use. *Academy of Management,* 28(1), 73-85.
Robey, D. & Farrow, D. (1982). User Involvement in Information System Development: A Conflict Model and Empirical Test. *Management Science,* 28(1), 73-85.
Saga, V.L. and Zmud, R.W. (1994). *The Nature and Determinants of IT Acceptance, Routinization, and Infusion. Diffusion, Transfer and Implementation of Information Technology* (A-45). 67-85.
Sainfort, P.A. (1990). Job Design Predictors of Stress in Automated Offices. *Behaviour and Information Technology,* 9(1) 3-16.
Scarberough, H. and Corbett, J.M. (1992). *Technology and Organisation,* Rutledge, NY.
Shneidermann, B. (1992). *Designing the User Interface: Strategies for Effective Human-Computer*

Interaction. Reading, MA: Addison-Wesley.

Sless, D. (1989). *Practical Solutions to the interface crisis. Keynote Address at the 25th Annual Conference of the Ergonomics Society of Australia,* Canberra.

Sprung R.C. (1990). US Exporters: Lounge tied Ambassadors in Chew J.C & Whiteside J (eds) *Empowering People Chi 90 Proceedings, Seattle,* 291 - 292.

Suh, K., Kim, S. and Lee, J. (1994). End-user's Disconfirmed Expectations and the Success of Information Systems. *Information Resources Management Journal,* 7(4), 30-39.

Swanson, E.B. (1974). Management Information Systems: Appreciation and Involvement. *Management Science,* 21 178-188.

Tait, P. & Vessey, I. (March 1988). The Effect of User Involvement on System Success: A Contingency Approach. *MIS Quarterly,* 91-108.

Treitler, I. (Spring 1996). Culture and the Problem of Universal Access to Electronic Information Systems. *Social Science Computer Review,* 14(1) 62-64.

Turner, J.A. (1982). Observations on the Use of Behavioral Models in Information Systems Research and Practice. *Information and Management,* 5, 207-213.

Udo, G. and Guimaraes, T. (1994). Improving Organization Absorption of Emerging Technologies: A Socio-Technical Approach in Khosrowpour M. *Information Technology and Organizations: Challenges of New Technologies,* Idea Group Publishing, Harrisburg Pennsylvania, 3-30.

Underwood J (1992) Information Systems Work Contradictions in Theory and Practice in MacGregor R.C., Clarke R.J., Little S.E., Gould E.L. & Ang A.Y. (eds) ISOP 92 *Proceedings Third Australian Conference on Information Systems,* Wollongong, 267 - 274.

Williams, J. (1991). Negative Consequences of Information Technology in Szewczak E., Snodgrass C. & Khosrowpour M. *Management Impacts of Information Technology: Perspectives on Organizational Change and Growth,* Idea Group Publishing, Harrisburg Pennsylvania, 48-74.

Williams, T.A. (1991). Sociotechnical Systems in the Information Technology Age in Aungles S. (ed) *Information Technology in Australia,* 1 - 25.

Williams, T.A. (1994). Information Technology and Self managing Work Groups. *Behaviour and Information Technology,* 13(4), 268-276.

Winner, L. (1986). *The While and the Reactor,* Chicago: Chicago University Press.

Wishnick, Y.S. & Wishnick, T.K. (1993). Relationships between school labor relations practitioners' personal and social beliefs and their propensity toward using an interest-based negotiations model in the public schools. *Journal of Collective Negotiations in the Public Sector,* 22(3), 215-231.

Wysocki, R. and Young, J. (1990) *Information Systems: Management Principles in Action.* John Wiley & Sons.

Zeithaml, V.A., Parasuraman, A., and Berry, L.L. (1990). *Delivering Quality Service: Balancing Customer Perceptions and Expectations,* New York: Free Press.

Zeithaml, V.A., Berry, L.L., and Parasuraman, A. (1993). The Nature and Determinants of Customer Expectations of Service. *Journal of the Academy of Marketing Science,* Winter, 1-12.

Chapter 8

An Attributional Analysis of the Rejection of Information Technology

John W. Henry
Georgia Southern University, USA

Mark J. Martinko
Florida State University, USA

The major relationships depicted by attributional models of the process by which individuals accept or reject new information technologies were tested with path analyses in a field setting. The results confirmed that attributions regarding ability were directly related to efficacy expectations, whereas attributions regarding task difficulty and effort were related to outcome expectations. The results further confirmed that both efficacy and outcome expectations were directly related to outcomes including both job performance and end-user satisfaction. In addition, the research showed how attributions affected outcome measures indirectly through expectations.

The factors associated with the successful introduction of New Information Technologies (NITs) are well known and include user involvement (Baroudi, Olson, & Ives, 1986; Boland 1978; Debrabander & Edstrom, 1977; Mankin, Bikson, & Gutek, 1985; Tait & Vessey, 1988), top management support (Leonard-Barton, 1988; Zmud, 1984), training (Glass & Knight, 1988), and realistic user expectations (Ginzberg, 1981; Martinko, Henry, & Zmud, 1996; Salloway, Counte, & Kjerulff, 1987). Specifically, NIT refers to any product, introduced for the first time to the end user, whose underlying technological base is comprised of computer or communications hardware and software (Cooper & Zmud, 1990).

Because these factors have been identified, it would seem that there would be little resistance to the implementation of NITs. Unfortunately, this is not the case and difficulties associated with introducing and training end-users on NITs in the work place have been

This chapter originally appeared in the Journal of End User Computing, vol. 9, no. 7.

Figure 1: An Attributional Model of Reactions to Information Technology

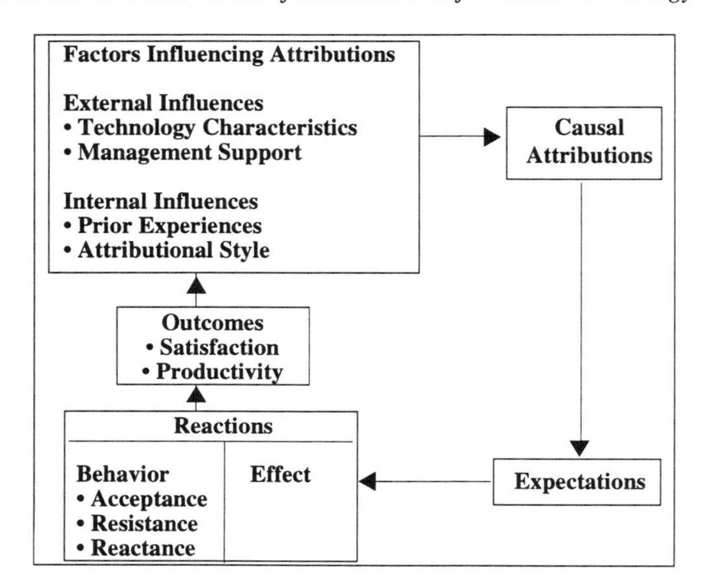

thoroughly chronicled (Argyris, 1971; Blackler & Brown, 1985; Cancro & Slotnick, 1970; Compeau, Olfman, Sein, & Webster, 1995; Dowling, 1980; Meier, 1985; Rosen, Sears, & Weil, 1987). However, as of yet, there does not appear to be any well-accepted or documented integrative explanation of the variables and the dynamics by which end-users decide to accept or reject NITs.

The purpose of this chapter is to address the needs identified above by both proposing and testing an attributional model of the dynamic process that determines end-user acceptance or rejection of NITs.

TOWARD A COMPREHENSIVE MODEL

Recently, several authors have proposed attributional explanations of the behavioral dynamics encountered by end-users when accepting or rejecting NITs (Henry, Martinko, & Pierce, 1993; Martinko, Henry, & Zmud, 1996). All of these explanations draw heavily on Weiner's (1979) work on achievement motivation as well as the work of Martinko and Gardner (1982) and Abramson, Seligman, and Teasdale (1978) describing the role of attributions in Learned Helplessness (LH). While there are some minor variations in the models and the explanations which have been proposed, the dynamics depicted in Figure 1 are representative of the relationships which have been described.

Essentially, the model depicts acceptance and rejection behavior as a function of user expectations. The predictive validity of expectations has been tested in previous studies (Henry & Stone, 1995a). These expectations are formed from users' attributions regarding the likely causes of their successes and failures in interacting with the NIT. The attributions are also influenced by the characteristics of the NIT as well as any similar experiences that the user may have had with other NIT implementations. In addition, individual dispositional differences such as attributional style are also proposed to influence user attributions.

Based on the LH model (Abramson, Seligman, & Teasdale, 1978; Martinko & Gardner, 1982), the following chains of relationships are predicted for acceptance versus rejection of

NITs. Those who accept NITs are more likely to have had positive experiences with prior information technologies and to have optimistic explanatory styles (Seligman, 1990). Similarly, in forming their expectations of the outcomes of their interactions with the NITs, people who are likely to accept the NIT are also more likely to believe (attribute) that their prior successes with information technologies were caused by internal and stable characteristics such as ability and expect that their outcomes with the NIT will be positive. On the other hand, those who are most likely to reject an NIT are much more likely to have had negative outcomes in interacting with prior information technologies, have pessimistic explanatory styles, attribute their likelihood of failures with the NIT to an internal and stable dimension such as lack of ability, and expect that their outcomes will be negative.

Several partial tests of the above model have been reported.
In a study of students enrolled in their first computer science course, Henry, Martinko, and Pierce (1993) found that students with optimistic attributional styles regarding writing computer programs achieved higher grades than those with pessimistic attributional styles. In addition, they found that final grades were related to causal attributions of ability. In a similar study of students enrolled in an introductory programming course, Henry, Stone, and Pierce (1993) found that students with positive expectations, operationalized as computer self-efficacy, were more likely to continue in the computer science or management information systems major and experienced less frustration while working on programming projects. Henry & Stone (1995a, 1995b) found that expectations greatly influenced end-users' self ratings of their job satisfaction and job performance.

Although the above studies provide some support for the attributional model of reactions to NITs, the support is clearly limited. The first two studies employed student samples and were concerned with attributions and reactions in an educational rather than a work setting where use is non-volitional. More importantly, the strength of the results in both studies was limited because of problems with sample sizes. The relatively small number of subjects in the Henry et al. (1993) study (69) reduced the probability of detecting significant relations. Thus, a more rigorous test of the attributional model in a field setting is needed.

Hypotheses

Rather than attempting an omnibus validation of the many relations depicted in the attributional model of reactions to NITs, the current study concentrates on two key relationships depicted by the model: 1) the relationship between attributions and expectancies and 2) the relationships between expectancies and outcome measures. More specifically, attributional models of the acceptance and rejection of NITs (Martinko, Henry, & Zmud, 1996), as well as other more general models of attributional processes (Abramson, Seligman, & Teasdale, 1978; Weiner, 1979, 1985), depict a sequential chain of causal relationships indicating that attributions cause expectancies and that expectancies cause the behaviors associated with acceptance or rejection. Thus, attributions do not directly influence acceptance or rejection. Their effects are mediated by expectancies and they are viewed as the primary cause of the expectancies.

An additional factor complicating the relationships between attributions, expectancies, and acceptance behavior is that expectancies are multidimensional. As Bandura (1977) and more recently Gist and Mitchell (1992) have pointed out, there are two types of expectancies: efficacy expectations and outcome expectations. Efficacy expectations are concerned with the individual's expectations that they are capable and competent of performing a specific task (Bandura, 1977; Gist & Mitchell, 1992; Hirscheim & Newman, 1988; Weiner, 1985). Outcome expectations are defined as a "... person's estimate that a given behavior will lead to certain outcomes" (Bandura, 1977). Thus, outcome expectations are concerned with whether or not individuals believe that they will be rewarded if they achieve a desired level of performance.

Although research has been limited regarding the relationships between attributions and specific types of expectations, it would seem that efficacy expectations would be most closely related to the stable and internal attribution of ability. On the other hand, it would seem that outcome expectations would be related to the external and stable attributions regarding task difficulty. For example, within the context of accepting and rejecting NITs, we would expect that those subjects who express the internal and stable attributions of low ability will have low levels of efficacy expectations. Conversely, those who attribute prior difficulties with the system to the system itself are likely to have low outcome expectations.

In order to address the issues of the relationship between attributions and expectations as well as the general flow of causal relations depicted by attributional models within the context of accepting and rejecting NITs, a study was designed to test the following four propositions:

1. Attributions have direct effects on expectancies and indirect or no effects on outcomes.
2. Internal and stable attributions of ability are directly related to efficacy expectations and only indirectly or not related to outcome expectations and outcomes.
3. External and stable attributions regarding the difficulty of the NIT will be directly related to outcome expectations but only indirectly or not related to efficacy expectations.
4. Both efficacy expectations and outcome expectations will be directly related to outcomes such as productivity and satisfaction.

METHODS

The Research Setting and Sample

This study may be characterized as a natural experiment (Weick, 1979) in that the target of the study was experiencing changes in information technology as a part of the normal business process. More specifically, the site selected was a nonprofit urban hospital located in the southeastern United States in which a new Order Communications and Results Reporting system was being implemented for use by the hospital staff. The new system, which will hereafter be referred to as the NIT, was designed to improve the accuracy, legibility and timeliness of interdepartmental communication. For example the system is designed to record all patient services including patient scheduling, X-ray scheduling, medication records, dietary procedures, surgical procedures (both planned and completed), diagnosis results, and prognosis. The system, a patient database, is completely controlled and maintained by the MIS department. End-users accessing the system must go through a series of screens to reach each function: however, with practice the sequential screen selection process can be bypassed by entering direct commands. It is also necessary to follow a specific menu selection for each function performed by the system. The first screen that usually appears at an access station is the unit census or "patient selection menu." Order selection screens are designed with multiple levels, within major categories. Upon selection of the patient, the most common services utilized by a department or nursing unit are automatically displayed on the "Common Order Screen." These common services are selected by the nursing station and service department personnel. Less frequently used orders or services are accessed from lower level menus. Similar procedures are followed for other selections from the Order Communications/Results Reporting Screen.

Table 1: Correlation Matrix for All Variables

	(Reliability)	M	SD	1	2	3	4	5	6	7	8
1. Ability		4.63	1.87	1.00	.177*	.563***	.158	-.208***	.151	.045	-.034
2. Difficulty of System		4.57	1.60	.177**	1.00	.191**	.230**	-.006	-.097	-.087	-.081
3. Effort		4.47	1.98	.563***	.191**	1.00	.205**	-.056	.220**	.170	.059
4. Luck		3.15	1.82	.158	.230***	.205**	1.00	-.163	.014	.044	-.107
5. Efficacy [E1]	(.83)	2.99	.691	-.208**	-.006	-.056	-.163	1.00	.256***	.275***	.565***
6. Outcome Expectancy [E2]	(.81)	3.30	.511	.151	-.097	.220**	.014	.256***	1.00	.454***	.537***
7. End-User Satisfaction	(.95)	5.30	1.00	.045	-.087	.170	.044	.275***	.454***	1.00	.655***
8. Job Performance	(.86)	5.02	1.39	-.034	-.081	.059	-.107	.565***	.537***	.655***	1.00

Table 2: Factor Analysis of Expectancy Scale

		E2*	E1**	E3	E4	E5	E6
3.	[R] Working with the system leads to a feeling of accomplishment.	.78	.07	.06	.07	-.02	-.11
22.	[R] I expect the system to be easier to use as time goes by.	.76	-.10	-.07	.12	.09	.13
11.	[R] I think I will be able to use the system to produce high quality work.	.71	.25	.09	.18	.14	-.13
1.	[R] My capability to use the system will lead to high quality work.	.65	.17	.22	-.03	.06	.06
4.	[R] Working with the system will result in my completing my work on time.	.63	.00	.35	-.09	.20	.04
16.	[R] I believe I can be more productive at work using the system.	.59	.07	.52	.06	.05	-.00
21.	[R] I believe my performance with the system increases my chances of promotion.	.44	.27	.25	-.10	-.04	-.39
20.	[R] I really have very little sense of how the system works.	.01	.76	.19	.12	.10	.06
17.	Compared to other people at work, I know very little about the system.	.14	.73	-.21	.06	.08	.09
9.	I feel incompetent when I try to use the system.	.05	.66	-.18	.24	.30	.16
6.	[R] At work I feel more competent with the system than most other people.	.09	.61	.15	.04	-.05	.02
2.	If I were sitting before the system, I would not know how to use it.	.09	.61	-.07	.06	.19	.18
12.	[R] I will avoid the system as much as possible.	.12	.59	.31	.28	.33	-.02
13.	Using the system will not solve any of the important problems related to patient care.	.08	-.01	.68	.18	.33	.03
8.	[R] I feel that if I am able to use the system, I will have more time for other hospital duties.	.41	-.08	.67	.00	-.11	-.02
7.	[R] If I don't learn how to use the system, it will be difficult to be successful in my career.	.39	.31	.47	.01	-.32	-.14
14	[R] I believe that I will be able to learn how to use the system.	.13	.13	.01	.85	-.01	.02
15.	I don't think I will be able to work with the system.	.05	.26	.17	.78	.21	.06
19.	I dislike the system.	-.11	-.19	-.15	-.07	-.81	-.08
10.	I find the system very frustrating.	.23	.39	-.05	.12	.67	-.13
18.	[R] I could access the menus on the system without any difficulty.	.10	.31	.04	-.04	-.02	.83
5.	Computer terminology is difficult to learn.	-.14	.34	-.02	.30	.02	.43
	EIGEN VALUE	5.66	3.27	1.35	1.17	1.09	1.01
	PERCENT OF VARIANCE EXPLAINED	25.7	14.9	6.2	5.4	4.9	4.6
	TOTAL VARIANCE	61.7					

[R] = Reverse coded Note: Variables ordered by factor and magnitude of loading. *E2 = Outcome Expectancy **E1 = Efficacy

Table 3: Factor Analysis of Satisfaction Scale

		S1	S2	S3	S4	S5
4.	Sufficient Information	.85	.15	.02	.27	.09
3.	Needed Reports	.81	.06	.00	.33	.09
2.	Info Meet Your Needs	.81	.19	.08	.29	-.06
6.	Info Is On Time	.77	-.04	.20	.24	-.03
1.	Precise Info You Need	.76	.28	.11	.22	-.08
7.	Up To Date	.75	.03	.15	.15	.16
16.	Information Easy to Find	.73	.23	.20	.10	.31
13.	Logically Organized	.71	.05	.17	.01	.29
9.	Organization of Information	.70	.14	.15	.13	.32
12.	Format	.69	.26	.10	.12	.05
10.	Screen Layouts	.69	.43	.29	-.27	.09
5.	Satisfaction with Accuracy	.65	.09	.12	.04	.08
18.	Prompts On Screen	.64	.44	.40	-.04	.03
11.	Where Info Is To Be Entered	.63	.49	.23	-.17	.20
14.	Easy To See and Read	.60	.19	.12	-.10	.56
17.	Instructions Are Consistent/Inconsistent	.58	.42	.41	.00	.01
23.	System Is Complex	.16	.75	.01	.04	.10
25.	Need Technical Person	.09	.71	-.03	.30	-.02
24.	[R] Easy To Use	.33	.61	.22	.36	.20
19.	[R] Message Specificity	.15	.19	.85	.00	.03
20.	[R] Ease of Movement Between Screens	.18	-.03	.79	.22	.15
21.	[R] Helpfulness of System to Work	.27	-.04	.61	.46	.11
22.	[R] I Like to Use System	.27	.28	.26	.69	.04
26.	System is Cumbersome to Use	.27	.37	.18	.63	.18
15.	Screens Appear Uncluttered	.39	-.16	-.07	.34	.62
8.	[R] Characters on Screen Easy to Read	-.07	.36	.29	.05	.61
EIGEN VALUE		11.82	2.05	1.62	1.41	1.09
PERCENT OF VARIANCE EXPLAINED		45.5	7.9	6.2	5.4	4.2
TOTAL VARIANCE EXPLAINED		69.2				

Table 4: Factor Analysis of Job Performance Scale

5. Are you able to use the system to get job done?	.90
4. Are you able to make use of all relevant capabilities of system?	.88
2. Is work support by system of high quality?	.81
1. Do you do a large amount of work with the system?	.77
3. Does system make it easier to perform other hospital duties?	.74
EIGEN VALUE	3.37
PERCENT OF VARIANCE EXPLAINED	67.3

Note: Variables ordered by magnitude of loading

The sample comprised subjects who were directly or indirectly involved in patient care (e.g., patient nursing staff, nursing staff in ancillary departments, and administrative staff) such that interacting with the NIT was a normal part of their work process. Two hundred and sixty-two questionnaires were sent to the end-users. One hundred and thirty-nine usable questionnaires were returned for a response rate of 56%. The mean age of the subjects was 42.1 years (s.d. = 9.27). Their mean tenure with the hospital was 2.67 years (s.d. = 1.16) and 56.1 percent were females.

A power analysis demonstrated that this sample was large enough to detect an effect size of r=.20, alpha=.05 (two-tailed) with a power of .66 and an effect size of r=.30, alpha=.05 (two-tailed) with a power of .95 (Cohen and Cohen 1983).

Measures

Time 1. Immediately after training for the NIT, all subjects received questionnaires designed to evaluate their attributions and expectations regarding the NIT. The attribution questionnaire asked the respondents to identify their specific causal attributions for unsuccessful experiences with the NIT during the training period (i.e., single item questions on a 7-point Likert (1932) scale regarding ability, task difficulty, effort, and luck/chance. The anchors were strongly agree and strongly disagree). They were then asked to rate the specific cause on a 7-point Likert scale along the underlying dimensions of internal/external and stable/unstable. This method of eliciting causal attributions is typical in attribution research (Weiner, 1985).

The self-efficacy/outcome expectancy questionnaire asked the subjects about their expectations for performance regarding the NIT and was based on Meier's (1988) computer aversion scale and expectancy measures developed by Sims, Szilagyi and McKemey (1976). A series of 22 statements were rated on a 4-point Likert scale (Likert 1932) from always true to always false.

Time 2. After the NIT had been in use for at least six weeks, a questionnaire was administered to assess job performance and end-user satisfaction. The hospital provided form numbers on all questionnaires to insure that a "match" was made on all questionnaires between Time 1 and Time 2. All respondents were guaranteed anonymity.

The first part of the user satisfaction measure was adopted from Doll and Torkzadeh's (1988) and Torkzadeh and Doll's (1991) measure of end-user satisfaction and assessed satisfaction in the areas of information content, accuracy, format, ease of use, timeliness, screen display, system usability, and system terminology. The second part of the measure was based on Shneiderman's (1987) and Ravden and Johnson's (1989) measures and was designed to measure users' perceptions of the value and usefulness of the screen displays and system terminology. Finally, five questions were added to measure the ease of use of the NIT. Seven-point Likert scales were used with all of the items. The anchors were strongly agree and strongly disagree.

In designing the job performance measure, Baronas and Louis's (1988) suggestions for measuring quantity and quality of work were followed. The form consisted of five questions with 7-point Likert scales with strongly agree, strongly disagree anchors. Questions assessed users' perceptions of quantity and quality of work as well as perceptions of their level of performance with the NIT.

Analyses

The primary method for analyses was recursive path analysis (Cohen & Cohen, 1983; Pedhazur, 1982). A separate analysis was performed for each dependent variable, i.e. job performance and end-user satisfaction, resulting in separate path analyses representing direct, indirect, and total effects of all variables measured in Time 1 and Time 2.

Path analyses were conducted using hierarchial regression allowing for the assessment of indirect as well as direct effects (Asher, 1983). The first step for each analysis was the specification of a hypothesized model which placed the variables in the causal order consistent with the theory being tested (See the hypothesized models in Figures 2 and 3). Then, for each analysis, the endogenous (i.e. dependent) variable was regressed on its direct determinant(s) (i.e., the independent variables) and the resulting standardized partial regression coefficients represented the path coefficients.

The use of path analysis was limited to recursive models: just-identified and over-identified models. A just-identified model reproduces the correlation matrix (R) and provides a perfect fit to the data. Over-identified models are models in which some of the paths have been deleted such that "...one may use the reproduction of R for the purpose of assessing the validity of a causal model" (Pedhazur, 1982). Thus, testing a hypothesized model implies a comparison to the just-identified model (Pedhazur, 1982). In addition, the technique of theory trimming (Pedhazur, 1982) was used to produce the final model. Theory trimming means that all nonsignificant paths of the just-identified model were assumed to be zero and eliminated from consideration. Both the hypothesized model and the theory trimmed model are compared to the just-identified model to determine which model best fits the data using a Q value model comparison statistic and by computing a W-value which tests the generalized squared multiple correlation against the just-identified model (Pedhazur, 1982). By examining both Q and the significance of W one can conclude whether or not there is support for the model. If the hypothesized model is correctly specified, the hypothesized model and the trimmed model should be the same. Since the study was exploratory in nature, all path coefficients were tested for significance at the .10 level.

RESULTS

Research Scales

All scales were factor analyzed using principal components analysis with varimax rotation (Stevens, 1986). A conservative criteria of .50 was used as a rule for the interpretation of factor loadings. This criteria provides significant loadings at an alpha=.01 (two-tailed test), N>=100. Thus the sample size for the study (N=139) meets minimum requirements for producing reliable factors (Gorsuch, 1983). In addition, an eigen value greater than one, percentage of variance explained, scree plots, and item analysis were also used as criteria for including a factor in this study. The internal validity was determined using Cronbach's (1951) alpha and a reliability criterion of .70 (Nunnally, 1970). The means, standard deviations, correlations, and reliabilities of the scales are presented in Table 1.

Expectancy Scale. The factor analysis of the expectancy scale revealed six factors with eigen values greater than one. Both the first and second factor contained six items and had loadings ranging from .59 to at least .76. The remaining factors all had two or less items. Based on the criteria specified above and the similarity of the content of the items, the first and second factors were used as measures of self-efficacy (E1) and outcome expectancy (E2) respectively. E1 and E2 are used to represent the measures and avoid repetition of the terms self-efficacy and outcome expectancy as much as possible. The complete results of the factor analysis of the expectancy scale are reported in Table 2.

Satisfaction Scale. The factor analysis of the 26 item satisfaction scale revealed five factors with eigen values greater than one. The first factor consisted of 16 items with loadings ranging from .58 to .85. The content of the first factor appears to be similar to the content of Doll and Torkzadeh's (1988) end-user satisfaction scale in that all questions related to content (items 1,2,3,4), accuracy (item 5), format (items 8,9,10,11,12), and timeliness (items 6,7). The other four items (13,14,17,18) were related to screen organization and prompts. However, the items did not represent separate constructs as predicted by Torkzadeh and Doll (1991). The other factors all consisted of two or less items. Applying the same criteria as were used for including factors on the expectancy scale, only the first factor was used to represent end-user satisfaction in this chapter. The complete results of the factor analysis of the satisfaction scale are reported in Table 3.

Job Performance Scale. The factor analysis for this scale revealed that all five items loaded on one factor. The loadings ranged from .74 to .90. The results of the factor analysis are provided in Table 4.

Path Analyses

Assumptions. Several analyses were conducted to test for a violation of assumptions of path models (Cohen & Cohen, 1983; Pedhazur, 1982). There was no evidence of multicollinearity, that is $r >= .80$ (Billings & Worten, 1978). Scatterplots of the residuals were developed to test for non-linearity. No violation of this assumption was found. Moreover, the reliabilities of all the scales exceeded .70 and were thus judged to be acceptable (Nunnally, 1970). Finally, the residuals of the endogenous variables were tested with the Durbin-Watson "d" test (1951). The values ranged from 1.66 to 2.21 indicating no major violations of this assumption.

Tests of Path Models. Since the results of the regression of E1 (efficacy) and E2 (outcome expectancy) on ability, difficulty, effort, and luck/chance are the same for both hypothesized models, and the trimmed models provided a better fit to the data, these results will be presented here and not repeated for each path model. Rather the results of 1) the regression of the dependent variables on E1 and E2 in the hypothesized model, 2) the comparison of the hypothesized and just-identified model, 3) the analysis of the trimmed model and 4) the subsequent results of the regressions of the trimmed models will be presented in the sections that report the results of dependent variables.

In all the hypothesized models E1 (efficacy) was regressed on ability, difficulty of system, effort, and luck/chance ($R2 = .072$, $p<.05$). E2 (outcome expectancy) was also regressed on ability, difficulty of system, effort, and luck/chance ($R2 = .074$, $p<.05$). Ability had a negative direct effect on E1 ($beta = -.254$, $p<.05$) and luck/chance had a negative direct effect on E1 ($beta = -.157$, $p<.10$). Difficulty of system had a negative direct effect on E2 ($beta = -.146$, $p<.10$), while effort had a positive direct effect on E2 ($beta = .219$, $p<.05$). However, there was no significant effect of difficulty of system and effort on E1. Additionally, there was no significant effect of ability or luck/chance on E2. These non-significant paths indicated that alternative models may fit the data better. Subsequently, upon examination of the just-identified models for each dependent variable, the paths from ability to E2, difficulty of system to E1, and effort to E1 were deleted. However, the just-identified models indicated that the path from E1 to E2 should be added.

End-User Satisfaction. In the hypothesized model user satisfaction was regressed on E1 (efficacy) and E2 (outcome expectancy) ($R2 = .230$, $p<.001$). Although the hypothesized model provided general support for the hypothesized paths (See Figure 2, panel A), the failure to confirm a good fit to the data ($Q = .8872$, $p<.01$), and the non-significant paths suggested an alternative model may fit the data better.

Figure 2: Path Diagram for End-User Satisfaction

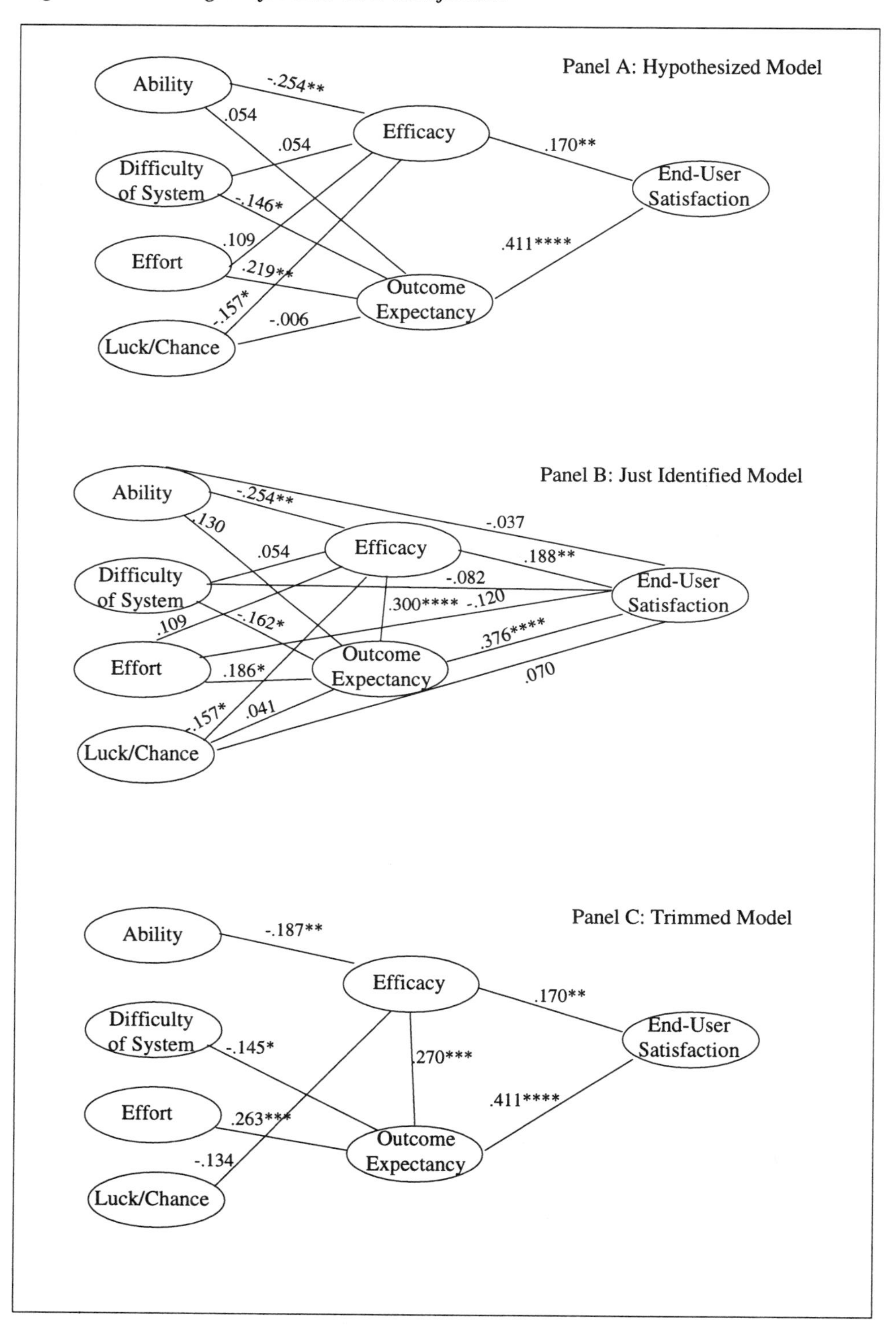

The just-identified model and the trimmed model are shown in Figure 2, panels B and C, respectively. The just-identified model suggests that there are no direct paths from ability, difficulty of system, effort, and luck/chance to user satisfaction. Non-significant paths are also suggested from ability to E2, difficulty of system to E1, and effort to E1.

Table 5: Summary of Causal Effects and Proportion of Variance Explained for End-User

Outcome	Determinant	Direct Effect	Indirect Effect	Total Effect	Zero r	Spurious
D.V.	Ability through E1		-.032			
Satisfaction	E2		-.021			
	E1 ->E2		-.053	-.053	.045	.098
	Difficulty of System through E1		-.059			
	E2		.-----			
	E1 -> E2		.059	-.059	-.087	-.028
	Effort through E1		.108			
	E2		.----			
	E1 -> E2		.108	.108	.170	.062
	Luck through E1		-.023			
	E2		-.015			
	E1 -> E2		-.038	-.038	.044 ***	.082
	E1 through E2		.111			
		.170	.111	.281	.275***	-.006
	E2	.411		.411	.454***	.043

Q=.9501 W=6.71, 8df, .50<p<.70

Direct Effects and Proportion of Variance Explained

Outcome	Determinant	Direct Effect	Indirect Effect	Total Effect	Zero r	Spurious
E1 ***	Ability	-.187			-.208***	-.021
(R^2 = .061)	Difficulty of System					
F (2,130) =	Effort					
4.20	Luck	-.134			-.163	-.029
E2***	Ability					
(R^2 = .141)	Difficulty of System	-.145			-.097	.048
F (3,130) =	Effort	.263			.220**	-.043
7.11	Luck					
	E1	.270			.256***	-.014
D.V. ****	Ability					
Satisfaction	Difficulty of System					
(R^2 = .230)	Effort					
F (2,123) =	Luck					
18.70	E1	.170			.275***	.105
	E2	.411			.454***	-.043

****p<.001 ***p<.01 ** p< .05 *p<.10 E1 Efficacy E2 Outcome Expectancy

In the trimmed model E1 was regressed on ability and luck/chance ($R2 = .061$, $p<.05$), E2 was regressed on E1, difficulty of system, and effort ($R2 = .141$, $p<.001$), and user satisfaction was regressed on E1 and E2 ($R2 = .230$, $p<.01$). In addition to the direct effects of ability on E1, difficulty of system and effort on E2, and E1 on E2, the trimmed model also supported the indirect effects of ability on user satisfaction through E1 (-.032), ability on user satisfaction through E1 and E2 (-.021), difficulty of system on user satisfaction through E2 (-.059), and effort on user satisfaction through E2 (.108). Additionally, the trimmed model supported the direct effect of E1 on E2 (beta = .270, $p<.01$), E1 on user satisfaction (beta = .170, $p<.05$), and E2 on user satisfaction (beta = .411, $p<.01$). Thus, the trimmed model showed significant paths from ability to E1, difficulty of system to E2, effort to E2, E1 to E2, and E1 and E2 to end-user satisfaction.

Table 5 shows the direct and indirect effects and statistical tests for the trimmed model. Note: In the table the dependent variable is labeled the "Outcome", E1 (efficacy) and E2 (outcome expectancy) are the endogenous variables, referred to as the "Determinants", the coefficients of the regression are reported under the column heading "Direct Effect". The effect of the Determinant through (mediated by) the endogenous variables is shown under the column "Indirect Effect" and represents the strength of the Determinant as mediated by the endogenous variables, i.e., efficacy and outcome expectancy. (See Figure 2.) The trimmed model provided a much better fit to the data ($Q = .9501$, $.50<p<.70$). An examination of the absolute difference between the estimated and original correlations also shows that the model fits the data. The trimmed model duplicated all the original correlations within .10 except the correlation of E1 and end-user satisfaction ($r=.105$). The trimmed model accounted for an additional 13% of the variance explained beyond that accounted for by the hypothesized model.

Job Performance. In the hypothesized model (See Figure 3) job performance was regressed on E1 and E2 ($R2 = .480$, $p<.001$). E1 (beta = .457, $p<.001$) and E2 (beta = .420, $p<.001$) had direct positive effects on job performance as predicted. However, although the hypothesized model was generally supported, it did not provide a good fit to the data ($Q = .8931$, $p<.01$).

The just-identified model was constructed and examined for significant paths. The analysis indicated that there were no direct paths from ability, difficulty of system, and effort to job performance. It also indicated that there are no direct paths from ability to E2, difficulty of system to E1, and effort to E1. In the trimmed model E1 was regressed on ability and luck/chance ($R2 = .061$), $p<.05$); E2 was regressed on E1, difficulty of system, and effort ($R2 = .141$, $p<.001$); and job performance was regressed on E1 and E2 ($R2 = .480$, $p<.001$). In addition to the direct effects of ability on E1, difficulty of system and effort on E2, and E1 on E2, the trimmed model also supported the indirect effect of ability on job performance through E1 (-.085) and the indirect effect of ability on job performance through E1 and E2 (-.021). Support was also provided for the indirect effect of difficulty of system on job performance through E2 (-.061) and the indirect effect of effort on job performance through E2. Support was also evident for the direct effects of E1 (beta = .457, $p<.001$) and E2 (beta = .420, $p<.001$) on job performance. As predicted, there were no direct effects of ability, difficulty of system and effort on job performance. All the paths mentioned above were significant in the trimmed model except the path from luck/chance to E1. The trimmed model showed significant paths from ability to E1, difficulty of system and effort to E2, E1 to E2 and E1 and E2 to job performance (See Figure 3).

Table 6 shows the direct and indirect effects and statistical tests for the trimmed model. Note: In the table the dependent variable is labeled the "Outcome" E1 (efficacy) and E2

Figure 3: Path Diagrams for Job Performance

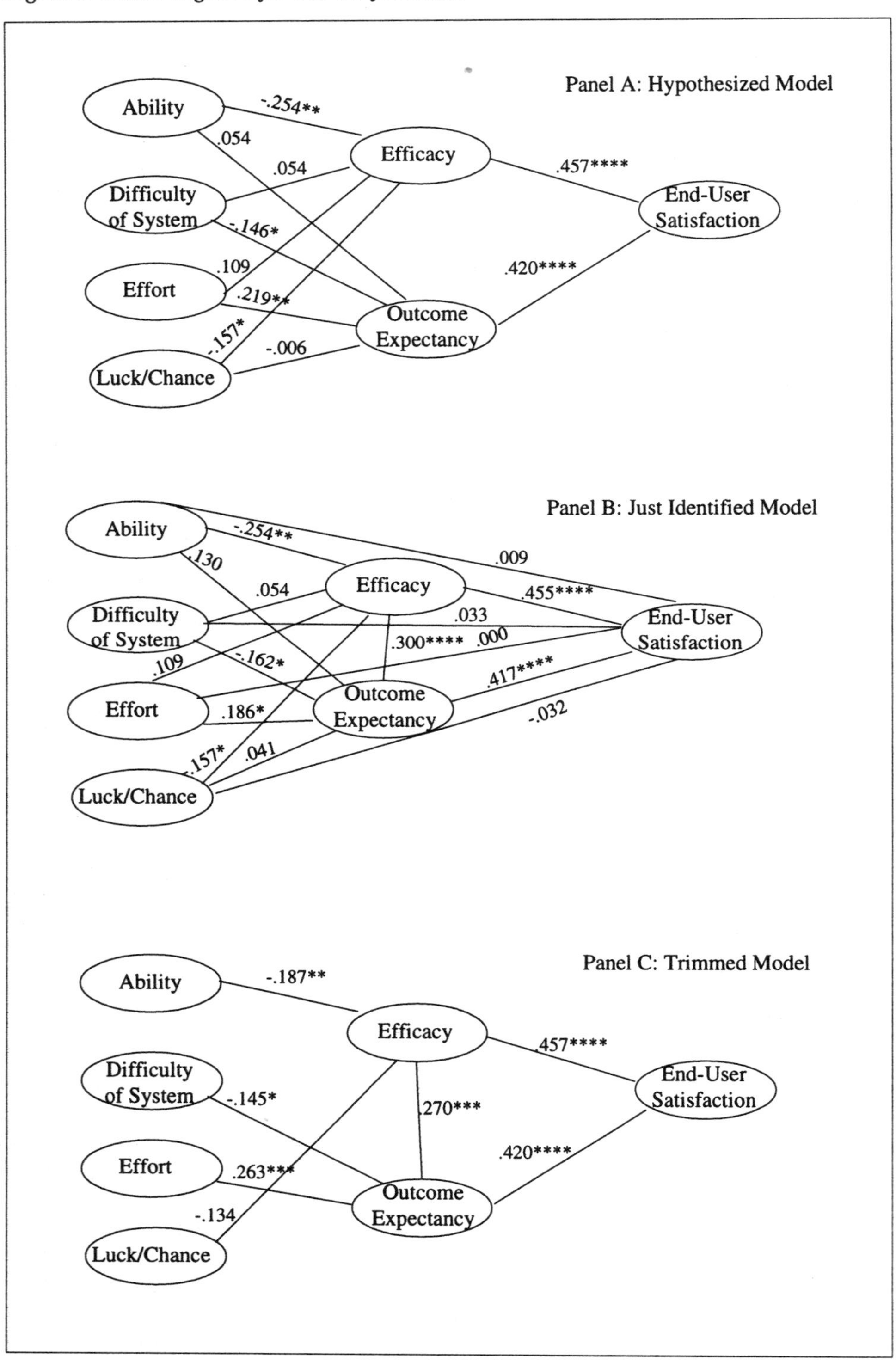

Table 6: Summary of Causal Effects and Proportion of Variance Explained for Job Performance Attributions

Outcome	Determinant	Direct Effect	Indirect Effect	Total Effect	Zero r	Spurious
D.V.	Ability thru E1		-.085			
Performance	E2		-.021			
	E1 ->E2		-.106	-.106	-.034	.072
	Difficulty of System through E1		-.061			
	E2		.-----			
	E1 -> E2		-.061	-.061	-.081	-.020
	Effort through E1		.110			
	E2		.----			
	E1 -> E2		.110	.110	.059	-.051
	Luck through E1		-.061			
	E2		-.015			
	E1 -> E2		-.076	-.076	-.107	-.031
	E1 through E2		.113			
		.457	.113	.570	.565***	-.005
	E2	.420	.420	.537***	.117	

Q=.9713 W=3.81 8df, $.80 < p < .90$

Direct Effects and Proportion of Variance Explained

Outcome	Determinant	Direct Effect	Indirect Effect	Total Effect	Zero r	Spurious
E **	Ability	-.187			-.208***	-.021
(R^2 = .061)	Difficulty of System					
F (2,130) =	Effort					
4.20	Luck	-.134			-.163	-.029
E2****	Ability					
(R^2 = .141)	Difficulty of System	-.145			-.097	.048
F (3,130) =	Effort	.263			.220**	-.043
7.11	Luck					
	E1	.270			.256***	-.014
D.V. ****	Ability					
Performance	Difficulty of System					
(R^2 = .230)	Effort					
F (2,133) =	Luck					
62.41	E1	.457			.565***	.108
	E2	.420			.537***	.117

****$p < .001$ ***$p < .01$ ** $p < .05$ *$p < .10$

E1 Efficacy

E2 Outcome Expectancy

(outcome expectancy) are the endogenous variables, referred to as the "Determinants", the coefficients of the regression are reported under the column heading "Direct Effect." The effect of the Determinant through the endogenous variables is shown under the column "Indirect Effect" and represents the strength of the Determinant as mediated by the endogenous variables, i.e., efficacy and outcome expectancy (See Figure 3). The trimmed model indicated a much better fit to the data (Q = .9713, .80<.90). An examination of the absolute difference between the estimated and original correlations also shows that the model fits the data. All correlations are within .10, except the direct effect of E2 on job performance. However, the trimmed model only accounted for an additional 5% of the explained variance beyond that accounted for by the hypothesized model.

DISCUSSION

The major contribution of this study is that it provides general confirmation for the attributional model describing the process by which individuals accept or reject NITs within a field setting. More specifically, with respect to the first proposition, it was found that attributions are directly related to expectancies and effect job performance and end-user satisfaction indirectly through expectations. Thus the notion that expectancies mediate the relationship between attributions and behavior was confirmed.

As suggested by the second proposition, it was found that attributions to ability were directly related to efficacy expectations in both models. Similarly, the third proposition was verified indicating that attributions regarding the difficulty of the system were directly related to outcome expectations. Finally, as expected, both efficacy (E1) and outcome expectations (E2) were directly related to job performance and end-user satisfaction. It should also be noted that although the hypothesized models did not provide optimal descriptions of the predicted relationships, they were nonetheless quite similar to the just-identified models. Moreover, there appeared to be little practical difference regarding the major relationships depicted by the hypothesized versus the trimmed models. Thus, the major relationships suggested by the attributional model describing the process of accepting or rejecting NITs were confirmed.

Some of the specific findings warrant additional comment. As anticipated and confirmed by the results, all of the attributions were not related to both expectancies. As both models show, when unsuccessful performance was attributed to lack of ability, it has a direct effect on self-efficacy expectations (E1), but not outcome expectancies (E2). This finding provides empirical support for the conceptual distinction made by Bandura (1977) between efficacy and outcome expectations. Corroborative results are reported by Hill, Smith and Mann (1987), who found that computer self-efficacy was related to computer usage independent of the individual's belief about the outcomes achieved through use. Within the context of the current study, it appears entirely plausible that although the users believed that using the NIT would result in improved job performance and other valued outcomes, i.e., outcome expectations, they also doubted their abilities to interact with the NIT resulting in low levels of self-efficacy expectations.

On the other hand, the analyses provide support for the direct effects of effort attributions and attributions regarding the difficulty of the system on outcome expectancies (E2), but not self-efficacy expectations (E1). Since effort is generally considered an internal and unstable attribution, it is not likely that failure experiences attributed to effort negatively affect end-users' expectations about outcomes since end-users probably believe that they can control the amount of effort expended. In fact the end-users may even expend more effort after failure in the belief that outcomes are achievable if they try harder (Wortman & Brehm, 1975). Thus, the finding that effort has a direct positive effect on outcome expectations is consistent with theory although this relationship was not specifically hypothesized.

Although the relationship between task difficulty and expectations has been documented in past research (Atkinson & Feather, 1966; Parsons & Ruble, 1972), research on attributions has generally confounded the effects of attributions on self-efficacy and outcome expectations by using ambiguous questions which fail to differentiate between the two types of expectancies (Eastman & Marzillier, 1984; Gist & Mitchell, 1992). We believe that our results are important because they confirm that attributions have differential effects on the two types of expectancies, i.e., self-efficacy and outcome expectancy. Moreover, the finding can be explained in that difficulties with the system are usually classified as stable and external attributions. Such attributions would not imply personal inadequacy and would, therefore, not be expected to adversely effect self-efficacy expectations.

Another finding which deserves additional comment concerns the significant positive direct paths from self-efficacy and outcome expectancies to end-user satisfaction (See Figure 2). The direct effect of outcome expectancy was more than twice as large as the direct effect of efficacy expectations on end-user satisfaction. Similar results were reported by Davis (1992) who found that system usefulness had a greater effect than ease of use on usage intentions. Thus, despite the problems inherent in learning NITs, it appears that the end-users may still have positive outcome expectations regarding the outcomes of the adoption of NITs if they perceive that a NIT will result in significant improvements in work performance and efficiency and assist them in achieving personal and work-related goals.

The indirect effect of attributions on outcome measures also deserves attention. As Figure 2 shows, the indirect effect of ability on end-user satisfaction was negative. The negative indirect effect of the difficulty of the system was generally as large as that of ability, indicating that both might be equally important in their effects on end-user satisfaction. However, the indirect effect of the difficulty of the system was through outcome expectancy. This is consistent with other findings in the implementation literature. For example, Baronas and Louis (1988) reported that end-users exposed to interventions designed to give them a sense of efficacy reported that they were not sure how the system would affect their jobs (outcome expectancy). This suggests that even though some end-users may believe they can learn the system, they may not be sure of how the system will affect their work outcomes.

Another finding which deserves comment is the indirect negative effect of ability attributions on job performance through efficacy and outcome expectancy. This finding is consistent with past research which has shown that unsuccessful experience with computers negatively affects future expectations. For example, Kraut, Dumais and Koch (1989) found that a group of service representatives who had unsuccessful experiences with computers tended to believe that the computers would not have a productive impact on job performance. On the other hand, the indirect positive effect of effort on job performance through outcome expectancy was the largest indirect effect in the current study. This finding emphasizes the importance of effort attributions for unsuccessful performance. It is also consistent with past research which shows that effort attributions do not necessarily result in lowered expectations for future performance (Fosterling, 1985). Thus, end-users who attribute their poor performance with a system to a lack of effort are less likely to demonstrate helplessness deficits than those who attribute their poor performance to their ability or the difficulty of the system. Moreover, this finding sheds some light on one of the most overlooked individual level outcomes — actual job performance, in terms of quantity and quality of work (Nelson, 1990).

Limitations

Several limitations of this research should also be noted. First, the sample size was relatively small for the number of variables that were included in the analysis. Future studies with larger, cross-organizational samples would enable more powerful analytic procedures such as LISREL so that the causal priority of the variables could be more clearly delineated. Moreover, larger sample sizes would also enable more complete tests of the model.

Second, although this study was cross-sectional, it must be classified as a natural field study (Weick, 1979) in that the intervention was a function of natural changes in the organizational environment, rather than the result of purposeful manipulations by the experimenters. Future studies should consider experimenter manipulations such as attributional training (Martinko & Gardner, 1982) to more clearly identify the relationships between attributions, expectancies, and outcomes.

Finally, although the factor analyses suggest that the dependent variables were reasonable measures of job performance and end-user satisfaction with the system, the results would be more convincing if hard measures of system usage such as the amount of time interacting with the system were used in future studies, although this may even present problems in non-volitional contexts.

Managerial Implications

These results clearly demonstrate the relationships between specific attributions, the two types of expectancies (efficacy and outcome expectancy), and outcomes associated with the acceptance/rejection of NITs, i.e. job performance and end-user satisfaction. Coupled with the other research which has been done on the acceptance and rejection of NITs as well as the attributional research which has discussed and tested the effects of strategies for behavioral change based on attributions (Gist, Schoerer, & Rosen, 1989; Martinko & Gardner, 1982; Martinko, Henry, & Zmud, 1996), several suggestions can be made regarding the implementation of NITs. First, it appears that system designers can enhance the acceptance of NITs by making sure that users who are experiencing difficulties receive feedback that will result in attributions that will facilitate rather than lead to LH in their interactions with the system. Designers need to be aware that initial expectations can be difficult to change and that they need to facilitate the "transfer-of-training" process (Tannebaum, Mathieu, Salas, & Cannon-Bowers, 1991). In explaining attributional counseling, Martinko and Gardner (1982) suggest that feedback which teaches end-users to attribute poor performance to unstable and external characteristics is helpful in that self-efficacy is not eroded. However, the current findings suggest that such feedback could also result in reducing outcome expectations. Thus, it would seem that a better strategy would be to design feedback suggesting that end-users are capable (i.e., have the ability) and that with more effort they can master the system even if it is difficult. As suggested by Martinko et al. (1992), role models who are perceived to have abilities which are similar to the end-users who are experiencing difficulties may be particularly helpful in communicating to end-users that they can succeed if they expend reasonable effort.

The current research also suggests that system designers should make concerted efforts to publicize the benefits of NITs, even if the NIT is difficult to learn, in order to heighten outcome expectancies. Any initial negative impressions of the system can be very difficult to reverse with post training. In other words, make sure the end-users know exactly what the system will do for them in terms of improving job performance and attaining personal and organizational goals.

Finally, immunizing end-users to LH by designing introductory experiences with NITs that are designed to facilitate optimistic attributions is an important aspect of system design which can increase the probability of system acceptance. Importantly, while these introductory experiences should primarily result in success, the end-users should also experience and learn to process failures in interacting with the system since the ability to respond positively to failure may be as important as how individuals respond to success (Clifford, 1978). Thus, the introductory aspects of system design should strongly emphasize that the end-users are efficacious and capable; unsuccessful experiences are generally due to a lack of effort, successful experiences are due to both ability and effort, and that the benefits of using the system with respect to both work performance and satisfaction are considerable. Such features should result in both positive efficacy and outcome expectations which should lead to optimal use of the NIT.

CONCLUSIONS

The principle contribution of this study is that it confirms the major relationships depicted by attributional models describing the process by which individuals accept or reject NITs within a field setting. To some, practitioners in particular, parts of the study may appear obvious. For example, the general management notion that "a happy worker is a productive worker" has been repeatedly disproved and generates a great deal of discussion and varying opinions. The point being that what may appear obvious still needs to be tested and validated. With this in mind, the current study clearly demonstrates that, at least within the context of this study, attributions shape expectancies and that these expectancies are related to important system outcomes including job performance and end-user satisfaction. Moreover, the study clearly shows that attributions are differentially related to both efficacy and outcome expectations. Ability attributions were clearly related to efficacy expectations whereas attributions to effort and task difficulty were related to outcome expectations. These findings are important, not only within the context of accepting or rejecting NITs, but also within the more general context of attribution and motivation theory.

Although there were a number of limitations regarding the current research, the results suggest that attributional explanations appear to be both valid and useful explanations of the process by which end-users accept or reject NITs. Given that the current research provided only a partial test of the attributional model, it would seem that further research designed to test other aspects of the model is warranted. In particular, research which incorporates larger sample sizes to more completely test the model would be appropriate. In addition, other relations suggested by the model such as the relationship between attributional styles and user acceptance of NITs may also be beneficial to consider.

REFERENCES

Abramson, L. Y., Seligman, M.E.P., & Teasdale, J.D. (1978). Learned helplessness in humans: Critique and reformulation. *Journal of Abnormal Psychology*, 87(1), 49-74.

Argyris, C. (1971). Management information systems: The challenge to rationality and emotionality. *Management Science*, 17, 6.

Asher, H. B. (1983). *Causal modeling,* Beverly Hills, CA: Sage Publications.

Atkinson, J. W., & Feather, N.T. (Eds.) (1966). *A theory of achievement motivation,* New York: Wiley.

Bandura, A. (1986). *Social foundations of thought and action: A social cognitive theory*. New Jersey: Prentice-Hall.

Bandura, A. (1977). Self-efficacy: Toward a unifying theory of behavioral change. *Psychological*

Review, 84(2), 191-215.

Baronas, A. K., & Louis, M.R. (1988). Restoring a sense of control during implementation: How user involvement leads to system acceptance. *MIS Quarterly*, 12(1), 111-126.

Baroudi, J. J., Olson, M.H., & Ives, B. (1986). An empirical study of the impact of user involvement on system usage and information satisfaction. *Communications of the ACM*, 29(3), 232-238.

Billings, R. S., & Worten, S.P. (1978). Use of path analysis in industrial/organizational psychology: Criticisms and suggestions. *Journal of Applied Psychology*, 63(6), 677-688.

Blackler, F. & Brown, C. (1985). Evaluation and the impact of information technologies on people in organizations. *Human Relations,* 38(3), 213-231.

Boland, R. J. (1978). The process and product of system design. *Management Science,* 24(9), 887-898.

Compeau, D., Olfman, L., Sein, M., & Webster, J. (1995). End-user training and learning. *Communications of the ACM,* 38(7), 24-26.

Cancro, R., & Slotnick, D. (1970). Computer graphics and resistance to technology. *American Journal of Psychotherapy,* 24, 461-469.

Cohen, J. & Cohen, P. (1983). *Applied multiple regression/correlation analysis for the behavioral sciences*, Hillsdale, NJ: Lawrence Erlbaum Associates.

Cooper, C. L., & Zmud, R. W. (1990). Information technology implementation research: A technological diffusion approach. *Management Science*, 36, 123-139.

Clifford, M. M. (1978). Have we underestimated the facilitative effects of failure? *Canadian Journal of Behavioral Science,* 10(4), 308-316.

Cronbach, L. J. (1951). Coefficient alpha and the internal structure of tests. *Psychometrika,* 16, 297-334.

Davis, F. D. (1992). Early user acceptance testing in information systems design. Unpublished manuscript.

Debrabander, B., & Edstrom, A. (1977). Successful information system development projects. *Management Science,* 24(2), 191-199.

Doll, W. J., & Torkzadeh, G. (1988). The measurement of end-user computing satisfaction. *MIS Quarterly*, 12(2), 259-274.

Dowling, A. F. (1980). Do hospital staff interfere with computer system implementation? *Health Care Management Review,* 5(4), 23-32.

Durbin, J., &, Watson, J. S. (1951). Testing for serial correlation in least squares regression. *Biometrika,* 38, 159-177.

Eastman, C., & Marzillier, J. (1984). Theoretical and methodological difficulties in Bandura's self-efficacy theory. *Cognitive Therapy and Research*, 8, 213-229.

Fosterling, F. (1985). Attributional retraining: A review. *Psychological Bulletin,* 98 , 495-512.

Ginzberg, M. J. (1981). Early diagnosis of MIS implementation failure: Promising results and unanswered questions. *Management Science*, 27(4), 459-478.

Gist, M. E., & Mitchell, T. R. (1992). Self-efficacy: A theoretical analysis of its determinants and malleability. *Academy of Management Review,* 17(2), 183-211.

Gist, M. E., Schwoerer, C., & Rosen, B. (1989). Effects of alternative training methods on self-efficacy and performance in computer software training. *J. Applied Psychology,* 74(6), 884-891.

Glass, C. R., & Knight, L. A. (1988). Cognitive factors in computer anxiety. *Cognitive Therapy and Research,* 12(4), 351-366.

Gorsuch, R. L. (1983). *Factor analysis.* Hillsdale, NJ: Lawrence Erlbaum.

Henry, J. W., Martinko, M. J., & Pierce, M. A. (1993). Attributional style as a predictor of success in a first computer science course. *Computers in Human Behavior*, 9, 341-352.

Henry, J.W., and Stone, R.W. (1995a). Computer self-efficacy and outcome expectancy: The effects on the end-user's job satisfaction. *Computer Personnel*, 16(4), 15-37.

Henry, J.W., and Stone, R.W. (1995b). A structural equation model of job performance using a computer-based order entry system. *Behaviour and Information Technology,* 14(3), 163-173.

Henry, J.W., Stone, R. W., & Pierce, M. A. (1993). The role of self-efficacy and outcome expectancy as determinants of student perceptions regarding programming courses. *Proceedings of the International Academy for Information Management*, Orlando, Fla, pp. 403-425.

Hill, T., Smith, N. D., & Mann, M. F. (1987). Role of efficacy expectations in predicting the decision to use advanced technologies: The case of computers. *J. Applied Psychology,* 72(2), 307-313.

Hirscheim, R., & Newman, M. (1988). Information systems and user resistance: Theory and practice. *The Computer Journal,* 31(5), 398-408.

Kraut, R., Dumais, S. & Koch, S. (1989). Computerization, productivity and quality of work-life. *Communications of the ACM,* 32(2), 220-238.

Leonard-Barton, D. (1988). Implementation characteristics of organizational innovations. *Communication Research,* 15(5), 603- 631.

Likert, R. (1932). A technique for the measurement of attitudes. *Archives of Psychology,* 140.

Mankin, D., Bikson, T. K., & Gutek, B. (1985). Factors in uccessful implementation of computer-based office information systems: A review of the literature with suggestions for OBM research. *Journal of Organizational Behavior Management,* 6(3/4), 1-20.

Martinko, M. J., & Gardner, W. L. (1982). Learned helplessness: An alternative explanation for performance deficits. *Academy of Management Review,* 7(2), 195-204.

Martinko, M. J., Henry, J.W., & Zmud, R.W. (1996). An attributional explanation of individual reactions to information technologies in the workplace, *Behaviour and Information Technology.*

Meier, S. T. (1988). Predicting individual differences in performance on computer-administered tests and tasks: Development of the Computer Aversion Scale. *Computers in Human Behavior,* 4, 175-187.

Meier, S. T. (1985). Computer aversion. *Computers in Human Behavior,* 1, 171-179.

Nelson, D. L. (1990). Individual adjustment to information-driven technologies: A critical review. *MIS Quarterly,* 14(1), 79-98.

Nunnally, J. C., Jr. (1970). *Introduction to psychological measurement.* New York: McGraw-Hill, 1970.

Parsons, J. E., & Ruble, D. N. (1972). Attributional processes related to the development of the achievement-related affect and expectancy. *Proceedings of the 80th Annual Convention of the American Psychological Association,* 1972.

Pedhazur, E. J. (1982). *Multiple regression in behavioral research: Explanation and prediction.* San Francisco: Holt, Rinehart and Winston.

Ravden, S., & Johnson, G. (1989). *Evaluating usability of human-computer interfaces.* New York: John Wiley and Sons.

Rosen, L., Sears, D., & Weil, M. (1987). *Computerphobia. Behavior Research Methods, Instruments & Computers,* 19, 167-179.

Salloway, J. C., Counte, M. A. & Kjerulff, K. (1985). The effects of a computerized information system in a hospital. *Computers and the Social Sciences,* 1, 167-172.

Seligman, M. E. P. (1990). *Learned optimism.* New York: Alfred A. Knopf, Inc.

Shneiderman, B. (1987). *Designing the user interface: Strategies for effective human-computer interaction.* Reading, MA: Addison-Wesley.

Sims, H. P., JR., Szilagyi, A. D., & MCKemey, D. R. (1976). Antecedents of work related expectancies. *Academy of Management Journal,* 19(4), 547-559.

Stevens, J. (1986). *Applied multivariate statistics for the social sciences.* London: Lawrence Erlbaum Associates, Publishers.

Tait, P. & Vessey, I. (1988). The effect of user involvement on system success: A contingency approach. *MIS Quarterly,* 12(1), 91-107.

Tannenbaum, S.I., Mathieu, J.E., Salas, E., & Cannon-Bowers, J.A. (1991). Meeting trainees' expectations: The influence of training fulfillment on the development of commitment, self-efficacy, and motivation. *Journal of Applied Psychology,* 76(6), 759-769.

Torkzadeh, G., & Doll, W. J. (1991). Test-retest reliability of the end-user computing satisfaction instrument. *Decision Sciences,* 22, 26-37.

Weick, K. (1979). *The social psychology of organizing* (2nd ed.). Reading, MA: Addison-Wesley.

Weiner, B. (1979). A theory of motivation for some classroom experiences. *Journal of Educational Psychology,* 71, 3-25.

Weiner, B. (1985). An attributional theory of achievement motivation and emotion. *Psychological*

Review, 92(4), 548- 573.

Wortman, C. B., & Brehm, J. W. (1975). Responses to uncontrollable outcomes: An integration of reactance theory and the learned helplessness model. In L. Berkowitz (Ed.), *Advances in Experimental Social Psychology* (Vol. 8). New York: Academic Press, pp. 278-336.

Zmud, R. W. (1984). An examination of 'Push-Pull' theory applied to process innovation in knowledge work. *Management Science*, 30(6), 727-738.

Chapter 9

The Relationship of Some Personal and Situational Factors to IS Effectiveness: Empirical Evidence from Egypt

Omar E.M. Khalil
University of Massachusetts, USA

Manal M. Elkordy
Alexandria University, Egypt

Most, if not all, of the empirical evidence on information systems effectiveness and its associated factors is confined to the use of data from developed countries, in particular from the USA. The findings of such research cannot necessarily be generalized to other environments where the social, economic, and cultural characteristics are different. Such evidence needs to be first validated using cross-cultural research before it can be used to manage global information systems effectively. This chapter reports on the results of research aimed at testing the relationship of user's age, tenure in the job, organizational level, education, training, duration of system use, and involvement in system development to information systems effectiveness, as measured by user satisfaction and systems usage. Data were collected from 120 managers in 22 Egyptian banks. Age, tenure in the job, and user involvement in systems development were found to be positively correlated with user satisfaction. However, age, organizational level and education were found to be negatively associated with system usage. While beneficial to the Egyptian IS managers, such evidence from developing countries should contribute to the building of a general theory of trans-national global information systems.

The ability of a corporation to compete effectively in a global economy depends on the effectiveness of the information systems (IS) function and its global orientation (e.g., Karimi & Konsynski, 1991). Information systems, however, may not be accepted and used by those individuals for whom the systems were designed and implemented (e.g., Swanson, 1988;

This chapter originally appeared in the Journal of Global Information Management, vol 3, no. 2.

Davis et al., 1989). Research findings suggest that IS problems are country-specific and are related to the country's unique political, legal, economic, cultural, and technological environments (e.g., Deans et al., 1991; Ein-Dor, Segev & Orgad, 1993). Thus, effective management of such systems requires identifying the issues that might be unique to certain cultures (Deans & Ricks, 1991; Palvia & Saraswat, 1992).

While it is important to understand the factors affecting information systems effectiveness, most, if not all, of the currently available empirical evidence is confined to data from developed countries, particularly from the USA (e.g., Lucas, 1975a, 1975b; Montazemi, 1988). Such studies have contributed little to our understanding of the factors that are associated with IS success in underdeveloped countries. Thus, there is a need for IS research to broaden the focus beyond ethnocentric and regional studies in order to build a general theory of trans-national global information systems (Palvia, 1993). A comprehensive model of information systems effectiveness that directly addresses the issue of culture is long overdue, especially with the continuous growth of multinational organizations and the challenges of managing global information systems.

Further, research findings obtained from organizations operating in a Western environment cannot necessarily be generalized to other environments where the social, economical, and cultural characteristics can be fundamentally different. Hence, if the external validity, especially its international dimension (Aharoni & Burton, 1994), of such evidence is to be strengthened, it needs to be validated using cross-cultural research. The investigation of IS issues in a particular area of the world (e.g., Hassan, 1994) emphasizes the possible impact of cultural differences on such issues (Wetherbe, Vitalari, & Milner, 1994).

The purpose of this chapter is to report on the results of an investigation of the relationship of some personal and situational factors to information systems effectiveness in Egyptian banks. The findings of this study should contribute to the efforts toward building a general theory of trans-national global information systems.

BACKGROUND

Much of the research on information systems effectiveness has focused on identifying factors conducive to the success or failure of such systems. These factors include, among others, personal characteristics (e.g., Igbaria, 1993, 1992; Mawhinney & Lederer, 1990; Ginzberg, 1981; Robey, 1979), task characteristics (Sanders and Courtney, 1985), user involvement (e.g., Amoako-Gyampah, 1993; Barki & Hartwick, 1989), user training (Nelson & Cheney, 1987), and management support (Leitheiser & Wetherbe, 1986).

Such factors may also be applicable as determinants of the success of systems that are implemented in developing countries. However, most, if not all, of the research findings are confined to systems that were implemented in developed countries. As mentioned earlier, one cannot assume such applicability without empirical evidence. Therefore, seven personal and situational variables were selected for investigation as possible determinants of systems effectiveness in Egypt as a developing country. The selection of the variables is based on the existence of literature supporting their relevance as likely determinants of systems effectiveness or success. User satisfaction and system usage, as the dependent variables and surrogate measures of system effectiveness, are discussed next, followed by a discussion of each of the independent variables and the rationale for research hypotheses.

Table 1: Summary of Prior Research on the Relationship of Personal and Situational Variables to Information Systems Effectiveness

Independent Variable	Study	Dependent Variable	Results
Age	Igbaria (1993)	user attitude	no direct influence
	Igbaria (1993)	system use	positive influence
	Igbaria (1992)	system use	negative relationship
	Mawhinney & Lederer (1990)	system use	no relationship
	Culnan (1983)	system use	negative relationship
	Lucas (1975a, b)	system use	negative & positive relationships
	Schewe (1976)	user attitude	positive relationship
	Schewe (1976)	interactive use	positive relationship
	Taylor (1975)	information quantity	positive relationship
Gender	Igbaria (1993)	user attitude	negative among female users
	Igbaria (1992)	system use	less use by female users
	Vasarhelyi (1977)	user performance	no relationship
Tenure in the company	Culnan (1983)	system use	negative relationship
	Lucas (1975a)	user attitude	positive relationship
	Schewe (1976)	user attitude	positive relationship
	Schewe (1976)	system use	no relationship
Tenure in the job	Lucas (1975a)	system use	negative relationship
	Lucas (1975b)	system use	negative relationship
	O'Reilly (1982)	use of info. sources	negative & positive relationships
	Schewe (1976)	user attitude	negative relationship
	Schewe (1976)	interactive use	positive relationship
Education level	Igbaria (1993)	user attitude	no influence
	Igbaria (1993)	system use	positive influence
	Igbaria (1992)	system use	positive relationship
	Mawhinney & Lederer (1990)	system use	no relationship
	Culnan (1983)	system use	positive relatinship
	Lucas (1975a)	system use	negative relationship
	Lucas (1978)	user attitude	negative relationship
	O'Reilly (1982)	use of info. sources	negative & positive relationships
	Schewe (1976)	user attitude	no relationship
	Schewe (1976)	system use	no relationship
	Vasarhelyi (1977)	user performance	positive relationship
Organizational Level	Mawhinney & Lederer (1990)	system use	no relationship
	Culnan (1983)	system use	negative relationship
	Eason (1976)	system use	negative relationship
	Lucas (1975a)	indirect use	positive relationship
	Lucas (1978)	interactive use	positive relationship
	Specht (1986)	flexibility	positive relationship
User training	Igbaria et al. (1995)	system use	positive influence
	Igbaria (1993)	user attitude	no influence
	Igbaria (1993)	system use	positive influcence
	Amoroso & Cheney (1991)	user attitude	no relationship
	Cronan & Douglas (1990)	user satisfaction	positive relationship
	Nelson & Cheney (1987)	user satisfaction	no relationship
	Montazemi (1988)	user satisfaction	positive relationship
	Rivard (1987)	user satisfaciton	positive relationship
	Rivard & Huff (1988)	user attitude	positive relationship
	Sanders & Courtney (1985)	user satisfaction	positive relationship
	Schewe (1976)	user attitude	positive relationship
	Schewe (1976)	system use	no relationship
Duration of system use	Gatian (1994)	use satisfaction	positive relationship
	Sanes & Courtney (1985)	user satisfacton	positive relationship
	Vasarhelyi (1977)	system acceptance	positive relationship
User involvement	Amoako-Gyampah & White (1993)	user satisfaction	positive relationship
	Montazemi (1988)	user satisfaction	positive relationship
	Schewe (1976)	user attitude	no relationship
	Schewe (1976)	system use	no relationship
	Swanson (1974)	system appreciation	positive relationship
	Nosehi (1984)	information quality	positive relationship
	Nosehi (1984)	information use	positive relationship

User Satisfaction and Systems Usage (the dependent variables)

Information systems effectiveness is a multidimensional construct (Delone & McLean, 1992). The measurement of such a construct is one of the issues that, over the years, has generated much interest among information systems (IS) researchers and practitioners (Srinivasan, 1985). Approaches that have been suggested and used to measure information systems effectiveness can be grouped into three categories (Delone & McLean, 1992; Ives & Olson, 1984; Zmud, 1979): performance-related measures, system usage measures, and user satisfaction measures. All the measures have advantages and disadvantages. However, user satisfaction and system usage are two of the oldest and most often used effectiveness measures in IS research that have attempted to identify IS success factors (e.g., Delone & McLean, 1992; Melone, 1990; Lucas, 1975a, 1978; Zmud, 1979; Schewe, 1976; Ives, et al., 1983).

The user satisfaction approach assumes that systems effectiveness can be determined as the extent to which the system has achieved its objectives from the user's point of view (Amoroso & Cheney, 1991; Delone & McLean, 1992; Ives & Olson, 1984). Therefore, user satisfaction reflects the user's attitude toward the system and its capacity to provide him/her with the needed information, which can be reflected in better decisions (Ives et al., 1983; Lucas, 1975a). A number of instruments have been developed and used to measure user satisfaction regarding systems with different characteristics, including batch/data processing systems (i.e., Bailey & Pearson, 1983; Ives et al., 1983), interactive systems (i.e., Swanson, 1974; Lucas, 1975a), decision support and modeling systems (e.g., Robey, 1979), and end-user computing (i.e., Doll & Torkzadeh, 1988).

Systems usage, on the other hand, has been recommended and widely used as a measure of systems effectiveness in IS research, particularly when the use of the system output is optional. Modes of use (e.g., batch, on-line) determine the type of system usage measures that should be used to measure effectiveness (i.e., Lucas, 1975a; Amoroso & Cheney,1991; Culnan, 1983). Some of the researchers (i.e., Lucas, 1978; Ginzberg, 1981; Robey, 1979; Swanson, 1974) measured usage by actually monitoring the use in terms of the number of log-in times, length of log-in time, number of system resources utilized, or number of records accessed and updated. Others used subjective measures by allowing users to estimate their own or their peers' usage of a particular system (i.e., Lucas, 1975a; 1978). Although less accurate (Davis et al., 1989), subjective measures have been commonly used in IS research (e.g., Melone, 1990).

Although IS literature is replete with arguments for and against the use of these two approaches (e.g., Thong & Yap, 1996; Ginzberg, 1978; Melone, 1990; Sanders & Courtney, 1985; Srinivasan, 1985; Delone & McLean, 1992), there is no absolute perceptual measure of information systems effectiveness which exists across varying technological and organizational contexts. Consequently, multiple measures of information systems effectiveness are required. This study adopts user satisfaction and system use as two measures of information systems effectiveness.

Personal and Situational Factors (The Independent Variables)

Personal and situational characteristics may influence one's perception of information (Lucas, 1982) and the way one processes such information. Individuals with distinct characteristics and backgrounds are expected to have unique ways of interacting with information systems and, consequently, have different attitudes and behavior toward such systems.

For instance, compared to their coworkers, individuals possessing a higher capacity for communications and information exchange (or gate keepers) are expected to have higher education, longer tenure in the organization, and to occupy higher managerial positions (Culnan, 1983). Further, individuals from the same age or gender groups are expected to share a common language and possess a common group attitude and behavior toward the information system output. Whether those attitudes and behaviors are positive or not depends on the system's capability to interact with the users in a language that is understandable to them (Zenger & Lawrence, 1989).

Additionally, Zmud (1979) identifies three groups of user-related variables that were investigated in IS research: cognitive style (i.e., complex/simplex, intuitive/analytic, heuristic/systematic), personality type (e.g., tolerance of ambiguity, field dependent/independent, etc.), and demographic factors (e.g., age, gender, profession, education, experience, organizational position). Zmud (1979) concludes that, compared with the other two groups, fewer studies investigating demographic variables were conducted. Table 1 summarizes prior studies on the relationship between personal and situational variables and system effectiveness as measured by user satisfaction and system use.

This study investigates the relationship of user's age, tenure in the job, organizational level, education, training, duration of system use, and involvement in system development to systems effectiveness, as measured by user satisfaction and system usage, in an Egyptian setting. Because of the lack of a theoretical base for this line of research in information systems, of consistent findings of the prior U.S.-based research (see Table 1), and of culture-based findings, these relationships are explored in this study in the form of null hypotheses testing.

RESEARCH HYPOTHESES

1. *Age.* A person's willingness to accept a new technology or a change may differ with the person's age (Davis et al., 1989). Since younger users generally display a more positive attitude toward the information system, they are more ready to accept the change. However, Schewe (1976) found a positive association of managers' age to their attitude toward the system's influence on productivity and to their system use. Igbaria (1993) found no direct influence of age on user's acceptance of microcomputers.

Additionally, age was found to be associated positively with information use and negatively with information processing speed (Taylor, 1975). Igbaria (1993) found a positive and direct effect of age on microcomputers usage. Age was found to have no correlation with the managers' use of microcomputers (Mawhinney & Lederer, 1990). Culnan (1983) found age to associate negatively with interactive and indirect use of systems, and found those who didn't use the systems to be older than those who did. In addition, using a sample of Taiwanese managers, Igbaria (1992) found age to negatively correlate with microcomputers use time. The relationship of age to system effectiveness was explored using the following two null hypotheses:

Ho 1-1: There is no relationship between the user's age and his/her satisfaction with the information system.

Ho 1-2: There is no relationship between user's age and his/her use of the information system.

Table 2: Personal and Situational Variables

	Mean (years)	S.D.
Age	48.00	8.65
Tenure in the job	4.21	3.60
Tenure in banking	25.46	13.90
Tenure in the bank	19.68	11.65
Duration of system use	5.36	2.88
	Frequencies	**Percent**
Organizational level:		
Bank manager	22	18.33
Division manager	46	38.33
Department manager	52	43.34
Functional specialization:		
Savings accounts	27	22.50
Credit accounts	22	18.33
Foreign accounts	13	10.84
Public accounts	36	30.00
Branch managers	22	18.33
Education background:		
Type:		
Business	110	91.67
Others	10	8.33
Level:		
High School	17	14.17
College	81	67.50
Above college	22	18.33
Training:		
No formal training	80	66.67
On-site training	26	21.67
Off-site training	14	11.66
Involvement:		
Yes	9	7.50
No	111	92.50

2. *Tenure in the job.* User attitude and behavior toward information systems are expected to vary with the user's work experience, measured as tenure in the industry, organization, or job. Schewe (1976) and Lucas (1978) found users possessing longer tenure within the industry and organization to display a more positive attitude toward systems. Also, Schewe (1976) found tenure in the job to positively correlate with system use. Culnan (1983) found work experience to negatively correlate with interactive and indirect use of database systems. Lucas (1975a, 1975b), however, found tenure in the job to negatively correlate with system use. O'Reilly (1982) found the relationship between tenure in the job and system use to vary with the investigated information source (i.e., written reports, oral reports). The relationship between tenure in the job and system effectiveness was explored using the following two null hypotheses:

Ho 2-1: There is no relationship between user's tenure in the job and his/her satisfaction with the information system.

Ho 2-2: There is no relationship between user's tenure in the job and his/her use of the information system.

3. *The organizational level.* The organizational level of the user's job determines his/her responsibilities and decisions and, consequently, his/her informational needs (Lucas, 1982). Thus, satisfaction with and use of a system may vary at different managerial levels. Specht (1986) found users at the higher levels of management to rank systems output flexibility above its quality (i.e., accuracy, timeliness). On the other hand, users at the lower levels of management rated output quality higher than its flexibility. Further, user attitude toward the system was found to correlate positively with his/her organizational level (Lucas, 1978).

On the other hand, Lucas (1975a, 1978) found a positive correlation between system use and the user's organizational level. Mawhinney & Lederer (1990) found organizational level of managers to have no correlation to microcomputer usage. However, Culnan (1983) and Eason (1976) found the relationship to be negative. The relationship of the user's organizational level to systems effectiveness was explored using the following two null hypotheses:

Ho 3-1: There is no relationship between the user's organizational level and his/her satisfaction with the information system.

Ho 3-2: There is no relationship between the user's organizational level and his/her use of the information system.

4. *Education.* Higher levels of formal education may increase an individual's capability to manage work problems and to use more information sources (O'Reilly, 1982), which, consequently, contribute to the development of the attitude toward and use of information systems. Education was found to have no effect on users' attitudes toward microcomputers (Igbaria, 1993). Lucas (1978) found education level to negatively correlate to user satisfaction. Schewe (1976), however, found education level to have no relationship with attitude toward the system's impact on the organization performance and work condition.

Furthermore, Igbaria (1993) found education to have a direct influence on microcomputer use. In another study using a sample from Taiwan, Igbaria (1992) found education to positively correlate with the number of microcomputer application packages used. Culnan

Table 3: Summary of user satisfaction and systems usage results

Effectiveness Measures	Mean	SD	Lowest Score	Highest Score
1. User Satisfaction Measures:				
Use satisfaction (overall)	1.76	.79	-.5	3
User satisfaction elements:				
Relationship with IS staff and systems flexibility	1.37	1.25	-2.02	3
Quality of systems output				
Understanding of systems and Involvement in systems development	2.34	.59	.36	3
2. System Usage Measures				
Usage of systems output	.59	.27	0%	100%
Importance of manual reports	1.95	.16	1	3
Importance of printed reports	2.35	.60	1	3
Importance of on-line information	1.0	1.26	1	3

(1983) found education level to correlate positively with interactive and indirect use of systems. Vasarhelyi (1977) found a positive relationship between education and decision support systems impact on work performance. O'Reilly (1982) found education to associate positively with verbal information sources and negatively with written information sources. However, Mawhinney & Lederer (1990) found no relationship of education to microcomputer usage; and Lucas (1975a) and Schewe (1976) found education to negatively correlate with system use. The relationship of education level to system effectiveness was explored using the following two null hypotheses:

Ho 4-1: There is no relationship between the user's formal education level and his/her satisfaction with the information system.

Ho 4-2: There is no relationship between the user's formal education level and his/her use of the information system.

5. *Training*. User training, particularly in end-user computing environment, is viewed as an important influence upon the effectiveness of information systems (Amoroso & Cheney, 1991). A better understanding of the system in use increases user satisfaction (e.g., Montazemi, 1988). Furthermore, training was found to increase user satisfaction with, or attitude toward, the system (e.g., Cronan & Douglas; 1990; Amoroso & Cheney, 1991; Sanders and Courtney, 1985; Schewe, 1976). Nelson & Cheney (1987), however, found no relationship of user satisfaction or user attitude toward the computer system to his/her training or computer competency.

On the other hand, in a sample from Taiwan, training was found to positively correlate with microcomputers usage (Igbaria, 1992). In another study, Igbaria , Guimaraes, & Davis (1995) found a positive influence of training on system usage. Nelson and Cheney (1987) found a positive relationship between computer competency and system use. However, Amoroso & Cheney (1991) and Schewe (1976) found no relationship between training and

Table 4: Pearson Correlation Coefficients Between Personal and Situational Variables and System Effectiveness Variables

Personal & Situational Variable	User Satisfaction Components: Relationship & Flexibility	User Satisfaction Components: Output Quality	User Satisfaction Components: Understanding & involvement	Overall User Satisfaction	Measures of System Use: System Usage	Measures of System Use: Importance of Manual Reports	Measures of System Use: Importance of System Reports	Measures of System Use: Importance of On-line Service
Age	.2091**	.0289	.2815***	.2275**	-.2275**	.1076	.1214	-.2456**
Tenure in the bank	-.0035	-.0407	.1481	.0406	-.0333	.2660**	.0361	-.3267***
Tenure in the job	-.1644*	-.0834	.0285	-.1263	.0452	.0043	.1459	-.1052
Organizational level	.2535***	-.0231	.2749***	-.2536***	.0798	.0283	-.0401	-.0401
Education	.0339	-.0758	-.0675	-.0345	-.1549*	.1332	-.0579	-.1251
Training	.0089	.0871	.2028**	-.1127	.0485	-.0411	-.0280	-.1627*
Duration of system use	.0098	.0245	.1439	.0688	.0765	-.1833**	.2137**	.1243
User involvement	.1938**	.1242	.1507*	.2027**	-.1278	-.1415	.0139	.0901

* p < .10 ** p < .05 *** p < .01

system use. Thus, the possible relationship between training and system effectiveness was explored using the following two null hypotheses:

Ho 5-1: There is no relationship between the user's formal training level and his/her satisfaction with the information system.

Ho 5-2: There is no relationship between the user's formal training level and his/her use of the information system.

6. *Duration of system use*. Lengthy use of an information system may strengthen the user's belief in its usefulness, which, consequently, may increase his/her satisfaction with the system. Duration of system use was found to associate positively with user satisfaction (Sanders and Courtney, 1985), with system acceptance (Vasarhelyi, 1977), and with the user's willingness to use the system (Yaverbaum, 1988). Duration of system use was found to have a positive influence on satisfaction with information quality (Gatian, 1994). Montazemi (1988), however, found no relationship between duration of system use and user satisfaction. The relationship of duration of system use to system effectiveness was explored using the following two null hypotheses:

Ho 6-1: There is no relationship between the duration of a user's use of an information system and his/her satisfaction with the system.

Ho 6-2: There is no relationship between the duration of a user's use of an information system and his/her usage level of the system.

7. *User involvement.* User involvement in information systems development is believed to be critical in the effective implementation of such systems (Ives & Olson, 1984). User involvement was found to positively correlate with user satisfaction (e.g., Amoako-Gyampah & White, 1993; Montazemi, 1988; Nosehi, 1984; Swanson, 1974). Schewe (1976) found no relationship between user involvement and his/her attitude toward the system.

Further, user involvement was found to influence system use (Nosehi, 1984). Schewe

(1976), however, found no relationship between the two. Additionally, in their review of the results of 22 studies on the effects of user involvement on systems success, Ives & Olson (1984) found that out of the 13 studies investigating the relationship of user satisfaction to user involvement, only eight showed a positive correlation. Similarly, four out of nine studies correlating user involvement and systems usage reported significant correlations. The following two null hypotheses were used to explore the relationship between user involvement and system effectiveness:

Ho 7-1: There is no relationship between the user's involvement in an information system development and his/her satisfaction with that system.

Ho 7-2: There is no relationship between the user's involvement in an information system development and his/her use of that system.

RESEARCH METHOD

Sample Design

The research sample was selected assuming that most computer-based information systems applications in Egyptian corporations are management information systems (MIS) that have transaction processing systems (TPS) and information reporting systems (IRS) capabilities. This assumption was partially validated by the findings of a pilot study of seven large organizations in Alexandria, Egypt. The sample was selected from just one type of industry (banking) for two reasons: (1) to control for the possible impact of industry and information systems type on research results, and (2) to be able to compare findings with prior research results which had utilized similar sample designs.

Initial interviews were conducted with managers of the information systems departments in various bank branches in order to identify those users that would be included in the sample. As a result, a convenient sample of 22 branches (11 public and 11 private) were selected for the study using the following criteria: (1) systems should have been in use for at least three years; (2) applications should have been covering the basic functional areas in the bank; (3) systems should have been multi-user systems; and (4) the banks should be willing to participate in the study.

Measurement

1. *Personal and situational variables:* A questionnaire was used to collect data on the independent variables of the study (age, tenure in the job, organizational level, formal education level, formal training level, duration of system use, and user involvement). In this study, user involvement refers to a subjective psychological state of the user and defined as the importance and personal relevance that a user attaches either to a given system or to MIS in general (Barki & Hartwick, 1989). Therefore, user involvement was operationalized using a single-item categorical measure.

Users were classified into three groups: branch managers, department managers, and divisions managers. According to the managerial hierarchy in the Egyptian banks, branch managers are classified as middle-level managers with management control as their main responsibility. Department and division managers, on the other hand, are classified as operations lower-level managers with operations control as their main responsibility. In addition to general management, four functional areas were identified: deposits, credit, foreign accounts, and public accounts.

2. *User satisfaction:* To measure user satisfaction, a slightly modified version of the user satisfaction short instrument originally developed by Bailey & Pearson (1983) and modified by Ives, Olson, & Baroudi (1983) was adopted. Although some of the studies have reported problems with this semantic differential instrument, it was utilized in this study because of its (1) general acceptance among IS researchers, (2) established record of reliability and validity testing and retesting, (3) multidimensional coverage of information systems characteristics, and (4) appropriateness for measuring user satisfaction with MIS applications (Baroudi & Orlikwiski, 1988).

The adopted instrument includes 15 elements: the 13 elements of the original instrument and two elements (information timeliness and information security) from Bailey and Pearson's (1983) instrument. These two elements were added as a result of the feedback received from the pilot study regarding their importance to users working in banking. The calculated overall reliability coefficient (Cronbach alpha) for the modified instrument is .82. In addition, the reliability coefficients were calculated for each of the three basic factors produced by the factors analysis: relationships with IS staff and system flexibility (alpha = .81), quality of output (alpha = .64), and user's understanding of the system and users involvement (alpha = .67). Since the overall alpha (.82) is above .70, the reliability of the instrument is satisfactory as an indicator of the level of user satisfaction (Nunally, 1978).

3. *System use:* User's assessment of the degree to which the information system service satisfies his/her information needs was adopted to measure system use. This subjective approach was used because of the lack of objective measures in the studied banks. Additionally, the system use instrument, which was derived from the instruments used by Cheney & Dickson (1982) and O'Reilly (1982), included questions for the purpose of identifying and ranking the information sources—printed reports, manual reports, and on-line information—that were being utilized by the users.

Data Collection Procedure

Data was collected through directed interviews with information systems users. The users responded to the questionnaires during these interviews, which were all conducted by the same researcher over a 7-month period.

RESULTS

Descriptive Statistics

1. *Sample profile.* The usable responses were 120 (n=120). All participants were middle and lower-level managers: 56% from publicly owned banks and 44% from privately owned banks. The majority (87.5%) of the sample are male, which is an accurate depiction of the actual gender distribution in the managerial ranks in Egyptian institutions. Moreover, approximately 57% of the users were using only printed reports while 43% were using printed reports and had access to on-line information as well.

2. *Personal and situational variables:* Table 2 displays the averages, standard deviations, and frequency distributions of the personal and situational variables. The average

age of the sample is relatively high (48 years), which reflects a relatively long tenure both in banking (25 years) and in the current bank (20 years). The fact that such longevity exists suggests that managers are well aware of all formal and informal information sources available to them at work. However, the average tenure in the current job is relatively short (4.21 years), which suggests a high job rotation among the employees in the same bank. Additionally, the average duration of system use in the sample is 5.36 years, which is considered long enough for the users to develop accurate attitudes toward the systems and to make realistic assessment of their usage of such systems.

With regard to the organizational level, the sample distribution represents the managerial hierarchy in the banks: 18.3% were branch (bank) managers, 38.3% division managers, and 43.4% department managers. The distribution of the sample according to functional specialization is: 22.5% Savings Accounts, 18.4% Credit Accounts, 10.8% Foreign Accounts, 30.0% Public Accounts, and 18.3% branch managers. Business is the educational background of 92% of the sample; and more than 85% of them have at least a college degree. Further, approximately 67% of the sample had no formal training on the applications, 21% had only on-site training, and 12% had only off-site training. One justification for such poor training is that most of the systems use was indirect through printed reports. Finally, only 7.5% of the sample reported an involvement in systems development activities, which reflects a poor user involvement practice.

3. *System effectiveness variables:* The mean score of overall user satisfaction is 1.76 (SD=.79). Because the scale ranges from -3 (very unsatisfied) to +3 (very satisfied), the average score (1.76) reflects a relatively high level of satisfaction with the systems available. The relatively high user satisfaction can be attributed to one or more of the following: (1) systems were able to suffice user needs, (2) systems were easy to be used with minimal training, and (3) users did not perceive the introduction of the systems as a threat to their job security.

The internal components of the user satisfaction measure suggest that users are highly satisfied with the quality of the systems outputs, but less satisfied with system flexibility, their understanding of the systems, their involvement in systems development and implementation, and their relationship with IS staff (see Table 3 for more details).

On the other hand, the system usage scores indicate a 59% average use of the systems. This score reflects the users' assessment of the degree to which the systems services satisfy their information needs. Printed reports, however, are the most important information source, followed by the manual and on-line access sources. The low importance placed on the value of on-line information source is perhaps explained by the fact that, when data was collected, only 43% of the users had access to on-line information services. Furthermore, a positive relationship was found between the overall user satisfaction measure and system use measure ($r=.359$, $p<.01$).

HYPOTHESES TESTING

The hypothesized relationships of personal and situational variables to system effectiveness variables were evaluated using Pearson correlation coefficients and a significance level of 90%. The following is a discussion of the findings, which are summarized in Table 4.

1. *Age:* There is a significant positive relationship between age and the user's overall satisfaction ($r=.228$, $p<.05$). This finding suggests the rejection of Ho 1-1. Older users

expressed a higher level of satisfaction with information system. Also, compared to younger users, older users displayed more satisfaction with their relationship with IS personnel and the flexibility of the systems ($r=.209, p<.05$) and with their level of system understanding and the relatively low involvement level in system development ($r=.282, p<.01$). This finding is consistent with Schewe's (1976) and inconsistent with the presumed resistance of older individuals to the new systems and their accompanying changes.

Further, age was found to have a significant negative relationship with system use ($r=-.228, p<.05$). This finding suggests the rejection of Ho 1-2. Age was also found to have a negative relationship with the users' perceived importance of on-line information access ($r=-.246, p<.01$). Compared to younger users, older users tend to use systems less and place less importance on on-line service as a source of information. This finding is consistent with Igbaria's (1992) and Culnan's (1983) findings and inconsistent with those of Igbaria (1993) and Schewe (1976).

2. *Tenure in the job:* Tenure in the job was found to have an insignificant relationship with overall user satisfaction. Thus, users' attitudes toward the systems seem to be insensitive to their job-related experience. Also, tenure with the bank was not found to have a significant relationship with overall user satisfaction or with any of its internal factors. This result is inconsistent with Lucas's (1978) and Schewe's (1976) findings which suggest a positive relationship between tenure in the bank and users' attitude toward the system.

Furthermore, tenure in the job was found to have an insignificant relationship with system use. This finding, which is inconsistent with those of Lucas (1975a; 1975b), can be attributed to the relatively low level of system use (59%) reported in the sample. Tenure with the bank, however, was found to correlate positively with the perceived importance of manual reports ($r=.266, p<.05$) and negatively with the perceived importance of on-line service ($r=-.327, p<.01$).

3. *Organizational level*: The organizational level of the user was found to positively associate with his/her overall satisfaction with the information system ($r=.230, p<.05$), which suggests the rejection of Ho 3-1. This finding is consistent with Lucas' (1978). Users at higher managerial levels are more satisfied with the information systems in use.

The organizational level at which the user operates was also found to associate negatively with system use ($r=-.254, p<.01$), which suggests the rejection of Ho 3-2. Further analysis of the data shows that the usage level of systems at the department level (the lowest level) is significantly higher than the usage level at both the division and branch levels. That is, the level of system usage increases with the decrease in the organizational level at which the user operates. However, this usage doesn't seem to associate with the perceived importance of the automated and manual information sources at the three levels of management. These findings are consistent with those of Culnan's (1983) and Eason's (1976), and inconsistent with those of Lucas' (1975a). One likely reason for such inconsistency with Lucas' findings is the type of systems that were investigated in this study (MIS), which supports the operational activities of middle and lower level managers.

4. *Education:* Education level was found to have an insignificant relationship with overall user satisfaction and with its internal components. One reason for this finding is the existence of a narrow dispersion of education in the sample since more than 85% of the users have at least a college degree. This finding is consistent with those of Igbaria (1993) and Schewe (1976). The type of education was also found to have an insignificant relationship with overall satisfaction and its internal components.

Education was found to associate negatively with system use ($r=.155, p<.10$), which suggests the rejection of Ho 4-2. Compared to users with a lower level of education, users with a higher level of education are more capable of finding and using other sources of information to satisfy their information needs. Additionally, managers at higher managerial levels, who were found to use systems less, compared to lower level managers, are more likely to have higher education. This finding is consistent with those of Lucas (1975a) and inconsistent with those of Igbaria (1993, 1992), Culnan (1983), and Vasarhely (1977).

5. *Training:* Training level was found to have an insignificant association with user's overall satisfaction. This result is consistent with those of Igbaria's (1993), Amoroso and Cheney's (1991), and Nelson & Cheney's (1987) and inconsistent with those of a number of other studies (e.g., Cronan & Douglas, 1990; Montazemi, 1988; Sanders & Courtney's (1985), which found positive relationship between training and user satisfaction.

Training level was also found to have an insignificant association with system use. This result is consistent with those of Amoroso & Cheney (1991), and Schewe (1976) and inconsistent with those of Igbaria et al. (1995), Igbaria (1993), and Nelson & Cheney (1987). This result can be attributed to the mostly indirect use of systems, which is determined by other factors, such as availability and usefulness, rather than training.

6. *Duration of system use*: Duration of system use was found to have an insignificant relationship with the user's overall satisfaction and its internal components. That is, the formulation of the user's attitude—positive or negative—toward the system is not necessarily associated with the duration of his or her use of the system. This result is inconsistent with those of Gatian (1994), and Sanders & Courtney (1985).

Also, duration of system use was found to have an insignificant relationship with the usage level of system output (or system use). This finding can be attributed to the relatively easy use of systems outputs, particularly when the use is mostly indirect, and users don't have to use the systems for a long time before they can fully utilize the systems' information service.

7. *User involvement:* User involvement in systems development was found to positively associate with the user's overall satisfaction ($r=.203$, $p<.05$), which suggests the rejection of Ho 7-1. These findings are consistent with those of Choe (1996), Amoako-Gyampah & White (1993), Montazemi (1988), Nosehi's (1984), and Swanson (1974), and inconsistent with those of Schewe (1976).

User involvement, however, was found to have an insignificant relationship with system use. This finding is consistent with those of Schewe (1976) and inconsistent with those of Nosehi (1984).

DISCUSSION OF THE RESULTS

In our sample, the overall user satisfaction was found to be relatively high although system usage was rather low (Table 3). One reason for such finding is that the IS issues that may be perceived as problems by managers in the U.S. business environment may be seen as expected or accepted operational difficulties by managers in other countries such as Egypt. Another reason is that the level of IS knowledge may vary across international environments, and the higher the level of IS knowledge, the higher the level of user expectation. Also, the use rate of an IS system would influence the level of user expectations, and the rate of use is expected to have a considerable range across countries and cultures. Since usage level among our sample is low, user expectation is expected to be low.

Further, the level of IS adoption in a given country can influence the way that an IS product and service would be evaluated. Where the IS has a high level of adoption, users could use a relative measure of satisfaction which would raise the level of expectation (Lascu et al., 1995). In countries like Egypt, where the level of adoption is low, the measure of satisfaction would tend to be absolute. This is particularly true since the Egyptian business system is relatively isolated from the global business community. Additionally, in a tightly integrated society or a collectivist society (Hofstede, 1983)—such as in Egypt, users are not expected to openly express their attitudes and beliefs about IS products and services, which could have influenced their perceptions of such products and services.

With regard to the hypotheses testing, the findings do not deviate from those found in the previous U.S.-based studies, since most of the investigated personal and situational variables had mixed relations with IS effectiveness measures (Choe, 1996). User age positively correlates with user satisfaction, although the introduction of computer-based information systems is expected to bring about significant organizational changes, and, consequently, resistance (Hirsheim & Newman, 1988). The introduction of the systems investigated in this study seemed to cause minimal threats of layoffs, changes of work procedures, and need for retraining. This phenomenon of job security is perhaps a result of the protective labor regulations and governmental policies which are applicable to Egyptian public and private organizations.

User age, however, negatively correlates with system usage. Older users, compared to younger users, normally occupy higher positions in the managerial ranks and are assumed to seek more information for decision making. However, older users in our sample seemed to prefer either to get their information through their subordinates, who are younger and are more willing to use the systems, or to rely on other internal or external information sources.

Tenure in the job does not correlate with either user satisfaction or system usage. One likely interpretation of such finding is that the information systems applications in the investigated banks did not significantly change the way the work was done, and consequently, users did not develop any particular attitude toward the systems. Additionally, the findings (Table 4) suggest that the higher the banking-related experience, the higher the appreciation of other sources of information ($r = .266, p < .05$), and the less the appreciation of on-line service as a source of information ($r = .327$, p , .01). This result is of no surprise since users with longer banking tenure are expected to hold higher positions which demand information that MIS are less likely to provide.

With regard to organizational level, it was found to correlate positively with user satisfaction and negatively with system usage. The findings suggest that the users' overall satisfaction is attributable to the satisfaction with the relationship with IS staff and system flexibility ($r=.254, p<.01$) and the satisfaction with system understanding and involvement in system development ($r=.275, p<.01$). However, output quality was not perceived as a contributing factor to overall satisfaction. One plausible reason for such a result is that data accuracy was viewed by the Egyptian managers in the sample as a "must" attribute in banking business.

It is also notable that, compared to lower level managers, higher level managers reported more positive attitudes toward the systems while they used these systems less. Higher level mangers' satisfaction with the systems may be attributable to the systems-related positive feedback they received from their subordinates and the systems' positive impact on the bank overall performance. As mentioned earlier, the relatively lower use of systems by higher level managers may be attributed to (1) the dependency of those managers on their subordinates' use of the systems to provide them with the needed information, and/or (2) the insufficiency of MIS applications as information sources that managers can depend on to satisfy their information needs.

Education does not correlate with user satisfaction and has a weak negative relationship with system usage. One possible reason for this finding is the existence of a narrow dispersion of education in the sample since more than 85% of the users have at least a college degree, and 91% of them a degree in business. Consistent with the above findings, managers who assume higher managerial positions are more likely to have higher education, longer tenure in the job, and less use of the system.

Also, training was found to have no correlation with either user satisfaction or system usage. This finding is inconsistent with the findings of many of the U.S.-based studies (see Table 1). This inconsistency may be explained by the fact that more than 66% of the users in this study had absolutely no formal computer training (Table 2). Further, only 43% of the users had access to very standardized on-line information services, which did not require a high level of formal training in order to be used. However, training was found to associate positively with satisfaction with system understanding and involvement in system development (r=.203, r<.05) and with the perceived importance of on-line access to information (r=.163, p<.10) (Table 4).

Developing countries like Egypt tend to introduce new systems without providing sufficient training or ensuring a user-friendly environment. The result is non-use, or under-utilization of the system, ultimately leading to user dissatisfaction. Therefore, user training and education are particularly necessary for user acceptance and understanding in the initial stage of information technology adoption when the application systems are first introduced. In a culture which is slow to react to technological change, ease of use and accessibility become significant factors in determining the success of information systems.

User satisfaction was found to be insensitive to duration of system use. This finding could possibly be attributed to the relatively limited use of on-line information service (only 43% of the sample) and the relatively extensive indirect use of the systems by higher level managers. This interpretation is further supported by the fact that the average level of systems use is generally low, since MIS applications satisfy only 59% of the users' information needs. Further, the duration of system use was found to associate positively with the perceived importance of system reports (r=.214, p<.05) and negatively with the perceived importance of manual reports (r=-.183, p<.10).

Finally, user involvement was found to positively associate with user satisfaction and to have no correlation with system usage. Such involvement seems to enhance users' satisfaction with the relationship with IS staff and system flexibility (r=.194, p<.05), and with their system understanding (r=.151, p<.10) (Table 4). Therefore, user involvement seems critical to the user's overall satisfaction with the system and the relationship with IS staff. However, the lack of such a relationship between user involvement and system use in our sample could be possibly attributable to the use of a single-item categorical measure instead of using a multi-item instrument to measure user participation (Doll & Torkzadeh, 1989). Another reason for such a finding is the relatively low user involvement level in the sample since only 7.5% of the users had been involved in systems development activities. Such low user involvement is perhaps due to the existence of less participative leadership and management styles in Egyptian organizations.

CONCLUSIONS

The main objective of this study was to explore the relationship of some personal and situational characteristics of information systems users to systems effectiveness in Egyptian banks. This study's findings suggest that user satisfaction and system usage, as the two measures of systems effectiveness, are associated with some of the investigated personal and situational variables. User satisfaction is associated positively with age, organizational level, and user involvement. Systems usage, on the other hand, is associated negatively with age, organizational level, and education. System usage was also found to vary from one functional area to another (i.e., high system usage in Savings and low system usage in Credit). Nevertheless, these findings should be cautiously interpreted given that most of the computer-based information systems that were investigated in this study were MIS applications.

The findings of this study provide some evidence that IS managers in Egyptian banks can improve the likelihood of information systems success by carefully considering the personal and situational factors in systems development and implementation. While some of the factors --i.e., age, organizational position, functional specialization--cannot be directly controlled, systems development managers can be more aware of potential systems implementation difficulties and attempt to preempt the likely problems. Plans should be developed to facilitate the development of more successful information systems applications. For instance, the limited, and mostly indirect, use of only MIS applications in Egyptian banks necessitates the development of plans to expand information systems applications horizontally in order to cover the basic bank-functional areas, and vertically in order to satisfy the information needs of higher level managers. Since user involvement and formal users' training were found to be lacking, improvement in these areas may call for substantial changes from what is happening today in Egyptian banks, especially in preparation for moving from the initial phase and entering into the contagion phase of IT adoption process.

REFERENCES

Amoako-Gyampah, K., & White, K. B. (1993). User Involvement and user satisfaction: An exploratory contingency model. *Information & Management,* 25, 1-10.

Aharoni Y., & Burton, R. M. (1994). Is Management Science international: In search of universal rules. *Management Science.* 40 (1), 1-3.

Amoroso, D. L., & Cheney, P. M. (1991). Testing a causal model of end-user application effectiveness. *Journal of Management Information Systems.* 8 (1), 63-89.

Bailey, J. E., & Pearson, S. W. (1983). Development of a tool for measuring and analyzing computer user satisfaction. *Management Science.* 89 (5), 530-545.

Barki, H., & Hartwick, J. (1989). Rethinking the concept of user involvement. *MIS Quarterly.* 13 (1), 53-63.

Baroudi, J. J., & Orlikwiski, W. A. (1988). A short-form measure of user information satisfaction: A psychometric evaluation and notes on use. *Journal of Management Information Systems.* 4 (4), 4-59.

Cheney, P. H., and Dickson, G.W. (1982). Organizational characteristics and information systems: An exploratory investigation. *Academy of Management Journal,* 25(1), 170-184

Choe, J. (1996). The relationships among performance of accounting information systems, influence factors, and evolution level of information systems. *Journal of Management Information Systems.* 12(4), 215-239.

Cronan, T. P., & Douglas D. E. (1990). End-user training and computing effectiveness in public agencies: An empirical study. *Journal of Management Systems.* 6 (4), 21-39.

Culnan, M. J. (1983). Chauffeured versus end user access to commercial database: The effects of task and individual differences. *MIS Quarterly.* 7 (4), 55-67.

Davis, F. D., Bagozzi, R. P., & Warshaw, P. R. (1989). User acceptance of computer technology: A comparison of two theoretical models. *Management.* 35 (8), 982-1003.

Deans, P. C., & Ricks, D. A. (1991). MIS research: A model for incorporating international dimension. *The Journal of High Technology Management Research,* 2, 57-81.

Deans, P. C , Karwan, K. R., Goslar, M. D., Ricks, D. A., & Toyne, B. (Spring 1991). Identification of key international information systems issues in U.S.-based multinational corporations. *Journal of Management Information Systems*, 7, 27-50.

Delone, W. H., & McLean, , E. R. (1992, March). Information systems success: The quest for the dependent variable. *Information Systems Research*, 3, 60-95.

Doll, W. J., & Torkzadeh, G. (1988). The measurement of end-user computing satisfaction. *MIS Quarterly.* 12 (2), 259-274.

Eason, K. D. (1976). Understanding the naive compute user. *Computer Journal.* 19 (1), 3-7.

Ein-Dor, P., Segev, E., & Orgad, M. (1993). The effect of national culture on IS: Implications for international information systems. *Journal of Global Information Management.* 1 , Winter, 33-44.

Gatian, A. w. (1994). Is user Satisfaction a valid Measure of system effectiveness? *Information & Management.* 26, 119-131.

Ginzberg, M. J. (1981). Early diagnosis of MIS implementation failure: Promising results and unanswered Questions. *Management Science.* 27 (4). 459-478.

Hassan, S. (1994). Environmental constraints in utilizing information technologies in Pakistan. *Journal of Global Information Management,* 2, 30-39.

Hirsheim, R., & Newman, M. (1988). Information system and user resistance: Theory and practice. *The Computer Journal.* 31 (5), 398-408.

Hofstede, G. H. (1983). *The cultural relativity of organizational practice and theories.* 14, 75-89.

Igbaria, M. (1993). User acceptance of microcomputer technology: An empirical test. *OMEGA International Journal of Management Science.* 21(1), 73-90.

Igbaria, M. (1992). An examination of microcomputer usage in Taiwan. *Information & Management.* 22, 1992, 19-28.

Igbaria, M., Guimaraes T., & Davis, G. B. (1995). Testing the determinants of microcomputer usage via a structural equation model. *Journal of Management Information Systems.* 11(4), 87-114.

Ives, B., Olson, M. H., & Baroudi, J. J. (1983). The measurement of user information satisfaction. *Communications of the ACM.* 26 (10), 785-793.

Ives, B., & Olson, M. H. (1984). User involvement and MIS success: Review of research. *Management Science.* 30 (5), 586-603.

Karimi, J., & Konsynski, B. R. (1991). Globalization and information management. *Journal of Management Information Systems,* 7 (Spring) , 7-26.

Lascu, D., Ashworth, N., Giese, T., & Omar, M. (1995). The user information satisfaction scale: International applications and implications for management and marketing. *Multinational Business Review.* 3(2), 107-115.

Leitheiser, R. L., & Wetherbe, J. C. (1986). Service support levels: An organized approach to end-user computing. *MIS Quarterly.* 10 (4), 337-349.

Lucas, H. C. (1982). *Information Systems Concepts for Management.* New York, McGraw- Hill.

Lucas, H. C. (1978). The Use of an interactive information storage and retrieval system in medical research., *Communications of the ACM.* 21 (3), 197-205.

Lucas, H. C. (1975a). *Why information systems fail?.* New York , NY: Columbia University Press.

Lucas, H. C. (1975b). Behavioral factors in systems implementation. In Schultz, R. L. and Slevin, D. P. (Eds). *Implementing Operations Research/Management science.* N.Y.: Elsevier.

Mawhinney, C. H., & Lederer, A. L. (1990). A study of personal computer utilization by managers. *Information & Management.* 18, 243-253.

Melone, N. P. (1990). A theoretical assessment of the user satisfaction construct in information systems research. *Management Science.* 36 (4), 76-91.

Montazemi, A. R. (1988). Factor affecting information satisfaction in the context of the small business environment. *MIS Quarterly.* 12 (2), 239-256.

Nelson, R. R., & Cheney, P. H. (1987). Training end users: An exploratory study. *MIS Quarterly.* 11

(4), 547-559.

Nosehi, A. M. (1984). An empirical investigation of systems analysis and design in some Egyptian corporations. Unpublished Ph.D. dissertation, Faculty of Commerce, Mansoura University, Egypt (in Arabic).

Nunally, J. C. (1978). *Psychometric Theory,* 2nd ed. New York, NY: McGraw-Hill.

O'Reilly, C. A. (1982). Variations in decision maker's use of information sources: The impact of quality and accessibility of information. *Academy of Management Journal.* 24 (4), 756-771.

Palvia, P. (1993). Preface. *Journal of Global Information Management,* 1, 3-5.

Palvia, S., & Saraswat, S (1992). Information technology and the transnational corporation: the emerging multinational issues. in Palvia, P., Palvia, s., & Zigli, R. M. (eds.). *The Global Issues of Information technology Management.* Harrisburg, PA: Idea Group Publishing, pp. 554-574.

Robey, D. (1979). User attitudes and management information systems use. *Academy of Management Journal.* 22 (3), 527-538.

Sanders, G. L., & Courtney, J. F. (1985). A Field study of organizational factors influencing DDS success. *MIS Quarterly.* 9 (1), 77-92.

Schewe, C. D. (1976). The MIS user: An exploratory behavioral analysis. *Academy of Management Journal.* 19 (4), 577-590.

Specht, P. H. (1986). Job characteristics as indicative of CBIS data requirements. *MIS Quarterly.* 10 (3), 271-287.

Srinivasan, A. (1985). Alterative measures of system effectiveness: Associations and implications. *MIS Quarterly.* 9 (3), 243-253.

Swanson, E. B. (1974). Management information systems: Appreciation and involvement. *Management Science.* 21 (2), 178-188.

Taylor, R. N. (1975). Age and experience as determinants of managerial information processing and decision making performance. *Academy of Management Journal.* 18 (1), 74-81.

Thong, J. Y. L., Yap, C. (1996). Information Systems Effectiveness: A User Satisfaction Approach. *Information Processing & Management.* 32(5), 601-610.

Vasarhelyi, M. A. (Spring 1977). Man-machine planning systems: A cognitive style examination of interactive decision making. *Journal of Accounting Research.* 138-153.

Wetherbe, J. C., Vitalari, N. P., & Milner, A. (1994). Key trends in systems development in Europe and North America. *Journal of Global Information Management,* 2 (Spring), 5-20.

Yaverbaum, G. J. (1988). Critical factors in the user environment: An experimental study of users, organizations and tasks. *MIS Quarterly.* 12(1), 75-88.

Zenger, T.R. & Lawrence, B.S. (1989). Organizational demography: The differential effects of age and tenure distributions on technical communication. *Academy of Management Journal.* 32(2), 353-376.

Zmud, R.W. (1979). Individual differences and success: A review of the empirical literature. *Management Science.* 25(10), 966-979.

Chapter 10

Tailoring Software Development Processes Along TQM Concepts:
A Way to Narrow User-Perceived Expectations Gap for Information Systems

George E.M. Ditsa
University of Wollongong, Australia

A number of researchers (e.g., Rockart and Scott-Morton, 1984; Porter, 1985, 1992; Gilmour and Hunt, 1993; Leonard-Barton and Sinha, 1993; Alter, 1996) have emphasised the potential that information systems have for providing the competitive edge. The perception that an organisation is at a competitive disadvantage without computer systems has significantly increased users' expectations for information systems. These expectations have been further increased by the sensational media promotions of new computer products and services in the marketplace. Some vendors, acting in their own self-interest, may make inflated claims about their products putting more gap between users' expectations for information systems and the actual services delivered by the systems. The information technology industry has come under growing pressure to produce high-quality systems quickly and inexpensively to satisfy the growing user expectations (Lederer and Mendelow, 1990). This chapter looks at how some of the concepts of TQM can be applied to narrow the user expectations gap for information systems.

The consequences of information systems (IS) failures become more acute as organisations continue to invest large amounts of resources in information technology and

This chapter originally appeared in Managing IT Resources and Applications in the World Economy (Proceedings of the 1997 Information Resources Management Association International Conference), pp. 33-40.

application development. These IS failures have been classified variously in the literature. Block (1983), for example, classifies IS failures into 12 categories (see Table 1), whereas Williams (1991) classifies them into development failures and operations failures, while others (e.g., Lyytinen, 1988; Szajna and Scamell, 1993) identify some IS failures as user expectations failures. Szajna and Scamell (1993, p.494) define user expectations for an information system as:

> "a set of beliefs held by the targeted users of an information system associated with the eventual performance of the IS and with their performance using the system,"

while Lyytinen (1988, p.46) describes expectation failure as representing:

> "a pluralistic and political account of IS failure [which] defines an IS failure as a gap between stakeholders' expectations expressed in some ideal or standard and the actual performance."

Lyytinen identifies two main categories of IS failures: development failures and use failures. These categories with their subcategories are shown in Table 2. Indeed, Szajna and Scamell suggest the realisation of user expectations as one possible means of assessing the eventual success or failure of an IS.

Whereas there are various models for software process and software process maturity and improvement, user expectations for IS are on the increase, while software development processes are not keeping up pace in order to satisfy the set of beliefs held for IS, resulting in high expectations gap (Sallis et al. 1995). Indeed, Sallis et al. (1995, p.29) reaffirm: "Only a quality software process will consistently produce quality software". It is, therefore, appropriate to take a look at software development processes and incorporate concepts that are necessary to arrive at a quality software process. Quality, according to the International Standard Quality Vocabulary (ISO 8402-1986) is:

> "The totality of features and characteristics of a product or service that bear on its ability to meet stated or implied needs."

Behavioural theories and models such as the expectancy theory, the cognitive dissonance theory, the theory of reasoned action (TRA), the technology acceptance model (TAM) and, of late, the service quality models (Pitt et al. (1995), have been proposed by a number researchers to be incorporated into software development processes to enhance user expectations' success of IS. For example, Guimaraes and Ramanujam (1986); Lee (1986); Doukidis, et al. (1992); and Igbaria's (1993) models are drawn upon users' perceptions and expectations of IS to improve efficiency, improve income, value for money, sufficient training, adequate vendor assistance, and sufficient manuals, while Nolan and Seward (1974); O'Reilly (1982); Jenkins and Ricketts (1985); Doll and Torkzadeh's (1988, 1994) models are drawn upon users perceptions and expectations of information content, accuracy, format, ease of use and timeliness of information from IS. Recently, the concepts of Total Quality Management (TQM) is being suggested by some researchers as worth incorporating into the software development process (e.g., Abel, 1992; Keyes, 1992; Zadrozny and Tumanic, 1992; Kan, 1995; Aggarwal and Lee, 1995).

This chapter discusses the application of TQM concepts in the software development process to narrow the user expectations gap for information systems. The chapter begins by briefly examining the causes of user perceived expectations gap for IS. The chapter then examines the shortfalls in software development processes leading to IS expectations failure. Finally, the chapter proposes the adoption of some concepts of TQM in the software development process to, at worst reduce user expectations failures, and at best eliminate them.

CAUSES OF HIGH USER PERCEIVED EXPECTATIONS GAP

Advances in computer technology and IS have created new opportunities as well as challenges to the management of information resources. A number of researchers (Rockart and Scott-Morton 1984, Porter 1985, 1992; Gilmour and Hunt, 1993; Leonard-Barton and Sinha, 1993; Alter, 1996) have emphasised the potential that IS has for providing the competitive edge. The growing business competition in light of technological advancement and globalisation of markets are encouraging companies to use new technologies to achieve higher productivity and product quality. Managements under competitive pressure think that computerisation will bring the ultimate solutions to all their business problems (Aggarwal and Lee, 1995). The perception that the organisation is at a competitive disadvantage without computer systems has significantly increased users' expectations of computer systems.

Additionally, user expectations have been stimulated and heightened by media promotions of the latest technological advances, as well as by the ever-increasing introduction of new computer products and services in the marketplace. Vendors, acting in their own self-interest, may make inflated claims about their products. Media coverage of new technology usually provides a positive picture. Vendors' claims and success stories published in trade journals may be true only for an ideal environment. An ideal environment for systems implementation rarely exists, therefore, systems delivered by a development team may be below expectations compared to vendors' claims. Inflated vendors' claims and media coverage have added to the gap between the expectations and the actual performance of information systems. End users and information systems professionals are often misled by the glitter of new technology or by vendors' inflated claims. In such circumstances, their focus shifts from problem solving to working with the latest technology and software packages. They are under the impression that new computer systems will solve their problems. Vendors and the media do not make clear that in most worthwhile endeavours more is involved than merely technology. As a result, users' expectations are not met (Aggarwal

Figure 1: Key Elements of Total Quality Management

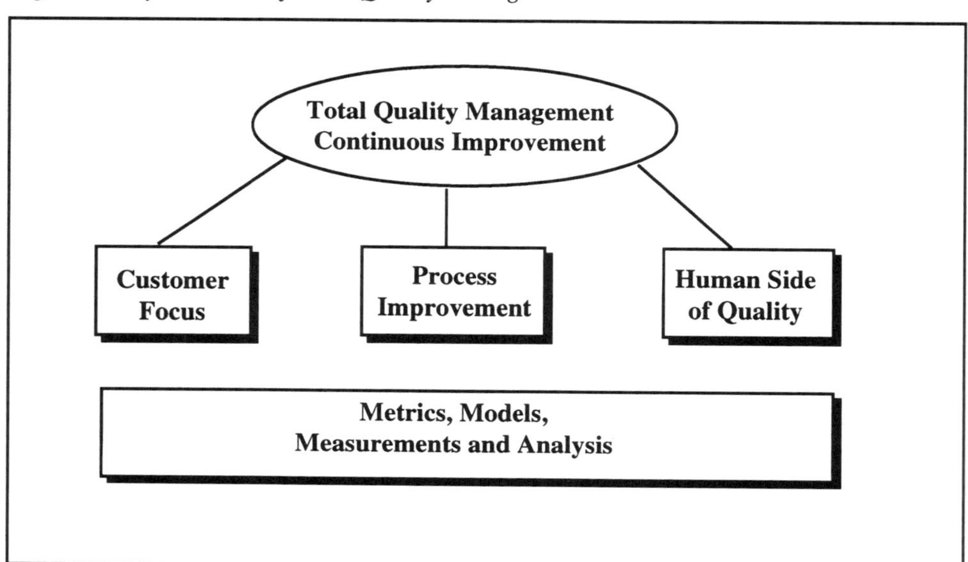

Source: Kan (1995)

and Lee, 1995).

SOFTWARE DEVELOPMENT PROCESS SHORTFALLS AND IS EXPECTATIONS FAILURE

While perhaps overstated, the quality of software has been the most concern of IS professionals since the birth of the information technology industry. Despite the many researches and practices so far in the area of software engineering, the field is yet a long way from meeting the ultimate satisfaction of its customers. Sanders and Curran (1994) restated that a software product displays quality to the extent that all aspects of the customer's needs are satisfied and suggest that this may be determined by:

- how fully the need is understood and captured by a requirements definition;
- how well that definition is transformed into a software product; and
- how well the software is supported.

They further suggest how the quality of software is lost through inaccurate requirements, support process defects and development process defects.

In addition, some of the other inadequacies in traditional systems development that have been pointed out in literature, which lead to loss of software quality include:

- inflexibility of design;
- inadequate analysis and design;
- improper planning and estimating;
- high turnover of development personnel;
- lack of user participation and involvement;
- lack of management participation and involvement; and
- long lead time, rendering systems obsolete before completion.

Aggarwal and Lee (1995) suggest that in the face of the negative credibility suffered by IS professionals in the past due to systems development processes, there is the need of devising strategies to narrow the expectations gap which has resulted from:

- unrealistically high expectations of users in the face of limited resources;
- unrealistic project completion date coupled with continually changing requirements;
- long lead time because of backlog problems, complexity of projects and manual developmental techniques;
- lack of user/management participation and involvement due to behavioural, organisational and political issues;
- improper planning, estimating, scheduling and monitoring because of the often too complex scope of systems being developed, lack of scientific methodology to correctly estimate resource requirements and the rapidly changing business environment of the contemporary world;
- inflexibility of design to incorporate unscheduled changes in requirements;
- unplanned absence of resources because of breakdowns of equipment and turnover of personnel; and
- inappropriate, incomplete and inadequate analysis and design because of lack of appropriate tools and resources.

Using the key elements of a TQM system described in the next section in addition to those other elements suggested in the following section, the loss in software quality and the other inadequacies in the traditional systems development mentioned above can be averted.

Figure 2: Demings Chain Reaction

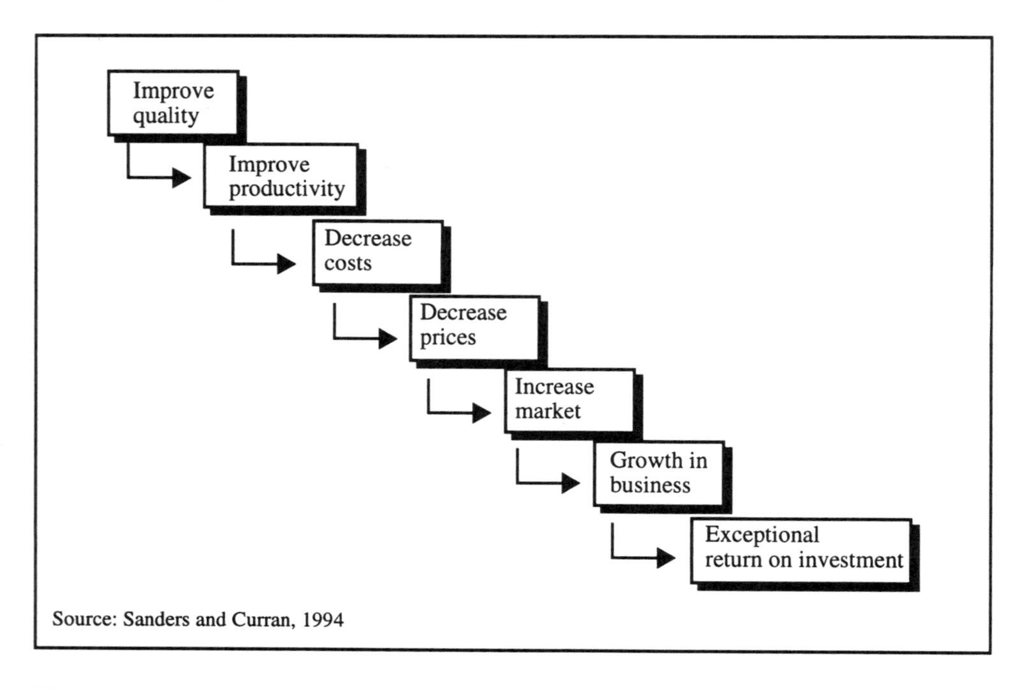

Figure 3: Application of TQM Concepts to Narrow User Expectations Gap

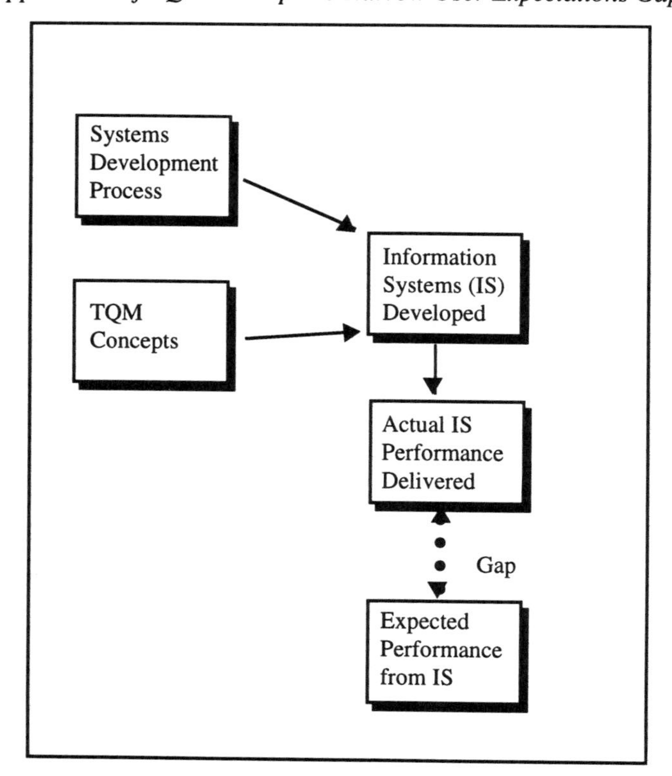

Table 1: Block's (1983) Twelve Categories of Information Systems Failures

Categories	Description
1. Resource Failures	Conflicts of people, time and scope; i.e., people and amount of time allotted are not sufficient to develop a required system. These failures are most often due to imposed deadlines combined with inability or unwillingness by management to provide adequate resources.
2. Requirements Failures	Result from incorrect, incomplete and unclear specification of system requirements.
3. Goal Failures	Result from inadequate or incorrect statements from system goals by management or from a misunderstanding of the goals by the system developers.
4. Technique Failures	Result from system developers attempting to use effective software development disciplines such as structured analysis and structured design. Poor techniques result in poor systems.
5. User Contact Failures	Result from lack of proper communication between developers and user community. The user may be someone within the organisation, a customer outside the organisation or all potential customers constituting the marketplace.
6. Organisational Failures	Result from an inability of the organisational structure to support the system development process. These failures can be internal or external to the system development group.
7. Size Failures	Mostly due to the size of the system. Big systems are usually functionally complex and demand high system development capabilities of an organisation.
8. Technology Failures	Result from hardware or software utilised by the system. Hardware or software does not work as described in its specification, the vendor unable to meet delivery schedule or product unreliable. Unthoroughly tested hardware or software usually results in these failures. Vendor support is another cause of this type of failure.
9. People Management Failures	Result from inability to motivate and maintain the morale of the system development group. Leads to time delays and budget overruns.
10. Methodology Failures	Result from failures to perform activities needed to build a system. May be due to lack of formal methodology as a guideline to system developers or to an overly rigid adherence to the adopted methodology.
11. Personality Failures	Result from clashes between people either within one system development group or between group members (often the leader) and members of an interfacing organisation.
12. Planning and Control Failures	Encompass planning, scheduling, task assignment and tracking of results. These failures result form vaguely defined assignments, inadequate tools to depict plans and schedules and failure to track progress to ensure that tasks are done. A poorly planned and controlled project results in uncertainty of tasks and task deadlines for members of the development groups.

Table 2: Lyytinen's (1988) Two Main Categories and Subcategories of IS Failures

	DEVELOPMENT FAILURES
Dimension	**Content**
1. Goals	A stakeholder's inability to state goals that are not ambiguous, narrow, conflicting and can be operationalised.
2. Technology	A stakeholder's inability to choose and implement technology so that design is cost-effective due to organisational policies, prior decisions, etc. A stakeholder's inability to avoid risks of technology change.
3. Economy	A stakeholder's inability to calculate accurately the economic impact of the system and to provide sound theoretical foundations.
4. View of organisation	A stakeholder's inability to predict behavioural, psychological and organisational impacts of the IS.
5. Process characteristics	A stakeholder's inability to participate in development that provides chances to influence, to communicate and express authentic opinions. A Stakeholder's inability to control and evaluate the quality of the IS from their point of view.
6. Self image	A stakeholder's inability to understand all aspects of IS design and the bias to regard it as a rational process.
	USE PROBLEMS
Dimension	**Content**
1. Technical solution	A stakeholder's inability to design and operate a technical solution that is fast, easy to use and reliable.
2. Data problems	A stakeholder's inability to maintain data that is correct, has relevance and is comprehensible.
3. Conceptual	A stakeholder's inability to solve his actual problems by the IS.
4. People's reactions	A stakeholder's inability to develop an IS without adverse effects on work, power shifts, or change in the job qualifications and content.
5. Complexity problems	A stakeholder's inability to create solutions that are not too complex to manage, understand, maintain, operate and change.

Equally, if these key elements of TQM are well applied, they will address the problems mentioned by Aggarwal and Lee above and subsequently narrow the user expectations gap.

THE CONCEPTS OF TQM

TQM is defined in the literature as an integrated management philosophy and set of practices that emphasises, among other things, continuous improvement, meeting customers' requirements, customer satisfaction, reducing rework, fewer errors, long-range thinking, increased employee involvement and teamwork, process redesign, competitive benchmarking, team-based problem solving, constant measurement of results, and closer relationships with suppliers (Zadrozny and Tumanic, 1992; Ross, 1993; Grant et al., 1994; Powell, 1995). Ultimate product quality to ensure ultimate customer satisfaction and gaining competitive advantage is the primary goal of TQM. This is to be achieved through a carefully well-planned management involving the total commitment of the whole organisation.

The perspectives on TQM as put forward by the proponents of the concept are shown in Table 3. The 12 TQM factors as outlined by Powell (1995) are also shown in Table 4. Deming's chain reaction for the adoption of the TQM concept is shown in Figure 2. According to Kan (1995), despite variations in the implementation of the concept of TQM, the key elements of a TQM system are:

- *Customer focus:* The objective of total customer satisfaction by studying customers' wants and needs, gathering customer requirements, and measuring and managing customer satisfaction.
- *Process:* The objective of reduction in process variations to achieve continuous process improvement.
- *Human side of quality:* The objective of creating an organisation-wide quality culture by good leadership, management commitment, total participation, employee empowerment, and other social, psychological, and human factors.
- *Measurement and analysis:* The objective of driving continuous improvement in all quality parameters by a goal-oriented measurement system.

These elements are represented diagrammatically in Figure 1.

Suffice to say that the concepts of TQM are applied implicitly in systems development to achieve the characteristics of quality software as set by the International Standards Organisation (ISO) and others such as Boehm et al. (1978). Equally, computer and software manufacturing companies, such IBM and Hewlett-Packard are seen to be implementing policies towards achieving quality software in their own right. However, it is my contention that adopting the TQM concepts explicitly, with the appropriate tools for systems development, will ultimately improve software quality and narrow the user expectations gap for IS.

TQM CONCEPTS FOR SYSTEMS DEVELOPMENT PROCESS

If we accept that the goals of TQM are ultimate quality of product and customer satisfaction, then it will be appropriate to consider adopting parts of the concepts that will help improve the quality of software. It is envisaged that the following concepts of TQM, if adopted in systems development processes, will improve software quality and narrow user expectations gap:

- Adopting TQM philosophy in crafting the day-to-day of systems development activities.
- Continuous quality improvement of systems by streamlining the development process using project management techniques and employee involvement.
- Emphasising teamwork; encouraging the participation of users, developers and senior managers with improved communication.
- Training, development programs and continuing professional education for users and systems personnel.
- Encouraging compliance with in-house quality control standards proclaimed by information resource management committee.

Table 3: Popular Perspectives on TQM

DEMING'S 14 POINTS[1]	THE JURAN TRILOGY[2]	CROSBY'S 14 QUALITY STEPS[3]
1. Constancy of purpose	I. Quality Planning	1. Management commitment
2. Adopt the philosophy	Set goals	2. Quality improvement teams
3. Don't rely on mass inspection	identify customers and their needs	3. Quality measurement
4. Don't award business on price	Develop products and processes	4. Cost of quality evaluation
5. Constant improvement	II. Quality control	5. Quality awareness
6. Training	Evaluate performance	6. Corrective action
7. Leadership	Compare to goals and adapt	7. Zero-defects committee
8. Drive out fear	III. Quality improvement	8. Supervisor training
9. Break down barriers	Establish infrastructure	9. Zero-defects day
10. Eliminate slogans & exhortations	Identify projects and teams	10. Goal setting
11. Eliminate quotas	Provide resources and training	11. Error cause removal
12. Pride of workmanship	Establish controls	12. Recognition
13. Education and retraining		13. Quality councils
14. Plan of action		14. Do it over again

Sources: [1] Walton, 1986; [2] Juran, 1992; [3] Crosby, 1970

Table 4: The 12 TQM Factors

1. Committed leadership: A near-evangelical, unwavering, long-term commitment by top managers to the philosophy, usually under a name something like Total Quality Management, Continuous Improvement, or Quality Improvement.
2. Adoption and communication of TQM: Using tools like the mission statement, themes or slogans.
3. Closer customer relationships: Determining customers' (both inside and outside the firm) requirements, then meeting those requirements no matter what it takes.
4. Closer supplier relationships: Working closely and cooperatively with suppliers (often sole sourcing key components), ensuring they provide input that conforms to customers' end use requirements.
5. Benchmarking: Researching and observing best competitive practices.
6. Increased training: Usually includes TQM principles, team skills, and problemsolving.
7. Open organisation. Lean staff, empowered work teams, open horizontal communications and a relaxation of traditional hierarchy.
8. Employee empowerment: Increased employee involvement in design and planning, and greater autonomy in decision making.
9. Zero-defects mentality: A system in place to spot defects as they occur, rather than through inspection and rework.
10. Flexible manufacturing: (applicable only to manufacturers) Can include just-in-time inventory, cellular manufacturing, design for manufacturability (DFM), statistical process control (SPEC) and design of experiments (DOE).
11. Process improvement: Reduced waste and cycle times in all areas through cross departmental process analysis.
12. Measurement: Goal orientation and zeal for data, with constant performance measurement, often using statistical methods.

Source: Powell, 1992, p. 19.

- Developing strategic planning and implementation techniques to achieve short-term as well as long-term quality goals for systems in the organisation.
- Promoting management by objectives in performance evaluation and understanding the process of motivation for systems staff.

Figure 3 shows a proposed model for adopting the TQM concepts in the software development process to narrow the user expectations gap.

CONCLUSION

TQM concepts strive to meet and exceed the expectations of users. User satisfaction depends on the degree to which the application software meets the users' current needs as well as the ease with which it can adapt to the changing business needs. Users are interested in systems that incorporate new business needs because requirements keep on changing in the dynamic business environment. TQM is more than a process of quality control. It is a commitment to the excellence of operations of a business in exceeding customer satisfaction. TQM allows the systems department to focus on its users in order to improve its performance and profitability, as well as reaching its goals of effective and efficient development of systems. TQM narrows the expectations gap by developing systems that meet users' needs, time requirements and resource constraints. The expectations gap is narrowed by continually improving all aspects of the systems development process, striving for the goals of 100 percent satisfied users and the participation of everyone in an effort to achieve zero defects.

Without doubt, a lot of successes have been scored in the information systems industry through research and practice, but user expectations gap for information systems continues to widen. There is the need, therefore, to continuously look at the systems development processes and incorporate concepts and practices that will narrow the user expectations gap. As depicted in Figure 3, the application of TQM concepts in systems development processes is believed will help narrow the user expectations gap for IS.

REFERENCES

Abel, J. (1992). Re-Engineering Treasury Processes for the '90s - Pennsylvania Power and Light Company's Blueprint. *Journal of Cash Management,* Vol. 12,10-14.

Aggarwal, R. and Lee, Jong-Sung. (1995). CASE and TQM for Flexible Systems. *Information Systems Management,* Vol. 12, 15-19.

Alter, S. (1996). *Information Systems: A Management Perspective*, Benjamin/Cummings.

Block, R. (1983). *The Politics of Projects*, Yourdon Press.

Boehm, B.W. (1978). *Characteristics of Software Quality*. Elsevier North-Holland, New York.

Crosby, P. (1979). *Quality is Free: The Art of Making Quality Certain.* McGraw-Hill, New York.

Doll, W.J. and Torkzadeh, G. (1988). The Measurement of End-User Computing Satisfaction. *MIS Quarterly*, 12(2), 258-274.

Doll, W.J. and Torkzadeh, G. (Jan 1994). The test-retest reliability of user involvement instruments. *Information and Management,* 26(1).

Doukidis, G.I., Smithson, S. and Naoum, G. (1992). Information Systems Management in Greece: Issues and Perceptions. *Journal of Strategic Information Systems*, Vol. 1, 139-

Grant, R.M., Shani, R. and Krishnan, R. (Winter 1994). TQM's Challenge to Management Theory and Practice. *Sloan Management Review,* 25-35.

Gilmour, P. and Hunt, R. (1993). *The Management of Technology*, Longman, Cheshire.

Guimaraes, T. and Ramanujam, V.(1986). Personal Computing Trends and Problems: An Empirical Study. *MIS Quarterly,* 10(2), 179-187.

Igbaria, M. (1993). User Acceptance of Microcomputer Technology: An Empirical Test. International *Journal of Management Science,* Vol. 21, 73-

Jenkins, A.M. and Ricketts J.A. (1985). The Development of an MIS Satisfaction Questionnaire: An Instrument for Evaluating User Satisfaction with Turkney Decision Support Systems. Discussion Paper#296, School of Business, Indiana University, Bloomington, August 1985.

Juran, J. (1992). *Juran on Quality by Design.* Free Press, New York.

Kan, S.H. (1995). *Metrics and Models in Software Quality Engineering*. Addison-Wesley Publishing Co.

Keyes, J. (May 1992). New Metrics Needed for New Generation. *Software Magazine*, Vol. 12, 42-56.

Lederer, A.L. and Mendelow, A.L. (1990). The Impact of the Environment on the Management of Information Systems. *Information Systems Research,* 205-222.

Lee, D.M.S. (1986). Usage Pattern and Sources of Assistance For Personal Computer Users. MIS Quarterly, 10(4), 313-325.

Leonard-Barton, D. and Sihna, D. K. (1993). Developer-User Interaction and User Satisfaction in Internal Technology Transfer. *Journal of the Academy of Management,* 36(5).

Lyytinen, K. (1988). Expectation Failure Concept and Systems Analysts' View of Information System Failures: Results of an Exploratory Study. *Information and Management,* Vol. 14, 45-56.

Nolan, R. and Seward, H. (1974). Measuring User Satisfaction to Evaluate Information Systems, in R. L. Nolan (ed.). *Managing the Data Resource Function,* West Publishing Co., 253-275.

O'Reilly, C.A. (1982). Variations in Decision Makers' Use of Information Sources: The Impact of Quality and Accessibility of Information. *Academy of Management Journal,* Vol. 25, 756-771.

Pitt, L.F., Watson, R.T. and Kavan, C.B. (June 1995). Service Quality: A Measure of Information Systems Effectiveness. *MIS Quarterly,* 173-185.

Porter, M. (1985). How Information Can Help You Compete. *Harvard Business Review,* Vol: 63, 149-160.

Porter, M. (1992). *The Competitive Advantage of Nations,* McMillan, London.

Powell, T.C. (1995). Total Quality Management as Competitive Advantage: A Review and Empirical Study. *Strategic Management Journal,* Vol. 6, 16-37.

Rockart, J.F. and Scott-Morton, M.S. (1984). Implications of Changes in Information Technology for Corporate Strategy. *Interfaces,* Vol: 14, 84-95.

Ross, J. (1993). *Total Quality Management: Text, Cases and Readings. S*t. Lucie Press, Delray Beach, Fl.

Sallis, P., Tate, G. and MacDonell, S. (1995). *Software Engineering: Practice, Management, Improvement,* Addison-Wesley Publishing Co.

Sanders, J. and Curran E. (1994). *Software Quality: A Framework for Success in Software Development and Support.* Addison-Wesley.

Szajna, B. and Scamell, R. (Dec 1993). *The Effects of Info Systems User Expectations on Their Performance and Perception.*

Walton, M. (1986). *The Deming Management Method*, Pedigree, New York.

Williams, J. (1991). Negative Consequences of Information Technology in Szewczak E., Snodgrass C. and Khosrowpour M. *Management Impacts of Information Technology: Perspectives on Organizational Change and Growth,* Idea Group Publishing, Harrisburg Pennsylvania, 48-74.

Zadrozny, M.A. and Tumanic, R.E. (1992). Zero-Defects' Software: Total Quality Management Approach to Software Engineering. *Chief Information Officer Journal,* Vol. 4, 10-16.

PART III: NEW STRATEGIES AND SOLUTIONS

Part III provides an analysis of the expected principles of software upgrades discussed in Part I of this book. The results of the survey were analyzed using multiple regression analysis, and as mentioned previously in the book, the details of the statistical analyses have been omitted to increase readability. Interestingly, some factors turned out to be critical factors, and others were found to be of much less importance in the upgrade process. An analysis of the reasons behind the differences in expected and actual outcomes provides profound insight into the upgrade process and suggests some new strategies, tips, and techniques that should be of great benefit to the practicing IT manager.

IT FACTORS

In general, IT factors were shown to be significant predictors of the transparency of software upgrades. Statistical tests give a strong indication that IT factors are an important predictor of the transparency of software upgrades. This finding is of particular importance for practitioners looking to compare the results of the current study with other published research. As mentioned previously in the book, the vast majority of IS researchers have claimed that technical issues can be largely ignored in an IS implementation; however, the results of the present research soundly refute those claims.

The change in user functionality is indeed an important factor in upgrades as shown by an extremely small (less than .0001) p-value for this variable in the regression model. The interesting point, however, is that the sign of the coefficient is the opposite of what one would expect. In other words, in this study, a higher degree of change in functionality was associated with a more transparent upgrade as perceived by the users. This is likely due to the fact that users were generally more satisfied with the upgrade if they perceived that it brought them additional benefits via the use of additional features.

Although the p-value for the user interface variable is quite small, the most interesting result for this construct comes from the interaction between it and the support given to the

Figure 1: Interaction Between User Interface and Support

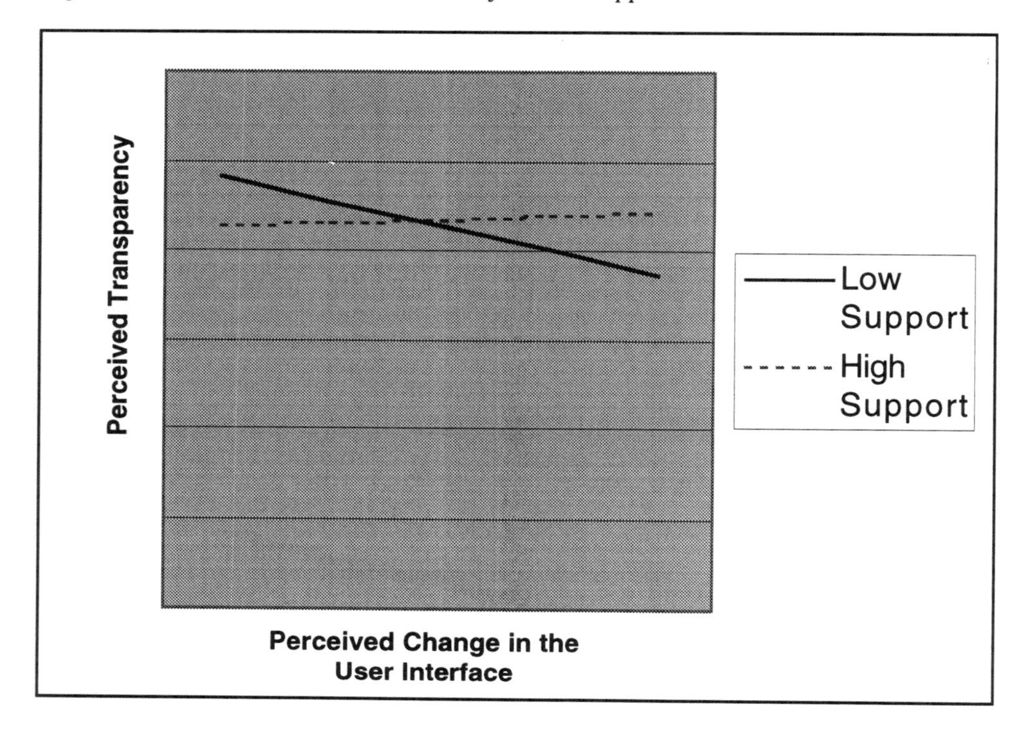

users in an organization during an upgrade. In other words, the effect of changes in the user interface on transparency depends upon the level of support given to the users. Figure 1 shows this effect graphically. Notice that when adequate support is given to users, changes in the user interface do not have a negative effect on transparency; however, if too little support is given, changes in the user interface become extremely important. This is a useful finding because it suggests the need to customize organizational support to the particular software package that is undergoing an upgrade. This finding suggests that an organization should allocate resources based upon changes in the user interface of a package, as opposed to changes in functionality, for example.

Surprisingly, the p-value for the external compatibility variable in the model is quite high (.3531), which indicates that compatibility might not be a major issue in the transparency of IS implementation. Logically one would have expected compatibility to play a larger role in determining perceived transparency; however, it is clear from the results of the study that if compatibility was really a problem, respondents were unable to distinguish the compatibility issues from other problems.

Technical quality is on the verge of significance at the .10 level with a p-value of .1115. Indeed it is surprising also that there is not a stronger relationship between the perceived quality of a software package and the perception of its implementation. This serves to make a strong case for deeper technological issues such as functionality and interface changes instead of quality as primary concerns for organizations.

ORGANIZATIONAL FACTORS

As with IT factors, there is a strong indication (p-value less than .0001) that organizational factors are an important consideration in a software upgrade. This result is consistent with previous studies of organizational innovation. The p-value for the variable representing conversion approaches (.3158) indicates that the difference in conversion approaches is most likely negligible. In such a case, the organization should choose the approach that will be least costly and thus most efficient. Similarly, the number of coping mechanisms used by an organization does not appear to be a significant predictor of the perceived transparency on the part of users. The p-value (.2246) shows that this particular factor might be a slightly better predictor than some possible alternatives, but still it is not small enough to warrant further consideration.

According to the results of the multiple regression analysis, the most important predictor is the change in functionality of the software package, as discussed previously. The next most important construct is the degree to which the organization depends upon the software that is undergoing change. The p-value (.0001) combined with the positive sign of the coefficient indicate that users are generally more satisfied with upgrades of critical software as compared to noncritical software. This result is contradictory to what was expected; however, in retrospect, it appears likely that an upgrade of software that is important to the organization will have more resources, better equipment, etc. that will in turn lead to an increase in perceived transparency. Although the organizational IT maturity construct is difficult to interpret because of the potential for misclassification of organizations by the respondents, it does not appear that the construct has a significant effect on the transparency of software upgrades since the p-value for the test is .2930. Again, however, this result must be used with caution.

USER FACTORS

User factors appear to be the least important group of factors in this particular study. The p-value for the partial F-test for the user factors is .0531, which is marginally significant at the .05 level. Thus, there is evidence to suggest that an organization should pay more attention to the other factors and then concentrate on the user factors as resources become available. .1085 is the p-value for the user acceptance variable in the multiple regression model. While this indicates marginal significance at the .10 level, it is certainly not enough evidence to conclude that user acceptance is a significant predictor of the transparency of software upgrades.

While user skill by itself does not contribute a great deal to the regression model, there is a significant interaction between the user skill and the amount of training given to users. In other words, users perceive training differently based upon their self-reported knowledge of computer systems. This relationship is explored more fully in the discussion of training given below; however, it is important to note that an organization should consider user skill in planning an upgrade, especially in conjunction with the amount of training required for employees. As discussed earlier, the primary importance of the support construct is in an interaction effect with the changes in the user interface. This should make organizations aware of the necessity of allocating support resources based upon the technological nature of an upgrade. Thus, support requirements might vary from one upgrade to another.

Figure 2: Interaction Between Training and User Skill

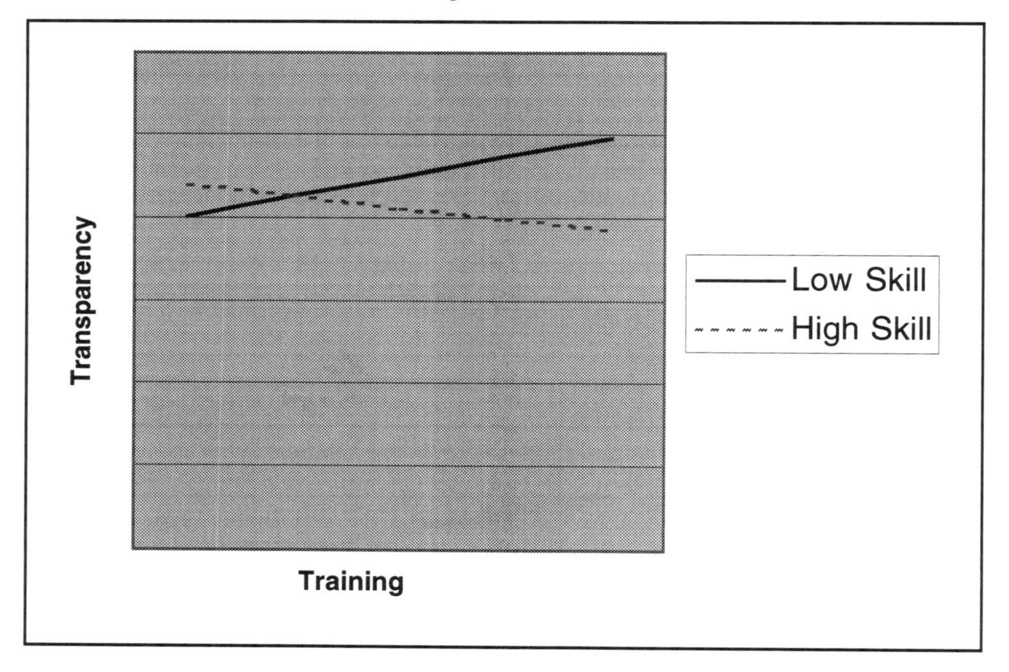

Similar to the user interface-support interaction effect described above, the effect of user training on transparency is dependent upon the skill level of the user. As shown in Figure 2 less skilled users prefer more training, while skilled users prefer less training.

SUMMARY

In summary, six of the 12 proposed factors have been shown to have a significant effect on the transparency of software upgrades. In addition, significant interaction effects exist between training and user skill, as well as between changes in the user interface and user support. To summarize the findings, a revised conceptual model is presented in Figure 3. This model can be used to identify potential problems in advance of an implementation and to plan for software upgrades in an organization.

The research presented in this book includes a number of significant advancements for IT managers. First and foremost, technical factors such as functionality and the user interface cannot be ignored in information systems implementation, contrary to widely published beliefs in the IS research community. Second, the extent to which an organization depends upon a particular technology is of great importance in determining the success of a technological change. Previously, the degree of dependence construct had been only theorized and not empirically tested (Shaw & Yadav, 1998). Organizations can use the degree of dependence measure to more accurately plan and sustain implementations that are both critical and noncritical. It is certainly likely, given the results of this study, that some IS implementations might overlook software packages perceived to be less important. If

Figure 3: Revised Model

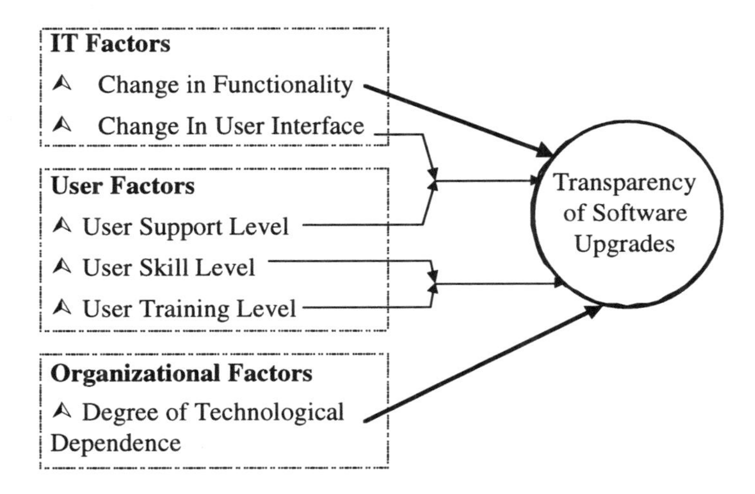

that is the case, possible dangers could arise if the software is actually more critical than originally thought.

Finally, two major interaction effects have been discovered. The effect of changes in the user interface of a software package can be moderated via the use of user support mechanisms, and the effect of user training is dependent upon the skill of the users to be trained. Thus, organizations would be wise to consider relaxing mandatory training statutes for skilled employees and to allocate resources to other training tasks or even to other areas. Also, existing rules-of-thumb might not be appropriate in cases where the level of one determinant depends on the level of another determinant. Such possibilities make a strong case for the treatment of each implementation, software upgrade, etc., as a special case instead of attempting to use a standard strategy for each case.

LIMITATIONS

The research in this book has two primary limitations which must be considered in order to properly interpret the results and conclusions of the study. The existence of these limitations does not invalidate the study, but anyone generalizing these results to other contexts or studies should realize and understand these limitations. It is certainly possible that these limitations could limit the generalizability of the results.

1. *Survey methodology*—As discussed earlier in the book, other research methodologies could have been used instead of a survey methodology. Case studies, field studies, or field experiments could certainly have been used to collect data for an empirical study to test the theoretical model. The survey methodology was chosen to improve generalizability and to study a broad range of phenomena (Benbasat, 1984); however, this methodology also limits the depth of the information that can be collected about a particular upgrade scenario. It is possible that the information collected in the survey omits important details about the organizational upgrade. Thus the survey methodology limits the richness of the information

that can be gathered. This should not significantly impact the conclusions of the study.

2. *Sample frame*—The true population of interest for this study is the set of all computer users in organizations; however, the sampled population for the study consists of IBM-compatible computer users who have filled out software and/or hardware registration cards at their company. Obviously these two sets are not equivalent. There are clearly a large number of computer users who never return a registration card for hardware or software. Similarly, many end-users in organizations never have an opportunity to fill out the cards if their hardware and software is installed by a centralized IS department. So, it is likely that the sampled population consists of a proportionately low number of end-users compared to managers and IS staff.

DETAILED RESEARCH

As shown by the study results, and as shown by many researchers previously, training is a critical factor in the success of any IS implementation. In the following chapter, Sein, Bostrom, and Olfman provide a hierarchical training model that can be used to update organizational training processes to fit more effectively with current technology. Similarly, their principles can be used to prepare properly for the installation of a new software package. Of course, training end-users is not the only problem for organizations when faced with an upgrade. The IT staff often has to be trained as well. Chapter 12, by Sherry Ryan, provides a model for "retraining" of IT employees that can help to improve training outcomes for IT staff.

The next three chapters, Chapters 13, 14, and 15, provide insight for IT managers into the inner workings of the people associated with upgrade projects, including systems analysts and end-users. These authors provide more detailed explanations and studies that support the basic claims made in the upgrade research presented earlier in the book. Also, the analyses provided by these authors suggest that understanding the motivations and attitudes of each individual in an upgrade project can significantly enhance the manager's effectiveness.

In the final chapter, an original article developed specifically for this book, Tiwana aids managers in coping with the upgrading of Internet-based software. The chapter presents a novel architecture for applying knowledge management to the problem of versioning of Internet applications, and the result is a useful mechanism for establishing and managing common characteristics of similar and dissimilar Internet software components. Specifically, the author proposes that the decomposition of Internet software packages facilitates an increased ability to manage and control relationships among the components of the package. Tiwana provides IT managers with a stimulating and thought-provoking approach to the management of Internet software development. As discussed earlier in the book, organizations need to be able to efficiently manage the transition from one package to another in order to minimize the disruption to end-users and to the organization. The method for decomposing Internet software is a unique approach that gives an organization the ability to upgrade components of software incrementally in order to minimize the negative impact on user and organizational productivity.

Chapter 11

Rethinking End-User Training Strategy: Applying a Hierarchical Knowledge-Level Model

Maung K. Sein
Agder College, Norway

Robert P. Bostrom
University of Georgia, USA

Lorne Olfman
Claremont Graduate University, USA

Training in information technology (IT) tools has traditionally been defined in terms of skills. Consequently, training methods and approaches have focused almost exclusively on ensuring that a trainee acquires the skills required to use an IT tool, and in a specific domain. With the advent and increasing use of enterprise-wide IT architectures, such as client/server, integrated processes such as workflow systems and integrated packages such as SAP, this narrow view of training will prove to be inadequate in preparing the workforce of the future. To train such a workforce, we propose a re-conceptualization of training based on a hierarchy of knowledge levels that a trainee will need. We then use this hierarchy to propose an integrated framework that can be used to develop a comprehensive training strategy. We offer directions for research that are needed to use our model to develop effective training strategies.

Traditional technology training is skills-focused. The goal is to teach programmers and users how to operate their tools and applications. In this chapter, we argue that such a narrow approach to training is not truly effective, and is inadequate for training the workforce of the future. We illustrate our thesis by the following example. Snell (1997) reports that an implementation of a client/server architecture at Carnegie Mellon University was a failure because it was limited to skills-focused training. Programmers did not see the need for the new development tools, and users could not distinguish between hardware and software problems.

The organizational landscape of future information technology (IT) use will differ

This chapter previously appeared in Journal of End User Computing, vol. 11, no. 1.

markedly from the traditional organizational function-based and end-user computing views of recent decades. The future workforce will be required to develop and operate applications based on enterprise-wide architectures, processes, and systems. These include integrative applications such as SAP that feature workflow systems and run on groupware platforms that depend on client/server architectures. IT will be integrated into the very fabric of organizations, which will be characterized by a focus on knowledge management and continuous learning.

In fact, the technologies noted above have been in use for some time, but are rapidly changing. This means that the learning process for computer users must be rapid and continuous. Rapid changes have led to enormous spending on IT training. Nelson, Whitener, and Philcox (1995) estimate it at over $5 billion in 1994. Still, the lack of successful implementation of new technologies often has been a lack of skilled personnel (Snell, 1997). Accelerated and continuous learning requires a different level of focus in IT training practices, one not found in traditional skills-focused training.

One of the aspects of a higher level of focus is that of conceptual training. Snell (1997) describes how Carnegie Mellon finally realized that in order to successfully deploy a client/ server system, both IT staff and end users had to be given a broad conceptual view of the overall architecture. In this chapter, we introduce a framework of knowledge levels that comprise a more complete range of knowledge outcomes for training the workforce of the future. The framework covers six types of knowledge from syntactical to meta-cognition. It is designed to serve as the cornerstone of developing an effective training strategy. We define a training strategy as the selection of a training method appropriate to a specific type of trainee and a specific IT tool given specific knowledge outcomes.

The rest of the chapter is organized as follows: The next section indicates the importance of conceptualizing IT training in terms of a set of knowledge outcomes rather than as a task of cost minimization. The following section presents prior research on the knowledge outcome, and introduces the "levels of knowledge" framework. Then a discussion of training research frameworks leads to the presentation of another framework, this one related to designing training strategies. The chapter concludes with a discussion of implications for practice and suggestions for further research.

CONCEPTUALIZING TRAINING IN TERMS OF OUTCOMES

We noted above that IT training is big business today. Doane (1996) describes an SAP implementation where training costs, including change management, were in the order of 10% of the total implementation costs. Some analysts believe that this figure can rise to as much as 20%. With burgeoning costs come attempts to devise innovative methods for cost minimization. A current popular approach is to develop or acquire computer-based training (CBT) packages. In addition, companies form partnerships with universities or even competitors to outsource some of the training burden (Blumfield, 1997). However, there is no evidence about the extent to which these cost reduction measures are influencing the effectiveness of training as reflected in use of the IT tools on the job. Cost minimization may reduce training benefits.

The potential intangible benefits of training can outweigh costs if the training is appropriate and effective. That is, the training must give the trainee appropriate knowledge and the motivation to use the system (Bostrom, Olfman, & Sein, 1990). It is evident that a traditional approach falls short in defining appropriate knowledge. Moreover, the traditional

Figure 1: A Research Framework for End-User Training (adapted from Bostrom et al., 1990)

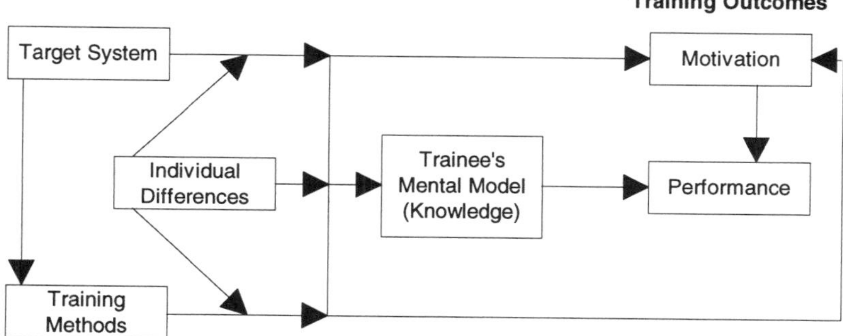

Table 1: Levels of Software Knowledge

Knowledge Level	Individual Productivity Software Example	Integrative Application Software Example
Command-Based *syntax and semantics*	Mouse click on a button to delete a sentence	Mouse click on a button to enter a transaction
Tool Procedural *combining commands to do generic tasks*	Create a document	Create a transaction
Business Procedural *application of tool procedures to a task*	Do a mail merge (produce letters for a group of people)	Query the database for other functional transactions
Tool Conceptual *the big picture of what to do with the tool*	Productivity tool	Workflow tool
Business Motivational *what can the tool do for the trainee and the organization*	Raises my skill level, I can do more in my job, my company can raise productivity	Enables consistent transactions across organizational functions
Meta-cognition: *learning to learn*	Teach learners to recognize and use a visual-kinesthetic pattern	Teach learners to use the learning cycle in exercises

approach cannot help devise a comprehensive training strategy because there is no known framework that can be used to develop such a strategy.

The value of a training strategy is that it can enable trainers to determine how to deliver training appropriately and effectively. A move to Web-based CBT and electronic performance support systems (EPSS) could be appropriate for certain users and IT tools given specific training outcomes. However, without a guiding framework, there is no clear indication about when and where CBT should be used in place of classroom instruction, or other forms of delivery (e.g., video), or what the contents of the training materials should be. Further, without a complete picture of the outcomes of training, knowing which training methods are right for specific users and tools may still make the training process fall short of achieving the organizational needs for a workforce that must perform continuous learning.

PRIOR RESEARCH ON KNOWLEDGE OUTCOMES IN TRAINING

Background

Bostrom, Olfman, and Sein (1990) presented a learning and training research framework. This framework specifies that the software to be learned, the training method used, and the trainee's individual characteristics act independently and in combination to determine training outcomes (see Figure 1). Training outcomes are defined as motivation and performance (ability to use the software on the job after training). These outcomes are predicated on understanding, that is the trainee's knowledge after training. Knowledge is defined in terms of a mental model, which is a "user's internal understanding of the system that guides interaction and helps solve problems" (Olfman & Sein, 1997, p. 3). The definition of the performance outcome is based on an in-depth view of individual learning, but it still emphasizes the tool (or the target system). Research carried out under the rubric of this model has mainly focused on testing methods that can efficaciously help a user develop accurate mental models (e.g., Santhanam and Sein, 1994; Sein and Bostrom, 1989). Key issues not addressed include how the tool fits into the strategies and processes of the organization.

The motivation outcome of training has been addressed in another stream of research. Olfman and Bostrom (1991) examined the use of personally relevant training to enhance learning and motivation. Webster and Martocchio (1992, 1995) studied the introduction of playfulness into the training process. Compeau and Higgins (1995a, 1995b) examined the impact of behavior modeling on trainees' self-efficacy.

These studies represent a major departure from viewing training solely in terms of the performance outcome. However, their main emphasis was to make training a motivationally satisfying experience. Olfman and Bostrom's work did emphasize the relation between the tool and the trainee's work situation. However, it did not address how the tool or the use of

Figure 2: The Training and Learning Process (from Compeau et al., 1995)

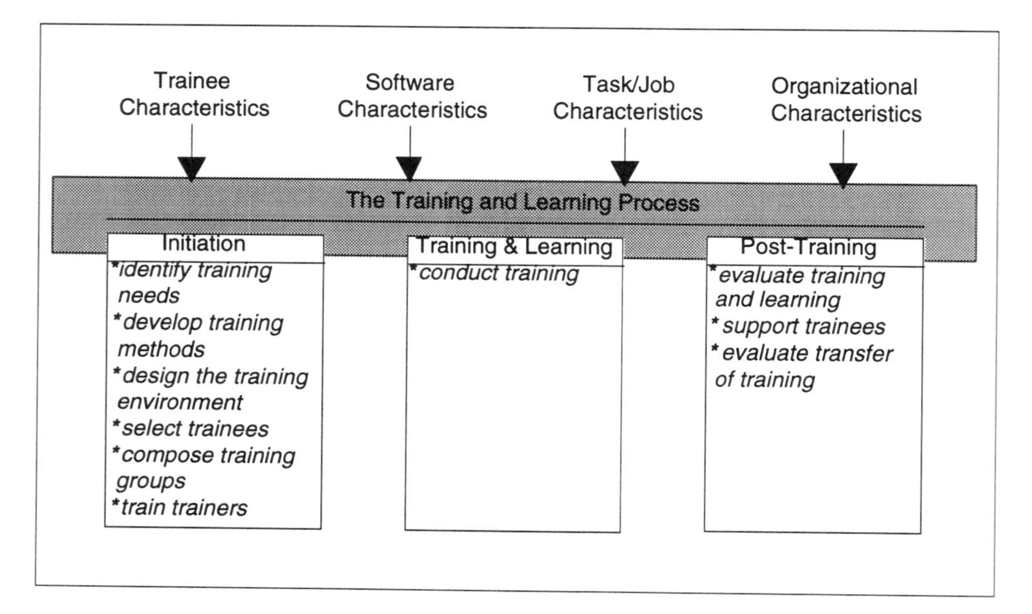

it fits into the organizational framework, or the individual's or the organization's objectives. Recently, Sein, Santhanam and Oliviera (1997) applied the theory of planned behavior to motivate trainees to learn the target system. While they were able to increase the trainees' motivational levels, they found no effect on the learning outcome.

Proposed User Knowledge Level Framework

One question that may arise is the kinds of links that exist between the motivational and performance outcomes. The Bostrom, Olfman, and Sein model indicates that motivation influences performance, but not vice versa. If one is motivated, does that automatically mean that one will also know more about the system at the end of the training? This presupposes that performance and motivational outcomes are distinct and independent outcomes of training. In our view, an individual's knowledge of a tool (or any object for that matter) can include the motivational component. This is explicitly stated in a hierarchy of knowledge levels that we propose below.

Shneiderman (1983) viewed knowledge content of a tool in terms of syntax (the language of interaction) and semantics (the meanings of the commands). In terms of the knowledge outcome, both levels were essential. Anderson's (1982) levels of declarative (what is it) and procedural (how to) extend the hierarchy further. However, both views deal entirely with the tool itself.

Using Rasmussen's (1986) abstraction hierarchy of physical systems, Ye (1991) developed a five-level knowledge content hierarchy to classify a user's understanding of a system. His levels are:

- physical — appearance of an object,
- logical — reasons for the physical existence of the object,
- functional— working relationships within the object,
- conceptual — abstractions that can be applied in different domains, and
- objective — goals and purposes of the object.

Ye's framework advances the concept of knowledge beyond the tool. Incorporating the conceptual and objective levels in training will definitely broaden its scope. However, whether the conceptual level of knowledge would lead to employees making inferences beyond the training context is not clear. Moreover, Ye's lower levels — physical and logical — are less distinct in terms of the use of IT tools than concepts such as syntax and semantics. There is a clear need to extend such knowledge hierarchies.

We propose a six-level knowledge content hierarchy. We make a major departure from the cited research by integrating motivation and meta-cognition as key knowledge components. Table 1 shows the framework. We use two types of software, individual productivity software and integrative applications, to illustrate the framework. We briefly describe each level of knowledge below.

Command-Based: This is knowledge of the syntax and semantics of IT (software) tools. The syntax of a tool is its set of commands and the command structures. Semantics are the meaning of those commands. Without this level of knowledge, users are unable to recover from errors or transfer knowledge from one system to another. Some training methods and manuals cover the semantic knowledge level. Generally speaking, end-user training focuses on command-based knowledge.

Tool Procedural: This level refers to grouping individual commands to perform a function such as creating a document. Tool procedural knowledge is needed to synthesize a set of commands into a method for accomplishing a generic task. As with command-based knowledge, most end-user training covers tool procedural knowledge.

Business Procedural: This is knowledge about applying tool procedures to business processes. For example, to prepare letters for a group of people, the "mail merge" function of a typical word processor could be taught in the context of this task. Another term for this level might be task-based knowledge. Business procedural knowledge has recently become of interest to software trainers, especially in the form of EPSS, which aim to provide just-in-time training on the job.

Tool Conceptual: This level of knowledge focuses on the big picture, that is, the overall purpose and structure of the IT tool. It provides a basis for being able to transfer learning to new situations. For example, a conceptual model of an ERP system is that it acts as a workflow tool. The concept of a workflow would be presented to trainees at the outset of training. Currently, tool conceptual knowledge is rarely provided in traditional training. If it is, it is almost always outlined in terms of command architecture. Providing appropriate tool conceptual knowledge can be expected to facilitate the learning of command-based, tool procedural, and business procedural knowledge because it acts as an "advance organizer" for understanding these knowledge levels.

Business Motivational: This is knowledge about what the IT tool can do for the trainee, the trainee's job, and the trainee's organization. In this sense, we differ from Ye's conceptualization of "objective," which refers to the tool itself. Business motivational knowledge typically requires instructor-led training to show how the software to be learned fits into the overall job function and the organization. One possibility is to have managers be involved in providing this type of knowledge.

Meta-Cognition: This level of knowledge focuses on learning to learn. One view of meta-cognition knowledge is that it provides learners with the ability to be successful in any type of learning environment. Another aspect is that learners can discover what they have

Figure 3: Training Strategy Framework

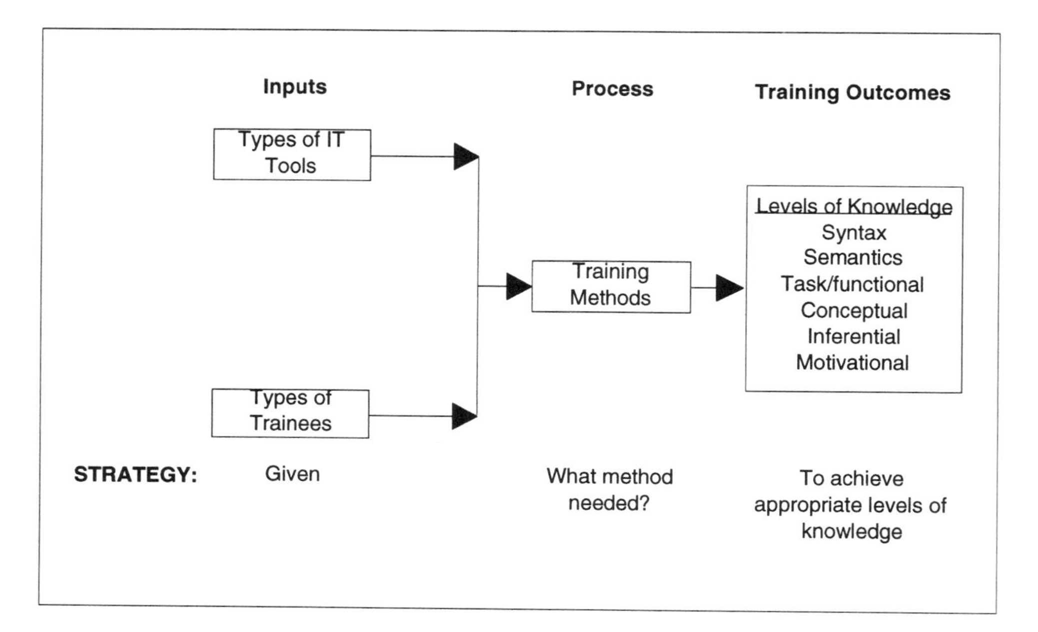

learned from a particular training. That is, they gain the ability to transfer their learning to other IT tools. This is important in an environment that stresses continuous learning.

Training literature and practices have almost exclusively stressed command-based and tool procedural knowledge, and to some extent business procedural knowledge. These levels define the traditional view of end-user training. In the context of current and future uses of IT (as outlined in the introduction), training methods need to be extended to include the tool conceptual, business motivational and meta-cognition levels of knowledge. This was the lesson learned by Carnegie Mellon University in their client/server architecture implementation (Snell, 1997). In addition, there is the problem that there is no stated comprehensive framework in the literature or in practice that can be used to develop appropriate training strategies.

PRIOR RESEARCH ON TRAINING FRAMEWORKS AND STRATEGIES

Background

The research literature on end-user training emphasizes that the most effective training of software users will be accomplished using a life cycle approach (Sein, Bostrom, & Olfman, 1987). The life cycle approach (see Figure 2) directs trainers to focus on stages before, during, and after the delivery of training. This approach has recently been reiterated by Compeau, Olfman, Sein, and Webster (1995), and by Olfman and Sein (1997).

The training and learning process cycle has three stages: initiation, training and learning (delivery), and post-training. In the initiation stage, the emphasis is on the design of training, matching trainees to appropriate training methods, and training the trainers. The delivery stage focuses on conducting training. Important rules to consider are: give trainees a strong grounding in tool conceptual knowledge and business motivational knowledge, and aim at building accurate and flexible mental models. In the post-training stage, the aim is to provide evaluation and support. It must be recognized that learning does not stop at the end of a training program.

Research on end-user training has examined the full range of the training life cycle. This includes work on assessing training needs (e.g., Nelson et al., 1995), assessing training materials (e.g., Carroll & Rosson, 1995), and matching learning styles with training approaches (e.g., Bostrom et al., 1990). However, research has not addressed the issue of developing effective training strategies. Moreover, a survey of the practitioner literature adds little value in this domain. Thus, there is no guidance on answering a question such as: How does a training organization decide whether a clerical user with a concrete learning style requires the same training content as a top executive with a concrete learning style? Without guidance for developing IT training strategies, trainers are left to design training based on personal experience or recommendations from benchmarking studies.

In fact, the issue of developing an IT training strategy is even more complex. A training strategy enables trainers to match methods to specific IT tools and trainees given specific knowledge outcomes. While most trade literature on end-user training describes the potential advantages of computer-based training technologies (e.g., multimedia presentations, Web-based training), there is little written about how they can be used effectively.

Training Strategy Framework

The literature cited in this chapter comes from a sample of studies that were published in mainstream information systems journals. As we noted, none of these studies provides a set of guidelines that can be used to establish a comprehensive training strategy for an organization. Nevertheless, they provide a rich source of information and ideas which we integrate here to develop such a strategy framework.

The crucial question a training strategy must address is: *Given an IT tool on which a specific user type needs to be trained, what training approaches and methods should be used to attain the appropriate level(s) of knowledge?* An effective strategy will match the appropriate method with the appropriate user for the appropriate tool. Therefore, our framework (see Figure 3) is based on a classification of trainees, specific training approaches for different classes of IT tools, and the level of knowledge required for using the tools. The output of the training process is defined by the levels of knowledge (discussed above) acquired by the trainees. Below, we discuss the other elements of the framework: the input elements of IT tools and trainees, and the process elements of training approaches and methods.

It is heartening to note that some vendors have recognized the need for an integrated strategy and are offering documents to their customers to that end. A recent example from SAP illustrates our model. This example outlines the content of recommendations from SAP to one of its clients who recently considered purchasing the software. One training strategy recommended by SAP is:

> *Transactional user* training should contain a high percentage of *hands-on exercises*, have *limited theoretical discussion about the application*, and if possible, the training should be led by a member of the organization that best understands the user work requirements.

(The italics are ours to exemplify different elements of our strategy framework.) The recommended SAP strategies are not always complete in terms of addressing all of the elements in our framework. However, the notion of articulating training strategies is important and should be supported by the research community. Research needs to evaluate and integrate these innovative strategies to form normative prescriptions. Below we discuss specific elements of our framework using the SAP strategy to illustrate them.

Types of Trainees

As discussed above, matching trainees to training approaches has been studied extensively. The Education Psychology literature, adapted by researchers in end-user training, promotes the aptitude-treatment-interaction paradigm (see Bostrom et al., 1990 for a review). Here, the goal is to tailor the training approach and contents according to the trainee's characteristics. Examples of such characteristics include prior knowledge, demographics, cognitive abilities and preferences, and learning style. What is not addressed by the aptitude-treatment interaction concept is which specific combination of content and aspects of IT tools should be taught to specific users. Rockart and Flannery (1983) classified computer users in terms of their level of direct relationships with the technology. Users ranged from those who only benefited from the outputs of a computer system to those who actually produced the outputs. While this classification was useful in the context of 1980s end-user computing, the IT landscape has undergone much change since then.

SAP proposes a topology that is in some ways similar to that defined by Rockart and Flannery. According to SAP, the first step in developing an "End-User Training Strategy" is to recognize various types of users, and define their needs. This is considered "all important to the success of a well-conceived training plan." The recommendations outline three kinds of user types:

- Transactional —a user who will use the software to carry out specific transactions.
- Casual — a user who will use the software to retrieve information.
- Power User — a user who has strong knowledge of computing and can act as an interface between the project team and the user community. (It appears that power users come from either of the first two categories.)

While these are useful conceptualizations, we believe that a classification of users must address end users' job features and functional levels. One possible approach is to categorize trainees as top management, middle management, staff, clerical and operational, and then according to abilities, learning styles, and motivation. It is also useful to consider that different types of end users may require different levels of knowledge about IT tools.

So, a top executive will need to know about the conceptual and business motivational levels of a tool in order to make decisions about using it to the company's advantage. A clerical end user may be more concerned with learning to use the tool, and thus should focus on the command-based and tool and business procedural levels. We believe that the business motivational and meta-cognition levels of knowledge must be incorporated into every type of training.

Training Methods

There is an abundance of research that evaluates various approaches to delivering training. Sein and Bostrom (1989) studied the types of conceptual models that can be used to produce the most effective mental models. Santhanam and Sein (1994) and Olfman and Mandviwalla (1994) compared conceptual and procedural approaches to training. Olfman and Mandviwalla (1995) studied different levels of documentation support for training. Compeau and Higgins (1995a) examined behavior modeling. These are but a handful of the studies in this stream of literature. The human-computer interaction (HCI) literature is rich in studies examining such innovative approaches as exploratory learning. However, all these studies focused on the performance outcome of IT tool training.

A related topic of interest is EPSS. These systems aim to provide just-in-time training, while minimizing instructor-led training (or put another way, while maximizing self-based training). A survey of users (Harp, Satzinger, & Taylor, 1997) notes that most feel they are self-directed in their learning styles. This seems to indicate that EPSS would be an effective training approach. However, some users prefer face-to-face training, especially on a one-on-one basis. Video training was not rated as effective as most other approaches. Snell (1997) describes how CMU used a team approach to training, where sessions were conducted by a team composed of users, systems engineers, and a trained trainer.

- Some general training issues that have recently appeared in the trade press are: a discussion of the advantages of classroom versus computer-based approaches to training where the authors recommend that classroom training is best for emotionally based training material (Gordon & Hequet, 1997) and total learning (Sims, 1996);
- a description of competency-based experiential learning (Ricks, 1997);
- a discussion of the benefits of on-the-job training (Filipczak, 1996a);
- a discussion of an approach to training that focuses on getting users up and running and able to explore features, that reduces travel costs, and aims to utilize low-cost community college courses (Filipczak, 1996b).

SAP recommends different training strategies for each of the training groups (i.e., transactional, casual, and power user). It is suggested that transactional users need more training than casual users, and should be trained with hands-on exercises, while getting little "theoretical discussion about the application." Casual users need to learn the structure of the complete business organization as well as how to do data retrievals. Power users are seen as potential trainers for the other two groups. With respect to training approaches, SAP recommends not producing reference manuals, and to stay away from self-study tutorials, lesson plans, and computer-based training. Instead, the approach is to use "mastery workshops" and "active learning tutoring". These suggestions contradict some of the directions being taken by end-user training organizations who are aiming to take the EPSS approach. It is evident that there is a need to develop a good classification of training approaches.

Types of IT Tools

Whether a training method that is efficacious for a specific IT tool and for a specific type of user will also work for another type of tool and another category of user is not certain. Research has focused mostly on the relationship between different types of software and the learning process. Davis and Bostrom (1993) examined the differences between command-line and graphical user interfaces. Sein, Olfman, Bostrom, and Davis (1993) also examined this relationship.

In addition to specifying how each category of tools requires specific tailoring of content, the more important question may well be the motivational aspect. For example, software differs in terms of its type of use: mandatory versus optional (voluntary). Since motivation is a key issue in providing training, it may be important to vary the kinds of training provided in terms of the required use of the tools.

To illustrate, we return to the example of SAP, which is an integrative software application. Use of this type of application package is mandatory. While workers are more likely to use software packages more often and in more mandatory situations (e.g., SAP's "transactional" users), managers' use of software will likely be much more critical and focused (e.g., SAP's "casual" users). Even in categories of IT tools whose use may appear voluntary (e.g., a suite of personal productivity tools), that may not be the case. For example, with SAP, some of the interactions can be performed through Microsoft Office applications.

RESEARCH DIRECTIONS AND CONCLUSIONS

Research Directions

We proposed a level of knowledge hierarchy based on prior research, our experience, and anecdotal evidence from practice. We then applied the levels of knowledge to create a training strategy framework. Our framework needs to be validated. To that end, we suggest some relevant research directions.

In order to help organizations develop effective training strategies, the research community needs to address five key issues:

- develop a classification of user types;
- develop a classification of IT tools;
- develop a framework of training methods and approaches;
- validate a framework of knowledge levels (such as the one proposed by us); and
- develop validated training strategies—given user type and IT tool, what are appropriate levels of knowledge needed and what training method(s) should be used?

The overarching research question that needs to be addressed is: How can training strategies facilitate IS professionals and end users to become effective users of information technology? Specifically, two broad research questions can be identified:

Research question #1: What specific methods exist for assessing the training needs of different categories of trainees of IT-based tools?

This question is related to needs assessment and developing the content of training within the context of the socio-technical environment of the organization. Specifically, what and how much (in terms of knowledge level classification) should specific trainees know about IT tools? What else, in addition to the tools themselves, should the different categories of end users know about the business processes? company policies? job requirements? functional needs?

Research question #2: What are the most appropriate training methods for specific types of trainees and specific IT tools?

We have identified several training approaches and methods in previous sections. The key issue here is given various types of users and IT tools, and the desired levels of knowledge to be achieved, which training methods should be applied to gain effective training outcomes?

A related question is: What are the best ways to design training so that the methods identified can be most effectively delivered? Several mechanisms exist to deliver training content: classroom training, one-on-one training, on-line tutorials, self-study manuals, etc. Which one is most effective for a specific class of end user? How can effective outcomes be most economically achieved? How can new technological innovations such as CBT and Web-based training be used to deliver training materials and assess training outcomes? Is in-house training more appropriate or should outside consultants be hired? If in-house training is used, what is the best way to train trainers?

While this paper emphasizes training of end users, several of our concepts can be applicable to training of IS staff. Which of these concepts are specifically relevant and how they apply to IS staff training are interesting and important areas of study.

Conclusions

This chapter emphasizes that for the workforce of the future, a broader view of end-user training is needed. Indeed, we show that this extended view has become imperative in today's fast-changing world of technological innovations. Examples from the field suggest that it is not enough to emphasize the skills/knowledge outcome of training. As Snell (1997, p. 21) concludes in his description of CMU's C/S roll out: "To make a dent in the client/server skills crisis, you've got to teach it all." In the traditional vernacular, training needs to move closer to education. Using our framework, or formulating their own, we invite researchers to develop a training strategies knowledge base that organizations can use to guide their training efforts. The objective is to develop a workforce who will successfully apply to their jobs what they have learned about IT tools. We invite the research community to take up the challenge of helping the practitioner community achieve this important goal.

Note: A previous version of this chapter (under a different title) was published in the Proceedings of the 1998 ACM SIGCPR Conference.

REFERENCES

Anderson, J. R. (1982). Acquisition of cognitive skill. *Psychological Review*, 4, 369-406.

Blumfield, M. (1997). Learning to share. *Training,* 34(4), 38-42.

Bostrom, R. P., Olfman, L., and Sein, M. K. (1990). The importance of learning style in end-user training. *MIS Quarterly*, 14(1), 101-119.

Carroll, J. M., and Rosson, M. B. (1995). Managing evaluation goals. *Communications of the ACM*, 38(7), 40-48.

Compeau, D. R., and Higgins, D. A. (1995a). Application of social cognitive theory to training for computer skills. *Information Systems Research*, 6(2), 118-143.

Compeau, D. R., and Higgins, D. A. (1995b). Computer self-efficacy: Development of a measure and initial test. *MIS Quarterly*, 19(2), 189-211.

Compeau, D., Olfman, L., Sein, M., and Webster, J. (1995). End-user training and learning. *Communications of the ACM*, 38(7), 24-26.

Davis, S.A. and Bostrom, R.P. (1993). Training end users: An experimental investigation of the roles of the computer interface and training methods. *MIS Quarterly*, 17(1), 61-85.

Doane, M. (1996). *In the path of the whirlwind.* Sioux Falls, SD: The Consulting Alliance.

Filipczak, B. (1996a). Who owns your OJT? *Training*, 33(12), 44-49.

Filipczak, B. (1996b). Training on the cheap. *Training*, 33(5), 28-34.

Gordon, J., and Hequet, M. (1997). Live and in person. *Training*, 34(3), 24-31.

Harp, C., Satzinger, J., and Taylor, S. (1997). Many paths to learning software. *Training and Development*, 51(5), 81-84.

Nelson, R. R., Whitener, E. M., and Philcox, H. H. (1995). The assessment of end-user training needs. *Communications of the ACM*, 38(7), 27-39.

Olfman L., and Bostrom, R. P. (1991). End-user software training: An experimental comparison of methods to enhance motivation. *Journal of Information Systems*, 1, 249-266.

Olfman, L., and Mandviwalla, M. (1994). Conceptual versus procedural software training for graphical user interfaces: A longitudinal field experiment. *MIS Quarterly*, 18(4), 405-426.

Olfman, L., and Mandviwalla, M. (1995). An experimental comparison of end user software training manuals. *Information Systems Journal*, 5(1), 19-36.

Olfman, L., and Sein, M. K. (1997). Ten lessons from research for end-user trainers. *End User Computing Management* (94-00-07), Auerbach.

Rasmussen, J. (1986). *Information Processing and Human-Machine Interaction: An Approach to Cognitive Engineering.* New York: North-Holland.

Ricks, D. M. (1997). How are your experiential components working? *Training*, 34(1), 138.

Rockart, J. F., and Flannery, L. S. (1983). The management of end-user computing. *Communications of the ACM*, 10, 776-784.

Santhanam, R., and Sein, M. K. (1994). Improving end-user efficiency: Effects of conceptual training and nature of interaction. *Information Systems Research*, 5(4), 378-399.

Sein, M. K., and Bostrom, R. P. (1989). Individual differences and conceptual models in training novice users. *Human-Computer Interaction*, 4, 197-229.

Sein, M. K., Olfman, L., and Bostrom, R. P. (1987). Training end users to compute: Cognitive, motivational and social issues. *INFOR*, 25, 3, 236-255.

Sein, M. K., Olfman, L., Bostrom, R. P., and Davis, S. A. (1993). The importance of visualization ability in predicting learning success. *International Journal of Man-Machine Studies*, 39(4), 599-620.

Sein, M. K, Santhanam, R. and Oliviera, M. (1997). Applying the theory of planned behavior to end-user training and learning. *Proceedings of the AIS Conference of the Americas*, 542-544.

Shneiderman, B (1983). Direct manipulation: A step beyond programming languages. *IEEE Computer*, 16(8), 57-69.

Snell, N. (1997). Why can't Johnny do Client/Server? *Inside Technology Training*, July/August, 21-26.

Sims, D. (1996). Who needs the classroom ... besides your students. *Training*, 33(11), 106.

Webster, J., and Martocchio, J. J. (1992). Microcomputer playfulness: Development of a measure with workplace implications. *MIS Quarterly*, 16(2), 201-226.

Webster, J., and Martocchio, J. J. (1995). The differential effects of software training previews on training outcomes. *Journal of Management*, 21(4), 757-787.

Ye, N. (1991). Development and validation of a cognitive model of human knowledge system: Toward an effective adaptation to differences in cognitive skills. Unpublished Ph.D. dissertation, Lafayette, IN: Purdue University.

Chapter 12

A Model of the Motivation for IT Retraining

Sherry D. Ryan
University of North Texas, USA

The skill-sets of many information technology (IT) professionals are becoming obsolete as IT changes accelerate. Organizations are retraining many software developers with legacy systems skills to skills required in the new Internet-based, client-server and object-oriented paradigms. This type of retraining is not incremental, but entails major cognitive, methodological and procedural shifts. Given its importance, cost, and currency, processes that impact the effectiveness of training should be considered. Trainee motivation is one such process that should be investigated because it is more malleable than other aspects, such as trainees' cognitive ability. This chapter proposes a model of motivational intentions and antecedents in this information technology retraining context. Theoretical background for the model is described. In addition, the implications of the model and its potential utilization in influencing motivational intentions, and ultimately improving retraining outcomes, is discussed.

Advances in information technology are providing organizations with exciting new opportunities. Organizations today can expand their market reach through globalized networks, augment their product lines with knowledge-based products and services, and use more agile organizational structures such as virtual teams. Yet, to leverage these new opportunities, firms are finding that they are requiring new and different skills from their information technology professionals. Most staffs are skilled in legacy systems application development, but are not versed in newer technologies (Chabrow, 1995; King, 1997). Because of the tremendous technological transitions, companies with in-house IT professionals are increasingly finding their skills obsolete (Gottlieb, 1993). Many companies, therefore, are retraining existing employees with skills that are appropriate for this new computing environment.

Because of the increased requirement for retraining due to technical advances and other

This chapter originally appeared in the Information Resources Management Journal, vol. 12, no. 4.

environmental factors, it is now more critical than ever that researchers examine the underlying processes that determine the effectiveness of IT retraining. Trainee motivation is one such process. Maier (1973) has maintained that training performance will most likely be poor if motivation is low, even if individuals possess the requisite ability to learn the content that is presented. Recently, researchers have focused on pretraining motivation because of the belief that, at least compared with general cognitive ability, motivation is more subject to marked change (Wlodkowski, 1985).

This chapter proposes a model of the individual motivation to retrain in IT, casting it as an intentional process, and specifying the antecedents of retraining intentions. This is an extension to prior research in several ways. First, this research specifically investigates *retraining*. That is, the training of employees whose current jobs, knowledge and skills have begun to become obsolete and will require significant, rather than incremental, change. The proposed model of motivation in this retraining context highlights salient antecedents that are proposed to be more intense than in a training environment in which the targeted skills to be acquired are incremental in nature. Next, this research specifically addresses the IT professional. Previous research concerning IT training and motivation has primarily concentrated on the end-user (e.g., Igbaria et al., 1996). However, in today's dynamic environment where technologies are rapidly changing, focus must also be given to the retraining of IT professionals. This research helps to fill the existing void. Finally, this chapter proposes a theoretical basis for further investigation of IT retraining. Many researchers have argued that much IS research lacks theoretical grounding (Lucas, 1991; Jarvenpaa et al., 1985). As suggested by Lucas (1991), this chapter draws upon existing studies from the information systems literature, as well as the reference disciplines of organizational behavior and human resource management.

This chapter will first investigate skill obsolescence issues. Second, prior research on the motivation to retrain will be reviewed. Third, the proposed model of motivation intention to retrain and its antecedents will be presented and discussed in an IT context.

SKILL OBSOLESCENCE

For many years, the IT environment was centered around the mainframe. As organizations are shifting to newer, more flexible technologies, such as Internet-based technologies, client/server and object-orientation, they are finding that their developers' skills are not sufficient to meet changing demands. For example, Chabrow (1995) indicates that only 30% to 50% of the applications developers in the U.S. possess the requisite client-server skills. Yet, industry surveys have shown that 75% of new multi-user applications are predicted to run on client/server platforms by 1999 (King, 1997).

This type of technological obsolescence is a key human resource (HR) dilemma (Gist et al., 1988). Fossum et al. (1986) define obsolescence as occurring "when the person requirements of a job which are demanded by its duties and responsibilities become incongruent with the stock of knowledge, skills and abilities currently possessed by the individual." In the context of the shift in software development from legacy systems to that of Internet-based, client/server and/or object-oriented, software developers are finding that the job requirements, and the requisite skills for essential job functioning, have indeed shifted. To implement technologically current systems, organizations must either retrain existing IT personnel or hire new IT professionals.

The human resource issues surrounding this staffing dilemma are complex. However, several salient factors are causing organizations to consider the retraining option. First, firms are finding that the availability of qualified programmers and developers with the requisite skill-set is inadequate to meet current market demands (Gottlieb, 1993; King, 1997). Second, hiring from outside the organizations brings individuals who may have certain technical competencies, but lack valuable company-specific knowledge regarding work processes and the competitive environment (Chabrow, 1995). Therefore, retraining has become a critical HR strategy for eliminating technological obsolescence and enabling employees with the requisite skills to fulfill future job-related requirements.

Retraining existing developers, however, is expensive and time consuming. The Gartner Group estimates the cost of retraining a programmer that earns $50,000 a year to be approximately $18,000. In terms of time, it is estimated that legacy developers require as much as 40 days of training to acquire new client/server skills (Chabrow, 1995), and between 6-18 months when moving to object-oriented methodologies (Scholtz et al., 1993). Part of the reason that the training time is so long is that the change in mindset required to move from a mainframe-based procedural programming background to that of newer environments is significant. Some indicate that the paradigm shift is the single biggest obstacle that IT professionals must overcome (Due, 1993). Especially in the case of object-orientation, Pinson (1994) found a strong resistance towards moving to the new paradigm. Because of the

Figure 1: Motivational Intentions and Antecedents in an Information Technology Retraining Context

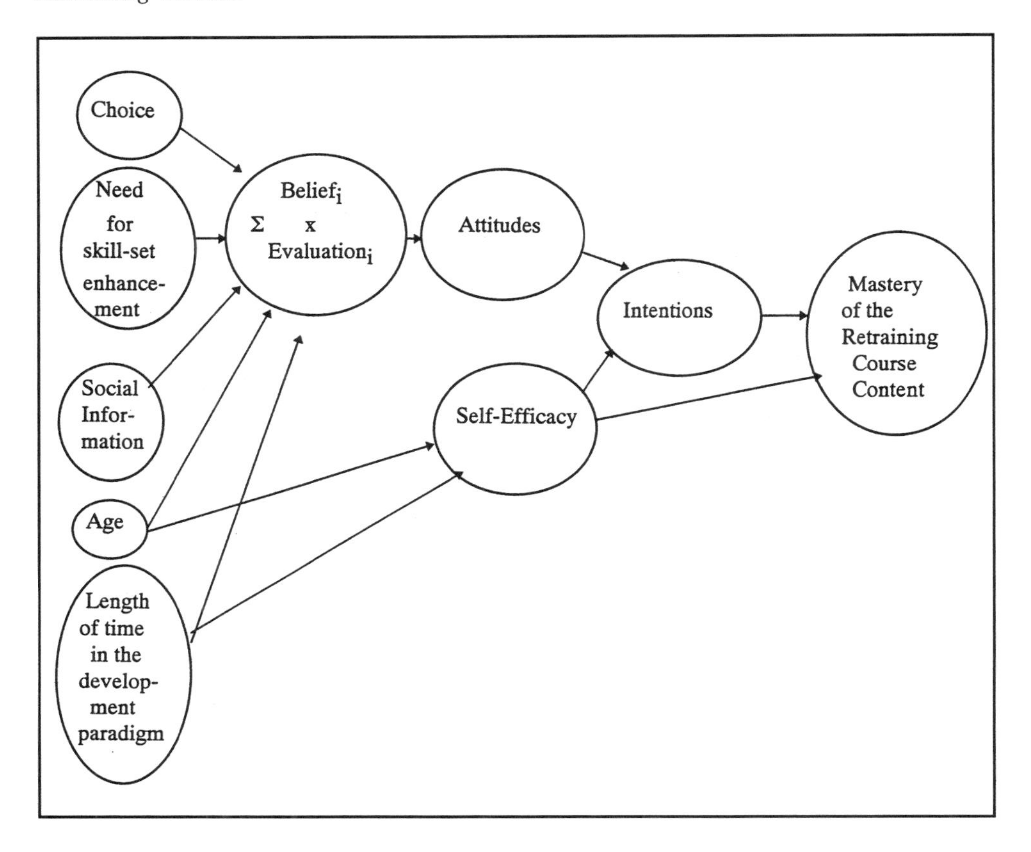

time, expense, and effort involved, it is important for organizations to consider ways in which retraining outcomes can be enhanced.

TRAINING MOTIVATION RESEARCH

In industry, retraining program strategies have focused on content, largely ignoring other factors such as motivation (Del Vecchio, 1994). Recently, however, academic researchers have focused on pretraining motivation because of its potential malleability (Wlodkowski, 1985). A number of studies have shown positive relationships between motivation and training outcomes. In a training program designed to improve skills in conducting performance appraisals and in providing feedback, Baldwin et al. (1991) found that pretraining motivation was related to learning. Facteau et al. (1995) found a significant relationship between pretraining motivation and trainee perceived skills transfer in a large-scale study of state government supervisors and managers. Also, Warr and Bunce (1995) found a significant correlation between pretraining motivation and a learning score in an open learning environment. While not all studies showed a significant relationship between learning outcomes and motivation (e.g., Noe & Schmitt, 1986), there is enough supporting evidence to indicate that training motivation is a useful dimension to study.

MOTIVATION THEORIES APPLIED IN TRAINING RESEARCH

Expectancy Theory

Vroom's (1964) expectancy model has been used in several studies as a theoretical basis for investigating the consequences of pretraining motivation. Expectancy theory consists of two types of probabilistic estimates that impact behavior: an effort-to-outcome evaluation (Expectancy I), and an outcome-to-outcome contingency (Expectancy II). These expectancies were described by Fossum et al. (1986) for a training context by stating that individuals would learn and apply relevant knowledge and skills if the individuals *believed*: (Expectancy I) they were capable of acquiring such skills and knowledge (Expectancy II) if having the skills and knowledge was instrumental in attaining valued rewards. Based upon expected relative costs and benefits, an individual may or may not be motivated to acquire new knowledge and skills. Employees are thus more likely to acquire and maintain those skills and knowledge which have the highest perceived future rewards.

Using the expectancy theory framework, Noe (1986) suggested trainee perceptions would influence trainee motivation to perform well. However, in a subsequent empirical study Noe and Schmitt (1986), using specific elements based on expectancy theory, found pretraining motivation was not significantly related to learning outcomes. Mathieu et al. (1992) also used expectancy theory as the theoretical basis for their research. Their initial model did not show a significant relationship between pretraining motivation and performance. However, in a post-hoc model the relationship was marginally significant. It should be noted that both these studies used pretraining motivation as a single construct rather than measuring and evaluating each of the two types of expectancies separately.

Theory of Planned Behavior

Ajzen's (1985; 1991) theory of planned behavior does differentiate between multiple motivational constructs. Although somewhat similar to expectancy theory, Ajzen's model was developed from a human behavior framework. The theory postulates that the direct antecedent of any behavior or any attempt of goal attainment is the intention to perform it.

Strength of intention has been equated with strength of motivation.

Three independent constructs are proposed as determinates of intention. The first is the *attitude* towards the behavior, which concerns the individual's evaluation of the favorableness of the particular behavior. Its meaning and proposed structure are nearly identical to Expectancy II. Second is a social factor entitled *subjective norms*. This entails the perceived social pressure from specific others in one's environment to perform or not to perform the behavior. The third determinate is *perceived behavioral control*, which is an individual's confidence in their ability to perform the behavior. It is similar to Expectancy I. In a training context, this theory implies that individuals would intend to successfully master the course content if he or she believed: a) positive outcomes would results from attending and learning the training course content (*attitude*); b) pressure would be applied from superiors, peers or other significant others to do well in the training course (*subjective norms*); and c) he or she was capable of acquiring the knowledge and skills (*perceived behavioral control*).

The predictive validity of the theory of planned behavior has been shown in many non-learning related contexts (e.g., Harrison et al., 1997; Taylor & Todd, 1995). Specifically in a learning context, Ajzen and Madden (1986) conducted a study in which the behavioral goal was earning an "A" in a particular course. Attitudes and perceived behavioral control, but not subjective norms, were significantly correlated with intentions. In addition, the intention to earn an "A" in a particular course was significantly correlated with the actual attainment of an "A" in the course.

RESEARCH MODEL OF MOTIVATIONAL INTENTIONS

Expectancy theory and the theory of planned behavior are general motivational models that have been used in a variety of situations. Researchers have customized these models for particular contexts to enhance their applicability and predictive capability. For example, Kurland (1996) modified the theory of planned behavior when considering the intention to behave in an ethical manner. Kurland's model included two constructs from the theory of planned behavior, attitude and perceived behavioral control, in addition to a moral obligation construct not included in Ajzen's original model. Subjective norms did not significantly predict intentions in this context, therefore it was omitted.

The following model of motivational intentions for an IT retraining context, shown in Figure 1, has its roots in the theory of planned behavior (Ajzen, 1985; 1991). Yet, it has been customized, based upon prior research, specifically for the retraining context. The model highlights salient antecedents that are proposed to be more intense than in a training environment in which the targeted skills to be acquired are incremental in nature.

As can be seen from Figure 1, the present model utilizes the attitudes construct and its antecedent $\sum$ beliefs$_i$ (b_i) x evaluations$_i$ (e_i) proposed in the theory of planned behavior. Ajzen (1991) suggested that a direct antecedent of a person's attitude is the summation of the strength of beliefs (b_i) that a behavior or action will lead to one or more important outcomes, multiplied by corresponding evaluations of those outcomes (e_i).

The self-efficacy construct used in this model is similar to Ajzen's construct of perceived behavioral control (Ajzen, 1991). However, because self-efficacy has been more frequently used in training research (Compeau & Higgins, 1995; Eyring et al., 1993) it is included in this model.

Unlike the theory of planned behavior, the subjective norm construct is proposed in this model not to have a direct effect on intentions. Instead, a construct called social information is suggested to be mediated by attitudes. This restructuring of the model for this retraining context is suggested by prior research.

In Ajzen and Madden's (1986) study of college students, subjective norms were not found to be significantly related to intentions. Results indicated that students did not feel social pressure to achieve the behavioral goal of earning an "A" in the course. Davis et al. (1989) argued that social pressures are not independent of outcomes. For example, a software developer might perceive pressure from his or her manager to successfully complete a retraining course because of a perceived outcome that if the retraining course were not completed successfully, a poor performance evaluation would follow. Therefore, social pressure contributes to the software developer's outcome evaluation, which in turn, impacts his or her attitude.

In other training research which has investigated the relationship between motivation and social support, the positive influence associated with a particular social relationship, results have been mixed. Maurer and Tarulli (1994) did not find a significant relationship between supervisor support or coworker support and motivation. Facteau et al. (1995) did find a significant relationship between supervisor support and pretraining motivation. However, the relationship between peer support and motivation was not significant.

From this research, it appears that there may not be a direct linkage between subjective norms and motivational intention in a training or retraining context. However, as suggested by Davis et al. (1989), the present model proposes that social information influences outcome evaluations which in turn influence attitudes. This will be discussed in more detail later in the section entitled Social Information.

Figure 1 shows that mastery of the retraining course content is the behavioral goal used in this model. This means that rather than merely attending the course, the trainee actually absorbs the course content and is able to demonstrate mastery of the material at or above some predetermined level. For example, a training course may have a performance-based final exam in which earning a minimum of 80% on this exam would be considered mastery of the course content.

Figure 1 shows that both motivational intentions as well as self-efficacy have a direct influence on achieving the behavioral goal. Attitudes and self-efficacy are direct antecedents of motivational intentions. Several salient antecedents of attitudes and self-efficacy are included. It is possible that other variables may be antecedents of attitude and self-efficacy, however, they are beyond the scope of this chapter. Attitudes, self-efficacy, and their proposed antecedents will be discussed in subsequent sections of this chapter.

Attitudes

In the theory of reasoned action, a predecessor of the theory of planned behavior, Fishbein and Ajzen (1975) proposed that each of an individual's beliefs regarding doing a behavior links that behavior to a particular outcome or to some other attribute (e.g., the cost of performing the behavior). Each outcome is positively or negatively valued by the individual. The strength of each belief is multiplied by this associated subjective evaluation (Σbelief$_i$ x evaluation$_i$). The resulting products are then added together to form a weighed belief index. This index is directly proportional to a person's attitude.

In the present retraining context, the outcomes of interest will concern the personal advantages and the disadvantages of mastery of the course content in the new technology retraining course. Implicit in these evaluations are the perceived costs and rewards associated with the acquisition of the course knowledge and skills. For example, an individual might believe that acquiring object-oriented skills would likely provide a reward of being more marketable or earning a higher salary. Conversely, the individual might also believe that acquiring the object-oriented skills would likely be overly time consuming, requiring a significant amount of after-hours study. The first outcome has a strong belief and a positive evaluation; the second outcome has a strong belief and a negative evaluation. All of these "belief x evaluation" products are aggregated over salient outcomes to form an overall attitude.

These beliefs and evaluations may be influenced by a number of personal, situational, or environmental factors. In the information technology retraining context, several of these factors are proposed to be stronger in intensity and more salient than in an incremental learning environment. The five factors shown as antecedents to beliefs and evaluations are: whether the individual is given the choice to participate in retraining, perceived need for skill-set enhancement, social information, age, and length of time within the development paradigm.

Choice. A number of empirical studies have supported the proposition that choice in attending training, rather than required compliance, is significantly related to motivational attitudes. Hicks and Klimoski (1987) found that individuals who had a high degree of choice demonstrated higher motivation to learn, had more positive reactions, greater satisfaction and higher performance achievement than those with little choice. Facteau et al. (1995) found that compliance, where individuals were required to attend training, was negatively correlated with pretraining motivation.

In the present IT retraining context, this indicates that individuals who have the choice of whether to attend training will have more positive attitudes. Yet, the issue of choice also has broader connotations. Certain individuals may be *mandated* to acquire new Internet-based, client/server or object-oriented skills. In essence, those software developers may not be given a choice of whether to attend retraining, but perhaps more significantly, may not be given a choice regarding the underlying basis of their job. In a compliance setting, where individuals are not allowed control over the decision process, beliefs, evaluations, and resulting attitudes can be strongly negative. The evaluations in this regard are likely to be even more extreme than in a training situation in which the new knowledge and skills are merely incremental.

Need for Skill-Set Enhancement. Noe (1986) identified reaction to skill assessments as an important determinant of motivation. When individuals receive information regarding their strengths and weaknesses, positive or negative reactions are likely to influence beliefs and evaluations towards improving or acquiring new skills in a training program. Noe and Schmitt (1986) conducted a study in which educators' administrative and interpersonal skills were evaluated in an assessment center. Educators were informed of the results, then attended a training session designed to strengthen administrative and interpersonal skills. No relationship was found between reaction to skill assessment and pretraining motivation.

In the proposed model, the construct involved is a *self-perception* rather than a reaction of a skill assessment performed externally. The degree to which an individual perceives that his or her skills are obsolete will impact attitudes in terms of the desire to acquire new, more current skills. If the individual does not perceive a need to update or acquire additional skills, he or she sees fewer incentives to obtain new skills.

Social Information. As discussed earlier, in a training environment, empirical evidence has been mixed in supporting a direct connection between subjective norms and motivational intentions. However, in an experiment conducted to investigate social influence in an end-user training context, Galletta et al. (1995) found that social information did significantly impact *attitudes,* especially in the negative direction.

Because retraining involves significant shifts in skills as well as in the work processes themselves, individuals or groups are likely to have strong opinions as to whether they support the retraining effort and whether or not success in the retraining endeavor has value. Coworkers' opinions may be influential in focusing attention on positive or negative aspects of the retraining. This will impact the evaluation and subsequent attitude of the individual. Likewise, the opinion of the immediate supervisor is likely to be influential because the supervisor can provide important inputs such as the relevancy of the retraining to the individual's continued career opportunities. So, social information highlights certain salient outcomes, shifts evaluations and strengthens or weakens beliefs.

Age. Age is important for both attitude and self-efficacy, especially because of the marked change in skills required in a retraining context. When considering the outcomes of retraining, an individual's age can influence evaluations. Several authors have suggested that age determines whether an individual is willing to learn new skills (Fossum et al., 1986; Chabrow, 1995). Kopelmen (1977) found that expectancies and outcomes valences (also known as ($belief_i$ x $evaluation_i$) were negatively related to age among engineers. Human Capital Theory (Becker, 1993) proposes that employees may differ in their desire to invest in training for new skills, as a function of age. Older individuals may be less willing to invest in updating because of a shorter stream of payoffs. However, if the payoff for making the skill investment is fully realized in the anticipated remaining portion of their work lives, then age should not be a contributing factor.

Length of Time in the Development Paradigm. Individuals who have worked in a traditional/legacy paradigm may be less willing to move to newer development paradigms than those with less experience. Individuals who have spent more time working with the processes and methodologies associated with legacy system development have a greater investment in terms of time and skills in this environment. Because of the sunk cost in the existing paradigm, shifting to a new environment may be viewed as more expensive. Therefore the beliefs, evaluations and attitudes will tend to be less favorable than those that have less invested in the older development methodology.

Researchers have labeled this type of behavior the "sunk cost effect" which occurs when decision makers consider the amount of money, time or effort already invested when making decisions (Staw & Hong, 1995). Singer (1993) applied sunk cost theory to individual decision making when individuals were not certain about the future but were reconsidering a partially implemented personal plan. The present situation is similar in that software developers may feel unsure about their future, or the future of the new technology, and may weigh the time and effort already expended in the present software development paradigm when considering the cost and benefits of moving to the new technology.

Self-Efficacy

The second major construct that impacts intentions to successfully retrain is self-efficacy (see Figure 1). While self-efficacy is similar to Ajzen's (1985; 1991) construct of perceived behavioral control, which in turn is similar to the effort-outcome relationship of expectancy theory, self-efficacy is thought to be more a comprehensive construct (Gist and Mitchell, 1992). Self-efficacy is not considered a static predictor of future behavior, but has a "generative" capability in that it can impact the manner in which an individual thinks, feels, and subsequently performs a task (Gist and Mitchell, 1992).

Bandura (1977) defined self-efficacy as people's beliefs in their ability to organize and execute the courses of action required to attain designated levels of particular task performance. This reflects an individual's subjective confidence in his/her capabilities to exercise control over events rather than an objective evaluation of skills or performance. Research has shown that self-efficacy leads to performance gains, even when the effects of underlying skills as represented in past performance have been partialed out (Locke et al., 1984). Bandura (1986) described several mechanisms through which self-efficacy can impact; performance: (a) the amount of effort an individual will exert toward initial task performance (b) the degree to which an individual will remain persistent despite poor performance; and (c) the degree to which an individual focuses on ways or strategies to perform the task, versus focusing on success or failure. In the retraining context, individuals are faced with the challenge of acquiring new knowledge, skills, methodologies, and procedures that are substantially different than those they have mastered in the past. Therefore effort and persistence appear to be necessary factors in achieving the criteria specified for passing the training course. Attentional resources must be expended to facilitate the paradigm shift in software development methodologies and techniques.

In the model in Figure 1, self-efficacy is proposed to have both an influence on intention as well as a direct influence on the successful achievement of learning criteria. This indicates that perceived ability to perform can impact behavior via intentions, however, it can also be used to predict behavior directly. Both of these assumptions have been validated empirically in other training contexts. Ajzen and Madden (1986) showed that their construct of perceived behavioral control significantly predicted intentions. Initially, the direct linkage from perceived behavior control to behavior added little additional predictive power. However, as more accurate perceptions of control were formed, the predictive validity became significant. Compeau and Higgins (1995), in a study of computer training methods, found that self-efficacy had a significant impact both on outcome expectations and on actual performance. Other studies have found a significant direct relationship between self-efficacy and performance for a behavior (Gist et al., 1991; Eyring et al., 1993).

As in the case of attitudes, there can be a number of antecedents to self-efficacy (see Gist and Mitchell, 1992). However, two that are particularly relevant to the retraining context are once again age and length of time in the development paradigm. These were also proposed by the model, and were previously discussed as antecedents of attitudes as well.

Age. The new technologies, such as those in the client/server and object-oriented paradigm, require different conceptualizations than in the traditional legacy system development (Scholtz et al., 1993). Development is more rapid and iterative in nature. Furthermore, in terms of object-orientation, rather than requiring purely analytical, deductive thought processes, inductive thought processes are required as well (Henderson-Sellers and Edwards, 1990). Because of the new cognitive skills required, older individuals may differentially lack confidence in their ability to make this transition.

Warr and Bunce (1995) suggest that older employees may not exert the effort to learn new skills unless they believe that they are capable of mastering the new skills. In addition, Knowles (1984) stated that older individuals may lack confidence in their abilities to master a new technology. Past empirical evidence has found that older workers were not as likely to volunteer for training programs because they had little confidence in their learning ability (Rosen et al., 1965). In a sample of 146 adult volunteers involved in an end-user IT training program, Gist et al. (1988) found that older trainees exhibited significantly lower performance than younger trainees. Results also showed that older employees who were trained with a self-efficacy enhancing training technique out-performed those who were trained with a technique that did not significantly impact self-efficacy. Therefore, bolstering older employees' confidence in their ability to successfully master the retraining course content may be a critical consideration for organizations.

Length of Time in the Development Paradigm. Those who have been using the same methods in their jobs for a number of years may lack confidence in the ability to switch. For example, anecdotal evidence suggests that some individuals experienced in the traditional development methodologies may have difficulty in switching to the object-oriented paradigm (Lee and Pennington, 1994). These individuals in IT not only have more invested in terms of time spent in legacy systems development, but many of these individuals may be considered experts in legacy system development. Going from a status of expert to one of novice may be unnerving. Again, the issue of confidence is a central concern.

IMPLICATIONS OF THE MODEL

This model proposes that attitudes and self-efficacy are key antecedents of the intention to retrain. Intention and self-efficacy are important determinates of mastery of the IT retraining course content. A number of antecedents were proposed to affect attitudes in this environment: choice, need for skill-set enhancement, social information, age, and length of time in the development paradigm. Age and length of time in the development paradigm are also shown in the model as antecedents of self-efficacy. This model can potentially help organizations focus on key antecedents in order to enhance motivation and subsequent achievement in new technology retraining courses. The remainder of this section will discuss the practical implications that can be derived from the model.

First, past research has shown that choice in attending training is significantly related to motivational attitudes. Therefore, whenever possible, those who are willing to attend retraining courses and move to new technologies should be given the first opportunities to do so. Providing employees with this choice enhances the belief that the employee has some control over his or her own destiny. Organizational rewards, such as bonuses based on skill-level, can also be provided so that the choice to keep one's skills current or to move to a technology will be more desirable.

Second, the need for skill-set enhancement is proposed to be significantly related to motivational attitudes. In order for employees to recognize that their skills are obsolescing, they must become aware of the gap between their skills and the current skill requirements. Organizations can hold informational sessions describing the latest skills, techniques and methodologies used in industry. Participation in IT conferences or industry meetings can also highlight desirable cutting-edge skills and make employees aware of their "skills gap."

Third, several methods of providing positive social information can enhance the beliefs and evaluations about retraining and moving to a new software development paradigm. Key opinion leaders, such as project managers and lead developers, can be targeted so that they clearly understand the advantages of the newer technologies. Other industry peers can also provide social information regarding the transition. Often industry meetings or conferences have new technology "experiences" sessions. While not all experiences are positive, they can give a potential trainee a realistic preview of the challenges and rewards of retraining and moving to a new technology. Managerial support is also important in setting an organizational climate that is conducive to retraining. Top managers can show support for retraining by allocating sufficient funds for the retraining effort and verbally communicating the importance of skill currency. Supervisors can express to potential trainees the significance of the retraining as it relates to the individual's current position and future career opportunities.

Fourth, older individuals or those with longer tenure in the legacy systems paradigm may believe that the benefits they will receive by retraining are not worth the costs or effort in making the transition. For example, a young employee may believe that moving into the object-oriented paradigm would increase his or her marketability and it is therefore worth the time and effort to make this transition. Yet, an older employee may not value increased marketability, especially if he or she is near retirement. To enhance beliefs and evaluations among older individuals or those with longer tenure in the legacy systems paradigm, the employee's manager should highlight the benefits of retraining that would be realized during the employee's career with the organization. This means that the organization should carefully consider what those potential benefits would be, and determine whether additional rewards should be offered as incentives. Possible rewards would be dependent on the particular situation; however, examples might include some type of monetary incentive, new computer equipment for the employee's use, or the retention of the employee in a leadership role on the project team.

In terms of self-efficacy, age and length of time in the legacy system paradigm were proposed to have negative impacts on self-efficacy. Organizations can adopt practices that impact self-efficacy both within and outside of the retraining program. Bandura (1977) proposed four sources of self-efficacy: 1) enactive mastery, 2) vicarious experience, 3) verbal persuasion, and 4) psychological arousal. The first three sources are most applicable to the retraining context. The discussion below considers these sources of self-efficacy as they apply, first, to the retraining program and then, outside of the retraining program.

First, enactive mastery relates to successful task accomplishment. If one has been able to successfully complete the task, or a similar task, in the past, Bandura (1986) found that the individual was more likely to believe they could accomplish the task in the future. Ensuring early successes and providing an abundance of efficacy-building tasks early in the program is especially important for older individuals or those steeped in the legacy systems environment. Therefore, in a retraining course, initial exercises should be simple to build confidence and establish a record of task successes. Exercises can then become more complex as the skills are mastered. Feedback must be provided in the exercises so that trainees recognize which elements of the exercise they have mastered and the specific elements they still must perfect.

Second, vicarious experience refers to bolstering self-efficacy by watching the successes of others. Seeing others successfully accomplish a task can engender the perception that "I can do that, too." An effective form of vicarious experience is behavior modeling by the instructor (Compeau and Higgins, 1995). The instructor should work through sample exercises, showing the trainees that the task can be successfully accomplished and demonstrating the steps required to do so. Other training methods, such as small-group or one-on-one mentoring, allow a trainee to see others successfully accomplish a task. If others need correction, the trainee can vicariously experience the "mistake," learning how to correct the problem without actually making the mistake themselves. The atmosphere must be positive and open, however, for the vicarious experiences of others to be beneficial.

Third, verbal persuasion involves others in verbally encouraging and persuading the trainee, giving the trainee confidence that he or she can successfully complete the retraining course. Creating a cooperative and encouraging atmosphere that is conducive to trainees attempting a task will help spawn a climate advantageous to the development of self-efficacy. A small group atmosphere in which the groups encourage each other may augment the encouragement given by the instructor.

Outside of the training program, managers and other peers can positively impact the development of self-efficacy through two of the sources proposed by Bandura (1977), first through vicarious experience. As individuals see other peers successfully complete the retraining and move to a new software development paradigm, their self-efficacy will be enhanced. The organization can publicize the past successes of others so that potential trainees will be aware of these "success stories." Another potential avenue for efficacy-building vicarious experiences is conferences. As mentioned above, conferences or industry meetings are often a good opportunity for IT professionals to interact with others who have successfully made the transition to the newest technologies. Second, self-efficacy can be impacted outside of the retraining program through verbal persuasion. Older employees or those steeped in the legacy systems paradigm may feel tentative about their abilities to successfully complete the retraining effort. Encouragement from respected co-workers and managers can reinforce their confidence.

CONCLUSION

As IT continues to evolve, organizations will be at a distinct competitive disadvantage without IT professionals who are current in requisite skills. Therefore, the effective retraining of IT personnel is a crucial issue.

This chapter has sought to extend prior work on IT training in several ways. First, this chapter specifically investigated the *retraining* of employees whose knowledge and skills had begun to obsolesce and required marked, rather than incremental, change. Next, while most prior research has concentrated on the end user, the focus of this investigation was the IT professional. Third, a model of individual motivation to retrain was proposed in an IT context. Because the requirement for retraining in the IT area continues to grow, a theoretical basis by which organizations can further investigate, understand and leverage motivation is useful and important. Fourth, practical and specific recommendations were given on how organizations can apply the principles set forth in the model to positively impact motivation and retraining outcomes. Empirical research in the retraining area is needed. This chapter provides a theoretical basis for such work and highlights the importance of retraining in the current environment of rapid technological change.

REFERENCES

Ajzen, I. (1985). From intentions to actions: A theory of planned behavior. In J. Kuhl & Bechmann (Eds.), *Action-control: From cognition to behavior.* Heidelberg: Springer, 11-39.

Ajzen, I. (1991). The Theory of Planned Behavior, *Organizational Behavior and Human Decision Processes*, 50, 179-211.

Ajzen, I. & Madden, T.J. (1986). Prediction of Goal-Directed Behavior: Attitudes, Intentions, and Perceived Behavioral Control, *Journal of Experimental Social Psychology,* 22, 453-474.

Baldwin, T.T., Magjuka, R.J., & Loher, B.T. (1991). The perils of participation: effects of choice of training on trainee motivation and learning. *Personnel Psychology*, 44, 51-62.

Bandura, A. (1977). *Social Learning Theory,* Englewood Cliffs, NJ: Prentice-Hall.

Bandura, A. (1986). *Social foundations of though and actions: A social cognitive view*, Englewood Cliffs, NJ: Prentice-Hall.

Becker, G.S. (1993). *Human Capital.* Chicago: University of Chicago Press.

Chabrow, E.R. (1995). The Training Payoff. *Information Week.* July 10, 36-46.

Compeau, D.R., & Higgins, C.A. (1995). Application of Social Cognitive Theory to Training for Computer Skills, *Information Systems Research.* 6(2), 118-143.

Davis, F.D., Bagozzi, R.P., & Warshaw, P.R. (1989). User Acceptance of Computer Technology: A Comparison of Two Theoretical Models. *Management Science.* 35, 982-1003.

Del Vecchio, M. (1994). Retooling the Staff Along With the Systems. *Best's Review,* March 1994, 98-

99.
Due, R.T. (1993). Object-Oriented Technology: The Economics of a New Paradigm. *Information Systems Management,* Summer, 69-73.
Eyring, J.D., Steele Johnson, D., & Francis, D.J. (1993). Cross-level units-of-analysis approach to individual differences in skill acquisition. *Journal of Applied Psychology.* 78(5), 805-814.
Facteau, J.D., Dobbins, G.H., Russell, J., E.A., Ladd, R.T., & Kudisch, J.D. (1995). The influence of general perceptions of the training environment on pretraining motivation and perceived training transfer. *Journal of Management*, 21(1), 1-25.
Fishbein, M. & Ajzen, I. (1975). *Belief, Attitude, Intention, and Behavior: An Introduction to Theory and Research*, Reading, MA: Addison-Wesley.
Fossum, J.A., Arvey, R.D., Paradise, C.A., & Robbins, ME. (1986). Modeling the skills obsolescence process: A psychological/economic integration. *Academy of Management Review*, (11), 362-374.
Galletta, D.F., Ahuja, M., Hartman, A., Teo, T., & Peace, G.A. (1995). Social Influence and End-User Training. *Communications of the ACM.* 38(7), 70-79.
Gist, M., Rosen, B., & Schwoerer, C. (1988). The influence of training method and trainee age on the acquisition of computer skills. *Personnel Psychology*, (41), 255-265.
Gist, M., Stevens, C.K., & Bavetta, A.G. (1991). The influence of self-efficacy and training condition on retention of learning. *Personnel Psychology*, (44), 837-861.
Gist, M.E., & Mitchell, T.R. (1992). Self-Efficacy: A theoretical analysis of its determinants and malleability. *Academy of Management Review*, 17(2), 183-211.
Gottlieb, L. (1993). Information technology: Do you have a human resources strategy for information systems in the '90s?. *CMA Magazine,* December/January, 8-9.
Harrison, D.A., Mykytyn, P.P., Jr., & Riemenschneider, C. K. (1997). Executive decisions about adoption of information technology in small business: Theory and empirical tests. *Information Systems Research*, 8(2), 171-195.
Henderson-Sellers, B. & Edwards J.M. (1990). The object-oriented system life cycle. *Communications of the ACM*, 33(9), 143-159.
Hicks, W.D. & Klimoski, R.J. (1987), Entry into training programs and its effects on training outcomes: A field experiment. *Academy of Management Journal.* 30(3), 542-552.
Igbaria, M. Parasuraman, S., & Baroudi, J. (1996). A Motivational Model of Microcomputer Usage. *Journal of Management Information Systems*, 13(1), 127-143.
Jarvenppa, S.L., Dickson, G.W., & DeSanctis, G. (1985). Methodological Issues in Experimental IS Research: Experiences and Recommendations. *MIS Quarterly*, June, 141-156.
King, J. (1997). Skills shortage delays projects. *Computerworld*, 31(2), 8.
Kopelmen, R.E. (1977). Psychological states of careers in engineering: An expectancy theory taxonomy. *Journal of Vocational Behavior*, (10), 270-286.
Knowles, M. (1984). *The adult learner: A neglected species.* Houston: Gulf Publishing.
Kurland, N.B. (1996). Sales agents and clients: Ethics, incentives, and a modified theory of planned behavior. *Human Relations*, 49(1), 51-74.
Lee, A. & Pennington, N. (1994). The effects of paradigm on cognitive activities in design. *International Journal of Human-Computer Studies*, 40, 577-601.
Locke, E.A., Frederick, E., Lee, C., & Bobko, P. (1984). Effect of self-efficacy, goals, and task strategies on task performance. *Journal of Applied Psychology,* (69), 241-251.
Lucas, H.C., (1991). Methodological Issues in Information Systems Survey Research, in K.L. Kraemer, (ed.), *Harvard Business School Research Colloquium*, Vol. 3, Boston, MA: Harvard Business School, 273-285.
Maier, N.R.E. (1973). *Psychology in industrial organizations*. Boston: Houghton-Mifflin, 1973.
Mathieu, J.E., Tannenbaum, S.I., & Salas, E. (1992). Influences of Individual and Situational Characteristics on Measures of Training Effectiveness. *Academy of Management Journal*, 35(4), 828-847.
Maurer, T.J., & Tarulli, B.A. (1994). Investigation of perceived environment, perceived outcome, and person variables in relationship to voluntary development activity by employees. *Journal of*

Applied Psychology, 79(1), 3-14.

Noe, R.A. (1986). Trainees' attributes and attitudes. Neglected influences on training effectiveness. *Academy of Management Review,* 11, 736-749.

Noe, R.A. & Schmitt, N. (1986). The influence of trainees attitudes on training effectiveness: Test of a model. *Personnel Psychology*, 39, 497-523.

Pinson, L.J. (1994). Moving from COBOL to C and C++: OOP's biggest challenge. *Journal of Object-Oriented Programming*, October, 54-56.

Rosen, N.A., Williams, L.K., & Foltman, F.F. (1965). Motivational constraints in an industrial retraining program. *Personnel Psychology*, 18, 65-70.

Scholtz, J., Chidamber, S., Glass, R., Goerner, A., Rosson, M., Stark, M., & Vessey, I. (1993). Object-oriented programming: The promise and the reality. *Journal of Systems Software*, 23, 199-204.

Singer, A.E. (1993). Strategy with sunk costs. *Human Systems Management*, 12(2), 97-113.

Staw, B.M., & Hong, H. (1995). Sunk costs in the NBA: Why draft order affects playing time and survival in professional basketball. *Administrative Science Quarterly*, 40(3), 474-494.

Taylor, S. & Todd, P. (1995). Understanding Information Technology Usage: A Test of Competing Models *Information Systems Research*, 6, 144-176.

Vroom, V.H. (1964). *Work and Motivation*. New York: Wiley.

Warr, P.B. (1994). Age and employment. In Triandia H.C., Dunnete M.D., Hough L.M. (Eds). *Handbook of Industrial and Organizational Psychology,* (4), Palo Alto: Consulting Psychologists Press, 485-550.

Warr, P., & Bunce, D. (1995). Trainee Characteristics and the Outcomes of Open Learning. *Personnel Psychology,* (48), 347-373.

Wlodkowski, R.J. (1985). *Enhancing Adult Motivation to Learn*. San Francisco: Jossey-Bass.

Chapter 13
Systems Analysts' Attitudes Toward Information Systems Development

James J. Jiang
Louisiana Tech University, USA

Gary Klein
University of Texas of the Permian Basin, USA

Joseph L. Balloun
Nova Southeastern University, USA

Certain researchers argue that systems analysts are too technical, a situation that may contribute to system failures. The results of this study, however, contradict this argument. By applying a framework of Dos Santos and Hawk (1988), analysts were found to have three primary orientations: technical, socio-political, and user. No one orientation dominated. Using the framework applied in this study, managers can consider the analysts' orientations in assigning development activities. Researchers can identify diverse orientations in future studies where attitudes may be significant predictors of system performance or development success.

Researchers and practitioners observe that systems analysts play a key role in systems development success (Lyytinen and Hirschheim, 1987; Markus, 1983; Zmud, 1979). Besides other factors (e.g., organizational management, technology, complexity, political influences), systems analysts' attitudes toward system development are consistently and significantly related to the quality of the final products (Bostrom and Heinen, 1977a, 1977b; Lyytinen, 1988; Zmud, 1979). A diagnosis of the attitudes of systems analysts may provide insights leading to future system success.

Certain researchers argue that systems analysts subscribe to too technical and economic design ideals (Kaiser and Srinivasan, 1982; Kumar and Welke, 1984). Alleged causes of system failures include the analysts' ignorance of social, political, behavioral, managerial, and psychological factors. Suggestions for improvements to system development include

This chapter originally appeared in the Information Resources Management Journal, Vol. 11 No 4. Copyright 1998, Idea Group Publishing.

Table 1: Abbreviated Statements

S1	Positive user attitude towards system
S2	User on project team during system definition phase
S3	Project should be carefully monitored
S4	Prototyping is useful
S5	Good communication is necessary
S6	Steering committee should manage project
S7	Top management support
S8	User on project team during system design
S9	User confident in system analysts
S10	Turnover in IS staff causes problems
S11	Technically competent IS staff avoids problems
S12	Large projects should be split into smaller projects
S13	Quantifiable benefit to projects
S14	Users initiate projects
S15	Realistic expectation from users
S16	Post implementation follow-up
S17	Walkthroughs with user is important
S18	Careful planning for changes for new system
S19	Turnover in top management
S20	IS staff's commitment
S21	Analysts should be in users' area
S22	Projects address important problems
S23	User interface is important
S24	Proper user training on new system
S25	System design should be frozen before programming
S26	Users integral part of development team
S27	IS staff's political skills
S28	The urgency of the systems
S29	Turnover among users leads to lack of commitment
S30	Dealing with many different user personalities
S31	Different personnel should be involved
S32	Use of structure technique is important
S33	Project leader managerial skills

formal training or education of systems analysts in managerial skills, behavioral ideas, and communications techniques (Benbasat, Dexter, and Mantha, 1980; Green, 1989). Others suggest improvements that include use of a socio-technical approach to system design (Bostrom and Heinen, 1977a, 1977b; Davis, et al., 1992; Markus, 1983). These approaches, however, are expensive and largely unproven. What is more important, the implicit assumption of these proposed solutions, that systems analysts have an undifferentiated technical attitude, may be incorrect. To clarify analysts' attitudes, Dos Santos and Hawk (1988) describe a survey study of 30 systems analysts. The study found that some systems analysts had a technical orientation, however, the majority had a user or socio-political orientation.

The intent of this study is to confirm or refute the identification of major attitudes toward system development held by systems analysts as identified by Dos Santos and Hawk (1988). This study will correct problems in the earlier study associated with the small homogeneous sample. Moreover, this study will describe analysts' attitudes, and examine relationships of several demographic traits to analysts' attitudes.

The sequence of issues follows a logical progression to help in addressing the following questions: 1) Do systems analysts possess diverse attitudes toward system development; 2) Which primary attitudes do systems analysts hold; and 3) are analysts' attitudes related to

Table 2: Respondents' System Development Experience

1. Experience in Designing & Implementing of IS:	
Less Than 2 Years	14 (5.9%)
2 - 4 Years	36 (15.1%)
5 - 8 Years	67 (28.0%)
More Than 9 Years	122 (51.0%)
Total	**239 (100%)**
2. Experience in Different Kinds of Applications:	
1 Application Area	9 (3.8%)
2 - 3 Application Areas	61 (25.5%)
4 - 5 Application Areas	58 (24.3%)
More Than 5 Appl. Areas	114 (46.4%)
Total	**239 (100%)**
3. The Average Complexity of Projects Involved in (Measured by Staff Year):	
1 Staff Year	47 (19.8%)
2 - 5 Staff Years	98 (41.4%)
6 - 10 Staff Years	43 (18.1%)
More Than 10 Staff Years	49 (20.7%)
Total	**237 (100%)**

Note: Responses may not total to 239 due to response omissions.

their demographic characteristics? Results of this study will have implications for information system (IS) practitioners and researchers by: 1) providing guidance for planning education and training programs for system analysts, 2) presenting information for effective development team formation, and 3) suggesting areas that IS researchers may wish to reevaluate and refine, such as current strategies for system development.

METHODS

This study used the instrument developed by Dos Santos and Hawk (1988). Exploratory principal components analysis was used to decide if the three categories of orientation (user orientation, socio-political orientation, and technical orientation) hold for a larger, more heterogeneous sample.

Questionnaire

The survey instrument was a set of 33 statements on various aspects of system development (Dos Santos and Hawk, 1988); abbreviated statements are presented in Table 1. The set included statements on user/analysts communication, individual differences among users, technical capabilities of the development staff, and systems that alter the balance of power in an organization. Instructions requested respondents to rate how strongly they believed the listed statements were critical to successful system development. A Likert scale was used with *strongly disagree* at the low anchor of one and *strongly agree* on the high anchor at five.

Table 3: Respondents' Demographic Information

1. Gender:		
	Female	69 (28.9%)
	Male	170 (71.1%)
Total		**239 (100%)**
2. Age:		
	Below 31	67 (29.0%)
	31 - 35	64 (27.7%)
	36 - 40	35 (15.2%)
	41 - 45	30 (12.9%)
	Above 45	35 (15.2%)
Total		**231 (100%)**
3. Education:		
	Community College/ Professional School Diploma	35 (14.7%)
	College Diploma	149 (63.0%)
	Computer Science	31 (13.0%)
	Information Systems	33 (13.9%)
	Others	86 (36.1%)
	Graduate Diploma	53 (22.3%)
	Computer Science	4 (1.7%)
	Information Systems	3 (1.3%)
	Others	46 (19.3%)
Total		**238 (100%)**
4. Management Level:		
	Executive/Manager of IS Department	43 (18.3%)
	IS Project Leader	68 (29.0%)
	IS Supporting/System Analysts	105 (44.6%)
	Others	19 (8.1%)
	Total	**235 (100%)**

Procedure and Sample

The questionnaire was pretested on a class of MBA students. Ambiguities in the instructions were corrected after the pretest. Questionnaires were then provided to six Chief Information Officers (CIO) from six organizations in the Kansas City metropolitan area. The number of employees in these organizations ranged from 2,500 to more than 25,000 employees with an approximate average of about 1,000 IS personnel. The CIOs in turn asked at least 40 of their staff members to complete the survey. Respondents were system analysts, IS project leaders, and IS department managers with experience in system development and were assured that their responses would be kept confidential. Apparently the direct request from the CIOs resulted in a full response. Two hundred forty four questionnaires were returned with 239 used in the data analysis due to question omissions.

Table 2 shows the respondents' working experience in information systems design and development. More than half of the respondents (51%) had more than nine years of work

Table 4: Rotated Factor Loading of Analysts' Attitude Orientation

Statement	Factor 1	Factor 2	Factor 3	Reliability[1]
S1	0.23	0.39	0.26	.99
S2	**0.56**	0.03	0.03	.99
S3	0.44	0.23	0.23	.99
S4	0.19	0.15	0.01	.97
S5	0.43	0.07	0.09	.99
S6	0.19	0.00	**0.55**	.95
S7	0.39	0.14	0.48	.98
S8	**0.55**	0.06	0.09	.98
S9	0.15	0.43	0.31	.98
S10	0.11	0.50	-.25	.97
S11	0.18	**0.57**	-.03	.98
S12	-.07	**0.51**	-.06	.93
S13	-.01	0.30	**0.49**	.97
S14	0.23	0.50	0.10	.94
S15	0.22	0.22	0.38	.98
S16	0.29	0.08	0.33	.98
S17	**0.58**	0.12	0.17	.99
S18	0.27	0.12	**0.55**	.99
S19	0.11	**0.53**	0.31	.96
S20	0.13	0.31	**0.55**	.99
S21	0.08	0.23	0.21	.90
S22	-.02	0.37	0.45	.97
S23	0.11	0.45	0.13	.96
S24	**0.64**	0.08	0.14	.99
S25	0.29	0.12	0.10	.96
S26	**0.76**	0.12	0.09	.99
S27	0.12	0.39	0.31	.97
S28	0.21	0.46	0.18	.95
S29	0.16	**0.70**	0.14	.97
S30	0.01	**0.71**	0.08	.97
S31	-.28	-.11	0.37	.82
S32	0.05	-.10	**0.56**	.97
S33	0.15	0.04	0.40	.98

Note: refer to Table 1 for statements.

experience, and about half the respondents (46.4%) had system experience in more than five application areas. Only 5.9 percent had less than two years of work experience and 3.8 percent had system experience in only one application area. The data showed that the respondents were experienced in the field of system development. Complexity of applications varied, suggesting that the analysts collectively had been involved in large and small projects.

The respondents were well educated, with 63 percent (149) having completed college and 22.3 percent (53) having completed a graduate degree program (Table 3). Within the 119 college educated respondents, 31 had a college diploma in Computer Science and 33 had a college diploma in Information Systems. Seventy-one percent (170) were male and 29 percent (69) were female. The sample was young, but still represented a wide age spectrum. The first, second and third quartiles of age were respectively 31, 34 and 41 years old. About half the respondents had management responsibilities.

Table 5: Attitude Groups

Group	Observed Subjects
A - user orientation (Factor 1)	53
B - socio-political (Factor 2)	54
C - technical (Factor 3)	47
D - user and socio-political (Factor 1 & 2)	17
E - user and technical (Factor 1 & 3)	16
F - socio-political and technical (Factor 2 & 3)	22
G - (All Factors)	30
Sum	239

Table 6: Analysis of Demographic Variables

Demographic	Test	Result
Gender	Chi-square on homogeneity*	significant at .05
Age	Chi-square on homogeneity (with breaks every 5 years)*	significant at .05
Education	Chi-square on homogeneity*	significant at .05
Management Level	Chi-square on homogeneity*	not significant
Design Experience	Chi-square on homogeneity*	not significant
Application Experience	Chi-square on homogeneity*	not significant
Project Complexity	Chi-square on homogeneity*	not significant

*(cross tabs analysis)

RESULTS

To classify respondents with similar attitudes, component analysis was done. First, principal components analysis was used to extract the dominant attitude components. Three components with eigen values greater than chance expectation were retained for further analysis (Lautenschlager, 1989). Components were then rotated by the varimax procedure (Table 4). The five highest loadings in each component served to identify associated questions.

Reliability of measurement for each component was computed as follows. First, the scores of the respondents on the rotated components were computed. The standardized scoring weights of the 33 questions were found for each rotated component. The reliability of each individual question was then estimated by its adjusted squared multiple correlation

Table 7: Orientations by Demographic Variables

Orientation	Female %	Male %	Average Age	<= Jr. College Education %	Undergraduate Degree %	Graduate Degree %
User	17	23	34.9	21	21	26
Soc-pol	12	27	38.3	38	20	19
Technical	22	19	34.5	6	22	20
User/Soc-pol	4	8	37.4	15	6	6
User/Tech	17	3	31.9	0	9	6
Soc-pol/Tech	12	9	35.5	6	11	7
All Three	16	11	38.3	15	11	17

with the other 32 questions (Table 4). Cliff (1988) provided the correct formula for the reliability of principal component scores. Component score reliabilities were 0.98, 0.99, and 0.98 for rotated components one, two, and three respectively. Component score reliability depends on the reliabilities of the questions that define it.

Examination of the rotated component analysis revealed that the three rotated components corresponded well to the three attitude orientations of Dos Santos and Hawk (1988). Component one corresponded to the user orientation, component two to the socio-political orientation, and component three to the technical/economic orientation. The interpretation of component three is equivocal, for it also seems related to political rationality.

Questions 2, 8, 17, 24, and 26 loaded strongly on component one. A high loading of a question on a component means that the question is correlated with other questions loading highly on that component. The common contents of questions loading most strongly on a component allow an interpretation of the meaning of the component. The questions loading most strongly on the first component included: "Users should be on the project team during system definition phase" (2), "users should be on the project team during system design"(8), "walkthroughs with users are important" (17), "proper user training on the new system" (24), and "users are an integral part of the development team" (26). These questions have a common theme of user project involvement. The questions of component one were concerned with taking measures to ensure the involvement of users. Affirmative answers to these questions showed a high importance of user involvement in the eventual success of an information system. Analysts dominant in this orientation have a user orientation.

Component two was most strongly related to questions 11, 12, 19, 29 and 30. These questions were "technically competent IS staff avoids problems" (11), "large projects should be split into small projects to ease development" (12), "turnover in top management can cause loss of critical support" (19), "turnover among users leads to loss of commitment" (29), and "dealing with many different user personalities complicates systems design and development" (30). These questions fell under the socio-political aspects of system design, except maybe number 12. The questions of component two were concerned with avoiding complications leading to problems, ensuring support and commitment, and were essentially social issues associated with development progress. There was a lack of questions about project economics, technology details, or any concern for detail. Analysts dominant in this orientation have a socio-political orientation.

Component three had high loadings with questions 6, 13, 18, 20, and 32. These were that "a steering committee should manage projects" (6), "quantifiable benefits are important" (13), "careful planning for changes for the new system is necessary" (18), "IS development staff should be committed to the project" (20), and "use of structured techniques is important" (32). Though these questions included project management and economic issues, they were detailed questions important to the success of system development. To be consistent with prior terminology, analysts dominant in this orientation have a technical orientation.

To classify each respondent, component scores were computed according to the procedure in Gorsuch (1983, pp. 262-263). From these component scores, a simple process would have been to select the highest score to categorize the individual. However, a respondent would have been able to exhibit only one attitude type under such a process. A second problem is that psychometric data of this type has been notoriously imprecise (McDonald, 1985). Still a third complication is that such comparisons suffer from reliability difficulties (Peter et al., 1992).

To overcome these three problems, we formed subgroups of respondents who were homogeneous in their endorsement of one, two, or three values as measured by their component scores. For example, if a respondent's second (and third) highest component score(s) did not differ from the first by a significant amount, the respondent also had the second (and third) orientation(s). Component score reliabilities were used to compute the standard error of measurement for the differences between each pair of component scores (Lord, 1958). The estimated standard error of the difference between component two and component three was .20, and the standard errors of the differences between the other two pairs of components were .17. For a given respondent, we considered a difference between two components to be nominally significant if it were at least twice the standard error of the difference (Lord, 1958).

For example, respondents were classified into group A (user orientation) when their component scores on component number one were significantly higher than their component scores on both component two and component three. Respondents were classified into group D (user and socio-political) when their component scores on component one and component two were not significantly different from each other, but both component one and component two were significantly greater than component three. Respondents showing no significant dominance pattern were placed into group G (all three orientations). Final groups (Table 5) were verified by a MANOVA with the component scores as the dependent variables and the group assignment as the categorical variable. The resulting model tested significant at .05.

Examination of the demographic variables is summarized in Table 6. Chi-square tests on homogeneity were conducted in a cross-tabs analysis on each primary demographic measure with orientations as the reference variable. Management level and experience were not related to the analysts' attitudes. Such lack of change throughout experience and managerial levels may be due to the constant updating required of IS professionals (Kirkley, 1988; Lucas, 1989). Gender, age and education, however, were found significant at .05. Each of these are detailed in Table 7.

DISCUSSION

The similarity of the groups found in this study to those found in the earlier study of Dos Santos and Hawk (1988) is encouraging. The improvements to technique and sample size have added significance to the groupings found earlier. These groups show an almost even distribution among the three major orientations but combinations were rarer. The data did not show that a technical orientation dominates systems analysts, but instead supported the hypothesis that multiple orientations were present in the profession as a whole and even in individual members of the profession. Such diversity can be important in achieving success (Klein and Aronson, 1996).

There was little gender difference in the user orientation and the technical orientation categories, but females showed much less socio-political orientation (Table 7). Perhaps of more interest is that females had a higher percentage in the combined groups, showing more complex or complete orientations. This latter trait is found in earlier studies where females believed more strongly in the need for a comprehensive scope in IS work (Smiths, McLean and Tanner, 1993). In the same report, males seemed to find themselves more goal oriented, a socio-politically oriented trait.

The relation between the older age groups and those having socio-political interests could be a result in the career growth of an individual over time, a reflection of one becoming more aware of social and political issues (Dalton et al., 1977). In addition, "getting young IS professionals socialized into the organization and work group may be a real challenge for IS managers" (Chusmir, 1989). This may be especially true for those technical professionals who enter the field for the challenge posed by the technology.

Major differences were found in the lower levels of education (Table 7). Lower levels of education had the higher number of socio-political analysts with a lessening in the number of technically oriented analysts. This is not surprising as IS educational programs are oriented to the technical aspects of IS delivery. The results are also consistent with the four-stage-career model which encourages a technical orientation in the early stages (Dalton et al., 1977).

CONCLUSION

A large sample replicates the attitude orientation structure of system analysts discovered by Dos Santos and Hawk (1988). Analysts are found to have a user orientation, socio-political orientation, technical orientation, or some combination of the three, and considerable attitudinal heterogeneity. The diversity of attitude orientation among systems analysts is supported. The results do not support the idea that most systems analysts hold a technical orientation as assumed by some researchers. This diversity discredits a common allegation that systems analysts are too technical in their orientation. Researchers must look elsewhere when searching for a cause of system failures.

Dos Santos and Hawk (1988) suggest that people with different orientations may be best assigned to particular types of projects. It may also be argued that each project should have each orientation represented to be certain all bases are covered. The success of a project involves aspects of all three orientations. Teams can be organized to incorporate systems analysts representing all major orientations, helping to ensure system success. Such a task requires further research into quick, reliable techniques for identification of individual orientations.

Age, gender, and education level were related to attitude categories. Females tended to be less socio-political and more complex than their male counterparts. Older analysts tended to have a more socio-political orientation. Those with higher education tended to replace a socio-political orientation by a technical orientation. These relations provide initial guidelines for the composition of complete teams. Not surprisingly, a good mix of backgrounds in education and diversity in age and gender will contribute to creating a group with diverse attitude orientations.

The results of the current study still need to be viewed with care. To our knowledge this is only the second study of this nature. Though a broad set of individuals is represented, the respondents are regional, and the survey examines them for a single time period. Possible shifts over time need to be investigated. The sample was also limited to large organizations. Small operations may require even more generalists (individuals with a mix of orientations) than do large firms.

Topics for future research include formalization of a metric for categorizing analysts by their orientations. Once an instrument is in place, confirmation studies can be conducted. Of particular interest would be studies regarding information system successes and failures as a function of the orientations and composition of project teams.

REFERENCES

Benbasat, I., Dexter, A.S., and Mantha, R.W. (1980). "Impact of Organizational Maturity on Information Skill Needs," *Management Information Systems Quarterly*, 4(1), .21-34.

Bostrom, R.P. and Heinen, J.S. (1977)."MIS Problems and Failures: A Socio-Technical Perspective - Part I: The Causes," *Management Information Systems Quarterly*, 1(3), 17-32.

Bostrom, R.P. and Heinen, J.S. (1977)."MIS Problems and Failures: A Socio-Technical Perspective - Part II: The Application of Socio-Technical Theory," *Management Information Systems Quarterly*,1(4), 11-28.

Chusmir, L.H. (1989), "Behavior: a Measure of Motivation Needs," *Psychology, A Journal of Human Behavior*, 26(2), 1-10.

Cliff, N. (1988)."The Eigenvalues-Greater-than-One Rule and the Reliability of Components," *Psychological Bulletin*, 103(2), 276-279.

Dalton, G. W., P. H. Thompson and R. L. Price (1977)."The Four Stages of professional Careers—A New Look at performance by Professionals," *Organizational Dynamics*, Vol. 6, Summer, 19 - 42.

Davis, G.B., Lee, A.S., Nickles, K.R., Chatterjee, S., Hartung, R., and Wu, Y.(1992)."Diagnosis of an Information System Failure: A Framework and Interpretive Process," *Information & Management*, 23(5), 293-318.

Dos Santos, B.L. and Hawk, S.R (1988). "Differences in Analyst's Attitudes towards Information Systems Development: Evidence and Implications," *Information & Management*, 24(1), 31-41.

Green, G.I. (1989)."Perceived Importance of System Analysts' Job Skills, Roles, and Non-Salary Incentives," *Management Information Systems Quarterly*,13(2),115-133.

Gorsuch, R. L. *Factor analysis*. (Second edition) (1983). Hillsdale, N.J.: Lawrence-Erlbaum.

Kaiser, K. and Srinivasan, A. (1982). "User-Analyst Differences: An Empirical Investigation of Attitude Related to Systems Development," *Academy of Management Journal*, 25(3), 630-646.

Kirkley, J. (1988). "MIS Professional is Not What It Used to Be," *Computerworld*, March 21, 80-81.

Klein, G. and Aronson, J. (1996). "Maximizing Diversity by Zero-One Programming," Working Paper, Terry College of Business, The University of Georgia, Athens, GA 30602.

Kumar, K. and Welke, R.J. (1984). "Implementation Failure and System Developers Values: Assumptions, Truisms and Empirical Evidence," *Proceedings of the Fifth International Conference on Information Systems*, Tucson, Arizona.

Lautenschlager, G. J. (1989). "A Comparison of Alternatives to Conducting Monte Carlo Analysis for Determining Parallel Analysis Criteria," *Multivariate Behavioral Research*, 24(3), 365-395.

Lord, F. M. (1958)."The Utilization of Unreliable Difference Scores," *The Journal of Educational Psychology*, 49(3), 150-152.

Lucas, H. C. (1989). *Managing Information Services*, New York, NY: MacMillan Publishing Company.

Lyytinen, K. (1988)."Expectation Failure Concept and Systems Analysts' View of Information Systems Failures: Results of an Exploratory Study," *Information & Management*, 14(1), 45-56.

Lyytinen, K. and Hirschheim, R. (1987). Information Systems Failure Revisited: A Survey and Classification of the Empirical Literature," in *Oxford Surveys in Information Technology*, Zorkoczy, P. (ed.), Oxford University Press, Inc.: New York, NY, Vol. 4, 257-309.

Markus, M.L., (1983). Power, Politics and MIS Implementation," *Communications of the ACM*, 26(6), 430-444.

McDonald, R. P. (1985). *Factor Analysis and Related Methods*, Hillsdale, NJ: Lawrence-Erlbaum.

Peter, J. P., Churchill, Jr., G. A. & Brown, T. J. (1993). Caution in the Use of Difference Scores in Consumer Research. *Journal of Consumer Research*, 19(4), 655-662.

Smiths, S.J., McLean, E.R. and Tanner, J.R. (1994)."Managing High-Achieving Information Systems Professionals," *Journal of Management Information Systems*, 9(4), 103-120.

Zmud, R. (1979)."Individual Differences and MIS Success: A Review of the Empirical Literature," *Management Science*, 25(10), 966-979.

Chapter 14

Utilization and User Satisfaction in End-User Computing: A Task Contingent Model

Changki Kim
Korea Advanced Institute of Science and Technology, South Korea

Kunsoo Suh
Soonchunhyang University, South Korea

Jinjoo Lee
Korea Advanced Institute of Science and Technology, South Korea

There has been much controversy regarding the relationship between utilization and user satisfaction. Moreover, conflicting empirical results on that relationship have been reported. Based on the information processing view, a new, alternative model which can resolve this conflict is suggested. The model includes the congruence of task uncertainty and utilization and the contingent effect of task uncertainty on the relationship between utilization and user satisfaction in the context of end-user computing (EUC). This new model is moderately supported by an analysis of data obtained from 134 end-users in 16 Korean business organizations. The results imply that we should pay attention to the fit between task uncertainty and utilization to promote user satisfaction. The results also provide a framework which resolves the inconsistent relationship between utilization and user satisfaction. Implications and future research directions are drawn for further research on MIS and EUC and for the management of EUC.

Utilization and user satisfaction have been used most extensively as the dependent variable to surrogate IS success (Amoroso & Cheney, 1991; Igbaria & Nachman, 1990). These two variables are also the primary measures of success in the study of end-user computing (EUC) (Ein-Dor & Segev, 1982; Schiffman et al., 1992). Taking these two variables into consideration, two issues prompt concern: the adequacy of them as surrogate measures and the relationship between them.

As a surrogate measure for IS success, utilization is an excellent measure in that it is

This chapter originally appeared in the Information Resources Management Journal, Vol. 11, No. 4.

more objective and easier to quantify than any other measures identified (DeLone & McLean, 1992). However, it has been argued that utilization is appropriate only when such usage behavior is voluntary (DeLone & McLean, 1992; Gatian, 1994). Researchers who insist on this argument have generally adopted the user satisfaction approach. User satisfaction instruments, however, have a significant problem in that they rely solely on cognitive dimension (beliefs about characteristics of a system) and affective dimension (attitudes towards a system or towards using a system) of IS success without accounting for the performance-related dimension (performance-related goals for which systems are designed) (Etezadi-Amoli & Farhoomand, 1996). In spite of weaknesses of these two measures, utilization and user satisfaction are the most frequently proposed alternatives.

In this chapter, the relationship between the two constructs is our primary concern. There has been inconsistency on that relationship. In addition, conflicting empirical results lead to the conclusion that the relationship may need further investigation (Igbaria & Nachman, 1990). Based on the information processing view, we make an effort to resolve this perplexing issue. A task contingent model to clarify the relationship between them is suggested and empirically tested in the context of EUC.

The information processing view of organizations is that organizational effectiveness is a function of the fit between the information processing requirements and the information processing capacity of the organization (Tushman & Nadler, 1978). In the context of EUC, the information processing requirements are largely determined by end-users' task uncertainty. In order to increase information processing capacity, one of the most important mechanisms is to invest in information technology (Ghani, 1992). At an individual level, end-users are able to increase their information processing capacity by being involved in EUC activities, which can be represented objectively by utilization measures. Task uncertainty, therefore, would be closely associated with utilization. And user satisfaction depends to some extent on the match between task uncertainty and utilization. In this perspective, we can argue that the match between task uncertainty and utilization is more important than the simple increment of utilization.

In summary, the purpose of this chapter is to suggest a task contingent model clarifying the relationship between utilization and user satisfaction. Based on empirical data, this study examines the model: the direct relationship between task uncertainty and utilization, and the moderating effect of task uncertainty on the relationship between utilization and user satisfaction.

THEORETICAL BACKGROUND

End-User Computing

In defining EUC, Rivard and Huff (1985) attempted to be more definitive by distinguishing between user developed applications (UDA) and the much broader set of activities termed EUC. Sipior and Sanders (1989) defined EUC as the development and use activities associated with the employment of computer resources to perform or facilitate job-related tasks and responsibilities. This study defines EUC more broadly as the direct, individual use of computers encompassing all the computer-related activities, by non-DP professionals, to accomplish or facilitate one's job (Rainer & Harrison, 1994; Sipior & Sanders, 1989; Doll & Torkzadeh, 1989; Ein-Dor & Segev, 1991). And this study defines end-users as the non-DP professionals who use and sometimes develop and manage computer-based applications to support their work in functional areas (Alavi, 1985; Benson, 1983; Sipior & Sanders, 1989;

Trauth & Cole, 1992).

As mentioned above, the broad set of activities associated with the use of the computer for job-related tasks have been referred to as EUC (Sipior & Sanders, 1989). End-users are involved in EUC activities in order to enhance their job effectiveness and/or to accomplish their tasks. So, task characteristics is one of the key variables affecting EUC success (Cheney et al., 1986; Ghani, 1992). However, few empirical studies have focused on task characteristics. In this chapter, task variability and analyzability, the basic dimensions of task characteristics, are key variables that explain utilization and user satisfaction.

Task Uncertainty and End-User Computing: An Information Processing View

A large number of organization theory researchers have made information processing the integrating or central concept in models that attempt to describe how organizations can match information processing requirements arising from task technology to information processing capacity arising from organization design and structure in order to achieve high organizational performance (Daft & Lengel, 1986; Galbraith, 1977; Keller, 1994; Tushman & Nadler, 1978). The basic idea of these models is that too much capacity will be redundant and costly, while too little capacity will not get the job done (Tushman & Nadler, 1978). Recent researchers have tested important contingency theory hypotheses between fit and performance, with fit conceptualized as a match between task technology and information processing (Keller, 1994).

The managerial information processing model or media richness theory is the best known formulation that extends this general information processing model to relationships between task characteristics, use of communication media, and performance. In this model, as similar to the general information processing model, the main proposition is that performance depends to some extent on the match between task uncertainty and the characteristics of the medium used.

Task uncertainty is defined as the difference between the amount of information needed to complete a task and the amount of information already possessed by the organization (Galbraith, 1977). Researchers in both MIS and organization theory recognize the close relationship between task uncertainty and organizational information processing (Ghani, 1992). Perrow (1967) originally proposed and described the two basic dimensions of task uncertainty: number of exceptions and analyzability. The first dimension refers to task variability. Task variability is defined as the number of exceptional cases, or unexpected and novel events encountered, which require different methods or procedures for doing the works (Perrow, 1967). The second dimension, task analyzability, is defined as the availability of concrete knowledge about task activities (Specht, 1986) and the degree of complexity of the search process in performing the task (Perrow, 1967). It concerns how individuals respond to problems that arise in the process of task completion.

In the EUC environment, end-users' task uncertainty is the major determinant of information processing requirements. While task variability affects the amount of information required to handle unexpected events, task analyzability affects the form of information necessary to resolve ambiguities (Ghani, 1992). Information processing needs arising from task variability require computing activities that can provide sufficient amount of information. Hence, highly variable tasks require diverse EUC activities. On the other hand, information processing needs arising from task analyzability require computing activities that can provide the relevant form of the information necessary to resolve ambiguities. Daft and Macintosh (1981) found that the reported amount of information processing increased with task variability and that the reported use of equivocal information decreased with task analyzability.

Less analyzable tasks require richer information that can be obtained by utilizing a rich medium. Daft & Lengel (1984) suggested that the three main factors associated with rich communication media involved cue variety, immediate feedback, and personalization. These criteria would also be appropriate in evaluating the richness of computing media. Generally, the PC is a richer computing medium than the mainframe for these three criteria. Software packages on the PC are usually better suited to providing immediate feedback (e.g., availability of user-friendly operating system, what-if analysis using a spreadsheet), multiple cues (e.g., ability to present information by audio and visual cues, ability to present data in graphical and tabular form), and personalization (e.g., ability to tailor an information output to user needs) than the packages available on the mainframe. On the mainframe, the user is often restricted to the use of a few corporate databases using specific application packages such as exception reporting and monitoring applications. On the PC, however, the user typically has more control over the data and can choose from a variety of user-friendly software tools. In Ghani's recent empirical research (1992), task analyzability was positively correlated with the use of mainframe (MF) computers—information-lean media—and negatively correlated with the use of personal computers (PC)— information-rich media.

Two Surrogates of Information Systems Success: Utilization and User Satisfaction

IS success can be ultimately defined as the extent to which the IS contributes to the organization in achieving its goals (Kim, 1990). Measuring IS success by this definition is especially important to IS practitioners. Nevertheless, MIS researchers have tended to avoid making these efforts because of the difficulty of isolating the effect of the IS from the numerous intervening environmental variables that may influence organizational performance (DeLone & McLean, 1992). Thus, surrogate measures for IS success which are assumed to relate to the organizational performance have been developed, such as user satisfaction, utilization, and decision-making effectiveness. Among various surrogate measures, utilization and user satisfaction are the most widely used measures of IS success and EUC success (Amoroso & Cheney, 1991; Ein-Dor & Segev, 1982; Igbaria, 1990; Schiffman et al., 1992).

Considering utilization and user satisfaction, two primary issues can be raised: the adequacy of them as surrogate measures and the relationship between them. The purpose of this chapter is not to discuss the first issue. Rather, our primary concern is the second issue. So, we make a parsimonious review about each issue and discuss various factors that may cause the lack of consistent research on the second issue.

In the first issue, the utilization variable may be the most objective and the easiest to quantify (DeLone and McLean, 1992). This may be why it is so frequently adopted as a measure of success. Although Ives and Olson (1984) argued that system utilization could be a good surrogate of IS effectiveness, it does not necessarily translate into improved organizational effectiveness, especially when utilization is mandatory (Gatian, 1994). So, as DeLone & McLean (1992) argued, utilization measure—either actual or perceived—is relevant as a surrogate measure only when such use is voluntary. Moreover, utilization of a poor system will not improve performance, and poor systems may be utilized extensively due to social factors, habit, availability, etc., even when utilization is voluntary (Goodhue and Thompson, 1995).

User satisfaction has, thus far, received greater support and served as the most popular measure in the literature for measuring IS success (Igbaria and Nachman, 1990; Ives et al., 1983; Melone, 1990). Researchers who advocate the user satisfaction approach have the implicit assumption that satisfied users should perform better than dissatisfied users and if the information system helps users perform better, the system is successful (Bailey & Pearson, 1983; Gatian, 1994). However, it is possible that users are unhappy with "bad" systems even when they have performed well. So, this implicit assumption should be reconsidered.

In the second issue, the relationship between utilization and user satisfaction has not been consistently proposed. And conflicting empirical results have been reported. While Ginzberg (1981) and Sanders (1984) found that there were low correlations, and no correlations in some cases, Robey (1979), Baroudi et al. (1986), and Igbaria and Nachman (1990) found a strong relationship between them. Schewe (1976) and Srinivasan (1985) found no significant relationship between user attitudes and system usage behavior. Srinivasan (1985) concluded that a strong relationship between the two constructs may not always exist.

The lack of consistent empirical results may be due to many factors. First of all, inadequate conceptualization of the constructs and weak theoretical background can be the major factors. Poor research methods and measures can cause much noise in empirical results. The fact that each researcher selected different information technologies and information systems makes it difficult to compare various studies. Utilization and user satisfaction measures have not yet been standardized, so many different measures are adopted according to the varying research objectives and unit of analyses. This can also cause inconsistent results.

In this chapter, well-established utilization and user satisfaction measures are selected and modified to suit EUC context. Also, using the task contingent approach, we suggest and examine a new theoretical model that includes task uncertainty, utilization, and user satisfaction.

HYPOTHESES

Task Uncertainty and Utilization

Since information acquisition represents one important means for reducing task-related uncertainty, the task-related uncertainty influences organization's information processing requirements to a large extent which subsequently influences the information needed by individuals in order to perform their jobs (Galbraith, 1973; Culnan, 1983). Numerous studies have found that either the amount or nature of information processing is associated with task uncertainty (Daft & Lengel, 1986; Keller, 1994; Rice, 1992). In the EUC environment, end-users will be able to increase their information processing amount or richness by the diverse and extensive utilization of computer systems. So, task uncertainty will be closely associated with utilization.

More specifically, task variability will require sufficient amount of information, hence it will be closely related to the diversity of utilization. Many studies provided support for a positive relationship between task variability and the amount of information processed (Tushman, 1979; Van de Ven and Ferry, 1980; Daft and Macintosh, 1981). End-users who are faced with unpredictable problems need to develop a variety of computing skills and be allowed the flexibility and discretion for handling these situations (Brass, 1985; Ghani, 1992). Therefore, it is expected that the opportunity to experiment with a variety of computing tools and application areas will be greater. And the nature of highly variable tasks requires large inclusion of computer analysis in problem-solving and decision-making. So, utilization will be more diverse in such a variable task than in one with few unexpected events.

This leads to our first hypothesis:

Hypothesis 1: Task variability will be positively associated with the diversity of utilization.

While task variability affects the amount of information demanded to handle unanticipated events, task analyzability affects the form of the information needed to resolve ambiguities (Ghani, 1992). Specht's (1986) empirical result supported that complex, nonroutine tasks with low analyzability required less precise information and more information processing than simple and routine tasks. In the EUC environment, the computing medium would mainly determine the form of the information. When task analyzability is low, end-users require richer information that can be obtained by utilizing a rich medium in order to clarify ambiguities. In other words, for unanalyzable tasks, end-users would be more inclined to use information-rich media (e.g., PC, general purpose user-friendly software) because there is a great chance of accomplishing the task for a given effort (Rice, 1992). When a task is analyzable, on the other hand, end-users' information requirements can be sufficiently satisfied with the information from information-lean media. In this situation, a mainframe-

Figure 1: Research Model

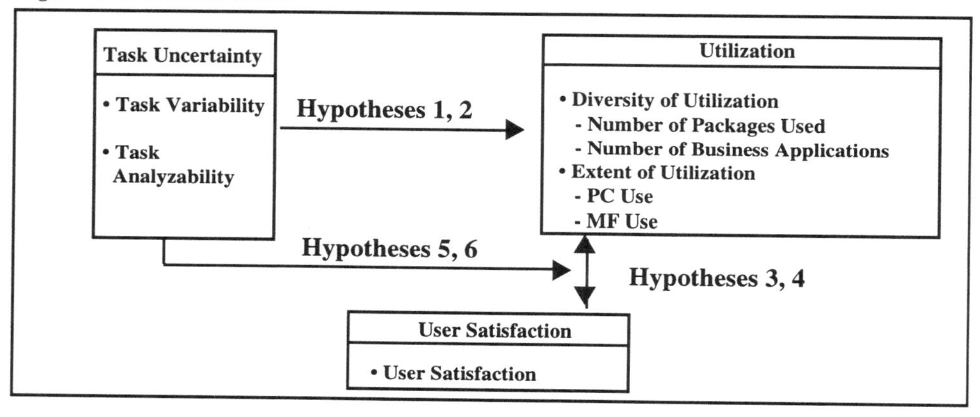

Table 1: Industry Distribution of Final Sample

Industry	Number of Respondents (companies)	Percentage
Manufacturing		
Chemicals & Petroleum	18 (2)	13.4%
Electrical, Electronic Machinery & Appliances	29 (3)	21.7%
Transport Equipment	3 (1)	2.2%
Wholesale and Retail	14 (2)	10.4%
Transport and Storage	12 (1)	9.0%
Banking and Insurance	19 (3)	14.2%
Information Services and Communications	16 (3)	11.9%
Other Services	23 (2)	17.2%
Total	134 (16)	100%

Table 2: Profile of Respondents

Job Categories		Organizational Level		Gender & Education	
Accounting & Finance	23.1%	Lower Employees	70.9%	Male	82.1%
Strategy & Planning	20.9%	Middle Managers	18.7%	Female	17.9%
Marketing & Sales	9.7%	Upper Managers	10.4%		100%
R&D Management & Technology Management	9.7%				
General Administration	9.0%			Undergraduate degree	53.0%
Production Management	6.7%			Graduate degree	33.6%
International Affairs	4.5%			Others	13.4%
Personnel Management	2.2%				
Others	14.2%				
Total	100%		100%		100%

Table 3: Measurement of Task Uncertainty and User Satisfaction

Measurement of Task Variability [a, b, c]

1. How many of these tasks are the same from day-to-day?
2. To what extent would you say your work is routine?
3. I do the same tasks in the same way most of the time.
4. Basically, I perform repetitive activities in doing my job.
5. How repetitious are your duties?

Measurement of Task Analyzability [a, b]

1. To what extent is there a clearly known way to do the major types of work you normally encounter?
2. To what extent is there a clearly known body of knowledge or subject matter that can guide you in doing your work?
3. To what extent is there an understandable sequence of steps that can be followed in doing your work?
4. To do your work, to what extent can you actually rely on established procedures and practices?
5. To what extent is there an understandable sequence of steps that can be followed in carrying out your work?

Measurement of User Satisfaction [b, d]

1. EUC helps me do my work better.
2. EUC has enabled me to carry out my work more easily and efficiently.
3. EUC has enabled me to carry out my work more effectively.
4. EUC has enabled me to make better decisions.
5. EUC is extremely useful.
6. All in all, I am now satisfied with EUC.

[a] Adapted from Withey et al. (1983)
[b] Seven-point scale
[c] Scores are reversed
[d] Adapted from Maish (1979), Ginzberg (1981), Sanders (1984), Lee & Kim (1992)

based hardware and a dedicated system designed to provide a specific solution would be extensively utilized. Accordingly, the following hypothesis is developed:

Hypothesis 2: Task analyzability will be negatively associated with the extent of PC use and positively associated with that of mainframe use.

Utilization and User Satisfaction

As discussed above, conflicting empirical results have been reported on the relationship between utilization and user satisfaction. Similar to the attitude-behavior relationship in psychology research, the path between utilization and user satisfaction has not been insisted as unidirectional. First, the influence of user satisfaction on utilization has been considered based on Fishbein & Ajzen's (1975) theory of reasoned action. Some empirical research supported that relationship by path analysis (Baroudi et al., 1986; Igbaria, 1990). Second, the influence of utilization on user satisfaction has rarely been considered (Melone, 1990). The point is that as end-users use the system for more tasks and application areas, they feel more comfortable and familiar with it, and they will discover new uses for it, which may lead to enhance user satisfaction with the EUC system (Igbaria & Nachman, 1990). However, the purpose of this chapter is not to investigate the path, but to examine whether there is a positive relationship between them. Accordingly, we propose the following hypotheses:

Hypothesis 3: The diversity of utilization will be positively associated with user satisfaction.

Hypothesis 4: The extent of utilization will be positively associated with user satisfaction.

Task Uncertainty, Utilization, and User Satisfaction

Based on the information processing model, we can discuss the moderating effects of task uncertainty on the relationship between utilization and user satisfaction. Daft & Lengel (1986) argued that the amount and richness of information processing and the media used

Table 4: Descriptive Statistics for Variables Studied (n=134)

Variables	Mean	S.D.	Min.	Max.
Task Uncertainty				
Task Variability	4.31	1.23	1.6	6.6
Task Analyzability	3.94	1.29	1.0	6.6
Utilization				
Number of Packages Used	3.78	1.68	0.0	8.0
Number of Business Applications	6.36	1.98	1.0	10.0
PC Use (hrs)	18.76	12.57	0.0	55.0
MF Use (hrs)	7.11	8.86	0.0	54.0
User Satisfaction	5.32	0.94	3.0	7.0

Table 5: Pearson Correlation Coefficients among Variables (n=134)

Variables	**1**	**2**	**3**	**4**	**5**	**6**
1. User Satisfaction						
Task Uncertainty						
2. Task Variability	.111					
3. Task Analyzability	-.164	-.721***				
Utilization						
4. # of Packages Used	.412***	.538***	-.523***			
5. # of Business Applications	.298***	.294***	-.267**	.417***		
6. PC Use	.279**	.198*	-.255**	.276**	.323***	
7. MF Use	.006	-.346***	.414***	-.310***	-.209**	-.266**

* p < .05; ** p < .01; *** p < .001

Table 6: Partial Correlation Coefficients between Task Uncertainty and Utilization

	Task Variability (controlling for analyzability)	**Task Analyzability (controlling for variability)**
Diversity of Utilization:		
Number of Packages Used	.294***	-.218**
Number of Business Applications	.150*	-.084
Extent of Utilization:		
PC Use (hrs)	.022	-.165*
MF Use (hrs)	-.067	.256***

* p < .10; ** p < .05; *** p < .01

should be matched to the level of task uncertainty. That is, performance effectiveness is related to the extent to which information processing capacity matches information processing needs. While an end-user's information processing needs arise from task uncertainty, information processing capacity depends to some extent upon utilization. When utilization matches task uncertainty, end-user's satisfaction level can be increased. Accordingly, the proposed relationships between utilization and user satisfaction may be greater when utilization is matched with task uncertainty. The contingent hypotheses to be tested are as follows:

Hypothesis 5: The higher the level of task variability, the greater the positive relationship between the number of packages used and user satisfaction.

Hypothesis 6: The higher the level of task variability, the greater the positive relationship between the number of business applications and user satisfaction.

Hypothesis 7: The lower the level of task analyzability, the greater the positive relation-

Table 7: Second-order Partial Correlation Coefficients Between Utilization and User Satisfaction

	User Satisfaction	
Diversity of Utilization:		
Number of Packages Used	.401***	(.412***)[a]
Number of Business Applications	.274***	(.298***)
Extent of Utilization:		
PC Use (hrs)	.256***	(.279***)
MF Use (hrs)	.064	(.006)

* p < .10; ** p < .05; *** p < .01
[a] ( ): Zero-order Pearson correlation coefficients

Table 8: Moderating Effects of Task Variability on the Relationship Between Diversity of Utilization and User Satisfaction

	R^2 Main Effects	R^2 Main and Interaction Effects		F-ratio of R^2 Increment
Diversity of Utilization:				
Number of Packages Used	187***	.208***	(.071*)[a]	3.527*
Number of Business Applications	.089***	.127***	(.071**)	5.789**

* p < .10; ** p < .05; *** p < .01
[a] ( ): Unstandardized regression coefficients of cross-product terms

Table 9: Moderating Effects of Task Analyzability on the Relationship between Extent of Utilization and User Satisfaction

	R^2 Main Effects	R^2 Main and Interaction Effects		F-ratio of R^2 Increment
Extent of Utilization:				
PC Use (hrs)	.084***	.086***	(-.003)[a]	0.291
MF Use (hrs)	.022	.043	(.013*)	2.918*

* p < .10; ** p < .05; *** p < .01
[a] ( ): Unstandardized regression coefficients of cross-product terms

ship between PC use and user satisfaction.

Hypothesis 8: The higher the level of task analyzability, the greater the positive relationship between MF use and user satisfaction.

To represent the relationship between the variables in this study more explicitly, the research model is depicted in Figure 1.

Table 10: Moderated Regression Analysis Results

H#	Regression Equations [a]		F-Value (sig.) [b]	R^2	Type of Moderator	Hypothesis Support
H5	US = 5.318	+ 0.277 PK - 0.119 TV (*)[c]	15.06 (0.000)	0.187	TV is a quasi moderator	Yes
	US = 5.240	+ 0.265 PK - 0.119 TV+ 0.071 PK*TV (*)	11.36 (0.000)	0.208		
H6	US = 5.320	+ 0.138 BA + 0.020 TV (n.s.)	6.43 (0.002)	0.089	TV is a pure moderator.	Yes
	US = 5.269	+ 0.152 BA + 0.039 TV + 0.071 BA*TV (**)	6.28 (0.000)	0.127		
H7	US = 5.342	+ 0.019 PC - 0.053 TA (n.s.)	5.91 (0.004)	0.084 0.084	—	No
	US = 5.331	+ 0.020 PC - 0.049 TA - 0.003 PC*TA (n.s.)	4.01 (0.009)	0.086		
H8	US = 5.335	+ 0.007 MF - 0.119 TA (n.s.)	1.47 (0.235)	0.022	TA is a pure moderator	Yes
	US = 5.276	- 0.005 MF - 0.097 TA + 0.013 MF*TA (*)	1.91 (0.131)	0.043		

[a] US = user satisfaction; PK = number of packages used; BA = number of business applications; TA = task variability; PC = PC use; MF = MF use; TA = task analyzability.

[b] The F-values and their significance levels are for the whole regression equation.

[c] Significance levels for individual regression coefficients; n.s.=insignificant; * p < .10; ** p < .05.

Methods

Sample

We conducted a cross-sectional field survey of a sample of companies in Korea which were large-sized companies (above 1,000 employees) and had IS departments. Eighteen companies were initially selected, based on stratified sampling, which took into account industrial sector. Eighteen companies belonging to eight industries, as listed in Table 1, responded to requests for cooperation. We visited these companies and a contact person for each company. We explained to the contact person that end-users should be selected randomly and cover diverse job categories. Each contact person distributed the questionnaire to 230 end-users and encouraged responses. A total of 152 responses (66.1% response rate) from 16 companies were obtained from the survey. Eighteen questionnaires were not used because either they were only partially completed (9) or responded by MIS professionals (9). As shown in Table 1, the final sample consisted of 134 end-users (58.3%) in 16 organizations.

Of the final sample, 82.1% were received from men, and 17.9% from women. Ages ranged from 19 to 39, with the average being 27.3 years old. A wide range of job categories, including

Table 11. Moderated Multiple Regression Results

Multiple Regression Equation	Increment in R^2
User Satisfaction (US) =	
Number of Packages Used (PK)	0.168***
+ Number of Business Applications (BA)	0.020*
+ PC Use (PC)	0.037**
+ MF Use (MF)	0.001
+ Task Variability (TV)	0.023**
+ Task Analyzability (TA)	0.000
+ TV*PK	0.007
+ TV*BA	0.017*
+ TA*PC	0.006
+ TA*MF	0.037**
Total R^2 (unadjusted)	0.316***

* $p < .10$; ** $p < .05$; *** $p < .01$

Figure 2: Task Variability, Diversity of Utilization and User Satisfaction

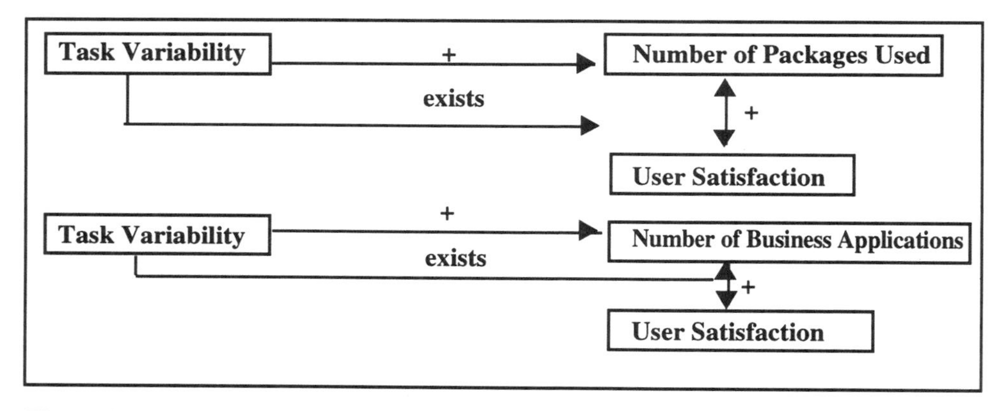

Figure 3: Task Analyzability, Extent of Utilization and User Satisfaction

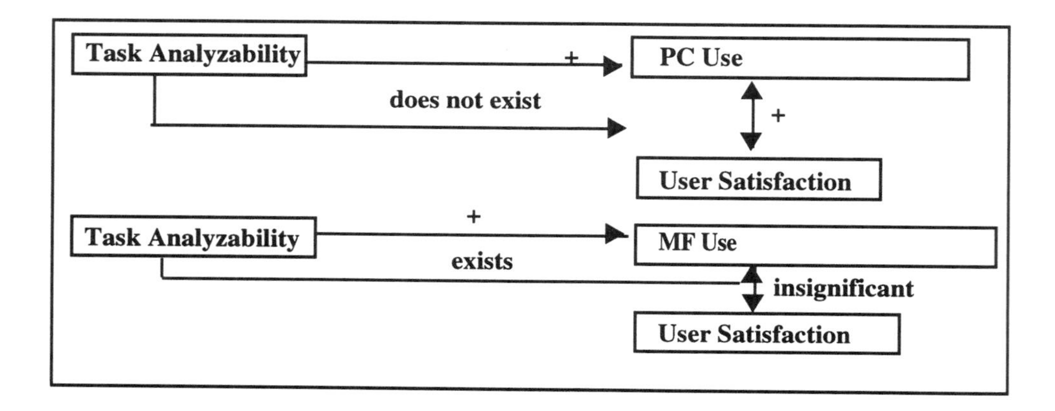

accounting, finance, planning, marketing, sales, R&D management, general administration, personnel management, etc., were represented. Table 2 presents the demographic profile of the sample.

Measures

Task Uncertainty. Withey et al. (1983) evaluated six of the most important studies in which various instruments were used to assess Perrow's dimensions of task technology. Based on these instruments, an improved measure was developed. This measure was used here to assess the two dimensions of task uncertainty. As presented in Table 3, each dimension consisted of five questions. Each question required the respondents to indicate their perceptions on task uncertainty. It was ranked on a 7-point Likert type scale ranging from (1) to a small extent to (7) to a great extent. The reliability of the instrument was assessed by computing Cronbach's alpha coefficient. The alpha coefficients were 0.895 for task variability (5 items) and 0.896 for task analyzability (5 items).

Utilization. Based on several studies, our study include two indicators of utilization: diversity of utilization and extent of utilization (Amoroso & Cheney, 1991, 1992; Igbaria et al., 1989). Diversity of utilization was measured by: (1) the number of different packages used by the participants; (2) the number of business applications performed with the help of EUC. To measure "the number of packages used," a list of nine different categories of packages was specified. Respondents were asked to count the number of categories that they were actually using. The list of categories consists of: word processors; spreadsheet; data management (e.g., dBase III, clipper); data analysis (e.g., SPSS, SAS); graphical presentation; modeling systems (e.g., IFPS); communication (e.g., via electronic mail); professional programming languages; and the fourth generation programming languages (e.g., SQL). For measuring "the number of business applications," ten application areas were presented: aiding in reporting to supervisors; historical reference; looking for trends; making decisions; planning; finding problems; communicating with others; budgeting; controlling and guiding activities; and aiding in the cutting of costs. Respondents were asked to indicate whether they used computers in these ten application areas. The total number of business application areas in which respondents reported utilization was used as an index of this measure. Extent of utilization was measured by PC use and mainframe use. Respondents were asked to specify the number of hours a week they typically spend directly using PC and mainframe, respectively.

User Satisfaction. A large number of user satisfaction constructs range from "satisfaction with the information output of a specific system" (Ives et al., 1983) to the "manifold of beliefs or attitudes about the value of the IS" (Swanson, 1974). The former conceptualization is termed user information satisfaction and the latter overall satisfaction or perceived effectiveness. According to research objectives and a level of analysis, appropriate measures should be selected. If a research takes a specific system as a unit of analysis, then user information satisfaction measures will be more appropriate. On the other hand, if a researcher is interested in measuring a user's general satisfaction with an IS contribution toward organizational effectiveness, then overall satisfaction measures will be better (Gatian, 1994).

In this chapter, user satisfaction is conceptualized as the affective attitude toward computing activities by any hands-on user of microcomputers or computers. We define EUC broadly as the direct use of computers encompassing all the computer-related activities. And user satisfaction with a specific system is not our concern. Therefore, end-user's perceived effectiveness and overall satisfaction measures are employed for evaluating user satisfaction. Table 3 presents the instrument. The Cronbach's alpha was 0.874 for user satisfaction measures (6 items).

RESULTS

General Findings

Table 4 shows the means, standard deviations, and other descriptive statistics for the variables studied. In this sample, end-users were spending more of their time with PC (mean = 18.76 hours) than mainframe (mean = 7.11 hours). Table 5 shows the zero-order correlation coefficients for the variables in this study. Task variability was significantly and negatively correlated with task analyzability (r = - 0.721). This is consistent with the results found in other empirical studies (Daft and Macintosh, 1981; Van de Ven & Delbecq, 1974). Perrow suggested that although conceptually distinct, the two dimensions might have a statistically significant correlation in real-world organizations. As expected, the correlation between user satisfaction and task uncertainty was not significant. Consistent with expectations, the data showed that task uncertainty was closely associated with utilization. Task variability positively correlated with the diversity of utilization (the number of packages used, the number of business applications) and PC use, while a significant negative correlation between task variability and mainframe use was found. The correlations between task analyzability and utilization were statistically significant and had opposite directions with the correlations between task variability and utilization. This may be partly due to the strong negative correlation between task variability and analyzability. Detailed analyses appear in later sections.

Relationship between Task Uncertainty and Utilization

In order to identify the relationship between task uncertainty and utilization, partial correlation coefficients were computed. The partial correlation coefficients between task

Figure 4: Task Uncertainty and Utilization

Low

High

Unanalyzable

Rich Media

Craft Technology

Examples: managerial work, money market trader

Nonroutine Technology

Examples: strategic planning, industrial R&D

Analyzability

Routine Technology

Examples: machine operator

Engineering Technology

Examples: accountant, engineer

Analyzable

Lean Media

Few Packages
Few Business Applications

Various Packages
Various Business Applications

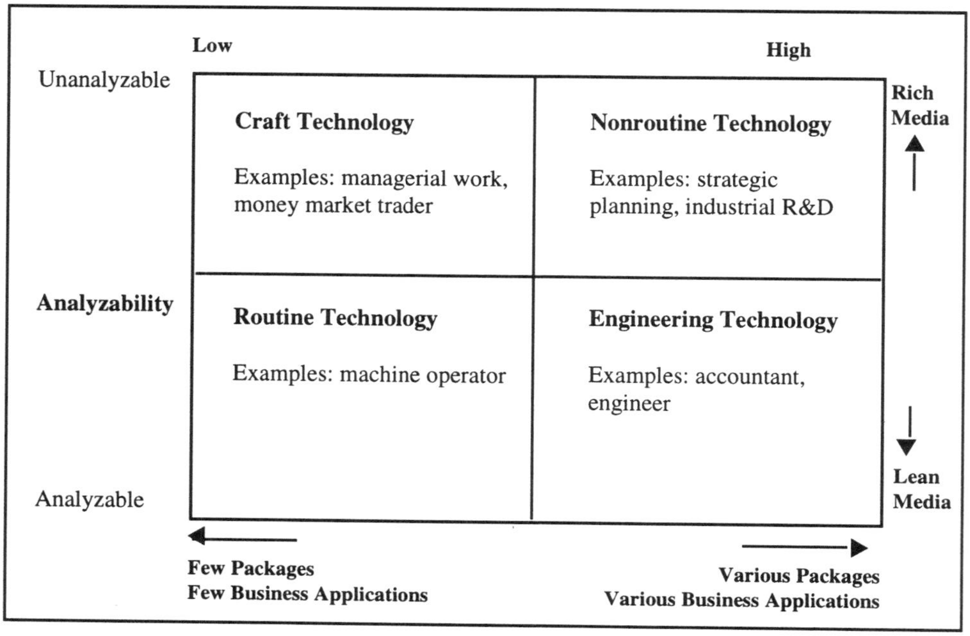

variability and utilization, controlling for task analyzability, are shown in the first column of Table 6. The partial correlation coefficients between task analyzability and utilization, controlling for task variability, are shown in the second column of Table 6.

The data indicate a positive relationship between task variability and the diversity of utilization. The coefficient between task variability and the number of packages used was 0.294 ($p < 0.01$) and the coefficient between task variability and the number of business applications was 0.150 ($p < 0.1$). This supports Hypothesis 1. When the frequency of exceptions and unexpected events increases, we expect end-users to have a wide variety of application software and to utilize computers for diverse business applications areas.

Data analysis revealed a negative correlation between task analyzability and PC use, but a positive correlation between task analyzability and mainframe use. This provides support for Hypothesis 2. As discussed in the previous section, PC is usually a richer medium than mainframe. So the more unanalyzable the task is, the more dependent upon PC end-users are. Under the condition of high task analyzability, in contrast, the information processing needs can be sufficiently met by mainframe use.

Unexpectedly, table 6 indicates a significantly negative correlation between task analyzability and the number of packages used ($r = -0.218$). This finding was not hypothesized. It means that end-users who face unanalyzable tasks tend to utilize diverse application packages. In other words, when the task is not well understood, it is difficult to resolve ambiguities by utilizing a few application packages.

Relationship Between Utilization and User Satisfaction

The simple correlation coefficients between utilization and user satisfaction are shown in parentheses on Table 7. Also, in order to examine the relationship between them while removing the effect of task variability and analyzability, the second-order partial correlation coefficients, controlling for these two variables, were computed.

The results showed that user satisfaction and the diversity of utilization were significantly and positively correlated. Thus, H3 was supported. In contrast, H4 was not supported because user satisfaction and mainframe use were not significantly correlated. The lack of significant relationship between mainframe use and user satisfaction might be due to the fact that mainframe tends to be a less rich medium than PC. This result suggests that there is not always a positive relationship between utilization and user satisfaction. It also suggests that multivariate contingent analyses are required to deeply examine the relationship between utilization and user satisfaction.

Moderating Effects of Task Uncertainty on the Relationship Between Utilization and User Satisfaction

In order to test the contingency hypotheses, H5-H8, moderated regression analysis (MRA) was used. In MRA, similar to the approaches taken by Schoonhoven (1981) and Gupta and Govindarajan (1984), two regression equations given below are run for each relationship:

$$Y = b_0 + b_1X_1 + b_2X_2 \quad (1)$$
$$Y = b_0 + b_1X_1 + b_2X_2 + b_3X_1X_2 \quad (2)$$

where Y is user satisfaction, X_1 is a variable of a particularly matched utilization, and X_2 is a moderating variable (task variability or analyzability).

In equation (1), task uncertainty (task variability or analyzability) and the variable of a particularly matched utilization were entered as predictors of user satisfaction. In equation

(2), the interaction term of task uncertainty and utilization was entered in addition to the main effects. A test was performed to see whether the addition of the interaction term resulted in a significant increment in the percent of variance explained in the criterion variable over that already explained by the main effect terms. If the addition of the interaction term increases R^2 by a significant amount and equations (1) and (2) are significantly different (i.e., b3= 0), then a moderating effect exists. As Hoffman et al. (1992) pointed out, mathematical arguments (Allison, 1978; Cohen, 1978; Cohen & Cohen, 1975) demonstrate that F-tests for increments in R^2 for product terms are valid even when the product terms are highly correlated with the component variables and when the scales are not ratio scales.

More specifically, as the criteria suggested by Sharma et al. (1981), if equations (1) and (2) are not significantly different and X_2 is related to Y (i.e., $b_3 = 0$; $b_2 \neq 0$), then X_2 is not a moderator variable but simply an independent predictor variable. For X_2 to be a "pure moderator" variable, X_2 should interact significantly with X_2 and should not be related to Y (i.e., $b_3 \neq 0$; $b_2 = 0$). For X_2 to be classified as a "quasi moderator" variable, X_2 should interact significantly with X_1 and should be related to Y (i.e., $b_2 \neq b_3 \neq 0$). In order to avoid the risk of multicollinearity problems due to the use of cross-product terms, all independent variables were centered (by subtracting their means) as suggested by Cronbach (1987).

Whether moderating effects existed or not, we checked the F-ratio of R^2 increment and the regression coefficients of cross-product terms. As shown in Table 8, there was evidence that task variability affected the relationship between the diversity of utilization and user satisfaction. The inclusion of the interaction term of the number of packages used and task variability significantly increased R^2 from 0.187 to 0.208 ($F = 3.527$, $p < .10$). And the inclusion of the number of business applications and task variability interaction term significantly increased R^2 from 0.089 to 0.127 ($F = 5.789$, $p < .05$). The coefficients of the two interaction terms were significantly positive.

On the other hand, as seen from Table 9, the moderating effects of task analyzability on the relationship between the extent of utilization and user satisfaction existed only in the case of mainframe use. The inclusion of the interaction term of PC use and task analyzability did not significantly increase R^2. In contrast, the inclusion of mainframe use and task analyzability interaction terms significantly increased R^2 from 0.022 to 0.043 ($F = 2.918$, $p < .10$). The coefficient of the interaction term was significantly positive.

Further MRA results are presented in Table 10. On the relationship between the number of packages used and user satisfaction, task variability was a quasi-moderator, because the coefficients of task variability and the interaction term were both significant. On the relationship between the number of business applications and user satisfaction, task variability was a pure moderator, because the coefficient of task variability was not significant while the interaction term was. Hypotheses H5 and H6 are supported, indicating that the positive relationship between the diversity of utilization and user satisfaction is contingent upon task variability. In contrast, the inclusion of the interaction term of PC use and task analyzability did not significantly increase R^2 and the coefficient of that interaction term was not significant. So, H7 is rejected. As hypothesized (H8), the coefficient of mainframe use and task analyzability interaction term was significant and task analyzability was not related to user satisfaction. Task analyzability was a pure moderator on the relationship between mainframe use and user satisfaction. Thus, H8 is supported.

The MRA technique tests the interaction effect of each moderating variable independently. As an additional analysis, Table 11 shows the results of introducing all utilization variables and four interaction terms into the multiple regression equation simultaneously. To determine the relative contribution of each of the variables in explaining variation in user satisfaction, the increment in R^2 was examined rather than the magnitude of the beta coefficients. The data in Table 11 show that the number of packages used ($R^2 = 0.168$; $p < 0.01$) explained the greatest variance in user satisfaction. Of other utilization variables, the number of business applications ($R^2 = 0.020$; $p < 0.10$) and PC use ($R^2 = 0.037$; $p < 0.05$) have significant main effects on user satisfaction. Of the cross-product terms, the cross-product term of task variability and the number of business applications ($R^2 = 0.017$; $p < 0.10$) and the cross-product term of task analyzability and mainframe use ($R^2 = 0.037$; $p < 0.05$) have significant interaction effects.

DISCUSSION

Conclusions

In this chapter, in order to clarify the conflicting empirical results between utilization and user satisfaction, we proposed a task-contingent model based on the information processing view. First, we found strong evidence that task variability was closely related to the diversity of utilization and task analyzability was closely related to PC use and mainframe use. Though not hypothesized, we found a strong relationship between task analyzability and the number of packages used. This result implies that end-users tend to utilize a large number of packages when a task is unanalyzable.

Second, there were not always positive relationships between utilization and user satisfaction. In this chapter, most utilization variables, except mainframe use, were significantly and positively correlated with user satisfaction. This is evidence that using information-lean media like mainframe may not be necessarily translated into user satisfaction and may even cause dissatisfaction.

Third, we found reasonably supportive evidence of moderating effects of task uncertainty on the relationship between utilization and user satisfaction. A task-contingent relationship between utilization and user satisfaction in our study's result can be represented by three situations. The first situation is represented in Figure 2. In this situation, utilization and user satisfaction are positively related, and task uncertainty affects the relationship between them. In our data, the positive relationship between the diversity of utilization and user satisfaction was greater when task variability was higher. The second situation is represented in the upper parts of Figure 3. In this case, utilization and user satisfaction are positively related and the moderating effect of task uncertainty on the relationship between them does not exist. In our data, PC use was closely associated with user satisfaction regardless of the level of task analyzability. The third situation is represented in the lower parts of Figure 3. In this situation, utilization and user satisfaction does not seem to be significantly related. However, this appearance may be due to the fact that the significant relationships in some task contingencies are concealed. In our data, though mainframe use and user satisfaction was not significantly correlated, the interaction term of mainframe use and task analyzability had significant interaction effect on user satisfaction.

Theoretical Implications and Managerial Implications

Theoretical implications of this chapter can be found in our new theoretical model that explains more comprehensively the relationship between utilization and user satisfaction. First of all, one of the most important implications is that the relationship between utilization and user satisfaction may vary. So, a contingent approach is required. Also, because utilization and user satisfaction constructs can be diversely defined and measured by many different measures, utilization and user satisfaction may have insignificant relationships in some utilization or user satisfaction variables. We should closely examine the insignificant relationships to see whether significant relationships in some contingencies are hidden. These possibilities should not be overlooked. For example, though utilization of information-lean media may be less influential than utilization of information-rich media in enhancing user satisfaction, it would be efficient under conditions of high task analyzability. In the opposite direction, user satisfaction may influence utilization more strongly when congruence between task uncertainty and utilization occurs.

Managerial implications of this chapter can be described with the following two points. First, for effective management of EUC in organizations, IS managers should consider the fit between end-users' task uncertainty and utilization in their EUC activities. Task uncertainty may vary widely within organizations, so a uniform company-wide EUC support policy will not suit all end-users. As illustrated in Figure 4, IS managers can classify end-users and user departments into Perrow's four categories of task technology. End-users who are under high task variability would be required to utilize diverse application packages and to involve diverse business applications. And end-users who are under low task analyzability would be required to use rich computing media, such as user-friendly software, analysis and inquiry application software, and personal computers. Of course, it could be argued that some tasks which are very unanalyzable or variable may not be aided by EUC. That is, Figure 4 represents the normative guideline for a desirable match between task uncertainty and utilization. For example, the work of strategic planning and industrial R&D falls under nonroutine technology and would best be supported by the utilization of various packages, various business applications, and rich media. On the other hand, machine operators and bank tellers fall under routine technology and would be sufficiently supported by the utilization of a few packages and lean media. Among the other diagonals, craft technology such as managerial work would be required to utilize rich media, but require only a few packages and a few business application areas. And end-users who are classified into engineering technology, such as accountants, would best be supported by diverse software packages and exception and monitoring applications generally available on mainframe computers.

The second point is the issue of measuring IS success or EUC success in the world of practice. IS managers would adopt utilization and user satisfaction most frequently as IS success or EUC success. However, they should be more cautious in using these measures. Both utilization measure and user satisfaction measure have their own weaknesses, so it is more desirable to use both measures complimentarily. When both measures are used simultaneously, our study results should be considered. For example, if end-users have diverse alternative systems for their tasks, they tend to utilize the system that fits their tasks. And when this fit occurs, the relationship between utilization and user satisfaction would be great. And IS managers should closely examine the situation in which utilization variables are not closely associated with user satisfaction.

Limitations and Future Research Directions

There are some limitations in this study, which need to be examined in further research. First, interpretation and generalization of our study's findings should be done cautiously. In particular, the participating firms were selected in a developing country, Korea, where the EUC phenomenon began to appear in 1989. The Korean situation may be different from firms in developed countries where EUC growth stages are relatively mature. Hence, further investigations of the study's model in other settings are encouraged to generalize our findings.

Second, the contingency variables were not exhaustive and should be extended. Further research could move toward clarifying under what contingencies the relationship between utilization and user satisfaction would be strong. These contingent variables include richness of hardware and software, voluntary nature of utilization behavior, computing abilities, work group norms for utilization, other social influences, etc. Incorporating these variables in an expanded research model could produce more comprehensive and sophisticated results.

REFERENCES

Alavi, M. (1985). End-User Computing: The MIS Manager's Perspective. *Information & Management*, 8(3), March, 171-178.

Allison, P.D. (1978). Testing for Interaction in Multiple Regression. *American Journal of Sociology*, 83, 144-153.

Amoroso, D.L. & Cheney, P.H. (1992). Quality End User-Developed Applications: Some Essential Ingredients. *Data Base*, Winter, 1-11.

Amoroso, D.L. & Cheney, P.H. (1991). Testing a Causal Model of End-User Application Effectiveness. *Journal of MIS*, 8(1), Summer, 63-89.

Bailey, J. & Pearson, S. (1983). Development of a Tool for Measuring and Analyzing Computer User Satisfaction. *Management Science*, 29(5), 530-545.

Baroudi, J.J., Olson, M.H. & Ives, B. (1986). An Empirical Study of the Impact of User Involvement on System Usage and Information Satisfaction. *Communications of the ACM*, 29(3), 232-238.

Benson, D.H. (1983). A Field Study of End User Computing: Findings and Issues. *MIS Quarterly*, 7, 35-45.

Brass, D.J. (1985). Technology and the Structuring of Jobs: Employee Satisfaction, Performance, and Influence. *Organization Behavior and Human Decision Processes*, 35, April, 216-240.

Cheney, P.H., Mann, R.I. & Amoroso, D.L. (1986). Organizational Factors Affecting the Success of End User Computing. *Journal of MIS*, 3(1), 65-80.

Cohen, J. (1978). Partial Products Are Interactions; Partial Powers Are Curve Components. *Psychological Bulletin*, 85, 858-866.

Cohen, J. & Cohen, P. (1975). *Applied Multiple Regression/Correlation Analysis for the Behavioral Sciences,* Hillsdale, New Jersey: Erlbaum.

Cronbach, L.J. (1987). Statistical Tests for Moderator Variables: Flaws in Analysis Recently Proposed. *Psychological Bulletin*, 69(3), 161-182.

Culnan, M.J. (1983). Chauffeured Versus End User Access to Commercial Databases: The Effects of Task and Individual Differences. *MIS Quarterly*, 7(1), 55-67.

Daft, R.L. & Lengel, R.H. (1984). Information Richness: A New Approach to Managerial Behavior and Organization Design. *Research in Organizational Behavior*, 6, 191-233.

Daft, R.L. & Lengel, R.H. (1986). Organizational Information Requirements, Media Richness, and Structural Design. *Management Science*, 32(5), May, 554-571.

Daft, R.L. & Macintosh, N.B. (1981). A Tentative Exploration into the Amount and Equivocality of Information Processing in Organizational Work Units. *Administrative Science Quarterly*, 26, 207-224.

DeLone, W.H. & McLean, E.R. (1992). Information Systems Success: The Quest for the Dependent Variable. *Information Systems Research*, 3(1), 60-95.

Doll, W.J. & Torkzadeh, G. (1989). A Discrepancy Model of End-User Computing Involvement. *Management Science*, 35(10), October, 1151-1171.

Ein-Dor, P. & Segev, E. (1991). Intensity of End User Computing. *Data Base*, Winter/Spring, 30-37.

Ein-Dor, P. & Segev, E. (1982). Organizational Context and MIS Structure: Some Empirical Evidence. *MIS Quarterly*, 6(3), September, 55-68.

Etezadi-Amoli, J. & Farhoomand, A.F. (1996). A Structural Model of End User Computing Satisfaction and User Performance. *Information & Management*, 30, 65-73.

Fishbein, M. & Ajzen, I. (1975). *Belief, Attitude, Intention and Behavior: An Introduction to Theory and Research,* Addison-Wesley, Boston, MA.

Galbraith, J.R. (1973). *Designing Complex Organizations*, Reading, MA: Addison-Wesley.
Galbraith, J.R. (1977). *Organization Design*, Reading, MA: Addison-Wesley.
Gatian, A.W. (1994). Is User Satisfaction a Valid Measure of System Effectiveness. *Information & Management*, 26(3), 119-131.
Ghani, J.A. (1992). Task Uncertainty and the Use of Computer Technology. *Information & Management*, 22, 69-76.
Ginzberg, M.J. (1981). Early Diagnosis of MIS Implementation Failure: Promising Results and Unanswered Questions. *Management Science*, 27(4), 459-478.
Goodhue, D.L. & Thompson, R.L. (1995). Task-Technology Fit and Individual Performance. *MIS Quarterly*, 19(2), June, 213-236.
Gupta, A.K. & Govindarajan, V. (1984). Business Unit Strategy, Managerial Characteristics, and Business Unit Effectiveness at Strategy Implementation. *Academy of Management Journal*, 27(1), 25-41.
Hoffman, J.J., Cullen, J.B., Carter, N.M, and Hofacker, C.F. (1992). Alternative Methods for Measuring Organization Fit: Technology, Structure, and Performance. *Journal of Management*, 18(1), 45-57.
Igbaria, M. (1990). End-User Computing Effectiveness: A Structural Equation Model. *OMEGA*, 18(6), 637-652.
Igbaria, M. & Nachman, S.A. (1990). Correlates of User Satisfaction with End User Computing: An Exploratory Study. *Information & Management*, 19(2), 73-82.
Igbaria, M., Pavri, F.N., & Huff, S.L. (1989). Microcomputer Applications: An Empirical Look at Usage. *Information & Management*, 16(4), 187-196.
Ives, B. & Olson, M.H. (1984). User Involvement and MIS Success: A Review of Research. *Management Science*, 30(5), 586-603.
Ives, B., Olson, M.H & Baroudi, J.J. (1983). The Measurement of User Information Satisfaction. *Communications of the ACM*, 26(10), October, 785-793.
Keller, R.T. (1994). Technology-Information Processing Fit and the Performance of R&D Project Groups: A Test of Contingency Theory. *Academy of Management Journal*, 37(1), 167-179.
Kim, K.K. (1990). Task characteristics, Decentralization, and the Success of Hospital Information Systems. *Information & Management*, 19(2), 83-93.
Lee, J. & Kim, S. (1992). The Relationship between Procedural Formalization in MIS Development and MIS Success. *Information & Management*, 22, 89-111.
Maish, A.M. (1979). A User's Behavior toward His MIS. *MIS Quarterly*, 3(1), 39-52.
Melone, N.P. (1990). A Theoretical Assessment of the User-Satisfaction Construct in Information Systems Research. *Management Science*, 36(1), January, 76-91.
Perrow, C.A. (1967). A Framework for the Comparative Analysis of Organizations. *American Sociological Review*, 32(2), April, 194-208.
Rainer, R.K. Jr. & Harrison, A.W. (1994). Toward Development of the End User Computing Construct in a University Setting. *Decision Sciences*, 24(6), 1187-1202.
Rice, R.E. (1992). Task Analyzability, Use of New Media, and Effectiveness: A Multi-site Exploration of Media Richness. *Organization Science*, 3(4), November, 475-500.
Rivard, S. & Huff, S. (1985). An Empirical Study of Users as Application Developers. *Information & Management*, 8(2), February, 89-102.
Robey, D. (1979). User Attitudes and Management Information System Use. *Academy of Management Journal*, 22(3), September, 527-538.
Sanders, G.L. (1984). MIS/DSS Success Measure. *Systems, Objectives, Solutions,* 4, 29-34.
Schewe, C. (1976). The MIS User: An Exploratory Behavioral Analysis. *Academy of Management Journal*, 19(4), December, 577-590.
Schiffman, S.J., Meile, L.C., & Igbaria, M. (1992). An Examination of End-User Types. *Information & Management*, 22, 207-215.
Schoonhoven, C.B. (1981). Problems with Contingency Theory: Testing Assumptions Hidden within the Language of Contingency Theory. *Administrative Science Quarterly*, 26(3), 349-377.
Sharma, S., Durand, R.M., & Gur-Arie, O. (1981). Identification and Analysis of Moderator Variables. *Journal of Marketing Research*, 18, 291-300.

Sipior, J.C. & Sanders, G.L. (1989). Definitional Distinctions and Implications for Managing End User Computing. *Information & Management*, 16(3), 115-123.
Specht, P.H. (1986). Job Characteristics as Indicants of CBIS Data Requirements. *MIS Quarterly*, 10(3), September, 271-287.
Srinivasan, A. (1985). Alternative Measures of System Effectiveness: Associations and Implications. *MIS Quarterly*, 9(3), September, 243-253.
Swanson, E.B. (1974). MIS: Appreciation and Involvement. *Management Science*, 21(2), 178-188.
Trauth, E.M. & Cole, E. (1992). The Organizational Interface: A Method for Supporting End Users of Packaged Software. *MIS Quarterly*, 16(1), March, 35-53.
Tushman, M.L. (1979). Work Characteristics and Subunit Communication Structure: A Contingency Analysis. *Administrative Science Quarterly*, 24, 82-98.
Tushman, M.L. & Nadler, D.A. (1978). Information Processing as an Integrating Concept in Organization Design. *Academy of Management Review*, 3(3), July, 613-624.
Van de Ven, A.H. & Delbecq, A. (1974). A Task Contingent Model of Work Unit Structure. *Administrative Science Quarterly*, 19, 183-197.
Van de Ven, A.H. & Ferry, D.L. (1980). *Measuring and Assessing Organizations*, Wiley Interscience, New York.
Withey, M., Daft, R.L. & Cooper, W.H. (1983). Measures of Perrow's Work Unit Technology: An Empirical Assessment and a New Scale. *Academy of Management Journal*, 26(1), 45-63.

Chapter 15

Understanding the End User: The Key to Managing End-User Computing

Donald L. Amoroso
University of Colorado, USA

The End-User Characteristics Matrix, a mapping of user characteristics onto four end-user taxonomies, provides a more detailed perspective on the end user as developer/operator of computer-based information systems. Understanding individual end users is probably the most critical element to effectively managing end-user computing. Yet many managers do not really understand the end user they are attempting to manage. The purpose of this paper is to develop a framework which will allow the manager of end users to identify and describe user characteristics which differentiate, define, and help us better understand the end user.

Previous literature on end users was discussed where four end-user taxonomies were presented, categorizing end users according to one or more characteristics, along with empirical research, which utilized those taxonomies. The Rockart and Flannery end-user taxonomy has been the most widely used framework since 1983. The most comprehensive taxonomy, Cotterman and Dumar's User Cube, was used as the basis for definitions in this research. The end user located in the developer/operator plane, identified as the fastest growing category of end users, was investigated in depth. Empirical research in end-user computing was examined to identify the set of user characteristics. Researchers studying end-user computing can use the matrix as a starting point to visualize how past research taxonomies and empirical studies are interrelated. Practitioners, anxious to develop policies to manage EUC, can concentrate their efforts on certain user characteristics they observe to be problematic.

After a decade of wild and rampant growth in end user computing (EUC), we are still searching for a set of principles which will allow us to more effectively manage it. A significant phenomenon of the 1980s, EUC continues to be an important issue for managers of tomorrow's organization. The increase in EUC literature provides evidence of this trend. Basically, managing end-user computing can only be more effective when we learn how to manage individual end-users. We will only be able to take great leaps ahead when we have

This chapter originally appeared in Managing Information Resources in the 1990s (Proceedings of the 1990 Information Resources Management Association International Conference).

a better understanding of the end users we are managing.

Despite the growth of EUC, practitioners, academics, and vendors have different understandings of the term "'end-user computing". This term is often substituted for "user" or the person that "uses" the reports generated by a computer. In addition to different definitions and assumptions, there is a variety of end-user classification schemes from which to organize research designs. A research base which does not share common definitions from which to investigate end-user computing creates a number of difficulties. First, the results are not comparable because the same language is not spoken. We simply do not understand the end users we are studying. Second, some study findings, using different definitions, are contradictory and inconclusive. Surely we do not want to recommend to managers of end-user computing that they establish corporate policies from inconclusive research results? Third, some researchers fail to utilize existing theoretical definitions in their variable operationalizations. As each of the frameworks offer differing perspectives on the end user, researchers in the end-user computing area have either been forced to choose one framework or create a new one in which to work.

Rockart and Flannery, early investigators of end-user computing, felt that top managers must understand their end users before they can even start to develop a strategy for effectively managing their EUC environment (Rockart and Flannery, 1983). Since 1982, several researchers have attempted to develop a categorization of end users in order to investigate a firm's EUC environment (Davis, 1985; Lefkovitz, 1979; Martin, 1979; Rivard and Huff, 1985; Rockart and Flannery, 1983). A framework is necessary to provide researchers and practicing managers with a common way of comparing the results of investigative research. Further, it creates a relevant context for readers of the research to evaluate and interpret the results. Finally, a framework promotes commonly used definitions. Unfortunately, the characteristics classifying end users vary significantly in literature. Frankly, another new typology is not needed; rather we simply need a better understanding of the end user using existing ones. In this research then, we will use the Cotterman and Dumar three-dimensional taxonomy of end users as a vehicle for our discussion in order to provide consistency of terminology (Cotterman and Kumar, 1989).

The purpose of this chapter is to identify and describe user characteristics, which differentiate, define, and help us better understand the end user. We will review the relevant literature on end-user computing in order to lay the groundwork for discussing those characteristics. Derived from the literature, four end-user taxonomies and then user characteristics will be used to develop an End-User Characteristics Matrix. The diversity of the end-user community lends even more evidence for differentiated training, supplements and software tools.

REVIEW OF THE LITERATURE

The MIS literature has portrayed the user in many different ways. Churchman and Schainblatt (1965) were the first to present a user/manager and analyst dichotomy. This dichotomy prompted the recommendation of the concept of "mutual understanding" between the user and the analyst. Users were categorized early in the MIS literature by the way they interacted with the computer in order to obtain outputs. In this section, several end-user taxonomies are presented along with empirical studies which utilized those taxonomies.

THE CODASYL END-USER TAXONOMY

In 1979, the CODASYL End-User Facilities Committee, commissioned in the late 1970s to study the explosive growth of end-user computer, initially classified users as direct or indirect, and later added the category of intermediary user (Lefkovitz, 1979). A direct user is one who interacts with a computer-based information system (IS) in either the batch or interactive mode to receive periodic computer reports. In contrast, an indirect user does not interface directly with the computer, but rather uses the outputs from the system to make decisions or perform tasks. An intermediary user interacts directly with the computer but does not utilize the output. Later, Joseph Davis (1985) developed a taxonomy of general MIS users from previous studies. He identified potential differences among the three COSASYL end-user categories, which include direct, indirect, and autonomous users. An autonomous user is one who acts on his/her own behalf to interact with the computer. It was found that most end users categorized in previous studies fall into Davis' autonomous users category.

Three early attempts to classify end users illustrates the interest among IS practitioners and academicians alike in deriving a working definition of the MIS user. The CODASYL report was the first effort to classify the growing subset of end users. From that report, McLean (1979) and Martin (1982) developed basic classification schemes, which included level of training, type of application, and level of technical understanding(Martin, 1985; McLean, 1979). Hackathorn and Keen (1981) describe end users as computer users who have exercised direct personal control over all aspects of information technology including equipment selection, software selection, software development, customization of applications, and data management. Hackathorn and keen state, "...emphasis is on the end user of the technology, acting as programmer, analyst, etc.,—without role differentiation". The emphasis of this research was on identifying user characteristics, which focused on the relationship between the user and the technology. Differences were observed to occur both in the system usage and in the system development process.

THE ROCKART & FLANNERY END-USER TAXONOMY

Rockart and Flannery (1983) took a broader view of end-user computing than previous research studies when they introduced six distinct classes of end users who differed significantly from each other in terms of computer skills, method of computer use, application focus, and the amount of support needed and obtained. Non-programming end users access computerized data through a limited, menu-driven application program usually provided by others. Command-level end users are able to specify, access, and manipulate data in order to generate unique reports. End-user programmers utilize both command and procedural languages directly for their own personal information needs. Functional support personnel support other end users and themselves in the development of applications. End-user computing support personnel and DP programmers, fluent in end-user languages, aid other end users in the development process.

Four studies utilized the Rockart and Flannery taxonomy as a means of classifying their respondents. In a study related to Rockart and Flannery, Quillard, et al. (1983) used the characteristics from the Rockart and Flannery study adding level of programming and level of technical understanding to their list. They derived a working definition of the end-user as the person who develops an application primarily for his or her own use utilizing end-user software tools. Brancheau, et al. (1985) conducted a field study to obtain the end user's viewpoint regarding the information center. End users were self-classified based upon user descriptions provided by Rockart and Flannery. Experience was regarded as an important user characteristic. Sumner and Kleppler (1987) investigated user programmer, and functional support categories. The primary user characteristics they examined were the degree of user involvement in application development, training and development of end users, and the nature of applications developed. Amoroso and Cheney (1987) investigated the end-user computing environment in 18 large North American insurance firms. The majority of end users (77%) fell into the command-level end user and end-user programmer categories.

THE RIVARD & HUFF END-USER TAXONOMY

Rivard and Huff (1985) delineated three end-user types based on distinct patterns concerning the reasons why users developed applications and for whom they were developed. Their study classified end users by functional area, type of application, and experience with end-user computing. Rivard and Huff examined only end users who developed their own applications. Their first end-user category, micro DP department users, includes users who respond to programming requests from other users in their departments. The second group are staff analysts who develop applications that they themselves use to solve problems or provide information to others. The third group includes opportunity seekers, who are users who have extensive expertise in their own functional area and some computer expertise. They typically develop decision support applications for their own use. In a follow-up article from the same research effort, Rivard and Huff (1988) reported the importance of the quality of data processing (DP) support for end-user development applications, user satisfaction, independence from DP, and the computer background of end users. The Rivard end-user taxonomy was not utilized by other researchers to date.

OTHER STUDIES

Davis and Olson (1985) reported four additional interrelated end-user characteristics than have been mentioned already. The first characteristic is the degree of software manipulation versus development. The second characteristic is level of technical understanding which involves two distinct concepts: 1) the general level of computer knowledge, and 2) the knowledge gained from using a specific system. The authors reported that novices and experts interact with a system in different ways. The third characteristic is developing applications. Rockart and Flannery defined a frequent user as one who utilizes the computer to perform tasks or solve problems in a reasonable timeframe. Quillard et al., answering Rockart and Flannery's need for a "reasonable timeframe" suggested that a frequent user is one who utilizes a specific application more than three hours weekly. The fourth characteristic distinguishes primary users from secondary users. This dimension is similar to the earlier DOSASYL (Lefovitz, 1979) classification of direct versus intermediary users. Davis and Olson define a primary user as one who benefits from the system's output. The secondary user is responsible for the input to the system, as is the intermediary user, but they do not use the output to perform their jobs.

Recently, three studies were conducted which investigated end-user usage patterns. Lee (1986) studied usage patterns and sources of assistance for personal computer users. He found that the extent of PC usage was correlated with prior knowledge of EUC tools. Support, specifically development assistance, was found to be critical, supplied by colleagues rather than traditional training methods. Application type was found to be a significant user characteristic, carried throughout Lee's study. The level of technical understanding was investigated with each end user. In a study investigating the management of personal computer use, Pyburn (1986) interviewed end users with at least one year of experience. Bergeron and Berube (1988) reported that the results of a study which examined user support structures, characterized end users by experience, type of application, degree of programming required, knowledge of microcomputer tools, and training acquired. None of these studies utilized a taxonomy or framework for categorizing end users.

THE USER CUBE TAXONOMY

Perhaps the taxonomies which were described above are too simplistic. In 1989, Cotterman and Kumar found "the lack of a clear-cut and commonly accepted definition and classification scheme for end users...". The argument for a comprehensive end-user classification scheme was made earlier. They offer the following definitions:

End User: Any organizational unit or person who has an interaction with the computer-based information system as a consumer or producer/consumer of information.

End-User Computing: The producer activities of end users relative to the organization's computer-based information system.

By definition, the data processing department, sole producers of information are excluded from their definition of the end user. Activities of producer/consumer of information in the EUC environment are summarized by operation, development, and control. Operation is the initiation and termination of system operation, monitoring or operation of hardware/software, and necessary manual tasks. Development is the performance of any or all tasks of the system development process, whether traditional systems development life-cycle or prototyping. Control is the decision-making authority to acquire, deploy, and use the resources needed to develop and operate the computer-based information system. Cotterman and Kumar state that, "Operation, development, and control are three key

Figure 1: The User Cube (Cotterman & Kumar, 1989)

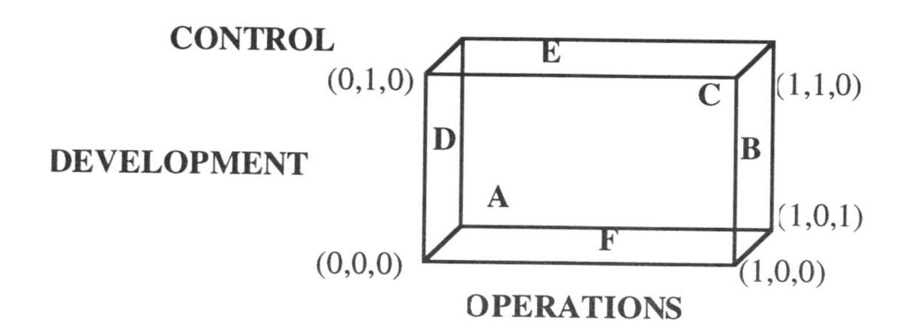

dimensions that allow us to distinguish between various types of end users. Figure 1 illustrates the User Cube as presented by Cotterman and Kumar. The letters on the cube represent the plane in which the user resides. The larger letters indicate a plane on the front, top or right side of the cube. Individual nodes or points are labeled with zeros and ones. For example, an end user who has direct access over computer operations while also developing the application would reside at point (1,1,0).

Following its presentation, the authors mapped existing definitions and classifications to the cube, face validating its comprehensiveness. To review their map, let us review each of the taxonomies below. The CODASYL categorization of intermediary user, specifying requirements for reports, would lie on the development line from points (0,0,0) to (0,1,0). Direct end users who operate computer equipment exist on the operations line from (0,0,0) to (1,0,0). The user described in the CODASYL taxonomy the, map to plane A in Figure 1. The users differentiated in the Rockart and Flannery taxonomy fall into the operator and/or developer dimensions, i.e., plane A in Figure 1. Control does not seem to enter into this taxonomy. The Rivard and Huff taxonomy dealing primarily with development would be described along the operations line, specifically around point (1,1,0).

BUILDING THE END-USER CHARACTERISTICS MATRIX

In the remainder of the chapter, we want to focus our discussion of user characteristics in the direction which will yield the largest impact on the end-user population. We will use the User Cube as the basis for definitions, but we want to primarily investigate plane A as the majority of users in previous studies fall into this space. Cotterman and Kumar did not identify where the bulk of end users presently lie on their User Cube nor where the growth in end-user computing will take place.

Three steps are discussed in the development of the End-User Characteristics matrix. First, a composite is developed of the end users that were investigated in previous studies. Second, a summarization and categorization of user characteristics presented earlier is presented. Finally, the is developed mapping the user characteristics described in previous studies to the taxonomies in plane A.Step 1: Composite of End Users Studied.

Articles were examined to identify those studies, which explicitly identified one of the previously identified taxonomies from which end users studied were categorized. Only five published studies reported using the Rockart and Flannery taxonomy, including, of course, the Rockart and Flannery study. Table 1 summarizes the user categorization in each of the

Table 1. Composite of End Users Studied Using the Rockart & Flannery Taxonomy

Types of End User	1983 Rockart & Flannery	1983 Quillard et al	1983 Bracheau et al	1987 Sumner & Klepper	1987 Amoroso & Cheney.
Nonprogramming end user	**9%**	**1%**	**4%**	**0%**	**3%**
Command-level end user	**22%**	**35%**	**26%**	**26%**	**41%**
End-use programmers	**30%**	**36%**	**41%**	**13%**	**34%**
Functional support	**53%**	**20%**	**29%**	**61%**	**16%**
EUC support	**7%**	**8%**	**0%**	**0%**	**4%**
DP programmers	**15%**	**0%**	**0%**	**0%**	**0%**
Reported sample size	**140**	**83**	**53**	**31**	**260**

five studies. All of the studies examined end-user computing in both microcomputing and mainframe environments.

The Rockart & Flannery and Sumner & Klepper studies indicated a large group of end users found in the functional support group. In a separate study, Quillard et al. reported only 20% in the functional support group, while 71% in the command-level end user and end-user programmer categories. Brancheau et al. and Amoroso & Cheney also found an extremely high concentration of end users in these two categories, 67% and 77% respectively. It appears from the five studies that the nonprogramming end user, which is defined along the operations line from points (0,0,0) to (1,0,0) on the User Cube, does not reflect a high growth category of end users. End -user categories apparently strongly reflect the development dimension. One might argue that the five studies represented in Table 1 were biased toward developing end users. However, the Brancheau et al. study investigated the information center, and the participants self classified themselves. Self-classification, in this study corroborated by IC managers in 75% of the cases, appears to be yielded a more unbiased categorization.

Both the Quillard et al. (1983) and Amoroso and Cheney (1987) research suggest that the growth in EUC would come from the command-level end user and end-user programmer categories. They found 71% of the end users randomly surveyed fell into these two categories. Davis identified the autonomous users as the fastest growing group of end users in the 1990s (1985). We find, by reading Davis' description of autonomous users that the autonomous user maps to Rockart and Flannery's command-level end user and end-user programmer categories. Perhaps the Sumner and Klepper data was skewed toward the functional support group as they were investigating information systems strategy in their research (1985). One cannot, however, deny the growth that will take place in the functional support group over the next decade. Other studies were not included in this analysis because they had not explicitly referenced specific end-user taxonomy.

Step 2: Summary of User Characteristics

After summarizing previous literature and categorizing the variety of user characteristics presented in those studies, ten characteristics emerged. Table 2 presents this summary information. Again, we are looking for explicit findings in the studies investigated indicating importance of a particular user characteristic. Descriptions of each of the user characteristics can be derived from the continuum measures. The continuum measures were taken from valid research instruments. Likert scales were used in the majority of studies investigated. Table 2 shows the Amoroso and Cheney study addressed all of the user characteristics derived from EUC literature. This was no accident; the user literature was reviewed prior to conducting that study. The study description can be found in Amoroso and Cheney (1987).

Step 3: Mapping of User Characteristics

The final step in the development of the involves mapping of the user characteristics in Table 2 onto the end-user taxonomies presented earlier. The data collected in the Amoroso and Cheney study was the primary source of information for the matrix (Amoroso and Cheney, 1987). Additionally, empirical studies were used to provide face validity for the matrix. The End-User Characteristics Matrix is presented in Figure 2. A taxonomy from McLean and Martin, derived from the CODASYL report, was separated out of the CODASYL classification as differences in user characteristics were noted.

End-user roles will continue to evolve as information technology advances ahead, despite researchers' attempts to classify them. For example, the greater the advances in

Table 2. Summary of User Characteristics

User Characteristic	Continuum Measure	Research Where Derived (refers to numbered references in the "Reference" section)
Computing skills	Low vs. high	2 10 11 16 19
Programming required	Yourself vs. others	2 4 8 10 16
Level of EUC support	Required by vs. provided to	2 11 16 18 19
Training/education	Few vs. multiple tools	2 4 10 13 14 20
Knowledge of EUC tools	Manipulation vs. development	4 8 10 11
Location of end users	Function vs. IS group	All of the studies
Nature of applications	Small/simple vs. large/complex	2 4 11 13 14 16 19 20
Technical understanding	Novice vs. expert	2 8 10 11 13 14 16
End-user attitudes	Positive vs. negative	2 18 20
End-user experience	Low vs. high	2 4 5 15 17 18

producing user-friendly software products, the greater the changes in user characteristics. These changes, in turn, will produce a shift in the characteristics over user types. We can certainly see that, with respect to the level of programming required, knowledge of EUC tools, and the nature of applications being developed.

CONCLUSIONS

The user has been represented in the MIS literature in many different ways. A working definition of the end user is crucial when attempting to understand the end-user computing phenomenon which is now occurring in most organizations. Cotterman and Kumar's User Cube takes important steps toward providing a comprehensive taxonomy for future research. However, within the User Cube taxonomy, a better knowledge of end-user characteristics is critical to managing end-user computing in organizations.

The End-User Characteristics Matrix, consisting of ten user characteristics mapped onto four end-user taxonomies, was primarily derived from previous research and a field study of 260 end users. The matrix is important in that it provides a framework for understanding the end user. IT supports the developer/operator dichotomy, located on Plane A within the User Cube. The fastest growing category of end users has been identified as the autonomous user who develops, designs, implements, and uses application programs to support personal or departmental information requirements. This type of end user is considered to be both a developer of applications and operator of computer-based information technology.

The major contribution of this article is the End-User Characteristics Matrix which provides a more detailed perspective on the end user as developer/operator. This matrix is useful to both researchers and practitioners. Researchers studying end-user computing can use the matrix as a starting point to visualize how past research taxonomies and empirical studies are interrelated. Practitioners, anxious to develop policies to manage EUC, can concentrate their efforts on certain user characteristics they observe to be problematic. Differentiated training, support, and software tools can be developed for a specific segment of the end-user population.

Figure 2. End-User Characteristics Matrix

End-User Categories	**Type 1**	**Type 2**	**Type 3**	**Type 4**	**Type 5**	**Type 6**
Rockart & Flannery (1983)	Non-programming End Users	Command Level Users	End-User Programmers	Functional Support	End-User Computing Support	Programming Support
McLean (1979) Martin (1982)	Non-DP Trained Users	DP Amateurs	*	*	DP Professionals	
CODASYL (1979)	Direct Users	Autonomous Users				
Rivard (1982)		Staff Analyst				
			Oppor. Seeker			
User Characteristics						
Computing Skills	Little	Low ◄	───	───	► High	
Programming Required	None	For yourself		For Others		
Level of EUC Support	Required by Users			Provided to Users		
Training/Education	Few Software Packages ◄─►			Multiple Software Packages		
Knowledge of EUC Tools	Manipulation	Manipulation/Development		Development		
Location of End Users	Functional Area					
Nature of Application	Small/Simple	◄ ───	─── ►		Large/Complex	
Technical Understanding	Novice ◄	───	─── ►		Expert	
End-User Attitudes	"Let Others Do It"		"I'll do it myself"		"Let me Help you"	
End-User Experience	Little	Low ◄	───	───	─── ►	High

REFERENCES

1. Amoroso, D. (1988). "Organizational Issues of End-User Computing, " *Data Base,* Fall/Winter, 49-58.
2. Amoroso, D., and P. Cheney (1987). "A Report on the State of End-User Computing in Some Larger North American Insurance Firms," *Journal of Information Management,* 8(2), 39-48.
3. Benson, D. (1983). "A Field Study of End User Computing: Findings and Issues", *Management Information Systems Quarterly*, 7(4), 35-45.
4. Bergeron, F. and C. Berube (1988). "The Management of the End-User Environment: An Empirical Investigation," *Information & Management,* 14(3), 107-113.
5. Bracheau, J., D. Bogel, and J. Wetherbe (1985). "An Investigation of the Information Center from the User's Perspective, " *Data Base,* 17(1), 4-17.
6. Churchman, C. and A. Schainblatt (1965)."The Researcher and the Manager: A Dialectic of Implementation", *Management Science,* 11(4), 869-887.
7. Cotterman, W. and K. Kumar (1989). "User Cube: A Taxonomy of End Users, " *Communications of the ACM,* 32(11), 1313-1320.
8. Davis, G.R. and M.H. Olson (1985). *Management Information Systems: Conceptual Foundations,*

*Structure, and Development.*2nd Edition, New York: McGraw-Hill.
9. Davis, J.(1985). "A Typology of Management Information Systems Users and Its Implications for User Information Satisfaction Research", *Proceedings of the 21st Computer Personnel Research Conference*, Minneapolis, May 1985.
10. Hackathorn, R, and P.G.W. Keen (1981)."Organizational Strategies for Personal Computing in Decision Support Systems," 5(3), 21-27.
11. Lee, D. (1986)."Usage Patterns and Sources of Assistance for Personal Computer Users," *Management Information Systems Quarterly*, 10(4), 313-325.
12. Lefkovitz, H.C., (1979). "A Status Report on the Activities of CODASYL End User Computing Facilities Committee (EUCF), *Information and Management,* Vol. 2, 137-163.
13. Martin, J., *Fourth-Generation Languages,* 1st Edition, Engewood Cliffs, N.J., Prentice Hall, 1985
14. McLean, E.R.(1979). "End Users As Application Developers", *Management Information Systems Quarterly,* 3(4), 37-46.
15. Pyburn, P.(1986/87). "Managing Personal Computer Use: The Role of Corporate Management Information Systems," *Journal of Management Information Systems,* 3(3) .49-70.
16. Quillard, J., J. Rockart, E. Wilde, M. Vernon, and G. Mock (1983). "A Study of the Corporate Use of Personal Computers", Working Papers, CISR-WP-109, Massachusetts Institute of Technology.
17. Rivard, S. and S. Huff (1985). "An Empirical Study of Users as Application Developers", *Information Management,* 8(2), 88-102
18. Rivard, S. and S. Huff (1988). "Factors of Success for End-User Computing," *Communications of the ACM,* 31(5), 552-561
19. Rockart, J.F., and L.S. Flannery (1983). "The Management of End User Computing", *Communications of the ACM,* 26(10), 776-784
20. Sumner, M.(1985). "How Should Applications Be Developed?: An Analysis of Traditional User Microcomputers", *Data Base,* 17(1), 25-33.

Chapter 16

Incremental Cross-Generation Versioning in Decomposable Internet Software Products: Opportunities for Knowledge Management in ISD

Amrit Tiwana
Georgia State University, USA

The most important factor distinguishing firms is the possession of knowledge, and the core differentiating skill is the ability to deploy that knowledge to their competitive advantage (Scott, 1998). Products of the turbulent information industries (Mendelson and Kraemer, 1998), especially those facilitated by the Internet, show the hitherto unseen promise of increasing returns. The flexibility to survive in turbulent technological environments, however, can only be achieved if positive feedback is not suppressed (Hall, 1997). This chapter examines incremental development and maintenance of software products designed to be used, delivered, and maintained through the Internet. Complex software products often go through a process of iterative evolution across several rapidly delivered versions, and the opportunities for knowledge management and application that arise in the midst of their evolution are discussed. We describe how both development and maintenance/upgrading of Internet software must be addressed in ways extending beyond traditional methods used for "traditional" information systems maintenance. Drawing on a diverse theory base, including information economics, emergence theory, and knowledge-based innovation, characteristics of Internet-based software applications are described; linkages between application modularity and decomposability with process knowledge are first explored; feasibility of managing component knowledge and renewing architectural knowledge is discussed; and finally, a conceptual model for managing process knowledge across generations and versions of decomposable applications to support software maintenance and evolution is presented.

CHARACTERISTICS OF INTERNET-BASED SOFTWARE APPLICATIONS

Internet software products exhibit several properties of conventional desktop software products—albeit less subtly—as well as several that are unique to this class of software (Iansiti and MacCormack, 1997). Software products delivered for use over public networks such as the Internet possess several characteristics, not all of which are common with their boxed equivalents. Each characteristic is discussed in further detail and summarized in Table 1.

The key characteristic distinguishing Internet-based software applications is their necessarily higher level of interoperability within the existing technological environment. Unlike traditional software products that run on standalone computers and are optimized for a particular, relatively stable operating system, these products depend on a complexly interwoven infrastructure to cooperatively function with other parts of the enterprise. To take a simple case, consider a Web-based site search application. This application might run on a Web server that is based on a particular operating system. This Web server must be accessible through a Web browser that might be running on a different operating system. Interactions occur through a protocol that is determined by an organization other than the one that might have developed the aforementioned components, which in turn depend on the network path provided by a networking service provider. Even though the software product may be located on a specific node on the network, the information system is constituted by the combination of several infrastructural components cooperatively and integratively distributed across the network. Unlike standalone software, changes in any one of these components might lead to loss of interoperability—and consequently operability.

The value of Internet-based software products to the consumer, much like Internet information products, is partially determined by their timeliness of delivery. Timely delivery encompasses two aspects: (1) the delay between a request initiated by the user and actual delivery of the product, and (2) cycle-time needed to deliver demanded functionality. This imposes two parallel constraints reflected in the need for faster development, upgrades, compressed time frames available for delivering new versions, and the need for optimizing over-the-network delivery time that takes available bandwidth into account.

Internet-based software products, like most products in the information industry, are characterized by a fast rate of change (Mendelson and Kraemer, 1998), as underlying technologies evolve rapidly, and often unpredictably (Davenport et al., 1996). Short product lifecycles, in turn, determine time-functional perishability of these products. Having to choose whether to optimize the application for one of multiple competing technological standards (e.g., W^3 Java versus Active Server pages) or to compromisingly ensure interoperability across conflicting standards; timing of commitments; and fundamental reservations about the nature, magnitude, and direction of shifts in consumer needs, create added market uncertainties and process instabilities both during development and during subsequent maintenance (Mullins and Sutherland, 1998; Shapiro and Varian, 1999).

Three broad categories of problems can be assimilated from extant literature: (1) distribution of work, (2) dynamic markets and unstable requirements, and (3) technological dynamism.

1. Distribution of Work: Software development teams are increasingly distributed, creating further challenges. As the wave of virtualization hits such engineering-oriented enterprises with full force (Rose, 1998), many aspects of the process that used to be implicit in organizational culture must then be supported and better explicated by enabling technol-

Table 1: Characteristics of Internet-based Software Products and Implications for Maintenance

Characteristic	Implications
Interoperability	Internet software operates in conjunction with existing infrastructure. Elements of this infrastructure come from different technology vendors implying the need for knowledge sharing among them (Song and Montoya-Weiss, 1998).
Timeliness of delivery	Determinant of the product's value to the consumer (Ballou et al., 1998).
Short product lifecycles	Subject to a fast rate of change (Mendelson and Kraemer, 1998). Underlying technologies evolve rapidly (Davenport et al., 1996).
Perishability	Decrease in the value of a product over a period of time.
Parallel Versioning	Multiple instantiations of the same basic product for different consumer segments facilitates quality discrimination [Varian, 1997 #482].
Market uncertainty	Such issues might include the appropriateness of the choice of a certain technology standard over another, the nature and extent of customer needs, uncertainty about the level of resources that must be invested and the timing of commitments create fundamental uncertainties about the target market (Mullins and Sutherland, 1998; Shapiro and Varian, 1999). These must be explicitly addressed and traced throughout the design, development, and maintenance process.
Complexity of description	Internet software is usually complex, possesses high levels of interoperability, and complexly interacts with other technological components. Complexity of description must be addressed to reduce customer uncertainty (Koppius, 1999).

ogy (Rose, 1998). Cultural impediments arising from geographic, functional, and organizational affiliations (Brown and Eisenhardt, 1995; Jassawalla and Sashittal, 1998) necessitate mechanisms for improved cross-disciplinary (Brown and Eisenhardt, 1995) and cross-institutional collaboration (Brown and Eisenhardt, 1995; Igbaria, 1998), explication of implicit process knowledge (Mowshowitz, 1997; Walsh, 1995), improved coordination (Boudreau, et al., 1998; Igbaria, 1998; Rose, 1998), and process synchronization (Rose, 1998) in distributed software teams.

2. *Market Instability*: Unstable and dynamic requirements (Truex et al., 1999), pressures for cost reduction (Rose, 1998), compressed development periods and timely delivery (Burchill and Fine, 1997; Meyer and Utterback, 1995), and tighter integration between software, hardware, and networks—all of which exhibit instability and rapid change (Rose, 1998)—poses additional challenges in maintaining and upgrading Internet software products.
3. *Technology Dynamism*: Increased complexity of design (Ungson and Trudel, 1999), compatibility issues (Iansiti, 1998), interoperability across multiple technological standards (Shapiro and Varian, 1998), performance expectations (Brown and Eisenhardt, 1995), and the need to incorporate unlearning (Walsh, 1995) as inter-sectoral technologies

and associated knowledge becomes obsolete (Tomas and Arias, 1995). Tighter integration of hardware and software causes version and configuration management problems (Rose, 1998), and overlap between technology domains necessitates higher collaborative synergy. Meyer and Utterback (1995) caution that the success of new technology products depends heavily on the team's ability to integrate dynamic technology components. Unlearning must accompany the design process to prevent disuse, follow decay, or overcome inefficient encoding of process knowledge (Walsh, 1995).

In addition to the aforementioned problems, discontinuance is a primary concern for electronically delivered products, as has also been noted for business-to-consumer online service markets (Parthasarathy and Bhattacherjee, 1998). Clientele, motivated by often-low switching costs of Internet-delivered software/services, are often fluid and increasingly switch when offered a viable transition path. Effective customer base can be thought of as a simple function that depends on the number of new initial adoption decisions and the number of discontinuers in that period (Rust and Zahorik, 1993). This has been often referred to as the "churn" rate.

Market share = f(Effective subscriber base)= Ψ(initial adoption level-discontinuance level)

Knowledge externalities and spillovers between client and allied organizations have also been observed (Bapista and Swann, 1998), which creates unique opportunities for lock-ins that can inhibit end users from switching to competing software products instead of choosing an upgrade to an existing application.

Dimensions of Complexity

Problems involved in Internet software product maintenance, as with many other complex products, can be classified into four cognitive complexity domains as described in Table 2 (based on Khurana, 1999).

Technological and environmental complexities are two aspects that can be better understood by decomposing the design of such software artifacts. It is within these two dimensions that most opportunities for ISD knowledge management lie.

Table 2: Software Application Complexity

Software application complexity	Causal description and influence
Logistical	Result of a high volume of transactions or tasks
Technological	System-level complexity inherent in both products and processes; two sub-characteristics: (1) interaction complexity and (2) nondecomposability
Organizational	Result of organizational forms, structures, and procedures that make organizational processes complex
Environmental	Results from events (interfaces, requirements evolution, and standards) outside the organization

Standalone Software Versus Internet-Based Software

Internet-based software products are distinguishable from traditional software products primarily based on their delivery mechanisms. These mechanisms carry on through subsequent iterations, and determine the manner in which they are usually maintained and upgraded. Standalone software products are typically installed on a computer and run either locally or on a shared memory location within a local network. These applications are distinguished by "big-bang" delivery mechanisms wherein compiled code is delivered after the entire application has been built, tested, and compiled. For our discussion, applications that are later updated through public networks (such as a software patches for productivity application suites and virus signature "patches") are also considered standalone applications. Significant modifications in functionality can be implemented only through the repetition of delivery whether through a network or through traditional storage media such as CD-ROM or floppy disks. Prototyping, end-user computing, and pilot implementation have cumulatively challenged Yourdon's notion of "big-bang" delivery wherein an information system is delivered by the ISD group after a long period of non-interaction between requirements analysis and delivery of the system.

Internet-based applications on the other hand are delivered—often continually streamed—through the Internet. Many Internet-based software applications follow the pay-to-use model as opposed to the previously dominant pay-to-own model of distribution and ownership. Application services delivered by application service providers (ASPs) are an increasingly common manifestation of the former model. Software buyers use such applications through a public network such as the Internet and pay based on their usage.

Application Service Providers (ASPs) are IS service firms that sell software and information systems as a "rental" service rather than a software product or license of ownership (Gillan and McCarthy, 1999). These service providers provide contractually-managed application services that collectively deploy, host, manage, and rent access to an application from a centrally managed facility; they are–directly or indirectly–responsible for providing all the relevant expertise and supporting specific activities targeted at managing this application set (Gillan and McCarthy, 1999). An ASP provides these software services to customers over a network, typically the Internet (Crowe, 1999), based on a contract between a service purchaser and provider that is structured around levels of service. Rather than having to choose technologies, customers get to choose *outcomes* such as functionality, acceptable performance levels, downtimes, transaction processing time bounds, response times, etc.

Upgrades, in such cases, become the responsibility of the software-service provider rather than the end-user organization. Because the application is streamed through the Internet *each time* it is used, and not stored or installed locally on the user side, it is more feasible to provide minor and major upgrades somewhat transparently to the end-user. Various application services such as customer service, CRM software, supply chain integration, billing and payment, security, network pipes, performance management, and enterprise integration (Keston, 1999) are being currently outsourced via the Internet using this model.

Trends of the "product" being replaced by meld of service and tangible components, with the latter having a feature set with fuzzy definition, have been reported in cross-disciplinary literature (Phillips et al., 1999). Application services as a manifestation of Internet-based software delivery are a good example of that shift. The software application is defined as an inseparable combination of service and software, hence a service-product mix described as an application-service.

Figure 1 compares the opportunities for learning in these two software delivery models,

Figure 1: A Comparison of Traditional and Internet-Based Software Application Upgrades

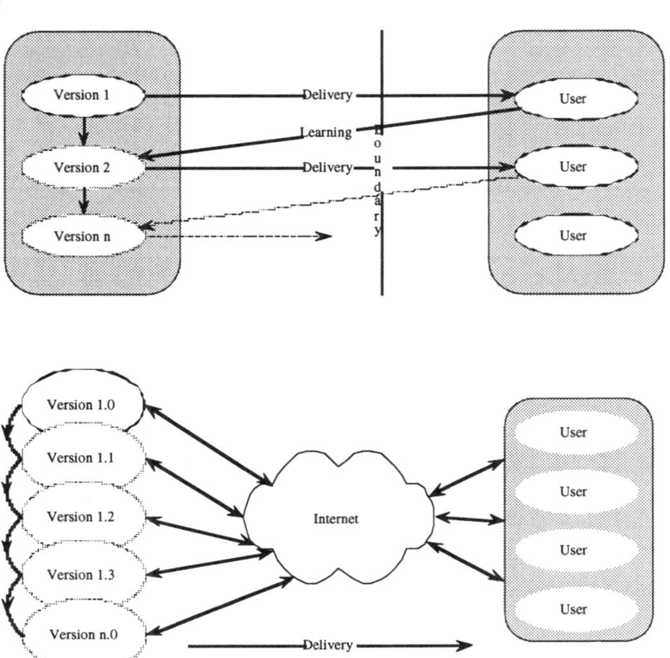

and in their subsequent upgrades. In the case of traditionally delivered software applications, there is a distinct boundary between the user and the application provider. As described in Figure 1(a), learning and feedback from preceding versions can actually be incorporated into the software products only when the subsequent version is released, even if such learning was assimilated over an intervening course of time. This is followed by the next version's delivery, and so on. While learning might occur in intermediate stages, there is no opportunity to incorporate it into the software product's design and translate it into new functionality until the next version is released.

In contrast, as illustrated in Figure 1(b), the aforementioned boundaries are blurred in the case of Internet-delivered software. A two-way interaction occurs every time the software is used (i.e., redelivered). Every instance of use therefore represents an opportunity for learning. Feedback and learning can be incorporated into the software almost on the fly, and new functionality can be delivered the next time a user requests the application. As Figure 2 illustrates, learning tends to be necessarily clumped, with most of it being incorporated only when the next major upgrade version is released in the case of "big-bang" delivered applications. However, if explicit measures are taken to incorporate learning into Internet-based software applications, knowledge integration can be a continuous process mediated by the more frequent interactions between the software-service provider and end users. Internet-based applications might follow the big-bang notion of functionality delivery only to a moderate extent, and many, if not all, subsequent versions are incremental.

Indeed, many known software applications fall somewhere between these two extremes (such as virus eradication applications that download updates through the Internet). However, for the sole purpose of our discussion, applications for which most functionality

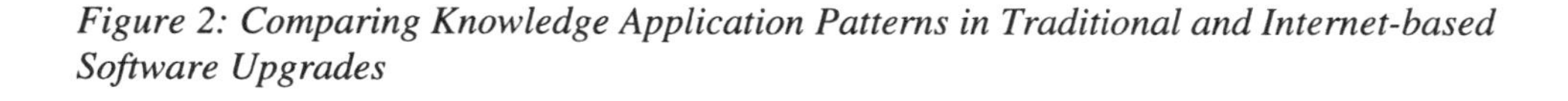

Figure 2: Comparing Knowledge Application Patterns in Traditional and Internet-based Software Upgrades

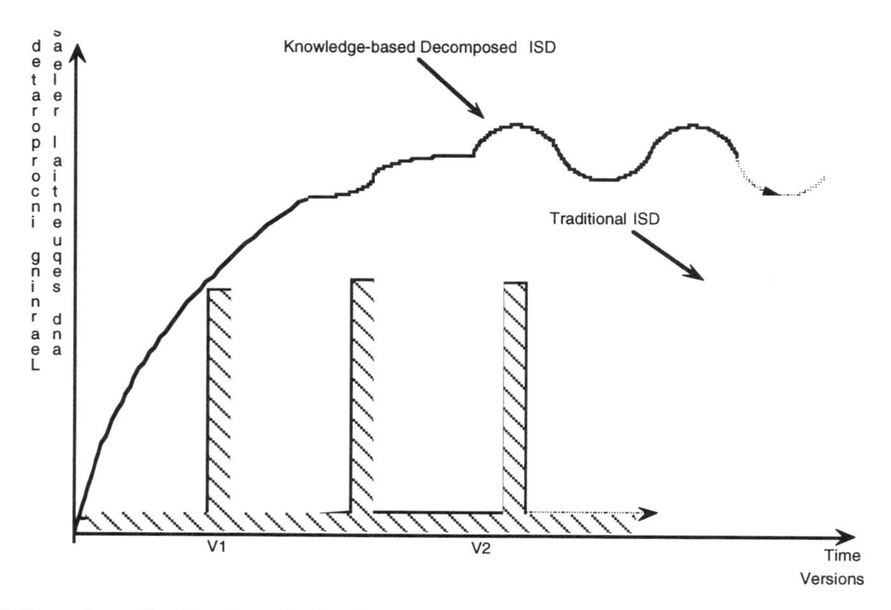

is delivered on the fly through the Internet are considered Internet-based. The range of software applications can therefore be viewed as a continuum, with standalone, "big-bang" delivered applications representing one end and real-time delivered applications exhibiting high levels of code volatility, the other extreme. The latter are available only during the course of a given session, often made available through a network-routed download on the fly.

Linking Emergence Theory and Software Upgrades

Emergence theory provides a powerful theoretical lens for analyzing Internet-based software. Emergence refers to an organizational state of constantly seeking stability, while never achieving it (Truex et al., 1999). Truex et al. describe this concept as implying that every feature of social organizations—culture, meaning, social relationships, decision processes—are continually emergent, following no predefined pattern. While temporal regularities might exist, these are only recognizable by hindsight, as they are "always in transition but never arriving." If emergence theory were taken into account, and the observed rapidity of organizational and business environment were to be accounted for, there would be increasing likelihood that the original goals of an ISD initiative and those at the time of delivery will be incongruent.

Recent ISD literature has reflected the need for taking an emergence theory-based perspective on software development, design, and delivery (e.g., Truex et al., 1999), suggesting that ISD practice must follow two rather unconventional objectives for software design: (1) software must be designed for high levels of maintenance, and (2) it must be optimized for short life spans. If an emergence-based perspective is adopted for software, systems must necessarily be optimized for short life spans and high levels of maintenance. It is argued that Internet-based software upgrades provide an apt opportunity for supporting organizational emergence in the context of information technology functionality. Life cycles of such software applications are necessarily short—usually limited to the period of a single use. Once the end-user exits a software application, she *can* (but need not) be offered a new version of the application the next time she instantiates it. By constantly interacting with end users and incorporating new knowledge through feedback—both solicited and unsolicited—software applications can be *optimized* for high levels of maintenance. It is argued that optimization for high maintenance must not necessarily translate to additional resource expenditures on the part of the end user—in terms of time needed to upgrade the application or in terms of loss of compatibility with other interacting applications. By shifting the burden of maintenance to the application-service provider, Internet-based software applications can viably facilitate emergent behavior that characterizes many organizational environments.

Many software applications often serve the needs of diverse user groups—needs that cannot be articulated during the analysis and design phase (Thayer et al., 1980). Adopting a knowledge-based approach to software upgrades allows for the subsequent incorporation of such emergent needs at a pace hitherto impossible in traditional software application deployments. Because of numerous micro-level, incrementally improved "sub-versions" of the application that may be delivered between major upgrade releases, we use the term versioning in preference over upgrading.

However, to be able to address issues arising from both technological and environmental complexities associated with software applications, especially when they interact within diverse user environments and information systems, upgrades must necessarily be knowledge-driven. This knowledge must span internal current, experiential, and external environmental knowledge. Especially because opportunities for two-way learning in the Internet versions of software applications abound, mechanisms for capitalizing on such learning must be put in place. Deliberately pursued mechanisms for knowledge management can facilitate time-pressured, complex decision making about software product versioning and upgrades.

Process Knowledge in Internet-Centric ISD

The firm's competencies, a cohesive set of skills and techniques, and knowledge are used to design, develop, distribute, support, and deliver a firm's offerings (Teece, 1986). Teece observed that market insights, product technologies, development processes, and distribution and support capabilities knowledge-based competencies provide a stable competitive basis to knowledge-intensive firms, such as software development organizations. In this section, I describe the role of process and declarative knowledge in ISD, and specifically interpret extant research in the context of maintenance and upgrade of existing software. Lacking factors in existing ISD practice support mechanisms and collaborative systems are then identified. Finally, the significance of veridicality in software maintenance and evolution is discussed.

Role of Knowledge in ISD

Knowledge management has received increasing attention, especially with its pronounced but empirically unverified influence on the competitiveness of the firm's products and services. Issues surrounding knowledge in software development have long been the focus of attention within many streams of information systems research including, but not limited to, design rationale (Ramesh and Dhar, 1992), reuse, requirements engineering (Ramesh and Dhar, 1992), and design traceability (Ramesh, 1998). Software development is a knowledge-intensive activity, one whose products are characterized by high levels of embedded knowledge content (Mendelson and Kraemer, 1998). As a firm gains experience through the development of information products, much of the lessons learned remain captured as information (Fielding et al., 1998; Robillard, 1999) that must be mobilized into knowledge and applied to guide future incremental versions.

Veridicality and Process Knowledge

The software design process consists of a series of interdependent design decisions that result in the creation of artifacts (Ramesh and Sengupta, 1995). These artifacts are interconnected in an interdependent manner to create the final product (Fielding et al., 1998). Most of these design decisions are made in a linear manner, and once reached, intermediate deliberations and knowledge associated with them are often lost.

Software development teams depend on two broad categories of knowledge: (1) declarative and (2) procedural. Figure 3 uses a concept map to describe these two dimensions of knowledge involved in software design teams (based on Robillard, 1999). Declarative knowledge is well supported by collaborative systems such as those used by software development teams, but process knowledge is not. Unfortunately, it is shared process knowledge—not declarative knowledge—that lays the foundation for coordinated action in teams (Zack, 1999a). The fundamental problem in design is that of discovering a process description that leads to a desired goal (Simon, 1991). Objects such as design artifacts are more meaningful if accompanied by process descriptions that led to their creation in the first place. While functional versioning of physical products can be expensive, relative costs of versioning information products to create artificial quality-based (e.g., for different market segments) differentiation is less expensive (Shapiro and Varian, 1998). With this end in mind, this chapter explores mechanisms for capturing—not necessarily codifying—a process description for each sequential and parallel software version.

Process knowledge is inherent, but its formal manifestations in software development are rather shallow (Rose, 1998). Neither collaborative technology nor organizational memory information systems currently support "rich" communications (Ramesh and Sengupta, 1995; Tomas and Arias, 1995), provide shared workspaces (Fielding, et al., 1998), or help

Figure 3: A Typology of Knowledge in Information Systems Development and Maintenance

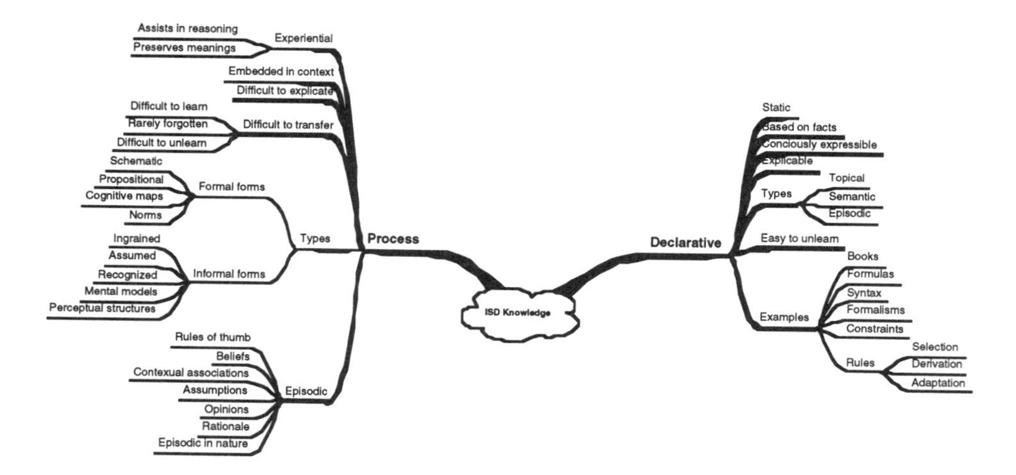

surface assumptions and previously held views of members in virtual teams. Coordination problems that have plagued traditional software development groups become even ominous in distributed teams (Favela and Connor, 1994). The predominantly tacit nature of process knowledge, group learning, members' beliefs, assumptions, and their cumulative impact on design has been well documented in software development literature (e.g., Ramesh and Sengupta, 1995; Rose, 1998; Stein and Zwass, 1995). Ad hoc teams also lack a collaborative history in which knowledge of past events is embedded (Anacona, 1990). The loss of permanence in often-distributed, ad-hoc ISD teams not only eliminate the social reservoir of the conventional team that has stored process knowledge created during design deliberations, but also prevents integration of spatially distributed team members' assumptions and beliefs about design, functionality, needs, and product vision. Therefore, mechanisms supporting such teams must help develop the missing sense of shared history, patterns of interaction, and normative formalisms. More importantly, most collaborative systems used to develop and maintain software applications often fail to capture valuable versioning knowledge that could later be leveraged to guide design decisions for subsequent application versions, and to bring knowledge to bear on present decisions. *Veridicality*—relationships between knowledge structures and information environments that they represent (Walsh, 1995)—must further be supported to retain context with design decisions and resulting artifacts. These issues must be addressed to facilitate versioning and incremental innovation in Internet-based software.

MODULARITY, DECOMPOSABILITY, AND KNOWLEDGE

Modularity of a software system's design has several implications for process knowledge management inherent in its development and maintenance. A modular design is one that is characterized by an intentionally high level of independence and loose coupling between components (Sanchez and Mahoney, 1996). Modularity is conceptually close to the notion of decomposability of complex systems, both at product and at organizational levels of analysis. A modular software product therefore is characterized by component subsystems, each of which can be independently developed, managed, and maintained. Through modularization of a software product, knowledge assets applied to deliver the final product operate at an architectural level instead of operating at a component level.

Using a modular design requires knowledge of interfaces—how components integrate and interact. Coordination and strategic flexibility benefits can be realized through a modular architecture, especially when the software application possesses high levels of knowledge of component interactions (Sanchez and Mahoney, 1996). Modularity facilitates partitioning of the development process into specific, discrete tasks (Von Hippel, 1990). Modularity decomposes the software product into a nearly independent system of components, each of which can be concurrently developed within loosely coupled organizational structures (Sanchez and Mahoney, 1996). Such organizational structures are representative of distributed, and often-virtual software development teams that characterize many IS development organizations and departments.

Managing design knowledge to facilitate upgrades, maintenance, and versioning is inherently more feasible when the software application is developed in a modular fashion. Each version or release can then be delivered as a combination of modules, interactions between them being cumulatively known through management of process knowledge. Different versions of modular components can be brought into the design as and when they are upgraded to include new technology or functionality, or to include end-user feedback or

Figure 4: Modularity and Component Knowledge Linkages in Internet-Based Software

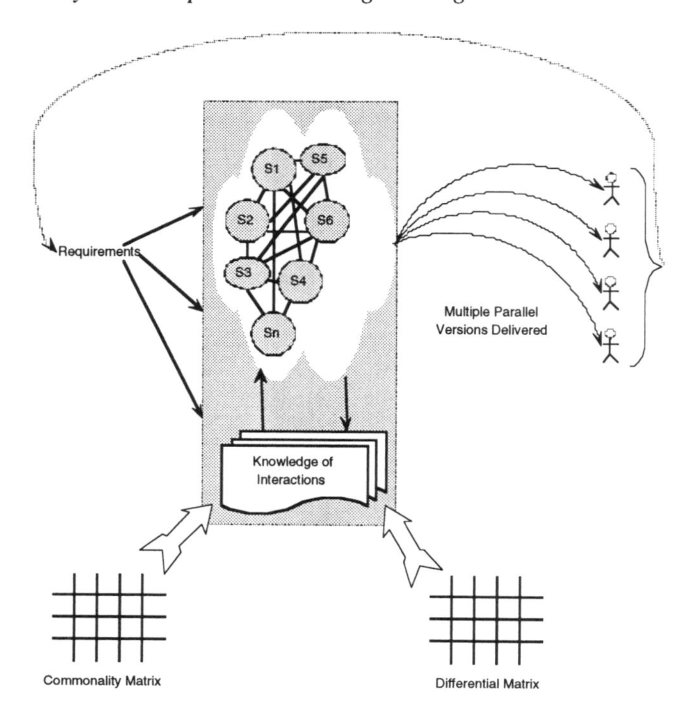

evolving needs. Such modular components can be left out or included to deliver multiple, parallel versions of the application. This facilitates versioning over time and across customer segments whose needs might differ—in effect introducing quality discrimination as described in a later section.

New knowledge about components and component interactions develops as software evolves through successive versions.

Figure 4 illustrates the conceptual architecture of a modular software application. S_1 through S_n represent subsystem-level components or modules. These modules are combined based on existing knowledge of their interactions to deliver a software application to the end user. Such combination can either be accomplished *a priori* or on the fly. As multiple, parallel versions are delivered to end users, new requirements might be generated as needs for new functionality emerge through feedback mechanisms. Such feedback may be explicit, such as through feedback Web pages or may be automated by means of functionality and usage analysis. Automated and relatively transparent feedback mechanisms are arguably easier to implement in Internet-delivered applications for two reasons: (1) end users instantiate and acquire application functionality each time they request the application from the provider's application server, therefore each event of use is an opportunity for delivering a new version; and (2) usage patterns and behavioral information can be aggregated over time.

Examples of modular architectures in software systems include ERP systems and electronic commerce platforms. In the case of electronic commerce platforms, various subsystem-level components such as order processing, credit verification mechanisms, customer order history, and Web-based inventory reporting subsystems can be integrated in various combinations to deliver functionality to build a Web store. Knowledge about integration and interactions associated with these components is used to design and deliver

Table 3: Characteristics of Component and Architectural Knowledge (Based on Matusik and Hill, 1998; Nelson and Winter, 1982; Nonaka and Takeuchi, 1995).

Knowledge Type	Characteristics
Component	• Relates to a subroutine, component, or discrete aspect • Relates to parts or components rather than a whole • Also defined as resources, knowledge, skills, and technical skills in literature • Can be held individually and collectively (individual/group/org level)
Architectural	• Relates to the "whole" • Organization-wide routines & schemas for coordinating component-level knowledge "pieces" • Result of path-dependent evolution (Nelson and Winter, 1982) • Can be used to upgrade component knowledge over time (Matusik and Hill, 1998) • Always held collectively; at an organizational level • Not comprehendible or articulable by a single individual • Tacit by default; relatively impervious to "leakages"

a customized solution to each customer. However, every solution is based on the same set of components. Such modularity might be viewed from different levels of analysis. One layer further down, a credit card verification component can be decomposed into a card-issuer communications subsystem and database storage subsystem, and so forth. Knowledge about individual components evolves with the evolution of their design; however, architectural knowledge remains relatively stable over time (Henderson and Clark, 1990).

COMPONENT VERSUS ARCHITECTURAL KNOWLEDGE

Knowledge in organizations exists at both architectural and component levels (Matusik and Hill, 1998), as described in Table 3. Innovation management literature suggests that innovations in technology can occur both incrementally and architecturally (Henderson and Clark, 1990). In either case, the system's core components remain unchanged even though linkages among them might, as in the case of architectural discontinuities. Architectural discontinuities are therefore beyond the scope of this chapter. Modular innovation is another category wherein linkages between core concepts and components remain stable even though the components themselves might change (Henderson and Clark, 1990). In the cases of incremental and modular development in Internet-based software that we are interested in, it is of consequence to note that architectural knowledge is necessarily path-dependent, i.e., it cannot be externally acquired (Matusik and Hill, 1998). Such knowledge is embodied in components and by a product architecture that defines the ways in which such components are integrated (Henderson and Clark, 1990). It is therefore posited that managing knowledge at a subsystem level will help build architectural knowledge that can further facilitate maintenance of Internet-based software applications.

FACILITATING UPGRADES AND VERSIONING THROUGH KNOWLEDGE MANAGEMENT

A knowledge-driven approach for managing versioning and upgrades in Internet-based software applications decouples knowledge creation activities associated with software development and maintenance from knowledge application activities. This decoupling has two critical implications on software upgrades:

1. *Maximization of knowledge application.* Decoupling knowledge creation and application processes helps the IS development organization in effectively exploiting its current stock of knowledge as suggested by organizational learning literature (March, 1991). Maintaining knowledge about commonality and differentially related attributes and their antecedent processes provide a mechanism for implementing and applying previously created knowledge. Simultaneously, in a loosely coupled manner, this knowledge is both maintained and renewed as components and their interactions are observed and recorded in such systems.
2. *Balancing knowledge exploitation and exploration.* Zack (1999b) suggests that organizations must strike a balance between the levels to which they explore and create new knowledge and those at which they exploit existing knowledge. Knowledge exploitation is conceptually analogous to knowledge application, i.e., use of existing knowledge in making upgrade and maintenance-level decisions. Using a modular architecture facilitates maintainability and upgradability (Sanchez and Mahoney, 1996) in addition to knowledge creation and management.

Figure 5: Real-Time Integration of Feedback and Learning in Internet-Based Software Upgrades.

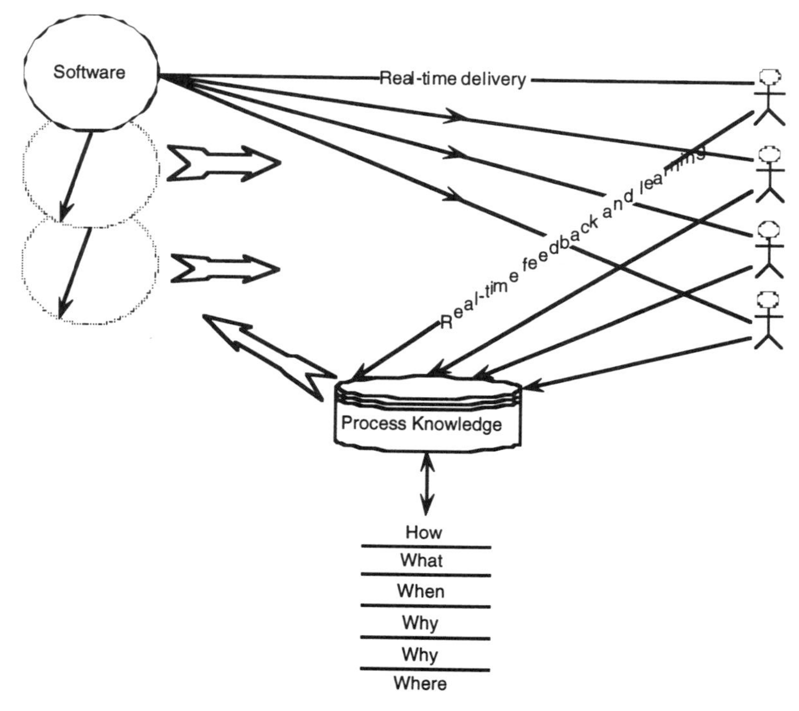

As described in Figure 4, knowledge management in Internet-based software products can be initiated by maintaining key common and differentiating attributes in components and packaged subsystems (delivered as a software application). This, in effect, creates a software platform to which design principles of product platforms (Meyer and Lehnerd, 1997; Robertson and Ulrich, 1998) can be applied. Commonalities refer to design aspects at the component level that remain the same across both temporally successive and spatially distributed versions of Internet-based software. Differential design decisions represent those that are explicitly changed across versions. The level of granularity at which such information is stored depends on the resource and cost overhead that the ISD organization is willing to expend, and on the time frame within which successive versions must be released.

Furthermore, by explicitly linking six dimensions of design traceability, such knowledge can be stored as process knowledge (see Figure 5). This can be accomplished through existing traceability mechanisms (e.g., Ramesh and Tiwana, 1999) that can link explicitly codified knowledge, external information (through hyperlinks), and pointers and rich multimedia-facilitated "captures" of some tacit knowledge underlying each decision. Each cell in the commonality and differentiating attribute matrix can be linked to its process history. When complex design decisions must be made under time constraints during subsequent upgrade and versioning initiatives, process knowledge from past initiatives and their outcomes can provide decision support. Therefore not only the decision but also its underlying process can be "revisited," effectively overcoming frequently reported problems of reinvention (associated with inaccessibility of past process knowledge) in technology-based organizations (Tiwana, 2000). Solution and development paths explored but rejected in previous versions are also made available along with the rationale underlying their rejection.

Real-Time Decision Support and Knowledge Integration

As derivative variants of software packages are developed from a base version, emergent learning occurs and over the course of several projects, a repository of design process knowledge begins to accumulate as shown in Figure 5. Applying the concept of traceability (Ramesh, 1998; Ramesh and Jarke, 1999) in large-scale software development, process knowledge about how, when, why, where, and by whom these service design decisions are made, accumulated process knowledge can be used to: (1) guide new development decisions, (2) create the next version of the software product, and (3) transfer knowledge across software generations. Because customization in Internet-based software *primarily* occurs at the time of delivery (Meyer and DeTore, 1999), how exactly this customization must be done can be guided by knowledge of past incremental development initiatives. In addition to guiding upgrade and maintenance, decisions based on past decision process paths, four additional benefits can accrue from managing experiential knowledge created in the process.

1. Component subsystem selection and architectural mass customization: Selection of specific components to provide requisite client functionality needs extensive cross-functional collaboration (Meyer and DeTore, 1999). This selection process is intensively knowledge-based, and given *very* short time frames within which such decisions must be made, process efficacy spells the difference between "good" and "bad" decisions.

2. Design and integration of subsystem-level service components: Besides using KM for tracking the differentiating attributes and commonality points among derivative software versions, architectural knowledge can also help set the bar at which standardized services and processes end and customization begins (Meyer and DeTore, 1999).

3. Integration of governance and maintenance mechanisms: Service firms have gained notoriety for ineffectual governance mechanisms. Many firms design their products first, and build mechanisms for governance later (Meyer and DeTore, 1999). By bringing past internal experiential knowledge and external knowledge, governance mechanisms can be designed in parallel with component upgrades.

4. Integration of external competencies: External competencies among suppliers, partners, developers of subsystem-level components, and complementary technologies are as important as internal organizational competencies. Many successful businesses develop a set of subcomponents that can be mixed and matched at the point of delivery (Heskett et al., 1997) (also reported in electronic publishing in Zack, 1996). Knowledge-based platforms can facilitate rapid, real-time "assembly" of customized software applications while applying experience gained from the preceding versions for (re)designing both temporally sequenced releases and parallel quality-discriminated versions addressing different end user segments; at the same time, external knowledge from developers and infrastructural suppliers that the application must interoperate with can also be integrated.

CONCLUSIONS AND FUTURE WORK

This chapter explored how software maintenance and upgrades can be driven by a knowledge-based approach. Characteristics, delivery methods, constraints, and knowledge intensity of Internet-based software were compared with traditional "stand-alone" software applications. Dimensions of complexity relevant to software maintenance were identified and linked to organizational emergence theory. Component- and architecture-level knowledge in application maintenance and upgrading was described and related to software modularity and decomposability. Drawing on the concept of product platforms, a mechanism for managing commonalties and differentiating attributes across sequential and parallel versions of Internet software was proposed.

Three areas warrant further research. First, an examination of the impact of discontinuities in software product platforms will provide better understanding of whether and how knowledge management-based approaches to software maintenance can provide mechanisms for coping with what Henderson (1990) describes as radical innovations. In such innovations, both architectural and component knowledge become obsolete. Second, an empirical analysis of architectural and component knowledge and their interplays will provide a better understanding of approaches that ISD organizations can take when the primary focus is on one. This will also provide further basis for developing tools and methods to support ISD knowledge management at various levels. Third, longitudinal analysis of a few ISD teams will better explain how knowledge transfer succeeds or fails in dynamic teams and unstable technological evolution.

APPENDIX: SURVEY INSTRUMENT

Welcome!!! This survey is designed to capture information about your perceptions of software upgrades. You will not be identified individually, and all data will be analyzed in aggregate.

We want you to think about the last software upgrade that took place at your organization. Specifically, we want you to think about the last time that your organization installed a new software package to replace an old one. Examples include replacing Windows 95 with Windows 98, replacing Windows 3.1 with Windows 95, replacing Microsoft Office 95 with Microsoft Office 97, or even replacing Microsoft Word with WordPerfect. These examples are certainly not the only ones that are of interest — any software upgrades are important for this study.

Please answer the following questions by circling or checking your response. If you do not know the answer to a question, or if it does not apply to you, simply leave that question blank.

1. Has your organization been involved in any software upgrades within the last 12 months?
   Yes | No

If you answered NO to question #1, please skip to question #62. If you answered YES to question #1, please continue with question #2.

2. What software package was replaced in your upgrade (What was the old software)? ____________________

3. What software package replaced the old software (What is the new software)? ______________________

4. How long (in months) has it been since the upgrade occurred? ________________

5. Was it your decision to adopt the software, or was the decision made for you?
   My Choice | Mandatory

6. Compared to other organizations, when would you say that your firm adopted the software?
   Before everyone else | About the same time as everyone else | After everyone else

For the next few questions, disruption should be defined as a negative change associated with the introduction of the new software. Thus, an upgrade that is disruptive causes more problems than an upgrade that is not disruptive.
Please indicate your level of agreement or disagreement with the following statements on a scale of 1-5 *(1=strongly disagree, 5=strongly agree).*

7.	The software upgrade was disruptive to my organization.	1	2	3	4	5
8.	The software upgrade was disruptive to my personal work.	1	2	3	4	5
9.	The upgrade was beneficial to my organization.	1	2	3	4	5
10.	The upgrade was beneficial to my personal work.	1	2	3	4	5
11.	My organization is more productive since the upgrade.	1	2	3	4	5
12.	I am personally more productive since the upgrade.	1	2	3	4	5
13.	I think the upgrade will be beneficial to my organization in the future.	1	2	3	4	5
14.	I think the upgrade will be beneficial to my personal work in the future.	1	2	3	4	5

15. Which of the following best describes the manner in which the software upgrade took place? *Please check only one.*

_____ Parallel — Both software packages were in operation at the same time for all users. The old package was either never removed or was only removed after the new package was successfully implemented.

_____ Phased — The new software was put into operation for some users while others still used the old software package.

_____ Modular - Only certain parts of the software were installed until it was certain that the new package would work correctly.

_____ Direct —— All users began using the new software at the same time.

_____ Other —— Please describe the implementation: ____________________________

____

____

16. The following list describes problems that sometimes occur with the implementation of new software packages. Please check all of the problems that you recall during the implementation of the software in your organization.

_____ Inadequate software training (lack of proper training for employees)
_____ Vendor oversell (false claims made by the software manufacturers and vendors)
_____ Integration (making the new software work with other software on your computer)
_____ Resistance (users who did not want to upgrade)
_____ Purchasing problems (problems obtaining the software)
_____ Vendor neglect (lack of support from the vendor after the sale)
_____ Support burden (information technology staff overburdened with queries from users)
_____ Cascading needs (purchase of new software forced purchase of other software or hardware)
_____ Unexplained failures (software or hardware crashes with no known explanation)
_____ Errors (known problems with the software, e.g. bugs)
_____ Poor performance (inefficient use of memory, processor, etc.)
_____ Other (please specify) ____

17. In your opinion, were the majority of the problems that occurred a result of technical problems (e.g. incompatibility, errors, etc.), organizational problems (e.g. poor management, lack of communication, etc.), or human problems (inability to learn new things, etc.)?

Human Organizational Technical

18. When problems did occur, what mechanisms did your organization use to cope with the problems (please check all that apply)?

_____ Education and training (formal and informal training, both on-site and off-site)
_____ Inaction (nothing was done to handle the problems)
_____ Internal support (information technology staff provided users with support)
_____ Vendor support (the vendor of the product was asked for help)
_____ New procedures (new policies and/or procedures were created)
_____ Persuasion (managers tried to persuade users and IT staff to accept the new technology)
_____ Endurance (users wanted external support, but resources for support were unavailable)
_____ Additional technology (additional software and/or hardware was purchased to support the upgrade)
_____ Consultants (external consultants were hired)
_____ Other users (users repeatedly asked other users for help with the new software)
_____ Staffing (additional staff were added to help with the problems)
_____ Other (please specify) ____

Please indicate your level of agreement or disagreement with the following statements on a scale of 1-5 (1=strongly disagree, 5=strongly agree).

19.	If I had a choice, I would prefer to have the old software back.	1	2	3	4	5
20.	I am comfortable using the new software.	1	2	3	4	5
21.	When I use the new software, I no longer think of it as new.	1	2	3	4	5
22.	I use the new software more than the old software.	1	2	3	4	5
23.	I would have liked to receive more training on the new software.	1	2	3	4	5
24.	The amount of training I received was adequate.	1	2	3	4	5

25.	I am satisfied with the training I received on the new software.	1	2	3	4	5
26.	I could not do my job without the software.	1	2	3	4	5
27.	The software is critical to the success of my organization.	1	2	3	4	5
28.	If the software was taken away from my organization, we could not continue operating.	1	2	3	4	5
29.	The software is not important to the success of my organization.	1	2	3	4	5
30.	I was unable to get help with the software when I needed it.	1	2	3	4	5
31.	I am satisfied with the support that I received for this new software package.	1	2	3	4	5
32.	Technical support for this software package was adequate.	1	2	3	4	5
33.	Our organization should have provided more support for this software.	1	2	3	4	5

On a scale of 1-5 (1=very low, 5=very high), please rate your skill in the following areas.

34.	Ability to learn to use new software packages quickly	1	2	3	4	5
35.	Ability to learn non-computer skills quickly	1	2	3	4	5
36.	Ability to program (e.g., in COBOL, FORTRAN, BASIC, etc.)	1	2	3	4	5
37.	Ability to use software packages (e.g. MS Word, WordPerfect, etc.)	1	2	3	4	5
38.	Ability to access data (e.g., data retrieval, queries, etc.)	1	2	3	4	5
39.	Ability to use and understand documentation (online help, manuals, etc.)	1	2	3	4	5
40.	Ability to use operating systems	1	2	3	4	5

41. Which of the following best describes the current state of computer applications in your organization? (Please check only one.)

______ Computers are mainly used for accounting purposes such as accounts payable, accounts receivable, payroll, and billing.

______ Computer applications are used heavily in all functional areas such as accounting, marketing, finance, etc. More and more new applications of all types are being added.

______ New applications are not allowed because things were getting out of control. The emphasis is on controlling and using existing applications instead of acquiring new ones.

______ Database applications are predominant. The majority of routine procedures have been automated into applications such as online order entry, online customer queries, and online personnel systems.

______ I do not know enough about the computer applications of my organization to answer this question.

42. Which of the following best describes the current state of computer personnel in your organization? (Please check only one.)

______ They have very little specialization (job titles such as programmer or analyst).

______ They have application development specialists (job titles such as scientific programmer, business programmer, systems analyst).

______ They have specialists for control and functional effectiveness (job titles such as systems programmer, maintenance programmer, accounting systems analyst, financial systems analyst, etc.).

______ They have specialists for database and telecommunications applications (job titles such as database analyst, telecommunications analyst).

______ I do not know enough about the computer personnel of my organization to answer this question.

43. Which of the following best describes the current state of computer management in your organization? (Please check only one.)
   ______ The computer department is a branch of another department such as accounting, and all computer personnel report to that department. The computer budget is informal.
   ______ The computer department reports to another department, but the highest level computing manager is promoted in the organization. Analysts and programmers work in accounting, finance, marketing, etc. The computing budget is informal.
   ______ The computer department is a separate department such as IS, IT, or MIS. Controls are implemented to prevent computer budget overflow. The computer budget is strongly controlled, but multi-year plans do not exist.
   ______ The computer department is a separate department such as IS, IT, or MIS. The highest level computing manager has a high level position in the organization, and 3-5 year plans exist for computer facilities, personnel, and applications.
   ______ I do not know enough about our organization's computer management to answer this question.

Please indicate your level of agreement or disagreement with the following statements on a scale of 1-5 (1=strongly disagree, 5=strongly agree).

44.	I can do more with the new software than with the old software.	1	2	3	4	5
45.	The new software has capabilities that the old software did not have.	1	2	3	4	5
46.	The number of new features was intimidating to me.	1	2	3	4	5
47.	The new software basically does the same things as the old software.	1	2	3	4	5
48.	The new software has features that the old software did not have.	1	2	3	4	5

The next few questions refer to the user interface of the software. Here, the term user interface refers to the manner in which you interact with the software. For example, the interface includes screens, menus, buttons, shortcut keys, etc. Please indicate your level of agreement or disagreement with the following statements on a scale of 1-5 (1=strongly disagree, 5=strongly agree).

49.	The user interface of the new software is different from that of the old software.	1	2	3	4	5
50.	The new user interface is basically the same as the old user interface.	1	2	3	4	5
51.	The new user interface included changes in menu options.	1	2	3	4	5
52.	The new user interface included changes in user screens.	1	2	3	4	5
53.	The new user interface caused changes in how I use the software.	1	2	3	4	5
54.	The new software had many technical problems, such as bugs, crashes, etc.	1	2	3	4	5
55.	The new software caused many technical problems on my computer.	1	2	3	4	5
56.	The new software caused many technical problems for my organization.	1	2	3	4	5

Please answer the following questions about software compatibility on a scale of 1-5 (1=incompatible, 5=compatible). Compatibility here refers to the ability of the software to interact with other components (e.g., file formats, protocols, etc.) All the questions ask "In your opinion, how compatible is the new software package with..."

57.	... other software on your computer?	1	2	3	4	5
58.	... the hardware in your computer?	1	2	3	4	5
59.	... the old software package that was replaced?	1	2	3	4	5
60.	... other software packages in the company that are not on your computer?	1	2	3	4	5
61.	... other software in the marketplace?	1	2	3	4	5

62. For approximately how many years have you been using computers? ___________

63. What is your job title? ________________

64. What is your primary job function? ______________

65. What is the highest level of education that you have attained? __________________

66. Which of the following industries is the primary industry for your organization?

    Financial | Manufacturing | Educational | Government | Computers |
    Other __________

67. If your firm is for-profit, what is the approximate annual revenue of your firm? If you do not wish to disclose this information, please leave this question blank. ______________

68. Approximately how many employees are in your company? ____________

(Optional) If you wish to have a copy of the survey results, please provide your name and address (postal or email), or attach a business card. All individual results will be kept strictly confidential. The survey number below is for tracking purposes only.

____
____
____
____
____

Would you be interested in learning more about research studies in this area? _______________

Please return the survey in the postage-paid reply envelope.
Thank you again for all of your help!!!

REFERENCES

Anacona, D. (1990). "Information Technology and New Product Teams," In *Intellectual Teamwork: Social and Technological Foundations of Cooperative Work*, J. Galegher, R. Kraut and C. Egido (Ed.), Lawrence Erlbaum Publishers, Hillsdale,191-220.

Ballou, Wang, Pazer and Tayi(1998). "Modeling Information Manufacturing systems to Determine Information Product Quality," *Management Science*, 44(4), 462-484.

Bapista, R. and Swann, P.(1998). "Do Firms in Clusters Innovate More?," *Research Policy* 27(4),525-540.

Boudreau, M.-C., Loch, K.D., Robey, D. and Straub, D. (1998). "Going Global: Using Information Technology to Advance the Competitiveness of the Virtual Transnational Organization," *The Academy of Management Executive*, 12(4), 120-128.

Brown, S. and Eisenhardt, K.(1995). "Product Development: Past Research, Present Findings, and Future Directions," *Academy of Management Review*, 20(2), 343-378.

Burchill, G. and Fine, C. (1997)."Time Versus Market Orientation in Product Concept Development: Empirically-Based Theory Generation," *Management Science*, 43(4), 465-478.

Crowe, E.(1999). "Online Software at Your Service," *Computer Currents*, December, 76-79.

Davenport, Jarvenpaa and Beers (1996). "Improving Knowledge Work Processes," *Sloan Management Review* :Summer, 53-65.

Favela, J. and Connor, J. (1994)."Accessing Corporate Memory in Networked Organizations," *Proceedings of the HICSS-27*, Hawaii, 181-189.

Fielding, R., Whitehead, J., Anderson, K. and Bolcer, G.(1998). "Web Based Development of Complex

Information Products," *Communications of the ACM*, 41(8), 84-92.

Gillan, C. and McCarthy, M.(1999). "ASPs are Real...But What's Right for You?," International Data Corporation Report, September.

Hall, R. (1997). "Complex Systems, Complex Learning, and Competence Building," In *Strategic Learning and Knowledge Management*, R. Sanchez and A. Heene (Ed.), John Wiley & Sons Ltd., Chichester, 39-64.

Henderson, R. and Clark, K. (1990)."Architectural Innovation: The Reconfiguration of Existing Product Technologies and the Failure of Established Firms," *Administrative Science Quarterly* (35), 9-30.

Heskett, J., Sasser, W. and Schlesinger, L. (1997). *The Service Profit Chain*, The Free Press, New York.

Iansiti, M.(1998). *Technology Integration: Making Critical Choices in a Dynamic World*, Harvard Business School Press, Boston, MA.

Iansiti, M. and MacCormack, A.(1997). "Developing Products on Internet Time," *Harvard Business Review* :September-October,108-117.

Igbaria, M. (1998). "Managing Virtual Workplaces and Teleworking in Information Technology," *Journal of Management Information Systems*, 14(4), 5-6.

Jassawalla, A.R. and Sashittal, H.C.(1998). "An Examination of Collaboration in High Technology New Product Development Process," *Journal of Product Innovation Management*, 15, 237-254.

Keston, G.(1999). "Application Service Providers," Faulkner Information Services Market Research Report 00017470, December.

Khurana, A.(1999). "Managing Complex Production Processes," *Sloan Management Review*, Winter, 85-97.

Koppius (1999). "Dimensions of Intangible Goods," *Proceedings of the 32nd Hawaii Internatioinal Conference on System Sciences*, Maui, Hawaii.

March, J. (1991). "Exploration and Exploitation in Organizational Learning," *Organization Science*, 2(1), 71-87.

Matusik, S. and Hill, C.(1998). "The Utilization of Contigent Work, Knowledge Creation, and Competitive Advantage," *Academy of Management Review*, 23(4), 680-697.

Mendelson, H. and Kraemer, K.(1998). "The Information Industries: Intorduction to the Special Issue," *Information Systems Research*, 9(4), 1-4.

Meyer, M. and DeTore, A.(1999). "Product Development for Services," *Academy of Management Executive*, 13(3), 64-76.

Meyer, M. and Lehnerd, A. (1997). *The Power of Product Platforms: Building Value and Cost Leadership*, The Free Press, New York.

Meyer, M. and Utterback, J.(1995). "Product Development Cycle Time and Commercial Success," *IEEE Transactions on Engineering Management*, 42(4), 297-304.

Mowshowitz, A.(1997). "Virtual Organization," *Communications of the ACM*, 40(9), 30-37.

Mullins, J. and Sutherland, D. (1998). "New Product Development in Rapidly Changing Markets: An Exploratory Study," *Journal of Product Innovation Management* , 15(3), 224-236.

Nelson, R. and Winter, S.(1982). *An Evolutionary Theory of Economic Change*, The Belknap Press of Harvard University, Cambridge, MA.

Nonaka, I. and Takeuchi, H.(1995). *The Knowledge-Creating Company: How Japanese Companies Create the Dynamics of Innovation*, Oxford University Press, New York.

Parthasarathy, M. and Bhattacherjee, A.(1998). "Understanding Post-Adoption Behavior in the Context of Online Services," *Information Systems Research*, 9(4), 362-379.

Phillips, F., Ochs, L. and Schrock, M.(1999). "The Product is Dead—Long Live the Product—Service!," *Research Technology Management*, July-August, 51-56.

Ramesh, B.(1998). "Factors Influencing Requirements Traceability Practice," *Communications of the ACM*, 41(12), 37-44.

Ramesh, B. and Dhar, V. (1992). "Supporting Systems Development using Knowledge Captured during Requirements Engineering," *IEEE Transactions on Software Engineering*.

Ramesh, B. and Jarke, M. (1999). "Toward Reference Models for Requirements Traceability," *IEEE Transactions on Software Engineering*.

Ramesh, B. and Sengupta, K.(1995). "Multimedia in a Design Rationale Decision Support System," *Decision Support Systems*, 15, 181-196.

Ramesh, B. and Tiwana, A.(1999). "Supporting Collaborative Process Knowledge Management in New Product Development Teams," *Decision Support Systems*, 27(1-2), 213-235.

Robertson, D. and Ulrich, K. (1998). "Planning for Product Platforms," *Sloan Management Review*, Summer,19-31.

Robillard (1999). "The Role of Knowledge in Software Development," *Communications of the ACM*, 42(1), 87-92.

Rose, T.(1998). "Virtual Assessment of Engineering Processes in Virtual Enterprises," *Communications of the ACM*, 41(12), 45-52.

Rust, R. and Zahorik, A. (1993). "Customer Satisfaction, Customer Retention, and Market Share," *Journal of Retailing*, 69(2),193-215.

Sanchez, R. and Mahoney, J.(1996). "Modularity, Flexibility, and Knowledge Management in Product Organization and Design," *Strategic Management Journal*, 17(1), 63-76.

Scott, M. (1998). *The Intellect Industry: Profiting and Learning from Professional Services Firms*, John Wiley & Sons, Chichester.

Shapiro, C. and Varian, H.(1998). "Versioning: The Smart way to Sell Information," *Harvard Business Review*, November-December, 16-114.

Shapiro, C. and Varian, H. (1999). *Information Rules: A Strategic Guide to the Network Economy*, Harvard Business School Press, Boston, MA.

Simon, H.A. (1991). "Bounded Rationality and Organizational Learning," *Organization Science*, 2(1), 125-134.

Song, M. and Montoya-Weiss, M. (1998)."Critical Development Activities for Really New versus Incremental Products," *Journal of Product Innovation Management*, 15,124-135.

Stein, E.W. and Zwass, V.(1995). "Actualizing Organizational Memory with Information Systems," *Information Systems Research*, 6(1).

Teece, D. (1986). "Profiting From Technological Innovation: Implications for Integration, Collaboration, Licensing, and Public Policy," *Research Policy*, 15(6), 285-306.

Thayer, R., Pyster, A. and Wood, R.(1980). "The Challenge of Software Engineering Project Management," *IEEE Computer*, 13(9), 51-59.

Tiwana, A.(2000). *The Knowledge Management Toolkit: Practical Techniques for Building a Knowledge Management System*, Prentice Hall, Upper Saddle River, NJ

Tomas, J. and Arias, G. (1995). "Do Networks Really Foster Innovation?," *Management Decision*, 33(9), 2-56.

Truex, D.P., Baskerville, R. and Klein, H.K. (1999). "Growing Systems in an Emergent Organization," *Communications of the ACM*, 42(8), 117-123.

Ungson, G. and Trudel, J.(1999). "The Emerging Knowledge-based Economy," *IEEE Spectrum*, May, 60-65.

Von Hippel, E.(1990). "Task Partitioning: An Innovation Process Variable," *Research Policy*, 407-418.

Walsh, J. (1995). "Managerial and Organizational Cognition: Notes from a Trip Down Memory Lane," *Organization Science*, 6(3), 280-321.

Zack, M.(1996). "Electronic Publishing: A Product Architecture Perspective," *Information & Management*, 31, 75-86.

Zack, M.(1999a). "An Architecture for Managing Codified Knowledge," *Sloan Management Review*, Summer, 45-58.

Zack, M.H.(1999b). "Developing a Knowledge Strategy," *California Management Review*, 41(3), 125-145.

About the Authors

BOOK EDITOR

Neal G. Shaw is an assistant professor in the Department of Information Systems and Management Sciences in the College of Business Administration at the University of Texas at Arlington. He holds a Ph.D. in Management Information Systems from Texas Tech University and has published his work in scholarly journals and international conferences. In addition, he has served an a consultant and advisor to a number of corporations in the area of software implementation. His current research interests focus on IS implementation, electronic commerce, and software upgrades.

CONTRIBUTORS

Donald L. Amoroso is assistant professor of information systems at the College of Business and Administration, University of Colorado at Colorado Springs. He has five years in industry as an information systems consultant and systems analyst. He has published in the *Journal of MIS Information and Management, Data Base, Information Resources Management Journal, and the Journal of Information Management.* Dr. Amoroso's research interests lie in the areas of information engineering, end-user computing, and measuring the effectiveness of emerging technologies.

Joseph L. Balloun is associate professor of Quantitative Analysis at Nova Southeastern University. He has a Ph.D. in industrial psychology from the University of California at Berkeley. His research interests include cluster analysis of objects, dimension analysis, ordinal response data, robust and resistant estimators, and general sciences. His papers on these and other topics have appeared in various leading journals. Besides being an active participant in national and international conferences, he has presented a variety of papers on statistical methodology in the social sciences.

Robert P. Bostrom is the L. Edmund Rast Professor of Business at the University of Georgia. He holds a Ph.D. in MIS from the University of Minnesota, USA. He has published several articles in leading journals such as *MIS Quarterly, Communications of the ACM, Management Science, International Journal of Human-Computer Studies.* His current research interests are focused on training, facilitation, group support systems, technology supported learning, and effective design of organizations via integrating human/social and technological dimensions.

Larry R. Coe is in his second year of the Management Information Systems Ph.D. program at the University of Illinois at Chicago. He earned his M.B.A. at the University of Chicago in 1992 and his B.A. at the University of Illinois-Urbana in 1974. He has had extensive systems experience in implementing major systems at IBM and Ameritech for the past 22 years.

Timothy Paul Cronan is Professor of Computer Information Systems and Quantitative Analysis at the University of Arkansas, Fayetteville. He received his D.B.A. from Louisiana Tech University and is an active member of the Decision Sciences Institute and The Association for Computing Machinery. He has served as Regional Vice President and on the Board of Directors of the Decision Sciences Institute and as President of the Southwest Region of the Institute. In addition, he has served as Associate Editor for MIS Quarterly. His research interests include local area networks, downsizing, expert systems, performance analysis and effectiveness, and end-user computing. Publications have appeared in *Decision Sciences, MIS Quarterly, OMEGA-The International Journal of Management Science, The Journal of Management Information Systems, Communications of the ACM, Journal of End User Computing, Database, Journal of Research on Computing in Education, Journal of Financial Research*, as well as in other journals and conference proceedings.

George Ditsa is a lecturer in the Department of Business Systems, University of Wollongong, Australia. His degrees include BSc (Computer Science) and MBA (IS) from the University of Wollongong. Mr. Ditsa has worked for several years in the information systems area in various organisations before taking up the lectureship position. His current research interests include user satisfaction of information systems, particularly executive information systems, information systems management and the use of information systems in small businesses.

Georgios Doukidis is an Associate Professor in the Department of Informatics at the Athens University of Economics and Business. His research interests include knowledge-based decision support systems, information systems management in small business and inter-organizational information systems. He is the author of 30 papers in international scientific journals and has published five books. He is a member of the editorial board of five international journals, including the *Journal of Strategic Information Systems* and the *European Journal of Information Systems* and has acted as guest editor on various occasions.

Manal M. Elkordy is currently a Ph.D student at City University Business School, UK. She is an assistant lecturer of Business Administration at Alexandria University, Egypt, from which she received a B. COM. and a Masters in Business Administration. She has published in IS refereed journals and proceedings. Her research interests include information systems effectiveness, and global information systems management.

John W. Henry (Ph.D. Florida State University) is currently an Associate Professor of Management at Georgia Southern University in Statesboro, Georgia. His teaching and research interests are information system implementation, end-user acceptance/rejection of information systems, hospital information systems, and computer ethics. Dr. Henry has published several research works, some of which have appeared in *Journal of Business Ethics, Computers in Human Behavior, Behaviour and Information Technology, Executive Development, Journal of Health Information Management Research, Computer Personnel, Information Resources Management Journal*, and national and regional proceedings.

James J. Jiang is an associate professor in the Computer Information Systems Department, Louisiana Tech University. He has a Ph.D. in Information Systems from the University of Cincinnati. His principal areas of research interest are decision support systems (DSS), DSS evaluation, computer-human interaction, and computer personnel. Dr. Jiang's work on these areas have appeared in *IEEE Transactions on Systems, Man & Cybernetics, Journal of Systems & Software, Computer in Human Behavior, Data Base, Information Systems Management, Computer Personnel,* and other outlets.

Omar E. M. Khalil is currently an Associate Professor of Information Systems at the University of Massachusetts at Dartmouth. He has a Ph.D. and an MS in Information Systems from the University of North Texas and MBA from Alexandria University, Egypt. He has taught graduate and undergraduate courses at Alexandria University, University of North Texas, Virginia Commonwealth University, and University of Massachusetts. He has publications in many refereed journals and peer-reviewed proceedings. His research interests include information systems effectiveness, information systems role in TQM and BPR, management of global information systems, and the human side of information systems.

Changki Kim is an advisory consultant at Samsung SDS Co., Ltd. in Seoul South Korea. His research interests include end user computing, measures of information systems success and management of information resources.

Gary Klein is dean of the School of Business at the University of Texas of the Permian Basin. He has a Ph.D. in Management Sciences from Purdue University's Karanert Graduate School of Management. His research interests include multiple criteria optimization, automated system design, integer programming, and model management and his papers have appeared in *Management Sciences, Decision Sciences, Naval Research Logistics, MIS Quarterly, Journal of Management Information Systems, IEEE Transactions on Systems, Man & Cybernetics, Information & Management, Data Base,* and other outlets.

Peggy L. Lane is an Assistant Professor of Information Systems at Indiana University and Purdue Univerity at Fort Wayne. Previously she was at Bradley University. She received her Ph.D. in information systems from the University of Arkansas and has published in the *Communications of the ACM* and the *International Journal of Computer Information Systems.*

Jinjoo Lee is a professor at the graduate school of management, Korea Advanced Institute of Science and Technology, South Korea. His research interests focus on innovation studies,

R&D management, and MIS implementation. He has published more than 30 articles in a variety of journals.

Takis Lybereas is a Ph.D. candidate at Warwick Business School, researching the effects of organizational culture on IS planning in less developed environments. His other research interests include strategic IS and business planning and IS growth models. Currently he is also the director of the Greek EDI Awareness Centre in Athens, Greece.

R.C. MacGregor is a senior lecturer in the Department of Business Systems, University of Wollongong. He is the founder and editor of the *Australian Journal of Information Systems* (AJIS). His degrees include BSc & M.Ed (Hons). Mr. MacGregor's current interests are in the area of small business, particularly the mechanisms for acquisition of computer technology by small businesses, as well as the effect of electronic commerce technologies on small business.

Mark J. Martinko is a Professor of Management at Florida State University. He received his Ph.D. from the University of Nebraska, M.A. from the University of Iowa, and undergraduate degree from Muskingum College. He teaches in the areas of organizational behavior, theory, management, change, and human resource management. His research is concerned with the development and testing of models for explaining and understanding intrapersonal and interpersonal behavior in organizations. This interest has resulted in research focusing on the observation of managerial behaviors, leadership behaviors, attribution theory, impression management, behavior management, personality, and emotion. In addition to his academic background, Dr. Martinko has experience in both private and public sector organizations including: Western Electric Corporation; Omaha Public Power District; the State of Nebraska; National Cash Register; Sheller-Globe Corporation; U.S. Steel; Florida Department of Law Enforcement; Appalachee Community Mental Health; Guinness Group Sales, Ltd., Ireland; and Wal-Mart Corporation. He is the co-author of *The Power of Positive Reinforcement, The Practice of Supervision and Management*, and *Attribution Theory: An Organizational Perspective* (St. Lucie Press, 1995). He is the author of more than fifty research articles and book chapters and has published in a variety of journals including the *Academy of Management Journal, Academy of Management Review, Journal of Management, Journal of Organizational Behavior,* and the *Journal of Management Studies.* Mark served two successive terms on the editorial board of the Academy of Management Review and is currently on the editorial boards of Organizational Dynamics and the Journal of Organizational Behavior Management. He served as the program chair for Southern Management Association in 1995 and is serving as the President of the Southern Management Association in 1996/1997.

Lorne Olfman is Professor of Information Science at Claremont Graduate University where he is the Chair of the Information Science Department. He holds a Ph.D. in Management Information Systems from Indiana University, USA. He has published several articles in leading journals such as *MIS Quarterly, Communications of the ACM,* and *International Journal of Human-Computer Studies.* Dr. Olfman's research interests involve three main areas: software training, the impact of computer-based systems on organizational memory, and the design and adoption of systems used for group work.

Jeffrey Palko is an Associate Professor of Computer Information Systems at Northwestern State University of Louisiana. He has taught graduate and undergraduate courses covering the entire development life cycle from systems analysis to program design. His research interests include human problem solving, systems development and computing education.

Sherry D. Ryan is an Assistant Professor of Business Computer Information Systems at the University of North Texas. She received her Ph.D. in Information Systems from the University of Texas at Arlington. Prior to pursuing her doctorate, she worked at IBM for11 years. Her current research interests include information technology investment decision processes, the human impacts of information technology, and IT training issues.

Maung K. Sein is Professor of Information Systems at Agder College. He holds a Ph.D. from Indiana University, USA. He has published several articles in leading journals such as MIS Quarterly, Communications of the ACM, Information Systems Research, and the International Journal of Human-Computer Studies. He is an Associate Editor of *MIS Quarterly* and the *Communications of the AIS*. His research interests include end-user training and learning, human-computer interaction, data modeling and IS management.

Steve Smithson is a lecturer in computing in the Information Systems Department of the London School of Economics. He has published numerous journal articles and conference papers on information systems management and the application of information technology in organizations. He has also co-authored two books in these areas. He is the editor of the European Journal of Information Systems and is on various other editorial boards.

Kunsoo Suh is an assistant professor at the department of management, Soonchunhyang University, South Korea. His research interests include end user computing, strategic use of information systems and software engineering. He has published articles in *Computer Personnel* (ACM SIGCPR) and *Information Resources Management Journal.*

Amrit Tiwana is completing his Ph.D. in information systems at J. Mack Robinson College of Business, Georgia State University. His research interests lie in the area of knowledge management in e-business settings. His ongoing work extends Knowledge-based Theory of the Firm at the team level in architecturally destructive business environments. Besides his publications in several journals and conferences, he has authored The Knowledge Management Toolkit (Prentice Hall, 1999).

Index

J

K

L

M

O

P

Q

R

S

T

U

W